AFRICAN EXPERIENCES OF CINEMA

African Experiences
of Cinema

Edited by
Imruh Bakari and Mbye B. Cham

BFI PUBLISHING

First published in 1996 by the
British Film Institute,
21 Stephen St, London W1P 2LN

The British Film Institute exists to promote appreciation, enjoyment,
protection and development of moving image culture in and throughout the
whole of the United Kingdom. Its activities include the National Film and
Television Archive; the National Film Theatre; the Museum of the Moving
Image; the London Film Festival; the production and distribution of film and
video; funding and support for regional activities; Library and Information
Services; Stills, Posters and Designs; Research, Publishing and Education; and
the monthly *Sight and Sound* magazine.

British Library Cataloguing-in-Publication Data
A catalogue record for this book is available from the British Library

ISBN 0–85170 510–3
      0–85170 511–1 pbk

Cover design and photograph by Nick Livesey

Set in 9½/11½ Sabon by Fakenham Photosetting Limited, Fakenham, Norfolk
Printed in Great Britain by St Edmundsbury Press Ltd, Bury St Edmunds,
Suffolk

Contents

The Continent of Africa

Preface and Acknowledgments

The documents, testimonies and essays in this book address significant aspects of the many experiences and challenges of cinema in various parts of the continent of Africa over a broad timespan. They reflect a complex plurality of experiences and challenges, as well as the responses – individual, collective, private, public, institutional, national, regional – to these. By no means an 'anthology of the best' that has been written on the subject, and by no means comprehensive in terms of geographic spread and coverage of films, authors and themes, this book brings together under one cover writings that have previously been published or presented elsewhere in an attempt to offer to a wide audience a critical map of the terrain of African film practice, broad views in parts, and specific and detailed in others.

The diversity, differences and areas of intersection that mark African film practice are reflected in the ensemble of documents, testimonies and essays. No one mode of apprehending African film practice is privileged here over others. We have sought to bring together histories, descriptions, analyses, theories and first-person narratives whose juxtaposition in this collection will enable clear and productive understandings of African experiences of cinema, its achievements as well as the problems and challenges which it has been, and is still, confronting and engaging in various ways.

The scope of the original plan of this project encompassed the continent, eschewing the customary division of the continent into North Africa and 'sub-Saharan' Africa. Even though this plan had to be modified slightly (hence the apparent dominance of references to sub-Saharan Africa), we are convinced that, fundamentally, the many issues engaged in the documents, testimonies and essays in the book are by no means relevant only to film practices of sub-Saharan Africa. In fact, all of the documents presented here were prepared by film-makers from all over the continent. Some of the testimonies are voices from Africa 'above the Sahara', and many of the essays use data from various locations across the continent. Thus, despite the absence of detailed attention to and analyses of particular films and film-makers from North Africa, we do believe that the book presents valid and compelling accounts of the material and non-material factors and forces historically at play in film practices across the entire continent of Africa.

The book is divided into five parts with an introduction which, among other things, highlights some recent developments not covered by some of the essays and documents. In a slight shift away from practices prevalent in some collections of this kind, we start the core of the book with the collective and individual voices of film-makers themselves. Part I consists of manifestos, declarations and resolutions generated collectively by film-makers at various gatherings over a period of time. As definitions of art, ideol-ogy, history, politics, economy, culture, society and their interrelations – as well as statements concerning strategy and material imperatives – these documents also enable us, at the present moment, to assess the nature of the continuities and transformations of African film practice. The collective voices of the documents in Part I resonate in various ways in the first-person testimonies and reflections of individual film-makers and one scholar-activist in Part II. Part III gathers together essays which describe and analyse critically the history of African and Black presences in various cinematic spaces, and the material, political and economic factors of production, distribution and exhibition, while Part IV focuses on questions of theory, approach and representation. In Part V, three essays are featured by way of studies on particular films, film-makers and issues. Parts II, III, IV and V contain suggestions for further readings which, we hope, will make up for gaps as well as engender further reflection.

This book follows on from the cinema season 'Screen Griots – The Art and Imagination of African Cinema', which formed a major part of the series of events organised by the British Film Institute's African Caribbean Unit for Africa '95, a presentation and celebration of the Arts of Africa held in London between August and December 1995. Financial assistance for these events and for this book was gratefully received from the EEC European Development Fund.

The editors would like to acknowledge the invaluable assistance of June Givanni of the BFI's African Caribbean Unit, and Paul Willemen and Sue Bobbermein of BFI Publishing. Our sincere gratitude to Lionel Ngakane, Rose Issa and Gaylene Gould, all of whom allowed various intrusions on their time and space. We would also like to thank all the contributors and publishers for their co-operation in making this publication possible. Finally, we would like to say thank you to Mahtarr Jobe of Gamtech, Gambia, for generously allowing us to use his office facilities and resources.

Introduction

MBYE B. CHAM

Although Africans in a few parts of the continent (mainly in Egypt, Algeria, Tunisia, South Africa and Senegal) were exposed to cinema from very early on, within five years of the invention of the art form, the practice of film-making by Africans on a significant scale is a relatively new phenomenon on the continent. Even though the first film made by an African, a short by Chemama Chikly from Tunisia entitled *Ain el Ghezal* (*The Girl from Carthage*), dates back to 1924, and even though Egyptians have been making films since 1928, it was only in the latter part of the 1950s and the start of the 60s, following political independence in many countries, that we began to witness the emergence of a significant corpus of films produced and directed by Africans. One of the first films directed by an African from the sub-Saharan region was not made until 1955, by a film-maker from Guinea, Mamadou Touré. That film, *Mouramani*, is an adaptation of a traditional oral narrative from Guinea. This was followed in the same year by another short film entitled *Afrique-sur-Seine*, which was the product of a collective of sub-Saharan African film-makers in Paris headed by the Senegalese Paulin Soumanou Vieyra. However, it was only in 1963 that the film that came to set a model for many African film-makers was made. This was *Borom Sarret*, a twenty-minute short by Ousmane Sembène from Senegal.

African film-making is in a way a child of African political independence. It was born in the era of heady nationalism and nationalist anticolonial and anti-neocolonial struggle, and it has been undergoing a process of painful growth and development in a post-colonial context of general socioeconomic decay and decline, devaluation (that is, 'devalisation') and political repression and instability on the continent. One is therefore talking here about a very young, if not the youngest, creative practice in Africa.

However, in spite of its youth and the variety of overwhelming odds against which it is struggling, cinema by Africans has grown steadily over this short period of time to become a significant part of a worldwide film movement aimed at constructing and promoting an alternative popular cinema, one that is more in harmony with the realities, the experiences, the priorities and desires of the societies which it addresses. A significant portion of the films that constitute African cinema share a few elements in common with radical film practices from other parts of the Third World, such as Third Cinema. Such films also exhibit similarities with part of the work of independent African American, Caribbean and Black British film-makers, and Indian film-makers such as

1

Satyajit Ray and Mirnal Sen. These parallels are manifested not only at the level of form and content but also in terms of the practices and challenges of production, distribution and exhibition. I shall use the label 'radical' to refer to this segment of African film practice.

Film-makers in this category consider film not only as popular entertainment, but more significantly as sociopolitical and cultural discourse and praxis. Ousmane Sembène, for example, has characterised cinema in Africa as a 'night school'. These film-makers deny conventional and received notions of cinema as harmless innocent entertainment, and insist on the ideological nature of film. They posit film as a crucial site of the battle to decolonise minds, to develop radical consciousness, to reflect and engage critically with African cultures and traditions, and to make desirable the meaningful transformation of society for the benefit of the majority. Hence the dominance of themes which reflect the social, political, cultural and economic concerns, challenges and contradictions of post-colonial African societies.

Some film-makers in this category proclaim themselves the modern-day equivalents of the traditional oral artists (the griot and/or the oral narrative performer) in the service of the masses, and they appropriate resources from their respective indigenous artistic heritages – oral, written and otherwise – in terms of both theme and technique, to create a cinema which engages a broad range of the personal, social, cultural, historical, political and imaginative experiences and challenges of their societies. These African film-makers seek to fashion a different film language with which to represent African realities and desires. Film-makers who champion this type of film-making include Yousef Chahine (Egypt), Ousmane Sembène (Senegal), Med Hondo (Mauritania), Souleymane Cissé (Mali), Lakhdar Hamina (Algeria), Haile Gerima (Ethiopia), Moufida Tlatli (Tunisia), John Akomfrah (Ghana), Safi Faye (Senegal), Sarah Maldoror (Guadeloupe/Angola), Djibril Diop Mambety (Senegal), Flora Gomes (Guinea-Bissau), Jilali Ferhati (Morocco), to mention only a few. The radical thrust of much of contemporary African cinema in the sub-Saharan region was fashioned historically by film-makers from 'arabophone', 'francophone' and, to some extent, 'lusophone' areas. As for the 'anglophone' countries, only Ghana and Nigeria have acquired any prominence in the field. Both north and south of the Sahara, film-making has been and continues to be a predominantly male activity. There are comparatively few women film-makers working in Africa, although this situation is changing.

There are two other categories of cinema that constitute significant forces in the history of African film-making. A second category of African cinema espouses creative values and practices associated with conventional Western films, particularly Hollywood films, and also with the patently commercial and entertainment-type films and melodramas from other parts of the Third World, especially India. Variously labelled 'imitative', 'failed Hollywood clones', 'escapist', 'cinéma digestif' and so on by critics, many of these films manage to seduce popular audiences through their ability to appropriate and revise motifs and formulae from the non-African films that have historically dominated and continue to dominate African screens. These non-African films – mainly Hollywood and Euro-Hollywood spectacles, Indian romances and melodramas, and kung fu movies – have been successful with popular African audiences because they are the only films that are programmed regularly in the majority of cinemas, which are owned by non-Africans who are beholden to foreign distribution companies. Many Africans grow up on this film diet, and what many of the African film-makers in the second category do is appropriate the adventure, the action, the romance, the melodrama, the spectacle, the fantasy and the general aura of these films and transpose them to Africa, investing them with recognisable African garb. For such film-makers, cinema is a refuge from the challenges of everyday life. Their films create an outlet for escape by serving as African versions and extensions of the foreign films which have such a hold over the African audience. Here the sociopolitical orientations of films of the radical category take a back seat to entertainment. Where such issues figure in these films, their treatment seldom goes beyond token gestures; the spectator is rarely challenged to probe further the implications of such issues for them as individuals and for their society as a whole.

Issues like the search for a new and more appropriate film language and the politics of representation are marginal in films in this second category. As pointed out earlier, they tend to be satisfied with received film forms, dramatic schemas developed and tested elsewhere. With the exception of the work of Chahine and Asma El Bakri and a few others, a good portion of the corpus of films from Egypt are part of this category, as are a large number of films from Nigeria.

The third, and perhaps most formidable, force in cinema in Africa is the hegemonic foreign, particularly Hollywood, film, which enjoys a virtual monopoly of African theatres, especially those in the sub-Saharan region. This continued hegemony has many implications. They include the perpetuation and/or the revision and refinement of traditional stereotypes and distortions of Africa and Africans, and the invention of new, more insidious ones. The dominance of the foreign film in Africa also means that the development of vibrant indigenous film industries in Africa is retarded, because when African films are not widely distributed and shown on their own turf not only are the prospects of recouping their production costs bleak (this is vital if other films are to be produced), but also their effectiveness in combating the negative film image of Africa and Africans inscribed in the foreign film and their aim to be an integral part of the development process in Africa become severely compromised. An integral factor in this hegemony of the foreign film is the re-emergence in recent years of the Africa film (understood as 'one that uses Africa as resource, but denies an African point of view') – *Out of Africa*, for example, shot in Kenya, or *King Solomon's Mines*, shot in Zimbabwe, not to mention the numerous other projects shot in South Africa. In such projects, mostly Western cast, crew and equipment are shipped in and out of location, and the benefits to the local industry are usually negligible.

What we have, then, in the landscape of African cinema as we enter the last decade of this century, is the coexistence of three principal competing modes of film thought and practice which are by no means uniform, fixed or stable, and which have historically interacted in various ways to shape the contours and contents of the landscape of cinema in Africa. It is a contested and dynamic terrain, one that is in constant flux, and continually subject to myriad internal pressures and demands as well as to the effects of a constantly changing global political and media economy.

In general, African film-making has been an activity *par excellence* of North

Africans and West Africans. In the north, much of the film activity takes place in Egypt, whose musical melodramas numerically dominate the field, in Algeria and Tunisia, with their more politically oriented films, and in Morocco, which is somewhat the poor relation in this group in terms of quantity of film productions. Libya is not generally known for any kind of significant film activity, even though it does possess the resources needed to launch a viable industry. As for Mauritania, the only well-known film-makers from here reside in and work out of Paris, although one of them, Med Hondo, is today one of the major forces in African film-making. (A much-heralded younger talent from Mauritania is Abderrahmane Sissako.) The north has relatively developed and modern production and post-production facilities and a significant pool of highly skilled technicians and professionals at various levels. These have greatly aided indigenous productions, and many African film-makers from the sub-Saharan region (Sembène with *Camp de Thiaroye* (1988), for example) have been increasingly making use of these facilities in an attempt to lessen their dependence on Western, especially French, facilities and technicians. This South/South co-operation in the area of film production is likely to be one of the major shifts in African film production practices in the 90s and beyond. In these moments of greater competition for shrinking local as well as global resources, in this era of devaluation ('devalisation') and rapidly disappearing film theatres (which are steadily being transformed into 'souks' or rice/flour/sugar/cement warehouses as IMF and World Bank-mandated liberalisation and privatisation of African economies become policy mantras), in these times of emergent trans-national media mega-corporations, the imperative for such a viable South/South axis becomes ever more compelling.

Below the Sahara, film-making has been dominated and continues to be dominated by cineastes from the francophone countries of Senegal, Mali, Côte d'Ivoire, Cameroon and Burkina Faso. Burkina Faso has over the years acquired the status of 'the capital of African cinema'. However, developments in the southern half of the continent, in Zimbabwe and South Africa, in particular, have begun to indicate possible changes in this situation. In the years to come, one can reasonably expect much more activity from this region, which already enjoys a fairly well developed production infrastructure. In fact, some film-makers in East and Southern Africa have already begun using the facilities of the Central Film Laboratories in Harare, Zimbabwe, and, surely, the promises of a post-apartheid South Africa are grounds for optimism.

Having provided this general overview of a few of the categories of African cinema, I would like now to consider what some of these films say and tell us about Africa, Africans and humanity in general. As I have indicated above, many African film-makers consider cinema as not only entertainment, but also – more significantly – as a vehicle for social, cultural, political and personal discourse and praxis. They use film to critically engage, celebrate and interrogate certain aspects of African cultural beliefs and traditions, and they use the resources of these traditions to make films which comment on the contemporary social, cultural, political, historical and personal realities, experiences and challenges faced by Africans. Thus, African cinema is integral to the wider social and collective effort on the part of Africans to bring about a better life for the majority of Africans. African cinema is, as the Fulani say of art in general, 'futile, utile, instructive'. It is entertainment, it is educational and it is functional.

The themes that dominate African film narratives mirror the problems, challenges, experiences and desires of African individuals and societies over time, with a particular emphasis on the operations and consequences of colonialism and its legacies. The conflicts and transformations that came in the wake of the encounter on African soil between African and Euro-Christian and Arab Islamic cultures and peoples have provided many African film-makers with narrative material. Equally prominent are themes that spin around the myriad challenges of post-colonial life and struggles in Africa. Themes such as disillusionment with political independence, declining quality of life for the majority, decaying production and service infrastructures, intransigent bureaucracy which frustrates common people, political instability and corruption, misuse of traditions and customs for individual gain, the requirement to question and revise certain aspects of tradition which are oppressive, anachronistic and exploitative, the need to rethink and change certain outmoded notions of gender and gender roles and expectations, especially where women are concerned, polygamy, caste and religion are all represented. African cinema also takes as its subject matter questions such as the need to rewrite African history from African points of view. This focus on history is a prominent feature in many recent African films, as is also the issue of the African environment. While many African films detail the difficult and miserable conditions under which the majority of Africans are struggling to make a decent living and survive, they also project a desire and hope for a different future by articulating the potential of people organised to transform the status quo.

Let me cite a few films in order to discuss in more concrete fashion some of the themes mentioned in the paragraph above. Many Africans believe that African cultures, societies and individuals suffered considerably more damage than positive gains when Arabs and Europeans set foot on African soil brandishing supremacist attitudes, beliefs and practices and superior armaments of various sorts which, over time, registered some success in subjugating some Africans to alien regimes of belief and social practices. The continued voluntary adherence of some Africans to these alien regimes of culture and their concomitant contempt for, and rejection of, African cultures constitute part of the focus of films such as *Xala* (1973) and *Ceddo* (1977) by Ousmane Sembène. Two of the most memorable characters in Sembène's oeuvre are found in these two films in the persons of El-Hadj Abdou Kader Bèye, the alienated and corrupt 'businessman' in *Xala* whose contempt for traditional prenuptial rites contributes to his condition of impotence, and the imam in *Ceddo*, the embodiment of an alien religion whose programme of radical cultural subjugation and transformation is wrapped around the cloak of religious conversion. These alienated figures, the like of whom are also encountered in films such as Kwaw Ansah's *Love ... Brewed in the African Pot* (1981) and *Heritage Africa* (1988), Saddik Balewa's *Kasarmu Ce* (1991) and many more, form the object of ridicule and strident criticism. They are mocked and projected as symbols of Africa betrayed, and they are presented as compelling reasons for the need for a radical and urgent project of African cultural rehabilitation and renewal.

Life in Africa some thirty or so years after political independence from European colonial rule is portrayed in many African films as one of continued struggle with and against basically the same forces as those in operation during the colonial era. For many film-makers, independence produced precious little

5

in terms of radical reorientation in the substance, structures and styles of rule, and even less in terms of the quality of life of the majority of the population, especially those in the rural areas. What one finds in many African countries today is the continued hegemony of structures, institutions, beliefs, practices and preferences which have their origins in non-African cultures, and which were put in place primarily to promote the interests of non-Africans. The undemocratic and even brutal methods that were formerly employed to establish, maintain and control such hegemonic structures before political independence are the same methods that have been fine-tuned, updated and deployed by the post-colonial state to maintain and control these same structures. Thus, in the eyes of the many Africans who feel disempowered, political independence has meant a further decline in the quality of their life, further alienation from state political power and a sense of betrayal and disillusionment. This has translated into a strong, albeit repressed, undercurrent of discontent and an injunction towards fundamental change, in addition to an increasing awareness of the potential and possible power of individuals when organised. A good number of recent African films such as Gaston Kaboré's *Zan Boko* (1989), Amadou Saalum Seck's *Saaraba* (1989), Jean-Marie Téno's *Afrique, je te plumerai*, and Souleymane Cissé's *Finyé* (1981) dramatise this post-colonial African condition.

Conducting the most mundane of transactions involving government bureaucracy anywhere usually elicits the proverbial red tape and frustrations. In Africa such activities have painful peculiarities all of their own. Dealing with post-colonial African bureaucracies, especially if one is not equipped with the requisite language tools (French or English, for example) and if one is not well connected or endowed with financial resources, is figured as a nightmare experience by some film-makers. Two films that look at and indict the cold impotence of the post-colonial bureaucracy are Ousmane Sembène's 1968 feature *Mandabi* and Clarence Delgado's 1992 first feature, *Niiwam* (an adaptation of a short story by Sembène).

Together these two Senegalese films show what it is like when an ordinary illiterate (in French) and poor Senegalese person, a peasant, comes face to face with a post-colonial bureaucracy which supposedly exists to serve all Senegalese. Ibrahima Dieng, the protagonist of *Mandabi*, is taken on a brutal eye-opening whirlwind tour of the Senegalese bureaucracy, and in the end not only does he lose the money entrusted to him by his nephew to another corrupt and dishonest nephew but he also loses his stature and self-esteem; his resolve to become a crook like everyone else is tempered by the postman, who articulates a different approach as to how to change things. Delgado's *Niiwam* condemns the sad state of medical and burial facilities available to ordinary people in the rural areas as well as in the city. Lack of adequate and good-quality health care, facilities and resources is a major theme in many African films, and the disastrous consequences of their absence in certain areas of a country is dramatised and alluded to in films such as *Certificat d'indigence* (Yoro Moussa Batchily, 1981), *Poko* (Idrissa Ouédraogo, 1981) and many others.

In *Niiwam*, Delgado uses the death of a child and the father's attempt to bury the corpse to take us on a critical guided tour through bustling Dakar and Senegalese modernity. With the dead body of his child wrapped in a cloth and held on his lap while seated in the bus, Thierno heads for the burial ground situated near the end of the bus route. In the course of the bus journey we are shown a cross-section of urban Senegal as people get on and off the bus at different stops. We are treated to the conversations and comments of these people on a variety of social, political and economic issues and concerns, but it is the voice of Thierno, in inner monologue, that provides the overall commentary, a most critical one at that, on the various characters and events in the course of the bus ride. Thierno, the peasant from a small fishing village just outside Dakar, is obliged by circumstances to deal with the modern city, and in this brief bus ride he encounters a gallery of characters – thieves, pickpockets, ordinary men and women honestly struggling to survive under difficult circumstances, young men and women with various sorts of dispositions and behaviours, and so on. The encounter with this different world occasions an invidious comparison with the world of his own village, and a critical reflection on modernity from the perspective of Thierno. *Yalla Yaana* (1995) by Moussa Sene Absa from Senegal and *Un Taxi pour Aouzzou* (1994) by Issa Serge Coelo from Chad bear some resemblance to *Niiwam* in their use of a 'car rapide' (a mini-bus), in the case of *Yalla Yaana*, and a taxi cab, in the case of *Un Taxi pour Aouzzou*.

The city as a site where traditional moral values and practices are tested, degraded, compromised or transformed is a theme that a number of African creative practitioners – oral narrative performers, writers, dramatists and film-makers – have privileged in many narratives. The very real phenomenon of rural–urban drift or migration, when young people, in particular, abandon their villages and farms and head toward the cities in search of better opportunities, and the effects of such migrations on rural and national economic productivity and on services and infrastructures in the urban areas have provided many film-makers with a great deal of narrative material. Usually, the narrative schema is one in which the protagonist is pushed out of the village or pulled towards the city, for one reason or another, and, once in the city, begins a struggle to adjust to and fit into a radically different world. A few make it, but the majority get dragged into an urban subculture of alcohol, drugs, prostitution, robbery, prison and, sometimes, death. A few get disillusioned and return to their village. Women subjected to this subculture become the objects of gross exploitation. The narrative of the Kenyan film-maker Anne Mungai's *Saikati* (1992) follows this schema to some extent. Earlier films which include this theme as part of their narrative include Tidiane Aw's *Le Bracelet de bronze* (1973), Drissa Touré's *Laada* (1991), and Idrissa Ouédraogo's *Le Choix* (1987) and *Samba Traoré* (1993).

Saikati casts a particular glance at this phenomenon in contemporary tourist Kenya, with a specific focus on women. Two different worlds are set up in this film, one inhabited by Saikati's cousin, Monica, and the other by Saikati and her parents and family members. Monica's world is the modern world of urban Nairobi skyscrapers, plush hotels, paved streets overflowing with people and vehicles of all makes, rural tourist spots, safaris in game parks, white male tourist companions/customers, Western-style dress and cosmetics, and a cramped one-room apartment in Nairobi. Saikati's world is the world of the Masai Mara surrounded by vast plains and animals of all sorts, a family enclosure within a small village, daily treks to and from school, and traditional Masai dress, cosmetics and jewellery. It is from this latter world that Monica fled some time back to go to Nairobi, where she lives the life of a sexually liberated woman working within the world of tourism. Within her world, Saikati is confronted with the exigencies of traditional lore and practices. She is being forced by her parents (her father in particular) to become the wife of the village chief's son for whom she has absolutely no feelings. On one of her visits back home, Monica offers Saikati a way out of this problem – to run away to Nairobi where the two of them can live and work together. Saikati's brief sojourn in Monica's world – and this is where the film turns into a promotional tourist piece – ends in rather bitter disappointment and disillusionment. Saikati rejects Monica's world and heads back to the Mara to deal with the challenges there. In *Saikati*, its technical and artistic shortcomings notwithstanding, Anne Mungai attempts a more balanced look at female prostitution in urban Kenya and at both the 'push' and the 'pull' factors that account for rural–urban drift. In doing this, she also levels a subtle indictment at the practice of forced marriage, whose victims are usually young girls who are thus robbed of opportunities to gain education and to experience youth.

Anne Mungai is one of a growing number of African women film-makers other than pioneers such as Safi Faye (Senegal), Assia Djébar (Algeria), Asma El Bakri (Egypt), Sarah Maldoror (Angola/Guadeloupe), Izza Gennini (Morocco), Thérèse Sita-Bella (Cameroon), Salem Mekuria (Ethiopia), and Flora M'Mbugu (Tanzania), and recent comers such as Mariama Hima (Niger), Moufida Tlatli (Tunisia), Ngozi Onwurah (Nigeria), Lola Fani-Kayode (Nigeria), Deborah Ogazuma (Nigeria), Funmi Osoba (Nigeria), Jane Lusabe (Kenya), Fanta Nacro (Burkina Faso), Khaditou Konaté (Mali), Anne Laure Folly (Togo), Wanjiru Kinyanjui (Kenya) and a few others. Like some of their male counterparts, these women film-makers engage the broad range of issues and topics thrown up by the experiences and challenges of life in post-colonial Africa. However, unlike many of their male counterparts, some of these women film-makers bring to these issues and topics a particular female and gender sensibility whose absence in previous male-directed films severely handicapped the filmic discourse on these issues and topics. Moreover, many of these women film-makers open up new spaces of discourse, focusing on subjects and raising questions on which many male film-makers maintained a long silence.

Kaddu Beykat (1975) by Safi Faye, for example, looks at the experience of Senegalese peasants with drought and their government's impotence and neglect *vis-à-vis* rural peasant conditions. She also privileges the voices of female peasants in ways that foreground their roles and work as primary agents in agricultural production, and as the people who bear an enormous part of the burden of dealing with drought within the household, a fact usually erased in many male-directed accounts of the effects of and responses to drought.

Salem Mekuria's *Sidet: Forced Exile* (1992) presents a compelling and moving portrait of women forced to flee from their homes by drought, hunger, political instability and war in the Horn of Africa region – Ethiopia, Eritrea, Sudan and Somalia. Mekuria makes present the absent faces and voices of the primary population which usually shoulders the brunt of the burden of the results of natural disasters and male misrule and destructive policies. In the voices of these involuntary residents of refugee camps, we also hear female assessments and indictments of customs and practices oppressive to women; we hear forceful articulations of the need for different conceptions of gender and gender roles;

8

and, above all, we see women actively struggling to construct a new life. So much for the conventional accounts of such mishaps, which focus on male heads of households only, and in which men are the only ones given the chance to speak, those narratives which project no hope at all! Equally significant along these lines is Sarah Maldoror's *Sambizanga* (1972), which shows women as primary agents in the Angolan war of liberation against Portuguese colonialism, and this at a moment when anticolonial liberation efforts were mistakenly figured principally as a male responsibility. Sembène in *Ceddo* (1977) and Med Hondo in *Sarraounia* (1986) also show African women in leadership roles in situations of combat and conflict.

African women today continue to be obliged, sometimes forcibly so, to comply with different practices sanctioned by 'tradition', many of which are blatantly oppressive, exploitative and harmful. These include spouse inheritance, in which the brother or some close male relative of a deceased husband can claim his widow as wife; polygamy, the practice of marrying more than one wife; forced marriage; various forms of genital surgery, wrongly named female circumcision; sexual and other forms of violence; adherence to codified and normative forms of dress, behaviour and comportment, especially in public; restriction to only certain forms of work; and exploitation and devaluation of female labour. These questions constitute a major focus in the work of some film-makers while others allude to one or more of them in their works. The Moroccan film-maker Jilali Ferhati's 1991 work, *La Plage des enfants perdus*, projects a refreshing and particulary complex and nuanced narrative of resistance by a young Morrocan woman to established gender norms and expectations, and the destabilising and transformative effects of such resistance on an entrenched patriarchy, while *Les Silences du palais* (1994) by the Tunisian filmmaker Moufida Tlatli deploys a metaphor of silence paradoxically to narrate loudly memories of royal subjugation and exploitation of female subjects and one young woman's response to such conditions.

Neria (1992), a film by the Zimbabwean Godwin Mawuru, dramatises the experience and response of one woman faced with the challenge of dealing with the practice of wife inheritance. Previously, Cheick Oumar Cissoko of Mali examined this aspect of traditional African customs in his 1991 film, *Finzan,* which also is one of the few African films, to date, along with Boureima Nikièma's *Ma Fille ne sera pas excisée* and Soraya Mire's *Fire Eyes* (1994), to engage the question of female genital mutilation. A newcomer, Mahamat Saleh Houroun from Chad, looks at the question of forced marriage in his first film, *Maral Tanie* (1994), the same topic engaged much earlier by Dikongue-Pipa's *Muna Moto* (1974), and which figures prominently in Cheick Oumar Cissoko's recent narrative of African totalitarianism in *Guimba* (1995).

Perhaps the African cultural practice that has so far received one of the most prominent treatments in film is polygamy. The one film-maker who has handled this theme with the greatest artistry and sophistication is no doubt Ousmane Sembène, whose 1974 film *Xala* not only subverts traditional definitions of African manhood but, more significantly, symbolically yokes the practice of polygamy to politics of gender, class, culture and neocolonialism. *Xala* is an allegory of post-colonial Africa. A different, but equally satirical, look at polygamy is to be found in *A la recherche du mari de ma femme* (1993) by Moroccan film-maker Mohamed Abderrahman Tazi and *Bal poussière* (1991) by Henri Duparc of Côte d'Ivoire. In the tradition of 'comédie de moeurs', Duparc takes a swipe at male excess in the figure of the incorrigible yet hard-to-dislike Demi-Dieu, whose foibles and struggles to keep six women under one roof inspire constant laughter in an audience which is simultaneously being dished a critique of this bastion of male privilege.

Other recent films which can be seen as distant cousins of *Bal poussière* include *Rue Princesse* (1993) by Henri Duparc, and *Gito l'ingrat* (1993) by Léonce Ngabo of Burundi. *Gito l'ingrat* recalls aspects of the 'been-to' syndrome found in some African novels of the late 60s and early 70s. This syndrome involves the African who goes abroad and returns home after some time, experiences readjustment problems and normally boasts of the places he has been to (in Europe or America, for example). *Back Home Again* (1994) by Kofi Nartey and Kwame Johnson from Ghana also plays out this syndrome. Ngabo's film extends the syndrome and invests it with a more comic twist. Gito's experience is the experience of many an African male who goes abroad and returns home after an extended stay. It is a comedy on modern urban youth culture and sexuality, a theme that also forms the basis of the narrative of another new film from Cameroon, *Quartier Mozart* (1993) by Jean-Pierre Békolo. Generational differences and emergent forms of African female resistance, self-affirmation and activism figure prominently in these new films as well as in Désiré Ecaré's controversial film *Visages de femmes* (1985) – one of the few African films, so far, to have engaged African female sexuality in explicit ways – in Djibril Diop Mambety's *Touki Bouki* (1973) and in Nouri Bouzid's *Bezness* (1992). The dynamics of modern urban youth culture and sexuality also constitute the narrative focus of Flora Gomes's *Les Yeux bleus de Yonta* (1993), a love story which also captures the cultural and political pulse of the post-war moment in urban Guinea-Bissau, a country still struggling with the myriad legacies and challenges of the long armed struggle against Portuguese colonial domination. *Les Yeux bleus de Yonta* extends and shifts the discourse inaugurated by Gomes in his first film on post-war Guinea-Bissau, *Mortu Nega* (1991).

While Ngabo's *Gito l'ingrat* focuses on the experience of return to the native land, *Toubabi* (1993), by the Senegalese film-maker Moussa Touré, revisits the theme of African emigration towards the metropolitan countries of the West, and the traumas, challenges and experiences of life as an immigrant in the cities of the former colonial powers such as France. This theme is present in films such as Med Hondo's *Soleil-O* (1973), Ben Diogaye Bèye's *Les Princes noirs de Saint Germain des Prés* (1971), Ousmane Sembène's *La Noire de ...* (1965), Abderrahmane Sissako's *Octobre* (1993), shot in Moscow, Mory Traoré's 1981 film, *L'Homme d'ailleurs*, a film shot in Japan about the story of a young African resident whose rejection by Japanese society compels him to commit suicide, and, more recently, in Idrissa Ouédraogo's chronicle of Black immigrant life in Lyons in *Le Cri du coeur* (1994). *Toubabi* emphasises the traps of the French urban subculture of drugs, pimping and prostitution, with a focus on its African victims who become ethically and morally debased even while professing superficially to hold on to their Africanness. This is the case with Soriba Samb's childhood friend, now a small-time pimp in Paris. Touré warns of the dangers of uncritical Westernisation, not unlike the manner in which other film-makers posit the city (discussed above) as a site of possible collapse and degradation of culture and identity. In contrast, Ouédraogo's *Le Cri du coeur* projects a different face of immigration and emergent new identities as he examines the life of a comparatively successful middle-class African immigrant entrepreneur and the challenges faced by third-generation African children born and bred in France.

Some films that deal with urban contemporary life also pay a great deal of attention to young, pre-adolescent people. The experience of coming of age, gaining a sense of one's sexuality, struggling to survive in harsh urban conditions – these are themes that one encounters in films such as Brahim Tsaki's sensitive portayal of youthful interracial relations in *Histoire d'une rencontre* (1985), Férid Boughédir's masterpiece, *Halfaouine* (1991), Mansour Sora Wade's delightful *Picc Mi* (1992), Ahmet Diallo's inventive and radically unconventional *Boxulmaleen* (1991) and Bouna Medoune Seye's *Bandit Cinema* (1993). The latter two films resonate with the style, tone and temperament of Djibril Diop Mambety's *Badou Boy* (1969), *Touki Bouki* (1973), *Hyenas* (1992) and *Le Franc* (1993). Notwithstanding the inordinate focus on young boys who often come to an awareness of their sexuality at the expense of women who are accorded marginal and stereotypical presence, these films show how young people see and deal with post-colonial urban environments and cultures in which traditional norms of responsibility, control and relations between elders and the young undergo severe strains to the point of total collapse. *Boxulmaleen*, in particular, constructs a counter-society ruled by pre-adolescent and young people, a counter-society which mirrors, yet simultaneously parodies and transgresses, the institutions, actors, norms, conventions and practices of established society. Wade's *Picc Mi* also comments on the effects of urbanisation on family and young people, and he achieves this through a most imaginative and skilful adaptation of traditional storytelling techniques. These urban-based narratives of adolescence complement the many stories of growing up young in rural Africa which are dramatised in the films of Gaston Kaboré (*Wend Kuuni*, 1982, *Rabi*, 1993), and those of Idrissa Ouédraogo (*Yaaba*, 1989), which situate themselves in predominantly rural African contexts away from the gaze and reach of Western-influenced modernist contexts of the urban-situated films.

Rural Africa is usually the setting of many narratives which dramatise the dynamics of life in pre-colonial Africa. Perhaps because it is usually figured as a zone of African cultural integrity and 'purity', uncontaminated by White culture, rural Africa is the favoured locale for films such as *Wend Kuuni* (1982), *Yeelen* (1991) and *Tilai* (1991), which privilege African versions of narratives and themes that are considered universal and symbolic of the human condition. In focusing on pre-colonial African conflicts, subjects and societies, with their share of joys, desires, virtues and vices, harmony and disharmony, triumphs and disappointments, these films seek to humanise Africans and to counter certain unrealistic constructs of pre-colonial Africa. Rather than depicting Africa as a place of perfect order and Africans as a special/unique species of humanity, these films find the following elements to be part of the reality of Africa: love, deception, lust and prejudice; father-son rivalry and fights for power; social cohesion, in relation to anti-social behaviour; adultery, violence against women, care for orphans, the indigent and the disabled; male chauvinist practices, exploitation, and oppression; religious piety and charlatanism of all sorts. A most eloquent narrativisation of these themes is to be found in Cheick Oumar Cissoko's *Guimba*.

The celebration and interrogation of Africa – past and present – which is evident in these films also informs Gnoan Mbala's film entitled *Au nom du Christ* (1993). Africans have always been confronted with crooks and confidence tricksters who exploit the deep-seated religious and spiritual disposition of Africans to advance individual secular interests and desires. Masked as holy men out to save souls and transform lives and fortunes, these religious charlatans use their gift of language, cunning and wit to win over dispirited, disempowered, alienated, frustrated and poverty-stricken victims of post-colonial misrule, who see in their discourse the promise of redemption from everyday misery. Urban Africa teems with revivalist, Pentecostal, Islamic and other such religious movements, many of which prey on the poor. Mbala's *Au nom du Christ* looks at this phenomenon in the Côte d'Ivoire. Magloire II, erstwhile thief, rapist and murderer, claims to have experienced a revelation from Jesus, whom he calls his cousin. He builds a following which gradually swells into a mini-empire over which he rules supreme. Magloire II's sovereignty over this mini-empire, his style of rule and his relations with his followers/subjects all echo the post-colonial state. Totalitarianism and a sense of omnipotence and immortality define Magloire II's style and person, but, paradoxically, it is the belief in his own self that spells his doom. In Magloire II, Mbala presents a double-edged parody and critique of both established religious and secular structures in contemporary Africa. He focuses particularly on the Côte d'Ivoire, whose late head of state spent billions constructing the famous basilica at Yamoussoukoro, his birthplace. *Au nom du Christ* is as much about religion as it is about politics in contemporary Africa.

The subject of African history is one which has commanded the attention of a number of films by Africans. There is a belief that stories of the African past have been rendered predominantly from the perspective of Europeans, and, as such, these versions of history exclude stories of Africa before the advent of Europeans and Arabs. These dominant European versions also focus predominantly on the story of Europeans in Africa and present these as authentic histories of Africa. In these versions, Europe is presented as the bringer of history and civilisation to an ahistorical Africa, thus justifying the project of imperial and colonial expansion, which is portrayed as benevolent, benign and sanctioned by God. A number of recent African films present versions of the African past from African perspectives, which contest and subvert conventional European accounts, and which present more complex and balanced histories, especially the histories of imperialism and colonialism. Some of these African films engage history in critical ways to reconstruct the past as well as to talk about the present in Africa. Examples of African filmic reconstructions of history include Ousmane Sembène's *Ceddo*, which presents a different version of how Islam came into Senegal and its effects, and *Emitai* (1971) and *Camp de Thiaroye* (1988), which deconstruct French colonial ideologies and practices of 'égalité, fraternité, justice'. Re-examination of the Algerian war of independence from France is evident in numerous films such as Mohamed Lakhdar-Hamina's 1975 classic *Chronique des années de braise*, Slim Riad's *La Voie* (1968), and more recently, Mohamed Chouick's *Youcef ou la légende du septième dormant* (1993). In a somewhat different vein, but with memory as its motor force, Moufida Tlatli's brilliant *Les Silences du palais* re-examines and rewrites a certain moment of Tunisian history, the period of the *beys*, the last rulers of Tunisia, from a female perspective and in refreshingly imaginative ways that accord a large place to individual lives and desires. Med Hondo's *Sarraounia* (1988) also presents a radically different version of French colonial policy and expansion in Africa through the story of Sarraounia, the nineteenth-century queen of the Azna of Niger, who successfully resisted French colonial domination and built a society based on equity, justice and tolerance. Most recently, Haile Gerima (Ethiopia) achieved in his latest film, *Sankofa* (1993), a most compelling rewrite of slavery from a Pan-African perspective. In *Keita, de bouche à oreille* (1994), the young Burkinabe film-maker Dany Kouyaté re-enacts the Mande 'master' narrative, the epic of Sundiata Keita, the thirteenth-century founding figure of the Mali Empire, in order to reflect on the necessity of producing more imaginative and productive uses of heritages of the past for the present as well as the future.

The final theme in African cinema that I want to dwell on briefly is the African environment and ecology. Concern with environmental issues such as drought and the consequences of prolonged lack of water (hunger, famine, death, displacement, migration, the breakdown of social structure and relations) has a long history in African creative practice. Many are the oral narratives that dramatise these issues, and a few African film-makers have engaged with these issues, some taking inspiration and models from the traditional narratives. Among the first African films to take up this issue is *Toula* (1973) by Mustapha Alassane from Niger, which is an adaptation of a story by Boubou Hama of Niger, juxtaposing African and Western approaches to drought control and problem solving. Western meteorological practices are placed side by side with the beliefs of an African traditional practitioner who prescribes sacrificing a human being to appease the water spirits. More recently, the increasingly devastating impact of drought on African lives, societies and economies in the Sahel and Horn of Africa regions, in particular, has commanded the artistic attention of a number of African film-makers.

Jom (1982), by the Senegalese film-maker Ababacar Samb Makharam, makes brief allusion to the drought in the Sahel in images of desertification, with the carcasses of dead animals, and in a sequence in which we are shown young women forced to migrate to the city to become maids for wealthier urban elites. Souleymane Cissé's *Yeelen* also presents graphic portraits of the drought-stricken Sahel as integral parts of his narrative, as does *Sigida* (1994) by Salif Traoré, also from Mali. We have also seen how the devastation of drought and famine constitute a major driving force of the narrative of Salem Mekuria's *Sidet*. Anne Mungai's *Saikati*, however, uses the Kenyan environment in a slightly different way, not unlike the manner in which Hollywood African productions set up the Mara, animals and game parks as backdrop to adventures and romances.

In 1987, Idrissa Ouédraogo of Burkina Faso made *Le Choix*, dramatising the options available to the inhabitants of a village afflicted with long periods without rains. The choice is between abandoning an unproductive zone and migrating south to more productive zones with better rainfall, on the one hand, and staying put in the drought-stricken village and depending on food aid from abroad, on the other. One family opts to leave and start a new life away from their traditional homes, while the majority are shown waiting for food donated by foreign agencies and governments. The dialectics of self-reliance

13

and dependence on foreign food aid, broached in *Le Choix* by Ouédraogo, receives a strong and most imaginative treatment in Ousmane Sembène's film, *Guélwaar* (1993).

Among the corpus of films dealing with the African environment, two short films by the Somali film-maker Abdulkadir Ahmed Said stand out in terms of imagination, inventiveness and effectiveness. In *The Tree of Life* (1989) and *La Conchiglia* (1992), Said positions human beings as the primary agents the depletion and destruction of environmental resources. These films address questions of deforestation and water pollution, and their effects – actual and potential–on human life, society and the environment in the Horn of Africa. In *The Tree of Life*, Said uses exaggeration to dramatise the potentially apocalyptic consequences of the practice of cutting down trees for firewood. In this film, a man who habitually engages in this practice has a dream in which his village undergoes a radical transformation from a community with adequate environmental resources to support life to one which is completely devastated and reduced to dust and rubble without any vegetation as a result of his constant depredation of the local trees. He is chased by a huge black dog as he attempts to cut down another tree. He wakes up from his dream/nightmare (which Said films in strikingly beautiful sequences) resolved to stop this practice. He assumes the role of a teacher and embarks on a project to educate his fellow citizens in order to control and, perhaps, totally eliminate the practice of indiscriminate and uncontrolled destruction of trees (which are figured here as a source of life).

Said's second film, *La Conchiglia*, adopts a similar style and approach – exaggeration, dream, surreal images, sounds and decor – to talk about the consequences of water pollution. This time, it is a young girl of no more than six years who assumes the role of narrator, but she is dead and we hear her voice mingled with the echo and sound of waves coming through a beautiful sea shell which a female painter picks up on a deserted beach. In her own voice, the young girl tells the story of her short and extremely difficult life, and memories of her village and the people who have also disappeared, victims of a terrible ecological disaster which contaminated the water and surrounding land. Said, however, projects a ray of hope when in the final sequence of the film we see a young girl stray away from the group of youngsters she is playing with, and directly invite the spectator to join in their game. So crucial and urgent is the question of the environment in Africa today that in 1991, for example, the 12th meeting of the biennial FESPACO chose as its theme 'Cinema and the Environment'.

The categories or 'tendencies' (to use Férid Boughédir's term) outlined above convey in a general way part of the diversity, complexity, dynamism and transformations of African experiences and encounters with cinema. As studied responses (individual and otherwise) to various artistic, material, cultural, political and socioeconomic challenges, opportunities and imperatives which are in a constant state of flux, these various categories are themselves also implicated in constant processes of change, adapting to different circumstances and, in many cases, engendering what seem to be new forms and directions.

PART I
Manifestos, Declarations and Resolutions

Resolutions of the Third World Film-Makers' Meeting, Algiers, Algeria, 1973

Committee 1: People's Cinema

The Committee on People's Cinema – the role of cinema and film-makers in the Third World against imperialism and neocolonialism – consisted of the following film-makers and observers: Fernando Birri (Argentina); Humberto Rios (Bolivia); Mañuel Perez (Cuba); Jorge Silva (Colombia); Jorge Cedron (Argentina); Moussa Diakite (Republic of Guinea); Flora Gomes (Guinea-Bissau); Mohamed Abdelwahad (Morocco); El Hachmi Cherif (Algeria), Lamine Merbah (Algeria); Mache Khaled (Algeria); Fettar Sid Ali (Algeria); Bensalah Mohamed (Algeria); Meziani Abdelhakim (Algeria). Observers: Jan Lindquist (Sweden), Josephine (surname unknown, Guinea-Bissau) and Salvatore Piscicelli (Italy).

The Committee met on 11, 12 and 13 December 1973, in Algiers, under the chairmanship of Lamine Merbah. At the close of its deliberations, the Committee adopted the following analysis.

So-called 'underdevelopment' is first of all an economic phenomenon which has direct repercussions on the social and cultural sectors. To analyse such a phenomenon we must refer to the dialectics of the development of capitalism on a world scale.

At a historically determined moment in its development, capitalism extended itself beyond the framework of the national European boundaries and spread – a necessary condition for its growth – to other regions of the world in which the forces of production, being only slightly developed, provided favourable ground for the expansion of capitalism through the existence of immense and virgin material resources, and available and cheap manpower reserves which constituted a new, potential market for the products of capitalist industry.

This expansion manifested itself in different regions, given the power relationships, and in different ways:

(a) Through direct and total colonisation implying violent invasion and the setting up of an economic and social infrastructure which does not correspond to the real needs of the people but serves more, or exclusively, the interests of the metropolitan countries;

(b) In a more or less disguised manner leaving to the countries in question a pretence of autonomy;

(c)   Finally, through a system of domination of a new type – neocolonialism.

The result has been that these countries undergo, on the one hand, varying degrees of development and, on the other hand, extremely varied levels of dependency with respect to imperialism: domination, influence and pressures.

The different forms of exploitation and systematic plundering of the natural resources have had grave consequences on the economic, social and cultural levels for the so-called 'underdeveloped' countries, resulting in the fact that even though these countries are undergoing extremely diversified degrees of development, they face in their struggle for independence and social progress a common enemy: imperialism, which stands in their way as the principal obstacle to their development.

Its consequences can be seen in:

(a)   The articulation of the economic sectors: imbalance of development on the national level with the creation of poles of economic attraction incompatible with the development of a proportionally planned national economy and with the interests of the popular masses, thereby giving rise to zones of artificial prosperity.
(b)   The imbalance on the regional and continental levels, thereby revealing the determination of imperialism to create zones of attraction favourable for its own expansion and which are presented as models of development in order to retard the people's struggle for real political and economic independence.

The repercussions on the social plane are as serious as they are numerous: they lead to characteristic impoverishment of the majority for the benefit in the first instance of the dominating forces and the national bourgeoisie of which one sector is objectively interested in independent national development, while another sector is parasitic and *comprador,* the interests of which are bound to those of the dominating forces.

The differentiations and social inequities have seriously affected the living standard of the people, mainly in the rural areas where the expropriated or impoverished peasants find it impossible to reinvest on the spot in order to subsist. Reduced in their majority to self-consumption, unemployment and rural exodus, these factors lead to an intensification of unemployment and increase underemployment in the urban centers.

In order to legitimise and strengthen its hold over the economies of the colonised and neocolonised countries, imperialism has recourse to a systematic enterprise of deculturation and acculturation of the people of the Third World.

That deculturation consists of depersonalising their peoples, of discrediting their culture by presenting it as inferior and inoperative, of blocking their specific development, and of disfiguring their history.... In other words, creating an actual cultural vacuum favourable to a simultaneous process of acculturation through which the dominator endeavours to make his domination legitimate by introducing his own moral values, his life and thought patterns, his explanation of history: in a word, his culture.

Imperialism, being obliged to take into account the fact that colonised or dominated peoples have their own culture and defend it, infiltrates the culture of the colonised, entertains relationships with it and takes over those elements which it believes can turn it to its favour. This is done by using the social forces

18

which they make their own, the retrograde elements of this culture. In this way, the language of the colonised, which is the carrier of culture, becomes inferior or foreign, it is used only in the family circle or in restricted social circles. It is no longer, therefore, a vehicle for education, culture and science, because in the schools the language of the coloniser is taught, it being indispensable to know it in order to work, to subsist and to assert oneself. Gradually, it infiltrates the social and even the family relationships of the colonised. Language itself becomes a means of alienation, in that the colonised has a tendency to practise the language of the coloniser, while his own language, as well as his personality, his culture and his moral values, become foreign to him.

In the same line of thought, the social sciences, such as sociology, archaeology and ethnology, are for the most part in the service of the coloniser and the dominant class so as to perfect the work of alienation of the people through a pseudo-scientific process which has in fact simply consisted of a retrospective justification for the presence of the coloniser and therefore of the new established order.

This is how sociological studies have attempted to explain social phenomena by fatalistic determinism, foreign to the conscience and the will of man. In the ethnological field, the enterprise has consisted of rooting in the minds of the colonised prejudices of racial and original inferiority and complexes of inadequacy for the mastering of the various acquisitions of knowledge and man's production. Among the colonised people, imperialism has endeavored to play on the pseudo-racial and community differences, giving privilege to one or another ethnic grouping.

As for archaeology, its role in cultural alienation has contributed to distorting history by putting emphasis on the interests and efforts of research and the excavations of historical vestiges which justify the definite paternity of European civilisation sublimated and presented as being eternally superior to other civilisations whose slightest traces have been buried.

Whereas, in certain countries, the national culture has continued to develop while at the same time being retarded by the dominant forces, in other countries, given the long period of direct domination, it has been marked by discontinuity which has blocked it in its specific development, so that all that remains are traces of it which are scarcely capable of serving as a basis for a real cultural renaissance, unless it is raised to the present level of development of national and international productive forces.

It should be stated, however, that the culture of the coloniser, while alienating the colonised peoples, does the same to the peoples of the colonising countries who are themselves exploited by the capitalist system. Cultural alienation presents, therefore, a dual character – national against the totality of the colonised peoples, and social against the working classes in the colonising countries as well as in the colonised countries.

Imperialist economic, political and social domination, in order to subsist and to reinforce itself takes root in an ideological system articulated through various channels and mainly through cinema, which is in a position to influence the majority of the popular masses because its essential importance is at one and the same time artistic, aesthetic, economic and sociological, affecting to a major degree the training of the mind. Cinema, also being an industry, is subjected to the same development as material production within the capitalist system and through the very fact that the North American economy is preponderant with respect to world capitalist production, its cinema becomes preponderant as well and succeeds in invading the screens of the capitalist world and consequently those of the Third World, where it contributes to hiding inequalities, referring them to that ideology which governs the world imperialist system dominated by the United States of America.

With the birth of the national liberation movement, the struggle for independence takes on a certain depth implying, on one hand, the revalorisation of national cultural heritage in marking it with a dynamism made necessary by the development of contradictions and, on the other hand, the contribution of progressive cultural factors borrowed from the field of universal culture.

The Role of Cinema

The role of cinema in this process consists of manufacturing films reflecting the objective conditions in which the struggling peoples are developing, that is to say, films which bring about disalienation of the colonised peoples at the same time as they contribute sound and objective information for the peoples of the entire world, including the oppressed classes of the colonising countries, and place the struggle of their peoples back in the general context of the struggle of the countries and peoples of the Third World. This requires from the militant film-maker a dialectical analysis of the socio-historic phenomenon of colonisation.

Reciprocally, cinema in the already liberated countries and in the progressive countries must accomplish, as their own national tasks, active solidarity with the peoples and film-makers of countries still under colonial and neocolonial domination and which are struggling for their genuine national sovereignty. The countries enjoying political independence and struggling for varied development are aware of the fact that the struggle against imperialism on the political, economic and social levels is inseparable from its ideological content and that, consequently, action must be taken to seize from imperialism the means to influence ideologically, and forge new methods adapted in content and form to the interests of the struggle of their peoples. This implies control by the people's state of all cultural activities and, in respect to cinema, nationalisation in the interest of the masses of people: production, distribution and commercialisation. So as to make such a policy operative, it has been seen that the best path requires quantitative and qualitative development of national production capable, with the acquisition of films from the Third World countries and the progressive countries, of swinging the balance of the power relationship in favour of using cinema in the interest of the masses. While influencing the general environment, conditions must be created for a greater awareness on the part of the masses, for the development of their critical senses and varied participation in the cultural life of their countries.

A firm policy based on principle must be introduced in this field so as to eliminate once and for all the films which the foreign monopolies continue to impose upon us either directly or indirectly and which generate reactionary culture and, as a result, thought patterns in contradiction with the basic choices of our people.

The question, however, is not one of separating cinema from the overall cultural context which prevails in our countries, for we must consider that, on the one hand, the action of cinema is accompanied by that of other information and cultural media, and, on the other hand, cinema operates with materials which are drawn from reality and already existing cultural forms of expression in order to function and operate. It is also necessary to be vigilant and eliminate nefarious action which the information media can have and to purify the forms of popular expression (folklore, music, theatre, etc.) and to modernise them.

The cinema language being thereby linked to other cultural forms, the development of cinema, while demanding the raising of the general cultural level, contributes to this task in an efficient way and can even become an excellent means for the polarisation of the various action fields as well as cultural radiation.

Films being a social act within a historical reality, it follows that the task of the Third World film-maker is no longer limited to the making of films but is extended to other fields of action such as: articulating, fostering and making the new films understandable to the masses of people by associating himself with the promoters of people's cinemas, clubs and itinerant film groups in their dynamic action aimed at disalienation and sensitisation in favour of a cinema which satisfies the interests of the masses, for at the same time that the struggle against imperialism and for progress develops on the economic, social and political levels, a greater and greater awareness of the masses develops, associating cinema in a more concrete way in this struggle.

In other words, the question of knowing how cinema will develop is linked in a decisive way to the solutions which must be provided to all the problems with which our peoples are confronted and which cinema must face, and contribute to resolving. The task of the Third World film-maker thereby becomes even more important and implies that the struggle waged by cinema for independence, freedom and progress must go, and already goes, hand in hand with the struggle within and outside the field of cinema, but always in alliance with the popular masses for the triumph of the ideas of freedom and progress.

In these conditions, it becomes obvious that the freedom of expression and movement, the right to practise cinema and research are essential demands of the film-makers of the Third World – freedoms and rights which they have already committed to invest in the service of the working masses against imperialism, colonialism and neocolonialism for the general emancipation of their peoples.

United and in solidarity against American imperialism, at the head of world imperialism, and direct or indirect aggressor in Vietnam, Cambodia, Laos, Palestine, in Africa through the intermediary of NATO, SEATO and CENTO, and in Latin America, hiding itself behind the fascist *coup d'état* of the Chilean military junta and the other oligarchies in power, the film-makers present here in Algiers, certain that they express the opinion of their film-maker comrades of the Third World, condemn the interventions, aggressions and pressures of imperialism, condemn the persecutions to which the film-makers of certain Third World countries are subjected and demand the immediate liberation of the film-makers detained and imprisoned and the cessation of measures restricting their freedom.

Committee 2: Production/Co-production
The Committee on Production/Co-production, appointed by the General

21

Assembly of the Third World Film-Makers Meeting in Algeria, met on 11, 12 and 13 December 1973, under the chairmanship of Ousmane Sembène. The Committee, which devoted itself to the problems of film production and co-production in Third World countries, included the following film-makers and observers: Ousmane Sembène (Senegal); Sergio Castilla (Chile); Santiago Alvarez (Cuba); Sebastien Kainba (Congo): Mamadou Sidibe (Mali); Benamar Bakhti (Algeria); Nourredine Touazi (Algeria); Hedi Ben Khelifa (Tunisia); Mostefa Bouali (Palestine); Med Hondo (Mauritania). Observers: Simon Hartog (Great Britain), representing the British film-makers' union, and Theo Robichet (France). Humberto Rios (Argentina) presented an information report to the Committee.

The delegates present, after reporting on the natural production and co-production conditions and the organisation of the cinema industries in their countries, noted that the role of cinema in the Third World is to promote culture through films, which are a weapon as well as a means of expression for the development of the awareness of the people, and that the cinema falls within the framework of the class struggle.

Considering:
- that the problems of cinema production in the countries of the Third World are closely linked to the economic, political and social realities of each of them;
- that, consequently, cinema activity does not develop in a similar fashion:
  (a) in those countries which are waging a liberation struggle,
  (b) in those countries which have conquered their political independence and which have founded states,
  (c) in those countries which, while being sovereign, are struggling to seize their economic and cultural independence;
- that those countries which are waging wars of liberation lack a film infrastructure and specialised cadres and, as a result, their production is limited, achieved in difficult circumstances and very often is supported by or is dependent upon sporadic initiatives;
- that in those countries struggling for their economic and cultural independence, the principal characteristic is a private infrastructure which enables them to realise only a portion of their production within the national territory, the remainder being handled in the capitalist countries;
- this leads to an appreciable loss of foreign currency and considerable delays which impede the development of an authentic national production.
- that in those countries in which the state assumes the responsibility for production and incorporates it in its cultural activity, there is, nevertheless, in a majority of cases, a lack of technical and industrial development in the cinema field and, as a consequence, production remains limited and does not manage to cover the needs for films in these countries. The national screens, therefore, are submerged with foreign productions coming, for the most part, from the capitalist countries.
- that, if we add as well the fact that world production is economically and ideologically controlled by these countries and, in addition, is of very mediocre quality, our screens bring in an ideological product which serves the interests of the colonisers, creating moreover the habit of seeing films in

22

which lies and social prejudice are the choice subjects and in which these manufacturers of individualistic ideology constantly encourage the habits of an arbitrary and wasteful consumer society;
- that co-productions must, first and foremost, be for the countries of the Third World a manifestation of anti-imperialist solidarity, although their characteristics may vary and cover different aspects. We do not believe in co-productions in which an imperialist country participates, given the following risks:
  (a) the imperialist country can shed influence through production methods which are foreign to the realities of our countries,
  (b) the examples of co-productions have given rise to cases of profit and the cultural and economic exploitation of our countries.

The participants in the Committee therefore concluded that it is necessary to seek jointly concrete means to foster the production and co-production of national films within the Third World countries.

In line with this, a certain number of recommendations were unanimously adopted:

- to provide the revolutionary film-makers of the Third World with national cinema infrastructures;
- to put aside the conceptions and film production means of the capitalist countries and to seek new forms, taking into account the authenticity and the realities of the economic means and possibilities of the Third World countries;
- to develop national cinema and television agreements for the benefit of the production and distribution of Third World films and to seek such agreements where they do not exist and to exchange regular programmes;
- to organise and develop the teaching of film techniques, to welcome the nationals of countries in which the training is not ensured;
- to use all the audiovisual means available for the political, economic and cultural development of the countries of the Third World;
- to promote co-productions with independent revolutionary film-makers, while leaving to each country the task of determining the characteristics of these productions;
- to include in the governmental agreements between countries of the Third World those measures likely to facilitate co-productions and film exchanges;
- to influence the establishment of co-productions between national organisations of the Third World in endeavouring to have them accepted by the governmental and professional institutions of their respective countries (through the influence, in particular, of the acting president of the non-aligned countries, Mr Houari Boumedienne);
- to propose the need for the creation of an organisation of Third World film-makers, the permanent secretariat of which should be set up in Cuba. While awaiting the creation of this organisation, the UAAV (Union of Audio Visual Arts of Algeria) will provide a temporary secretariat;
- the film-makers will henceforth keep each other informed of their respective approaches undertaken within the framework of the FEPACI (Fédération Pan-Africaine des Cinéastes).

Committee 3: Distribution

The Committee in charge of the distribution of Third World films, after consideration of the different remarks of the members present, proposes: the creation of an office to be called the Third World Cinema Office.

It will be composed of four members including a resident co-ordinator and one representative per continent. The Committee, in reply to the offer made by Algeria, proposes that the permanent headquarters of the office be established in Algiers.

The goals of the office will be:

1 To co-ordinate efforts for the production and distribution of Third World films.

2 To establish and strengthen existing relations between Third World filmmakers and cinema industries by:
   (a) the editing of a permanent information bulletin (filmography, technical data sheets, etc.) in four languages: Arabic, English, French and Spanish;
   (b) making a census of existing documentation on Third World cinema for the elaboration and distribution of a catalogue on the cinema production of the countries of the Third World;
   (c) fostering other festivals, film markets and film days on the Third World level, alongside the other existing events;
   (d) the editing of a general compilation of official cinema legislation in the Third World countries (problems of censorship, distribution of film copies, copyright, customs, etc.).

3 To take those measures required for the creation of regional and continental organisation leading to the creation of a tri-continental organisation for film distribution

4 To prospect the foreign markets in order to secure other outlets for the productions of the Third World countries (commercial and non-commerical rights, TV and cassettes).

The office will approach the authorities of the OAU, the Arab League and UNESCO in order to obtain from these organisations financial assistance for its functioning. It will also approach the authorities of those countries having effective control of their cinema industries, namely Algeria, Guinea, Upper Volta, Mali, Uganda, Syria and Cuba, as well as other countries which manifest a real desire to struggle against the imperialist monopoly. In addition to the above-mentioned assistance, the operating budget of the office will be composed of donations, grants and commissions on all transactions or Third World films entrusted to the office.

The Algiers Charter on African Cinema, 1975

For a responsible, free and committed cinema

This charter was adopted at the Second Congress of the FEPACI (Fédération Panafricaine des Cinéastes) in Algiers, January 1975.

Contemporary African societies are still objectively undergoing an experience of domination exerted on a number of levels: political, economic and cultural. Cultural domination, which is all the more dangerous for being insidious, imposes on our peoples models of behaviour and systems of values whose essential function is to buttress the ideological and economic ascendancy of the imperialist powers. The main channels open to this form of control are supplied by the new technologies of communication: books, the audiovisual, and very specifically the cinema. In this way the economic stranglehold over our countries is increased twofold by a pervading ideological alienation that stems from a massive injection of cultural by-products thrust on the African markets for passive consumption. Moreover, in the face of this condition of cultural domination and deracination, there is a pressing need to reformulate in liberating terms the internal problematic of development and of the part that must be played in this worldwide advance by culture and by the cinema.

To assume a genuinely active role in the process of development, African culture must be popular, democratic and progressive in character, inspired by its own realities and responding to its own needs. It must also be in solidarity with cultural struggles all over the world.

The issue is not to try to catch up with the developed capitalist societies, but rather to allow the masses to take control of the means of their own development, giving them back the cultural initiative by drawing on the resources of a fully liberated popular creativity. Within this perspective the cinema has a vital part to play because it is a means of education, information and consciousness raising, as well as a stimulus to creativity. The accomplishing of these goals implies a questioning by African film-makers of the image they have of themselves, of the nature of their function and their social status and of their general place in society. The stereotyped image of the solitary and marginal creator which is widespread in Western capitalist society must be rejected by African film-makers, who must, on the contrary, see themselves as creative artisans at the service of their people. It also demands great vigilance on their part with regard

25

to imperialism's attempts at ideological recuperation as it redoubles its efforts to maintain, renew and increase its cultural ascendancy.

In this context, African film-makers must be in solidarity with progressive film-makers who are waging anti-imperialist struggles throughout the world. Moreover, the question of commercial profit can be no yardstick for African film-makers. The only relevant criterion of profitability is the knowledge of whether the needs and aspirations of the people are expressed, and not those of specific interest groups. This means that all the structural problems of their national cinema must be of paramount importance to African film-makers.

The commitment demanded from African film-makers should in no way signify subordination. The state must take a leading role in building a national cinema free of the shackles of censorship or any other form of coercion likely to diminish the film-makers' creative scope and the democratic and responsible exercise of their profession. This freedom of expression for film-makers is in fact one of the prerequisite conditions of their ability to contribute to the development of a critical understanding among the masses and the flowering of their potentialities.

Niamey Manifesto of African Film-Makers, 1982

First International Conference on Cinema Production in Africa (Niamey, Niger, 1–4 March 1982)

The first international conference on cinema was held in Niamey, 1–4 March. The participants were film-makers, critics, officials from several African countries and international cinema experts.

The participants recognised the underdevelopment of cinema, including irregular film productions, in the majority of African countries.

Convinced that African cinema must have a commitment to assert the cultural identity of African peoples; be a means for international understanding; an effective means of education and entertainment; an incentive for development, contributing to national and regional economic policies –

The Conference started by making a serious evaluation of African and international policies on cinema.

The participants then studied proposals for the development of African cinema, production and the financing of productions and the possibilities of legislation that would promote pan-African strategies for the development of African cinema industry. They examined ways of implementing the proposals.

The Conference finally adopted the following resolutions and recommendations:

General Principles
The participants considered and set up the following principles:

- The viability of cinema production is closely tied to the complementary viability of the other four main sectors of cinema, namely the exploitation of cinema theatres, importation of films, distribution of films, technical infrastructure and training.
- There cannot be any viable cinema without the involvement of African States for the organisation, the support, the stabilisation of cinema and the encouragement and protection of private and public investment in cinema.
- It is not possible to have a viable cinema industry on a national level in Africa. The development of national cinema should take into consideration regional and pan-African co-operation by integrating cinema to political and economic ties that already exist between states.
- At the present stage of development of audiovisual facilities in the world and particularly in Africa, television should be complementary to cinema.
- It is possible to finance African film productions from the present revenue

27

from the millions who patronise cinemas in Africa. What is required is a strategy that will ensure that part of this revenue legitimately returns to the production of films. Production should not rely solely on patronage.

Recommendations

1. Cinema Market (Exploitation and Projection)
Every state should organise, support, safeguard and develop its movie theatre market and encourage and collaborate with neighbouring states to form a regional common market for the importation and exploitation of films.

Measures to be taken
(a) The setting up of national ticket agencies to monitor receipts of cinemas for the benefit of the exchequer, the cinema owners and film producers.
(b) The provision of cinemas and other appropriate film projection venues and facilities.
(c) To make available funds from cinema taxes to encourage exhibitors to expand their cinema circuits, thus enlarging the market.
(d) States to exempt taxation on equipment imported for film projections.
(e) States to encourage investment to build cinemas by creating incentives for would be investors.

2. Importation and Distribution of Films
We have to control and organise the importation and distribution of foreign films to ensure the projection of African films on national, regional and continental levels. We have to limit the dependence on foreign suppliers, and ensure cultural diversification of foreign films, thus preventing the domination of films from particular areas. All this must be done with the aim of reconquering and enlarging our cultural and economic space.

Measures to be taken
(a) The setting up of national distribution corporations in countries where they don't already exist, be they state-run or in the private sector.
(b) The setting up of regional film importation companies that would function as co-operatives, for example CIDC.
   Where possible representatives of film purchasing companies based in foreign countries should have African status so that taxes related to their activities be paid in Africa. These companies should promote African films abroad and their diffusion.
(c) To strengthen existing importing companies like CIDC by the participation of other states.
(d) Enact laws on distribution to favour African films nationally, regionally and continentally. This can be achieved by decreasing the share of revenue to the distributors when dealing with African films. This would contribute to the financing of future productions.

3. Production
Cinema productions, whether national, regional or inter-African, should be financed, not necessarily by state funds, but mainly by revenue from distribution

28

and from various forms of cinema taxation, including taxes on earnings by foreign films. Thus cinema will finance cinema.

Measures to be taken to finance productions
(a) The creation of film finance corporations funded by revenue from cinema.
(b) The creation of support funds to be administered by the corporations. The support funds help the production of film on the approval of scenarios.
(c) Increase of African producers' shares of box-office receipts.
(d) Advance payments to producers by distributors.
(e) Governments to legislate that television participate in financing of film production in various ways.
(f) To create by legislation incentives for capital investments in film productions. This can be accomplished by offering tax exemptions.
(g) To make bank loans at low interest available to producers by national banks. These loans to be guaranteed by support funds.
(h) To have intergovernmental agreements, bilaterally, regionally and continentally, for the free circulation of technicians, equipment and other production facilities, and with regard to reciprocal support funds and to infrastructure.
(i) To reinforce and encourage the activities of existing production organisations such as CIPAOFILMS (International Centre for Film Production), through participation by states, by paying subscriptions and by contributions from revenues acquired through cinema taxes.
(j) To support the production of short feature films through finance from support funds. These will give added experience to film-makers and be an additional source of labour for technicians. Cinemas should also be compelled to screen these films.
(k) Another source of finance for productions can be obtained from theatrical and non-theatrical rights from distributors and television.

4. Technical Infrastructure
Measures to be taken
(a) The last twenty years' experience having proved that technical infrastructure could not be maintained and made profitable on a national level because of the high costs of maintenance and management, the conference recommends that the future establishments of these structures should be on regional levels after joint studies and agreements between parties involved.
(b) To create archives and film libraries on regional and continental levels.

5. Training
It is preferable that the training of technicians and other disciplines related to cinema be in centres established in regions and within the framework of any cinema activities in Africa. Wherever foreign technicians are employed it should be obligatory that African technicians are attached.

African film-makers and technicians working abroad should be encouraged to return to the continent to contribute to the development of African cinema.

29

Measures to be taken
(a) Vocational training centres should be established to ensure the training of film and television technicians and their absorption in both media.
(b) Ensure the training of managerial staff and other non-technical personnel, for example lawyers, producers, production managers.
(c) Training in programming, promotion and public relations in order to facilitate efficient distribution.
(d) Ensure the training of projectionists, cinema managers and other activities related to exhibition of films.
(e) The development of film critics through continuous dialogue between film-makers and critics.

6. Legislation
Cinema legislation of any state should take into consideration the joint development of its cinema industry with that of its neighbouring states and also of the region.

7. National Film Corporations
National film corporations should be established in every country. The corporations should be autonomous in decision making but under a ministry. The role of these corporations should be to centralise all activities and matters relating to cinema in the country. There can be a management committee representing the government and the corporation.

A complementary authority should be established on a regional level to ensure the co-ordination of cinema policies of regions.

Final Recommendation
Any decision made executively or regarding legislation on cinema, nationally or regionally, should be considered by a committee representing the state, film-makers, cinema professionals and investors and cinema owners, to avoid individual or bureaucratic decisions arbitrarily taken against the interests of African cinema. On the other hand film-makers should maintain a sense of responsibility and morality in dealing with their governments and others they have dealings with.

Final Communiqué of the First Frontline Film Festival and Workshop, Harare, Zimbabwe, 1990

The First Frontline Film Festival and Workshop, held in Harare, Zimbabwe, 15–21 July 1990, under the aegis of the Ministry of Information, Posts and Telecommunications and with the unique support of the OAU, SADCC Secretariat and FEPACI, was a result of the need to identify actions in co-operation in order to reinforce solidarity and friendship among SADCC member states, particularly in the cultural field. It was also motivated by our recognition of the unique geographic and historic nature of this sub-region of the African continent.

While being held under the seemingly 'optimistic' atmosphere in the region as regards the liberation of South Africa, the Workshop still regards the situation there as being far from the desired goals of the liberation of Africa.

The Festival was attended by delegates from Angola, Botswana, Lesotho, Malawi, Mozambique, Namibia, Tanzania, Swaziland, Zambia and Zimbabwe, members of the SADCC subgroup of the continent, as well as delegates from the ANC.

We also note the continued and valuable support of the Nordic Council and the Commonwealth Foundation for the development of cinema in the region.

The Festival was also attended by personalities and eminent film-makers from Africa, who brought to the Festival their rich experiences for the benefit of the development of the cinema in the region.

Representatives of progressive forces in the cinema field from Africa and Europe also participated in the Festival.

Being a follow-up of earlier fora and the Niamey and Harare Declarations discussing the film industry in Africa and the Southern African region in particular, the Workshop could not but feel disappointed by the inadequate steps taken towards solving the long-exisiting problems facing cinema in Africa.

Analysing the existing conditions of cinema in the region the participants note:

1.   That there is yet no regional policy and strategy for the development of culture and communication. There is also the absence of viable structures and mechanisms to develop real co-operation within the region. That situation does not permit the valorisation of the cultural-historical heritage and potential existing in the region. The little co-operation that has been undertaken to date has been mainly bilateral and on an ad hoc basis.

31

2.   That there is quite a substantial stock of film equipment in the region which is grossly underutilised due to lack of knowledge of its availability and lack of communication between the owners and prospective users.

3.   That in the field of training there doesn't exist a regional policy and programmes to enable the use of the existing facilities and institutions.

4.   That there is a total absence of African and even Southern African films being distributed in the region due to the inherited and yet unchanged distribution structures and the lack of promotion of the exhibition of those kinds of films.

5.   That the aesthetic development of the African cinema is still very disturbing, requiring greater efforts at instilling an African identity, more so in the areas of language, censorship and the role of women in the cinema.

6.   That there is yet no permanent programme for the co-production of films and videos in order to promote the culture and the potential of the region.

7.   That the national television networks in the region need to re-orientate themselves and their role in the cultural development of the peoples of this region.

8.   That to date national film workers' associations do not exist in most of the countries of the region to help rally film workers towards film development in their countries in the region and continent as a whole.

Therefore, we SADCC delegates to the First Frontline Film Festival and Workshop recommend that:

1.   The SADCC Council of Ministers adopt a Declaration on Culture for the SADCC region, outlining and clarifying the relationship between national and regional policies, objectives and responsibilities of member states in the development of film, information, culture and the arts.

2.   Regional film-makers and artists and experts from other cultural disciplines wishing to participate be included in the drafting of the proposed Declaration on Culture for the SADCC.

3.   Regional film-makers and artists and experts from other cultural disciplines be charged with drafting a programme of action to implement the proposed Cultural Charter for SADCC in such a way that short-term, medium and long-term phases and projects are detailed.

4.   All member states of the SADCC which have not yet done so adopt national policies on culture and information incorporating the principles of the OAU Cultural Charter for Africa.

5.   All member states of the SADCC place levies on all films, film projects, videos and television programmes from outside Africa in order to create a national film fund for financing training programmes, refurbishment of non-commercial cinema halls, construction of new halls, film production and film distribution.

6. All member states create national film boards with representatives from all sections of the film industry and relevant policy-making bodies.

7. The SADCC Council of Ministers, through the Culture and Information sector, set up a regional revolving fund for film production to be financed from SADCC-sourced funds.

8. All SADCC states set up national structures for distributing films which should be integrated into regional, pan-African and international systems.

9. All SADCC states reach agreement to join one film market for purposes of:

(a) Acquiring international films;
(b) Establishing a reasonable credit system acceptable to all regional film establishments for encouraging SADCC film-makers to use regional facilities in film production:
(c) Making the UAPTA acceptable to all regional film establishments as payment for film production and other costs.

10. All SADCC states guide and rationalise donor-funded projects in order to safeguard the interests and objectives of the region and to prevent duplication and harmful competition.

11. SADCC ministers of commerce and industry ensure that film is classified and registered as a trade commodity in all PTA directories or registers.

12. SADCC states stipulate minimum quotas for national, regional and pan-African programme content in television, film and radio broadcasting for the purpose of countering the overwhelming dominance of foreign programmes.

13. The SADCC Council of Ministers, through the cultural/information sector, sponsor an inventory and assessment of existing regional facilities, skills and equipment in the fields of film, television and communications.

The inventory and assessment should include projects as well, whether they are near completion, pending or in the planning stage.

All major infrastructural projects in film be undertaken only after thorough feasibility studies involving film-makers, and governments should undertake the full implications of their decision on the projects in order to ensure their permanent support and commitment.

14. Following the regional survey of facilities and skills and the production of a thorough feasibility study, a regional film training school be established for film-makers at all levels.

15. The First Frontline Film Festival set up a steering committee of regional film-makers to be co-ordinated by the Zimbabwe Film, Television and Allied Workers Union and include one member each from Zambia, Mozambique and Angola.

The responsibilty of the steering committee will be to set up a Regional Bureau of Film and Video which shall be responsible for:

(a) Organising a regular Southern African Film Festival in conjunction with FEPACI;
(b) Following up the recommendations of the workshop;

(c) Encouraging SADCC film workers to form national unions affiliated to FEPACI and which should mobilise for their own protection and empowerment and for the creation of a regional film workers' association.

(d) Compiling and publishing a directory of film-makers, skills, services and facilities in the region;

(e) Creating and administering a computerised database for the film industry;

(f) Establishing a newsletter on film-making and film activities for the SADCC region;

(g) Request and obtain observer status in the SADCC consultative annual conferences;

(h) Advocate regional co-operation and co-production while providing advice on such matters as insurance, customs and immigration;

(i) Liaise with the SADCC culture/information sector and the SADCC Business Council on matters of film.

16. In each SADCC state, film-makers, film experts and other cultural workers initiate a thorough review of existing censorship legislation and censorship structures as a prelude to the launching of national debates on censorship.

17. SADCC film-makers and their associations commit themselves individually and collectively to exercise positive discrimination in favour of women film-makers when considering training, employment, leadership and other opportunities in film.

In conclusion, we the delegates to this Workshop and First Frontline Film Festival call upon film workers in the region individually and collectively to address themselves continually to the issues raised in this communiqué and to persuade their governments and institutions to implement these recommendations.

Statement of African Women Professionals of Cinema, Television and Video, Ouagadougou, Burkina Faso, 1991

After fifty years of cinematographic production and twenty-five years of televisual production, how many women are involved? What positions do they occupy and what roles do they play?

After fifty years of cinematographic production and twenty-five years after televisual realisation, what images of African women are shown to women of this continent, and how much have the latter contributed to challenge the 'established' clichés ... without women's participation in supervisory positions?

After a half-century of cinematographic production and a quarter-century of televisual productions, how many pioneers are there? And where are those female pioneers and film directors who could have been in a position to give their own vision of the world?

The African women's workshop held within the framework of the 12th edition of FESPACO in Ouagadougou from 25 to 27 February 1991 gathered together a diversity of African film, television and video professionals.

They came from various African countries and from the Black diaspora: Kenya, Tanzania, Zimbabwe, Ghana, South Africa, Nigeria, Burkina Faso, Benin, Tunisia, Cameroun, Niger, Côte d'Ivoire, Mali, Rwanda, Congo, Morocco and Chad.

These women fulfil the functions of editors, camerawomen, directors and producer of televisual programmes, video-makers, film-makers, distributors, compères-producers in television, producers, actresses.

But even after fifty years of cinematographic productions and twenty-five years of televisual production, though they fulfil various functions in cinema and television, the analysis of African women's situation during this workshop has emphasised their insignificant number in audiovisual professions and their difficulty in getting access to training and funds.

It is evident from the testimonies presented over these last three days that even when a woman wants to work in cinema and television professions she is often advised to stick to the latter because they suit her better as they require an attention to detail which is believed to be specifically part of women's character.

So half a century after the beginning of African cinema, a quarter of a century after those of television, the position of women in the various posts in cinematographic and televisual production is far from being satisfactory! Far from being up to the challenge of the third millennium.

35

And if this situation continues the cinematographic and televisual industry's growth, and even its development, could be hampered.

For if pictures produced by African women do not give another view on African women's reality, then there is a great risk that women themselves, because they are the main educators of children – the citizens of tomorrow – will not be able to show an alternative vision of the world.

Fifty years after the beginning of cinema, twenty-five years after that of television, inequalities and obstacles still persist.

In 1991, almost ten years before the year 2000, African women are still victims of pressures at their place of work, and exploited both as women and as professionals.

In 1991, almost ten years before the third millennium, because they are deprived of their citizenship rights, their access to cinema and television professions remains selective, discriminatory and minimal!

Nevertheless, in 1991, African professional women of cinema and television and video decided to meet in order to exchange their views, to create a framework for free expression, to elaborate an action programme to speed up their integration at all the levels of the production process of cinema and television.

A half-century after the birth of cinema, a quarter of a century after that of television, about fifty women from various areas of the continent, fifty women of different political, religious and philosophical backgrounds united for the sake of their professional requirements to express their will to struggle unflinchingly:

- to put forward their female vision of the world;
- to have a controlling position on their pictures.

They decided to set up a working group, a programme of action, in order to continue the action of a few isolated pioneers so that in the future, in the year 2000, there are 10, 50, 100 . . . 1,000 of them and more in the professions of cinema and television.

They call on funding and commissioning organisations from the South and the North, on institutions and associations to give their active, constructive and collaborative support for the development of their projects.

They know that a mobilisation of funds, of human resources, from the South and the North, and mainly women's determination, initiative and responsibility may help to overcome the obstacles!

The working panel is made up of the following members: Aminata Ouédraogo (Burkina Faso), director-producer; Grace Kanyua (Kenya), director-producer; Juanita Ageh-Waterman (Nigeria/London), actress; Alexandra Akoto Duah (Ghana), actress; Sepati Bulane-Hopa (South Africa), director-distributor; Chantal Bagilishya (Rwanda/Paris), distributor; Rose-Elise Mengue-Bekale (Gabon), editor; Kahena Attila (Tunisia), editor.

PART II
African Cinema and Society: Some Voices

What Is Cinema for Us?

MED HONDO

Reprinted from *Framework* II (Autumn 1979).

Throughout the world when people use the term 'cinema' all refer more or less consciously to a single cinema, which for more than half a century has been created, produced, industrialised, programmed and then shown on the world's screens: Euro-American cinema. This cinema has gradually imposed itself on a set of dominated peoples. With no means of protecting their own cultures, these peoples have been systematically invaded by diverse, cleverly articulated cinematographic products. The ideologies of these products never 'represent' their personality, their collective or private way of life, their cultural codes, or, of course, the least reflection of their specific 'art', their way of thinking, of communicating – in a word, their own history ... their civilisation.

The images this cinema offers systematically exclude the African and the Arab. It would be dangerous (and impossible) to reject this cinema as simply alien – the damage is done. We must get to know it, the better to analyse it and to understand that this cinema has never really concerned the African and Arab peoples. This seems paradoxical, since it fills all the cinemas, dominates the screens of all African and Arab cities and towns. But do the masses have any other choice? 'Consuming' at least fifty films in a year, how many films does the average African see that really talk to him? Is there a single one which evokes the least resonance, the least reflection of his people's life and history – past, present and future? Is there a single image of the experiences of his forefathers, heroes of African and Arab history? Is there a single film inscribed in the new reality of co-operation, communication, support, and solidarity of Africans and Arabs?

In *Lawrence of Arabia* an image of Lawrence – not of the Arabs – is disseminated. In *Gentleman of Cocodie* a European is the gentleman hero, and not an Ivorian. This may seem exaggerated. Some will say that at least one African country, Egypt, produces some relatively important films each year; that since independence in African countries a number of cineastes have made a future for themselves. In the whole continent of Africa, Egypt is only one country, one cultural source, one sector of the market – and few African countries buy Egyptian films. They produce too few films, and the market within Egypt is still dominated by foreign films.

African and Arab film-makers have decided to produce their own films. But despite their undoubted quality they have no chance of being distributed normally, at home or in the dominant countries, except in marginalised circuits –

the dead-end art cinemas. Even a few dozen more film-makers producing films would only achieve a ratio of one to ten thousand. An everyday creative dynamic is necessary for a radical change in the relationship between the dominant Euro-American production and distribution networks and African and Arab production and distribution, which we must control.

Only in this way, in a spirit of creative and stimulating competition between African and Arab film-makers, can we make artistic progress and become competitive in the world market. We must first control our own markets, satisfy our own peoples' desires to liberate their screens, then establish respectful relations with other peoples, and balanced exchange.

We must change the humilating relationship between dominating and dominated, between masters and slaves.

Some flee this catastrophic state of affairs, thinking cinema restricted to Western, Christian and capitalist elites, or throwing a cloak of fraternal paternalism over our film-makers, ignoring and discrediting their works, blaming them, in the short term forcing them to comply with a formal and ethical mimesis – imitating precisely those cinemas we denounce – in order to become known and be admitted into international cinema, in the end forcing them into submission, into renouncing their own lives, their creativity and their militancy.

Since the independence of our countries, a sizeable number of our film-makers have proved their abilities as auteurs. They encounter increasing difficulties in surviving and continuing to work, because their films are seldom distributed and no aid is forthcoming. Due to the total lack of a global cultural policy, African and Arab cinema is relegated to being an exotic and episodic subproduct, limited to aesthetic reviews at festivals, which, although not negligible, are undoubtedly insufficient.

Each year millions of dollars are harvested from our continents, taken back to the original countries, then used to produce new films which are again sent out onto our screens. Fifty per cent of the profits of multinational film companies accrue from the screens of the Third World. Thus each of our countries unknowingly contributes substantial finance to the production of films distributed in Paris, New York, London, Rome or Hong Kong. They have no control over them, and reap no financial or moral benefit, being involved in neither the production nor the distribution. In reality, however, they are coerced into being 'co-producers'. Their resources are plundered.

The United States permits a penetration of foreign films in its domestic its market of less than 13 per cent – and most of these are produced by European subsidiaries controlled by the US majors. They exercise an absolute protectionism.

Most important is the role of the cinema in the construction of peoples' consciousnesses. Cinema is the mechanism *par excellence* for penetrating the minds of our peoples, influencing their everyday social behaviour, directing them, diverting them from their historic national responsibilities. It imposes alien and insidious models and references, and without apparent constraint enforces the adoption of modes of behaviour and communication of the dominating ideologies. This damages their own cultural development and blocks true communication between Africans and Arabs, brothers and friends who have been historically united for thousands of years.

This alienation disseminated through the image is all the more dangerous for

40

being insidious, uncontroversial, 'accepted', seemingly inoffensive and neutral. It needs no armed forces and no permanent programme of education on the part of those seeking to maintain the division of the African and Arab peoples – to enforce their weakness, submission, servitude, their ignorance of each other and of their own history. They forget their positive heritage, united through their forefathers with all humanity. Above all, they have no say in the progress of world history.

Dominant imperialism seeks to prevent the portrayal of African and Arab values to other nations; were those responsible for this imperialism to appreciate our values and behaviour, they might respond positively to us. We are not proposing isolation, the closing of frontiers to all Western film, nor any protectionism separating us from the rest of the world. We wish to survive, develop, participate as sovereign peoples in our own specific cultural fields, and fulfil our responsibilities in a world from which we are now excluded. The night of colonialism caused many quarrels among us; we have yet to assess the full consequences. It poisoned our potential communications with other peoples; we are forced into relations of colonial domination. We have only preconceived and false ideas of each other imprinted by racism. Those who dominate us believe themselves 'superior'; they are unaware of our peoples' roles in world history.

We have been colonised and then subjected to even more pernicious imperialist domination. Although we are not entirely responsible for this state of affairs, some intellectuals, writers, film-makers, thinkers – our cultural leaders and policy-makers – are responsible for perpetuating this insatiable domination. It has never been enough simply to denounce our dominators, for they dictate the rules of their game to their own advantage. Some African and Arab film-makers realise that the cinema alone cannot change our disadvantaged position, but they know that it is the best means of education and information and thus of solidarity.

It is imperative to organise our forces, to reassert our different creative potentialities, and to fill the void in our national, regional and continental cinemas. We must establish relations of communication and co-operation between our peoples, in a spirit of equality, dignity and justice. We have the will, the means and the talent to undertake this great enterprise. Without organisation of resources we cannot flourish at home, and dozens of African and Arab intellectuals, film-makers, technicians, writers, journalists and leaders have had to leave their countries, often despite themselves, to contribute to the development and overdevelopment of countries that don't need them, and that use their excesses to dominate us. This will continue until we grasp the crucial importance of this cultural and economic strategy, and create our own networks of film production and distribution, liberating ourselves from all foreign monopolies.

41

African Cinema and the Headshrinkers: Looking Back at a Strategy for Liberation

TAHAR CHÉRIAA

Translated by Paul Willemen from *Afrique littéraire et artistique,* no. 49, 3rd quarter 1978.

If you look back on the last twelve or fifteen years of African cinema, taken as a whole, you arrive at a series of specific points. The first is that, for different reasons in each case, the Egyptian, Algerian and Guinean cinemas stand apart from the others. The second point is that all emerged from the political independence of the African states; some did so later than others, but all were the direct cultural offspring of that event. This is why the structures of these cinemas, economic, administrative and political, vary according to the different regimes. The third point is that, in spite of the diversity of the local situations, these cinemas share a number of common features.

First, one can describe each of them as structurally, and therefore economically and politically, a kind of monster, or a biological anomaly. They consist of heads (the authors and their films) without bodies (no markets in which to make the films pay), and no audiences because there are no normal distribution and exhibition structures. Even the nationalised markets remain dominated by foreigners who monopolise the system of imports and distribution.

And yet each of the national African cinemas constitutes, from the cultural point of view, a living reality which unmistakably belongs to the domain of artistic creation.

These African cinemas, regardless of their size or their respective qualities, are the tangible fruit, the public expression, of the convergence of two desires or two kinds of thrusts for change: the cultural one of the film-maker or the small group of cineastes animated by a desire to say something, to bear witness or to assert themselves through cinema; and the less obvious one of a power which, with the consent of the film-makers and whenever possible through their films, pursues its own political objectives. The relationship between these two desires resembles that of patronage in the history of the arts. That is why I say that the African cinemas, although a genuinely living reality, are only artistic creations, whereas other national cinemas are also industries and sectors of a broader national economy. I do not need to dwell on the first of these two desires since the voices of other African film-makers inhabit this collection and have their own say in it.

The second desire emanates either from a national state or from a foreign state linked to it by means of a bilateral co-operation agreement, or from an international organisation to which the national state adheres. That is why in so-called francophone Africa most films were produced with the help of the

French Ministry of Co-operation, 27 rue Oudinot, Paris; or, more modestly, with the Cultural and Technical Co-operation Agency set up in Niamey in 1970, the headquarters of which is located at 19 avenue de Messine, Paris. So one can say that in one way or another the national states are involved in the production of the films. Only a tiny minority could be realised against the wishes of those in power.

To the extent that African films cannot be regarded as normal productions, one might almost say, paradoxically, that they are films made to order. This conclusion is confirmed by the fact that one sees governments claiming the privilege of using the national films freely in their international exchange programmes or in other prestige events while at the same time refusing to assist film-makers 'for lack of money'.

Fine, you might say, but what has been achieved today as a result of the actions of African film-makers over the last decade and a half? Let me summarise it in four points:

1. In the 60s, thanks largely to a process of collective reflection made possible by pan-African festivals, African film-makers did make a fairly realistic assessment of their situation in their own societies, abroad as well as in their own states. In a context free of any structures or national film traditions, they were under the impression that all they had to do was to add to their own desire to make films the reinforcement of the state's desire, which, they hoped, was set on creating national cinemas. Feeling themselves so rich with things to say and imagining themselves to be free to say them, they believed the states to be similarly disposed and never doubted their freedom of action.

2. Although this analysis was realistic, it wasn't wholly adequate partly, no doubt, because political independence did not mean real economic autonomy. With a few exceptions, most of the film-makers did not manage to connect up sufficiently or accurately enough their thoughts about the problems of a national cinema with the global framework which determined a state's options as far as economic, political or international relations are concerned. Experience has shown, for instance, that what to the most militant film-makers between 1966 and 1972 seemed to be 'state deficiency' that could be corrected by means of a better understanding and awareness, was in fact due to a coherent, global political strategy which was in no way accidental.

3. It is the inadequacy of this analysis which is probably the main reason for the bankruptcy of the tri-axial strategy adopted by the film-makers who joined together in 1970 in the pan-African Federation which was particularly active until 1975, thanks to its general secretary, Babacar Samb. I call it a tri-axial strategy because it sought to achieve its objectives, for all the African cinemas, through three types of action:
(a) on the national level, by raising the consciousness of the film-makers, organising them and creating a force, by their very presence if not by the pressure they were able to exert, intended to become a worthy and legitimate interlocutor for the relevant authorities;
(b) on the double national and inter-African level, by proliferating mutual contacts, lobbying activities, the formulation of demands and the pursuit

of dialogue in any manner possible with governments and intergovernmental institutions in order to favour and foster the emergence of African cinemas;

(c) on the continental level, to create (with whatever means available) events which would enable film-makers to meet regularly and to submit their films to audiences and critics, and to get in touch with the mainstream press as well. That was the function of events such as the Carthage and the Ouagadougou festivals. They had a truly strategic role which, in my opinion, they discharged with honour.

4. I have suggested that this strategy seemed to go bankrupt and that the main reason for this was a defective analysis of the situation. However, I am not at all sure that it was a failure and I want to nuance that judgment somewhat. I think that the analysis was too narrowly cinematographic and insufficiently integrated into a wider understanding. I do not think that the strategy was fundamentally mistaken. Basically, if the film-makers who militated most energetically for this strategy made a mistake, it was because of their excessiveness: they placed excessive trust in the state powers' alleged desire to support their struggle to develop a national cinema; and they were excessively optimistic in their confidence in their own ability to overcome the foreign, head-shrinking monopolies which condemn African cinemas to be heads without bodies.

We underestimated the inexhaustible adaptability of the monopolies involved.

To Make a Film Means to Take a Position

SARAH MALDOROR

This is an edited version of the chapter 'On Sambizanga' in K. Kay and G. Peary (eds), *Women and the Cinema* (New York: E. P. Dutton, 1977).

The prominent figure of Sarah Maldoror within the landscape of African cinema is a pertinent reminder that intrinsic to this cinema are profound implications for the critical approaches to cinema itself as well as issues of human concern globally. Placing Maldoror within the context of African cinema more often than not prompts an apologetic tone in response to the fact she was born in France. But this seeming incongruity should serve as a reminder of the important relationship between the emergence of African cinema and ideas of pan-Africanism and liberation struggles which have been part of the continent's history in the 20th century.

Sarah Maldoror was born in 1939 in Candou in the south of France. Her parents were from Guadeloupe in the French Caribbean. In the 1950s Maldoror – with others, including Ababacar Samb, Toto Bisaninthe and Bassori Timite – was part of a theatre group in Paris called Les Griots. Later she studied film in Moscow, where Ousmane Sembène was one of her fellow students. In 1963 Maldoror was working in Algeria, most notably with Ahmed Lallem on Elles. *It was here she made her first short,* Monangambee (1969), *from a novel by the Angolan writer Luandino Vieira. In 1972 Maldoror made* Sambizanga, *also based on a novel by Vieira –* The Real Life of Domingos Xavier. *This is a story from the experience of the Angolan liberation struggle against Portugal in the 1960s. It was one of a number of bloody anticolonial wars in Africa during the 1960s and 70s.*

Set at the beginning of the liberation war, Sambizanga *tells the story of Domingos Xavier, an Angolan construction worker who is arrested by the colonial secret police. He is tortured and finally killed when he refuses to betray a white comrade who has joined the anticolonial struggle. The film is more a study of how people become politically conscious than of the liberation war itself. The story evolves by tracing the path of Xavier's wife, Maria, as she goes from village to village trying to find him. In this quest she discovers what it means to begin to struggle against colonialism. (Eds)*

I am one of those modern women who try to combine work and family life, and, just as it is for all the others, this is a problem for me. Children need a home and a mother. That is why I try to prepare and edit my films in Paris during the long summer vacation when the children are free and can come along.

45

My situation is a very difficult one. I make films about liberation movements. But the money for such film production is to be found not in Africa but in Europe. For that reason, I have to live where the money is to be raised, and then do my work in Africa.

To begin, *Sambizanga* is a story taken from reality: a liberation fighter, one of the many, dies from severe torture. But my chief concern with this film was to make Europeans, who hardly know anything about Africa, conscious of the forgotten war in Angola, Mozambique and Guinea-Bissau. And when I address myself to Europeans that is because it is the French distribution companies who determine whether the people in Africa will get to see a certain film or not. After twelve years of independence, it is your companies – UGC, Nef, Claude Nedjar, and Vincent Malle – which hold in their hands the fate of a possible African distribution for *Sambizanga*.

At any rate, I don't want to make a 'good little Negro' film. People often reproach me for that. They also blame me for making a technically perfect film as any European could. But technology belongs to everyone. 'A talented Negro' – you can relegate that concept to my French past.

In this film I tell the story of a woman. It could be any woman, in any country, who takes off to find her husband. The year is 1961. The political consciousness of the people has not yet matured. I'm sorry if this situation is not seen as a 'good one', and if this doesn't lead to a heightened consciousness among the audience of what the struggle in Africa is all about. I have no time for films filled with political rhetoric.

In the village where Maria lives, the people have no idea at all what 'independence' means. The Portuguese prevent the spread of any information and a debate on the subject is impossible. They even prevent the people from living according to their own traditional culture.

If you feel that this film can be interpreted as being negative, then you're falling into the same trap as many of my Arab brothers did when they reproached me for not showing any Portuguese bombs or helicopters in the film. However, the bombs only began to rain on us when we became conscious; the helicopters have only recently appeared – you sell them to the Portuguese and they buy them precisely because of our consciousness. For, not too long ago, people here believed that all that was happening in Angola was a minor tribal war. They didn't reckon with our will to become an independent nation: could it be true that we Angolese were like them, the Portuguese? No, that wouldn't be possible!

I'm against all forms of nationalism. What does it in fact mean to be French, Swedish, Senegalese, or Guadeloupian? Nationalities and borders between countries have to disappear. Besides this, the colour of a person's skin is of no interest to me. What is important is what the person is doing. I'm no adherent of the concept of the Third World. I make films so that people – no matter what race or colour they are – can understand them. For me there are only exploiters and the exploited, that's all. To make a film means to take a position, and when I take a position I am educating people. The audience has a need to know that there's a war going on in Angola, and I address myself to those among them who want to know more about it. In my films, I show them a people who are busy preparing themselves for a fight and all that that entails in Africa: that continent where everything is extreme – the distances, nature, and so on. Liberation fighters are, for example, forced to wait until the elephants have passed them by. Only then can they cross the countryside and transport their arms and ammunition. Here, in the West, the Resistance used to wait until dark. We wait for the elephants. You have radios, information. We have nothing.

Some say that they don't see any oppression in the film. If I wanted to film the brutality of the Portuguese, then I'd shoot my films in the bush. What I wanted to show in *Sambizanga* is the aloneness of a woman and the time it takes to march.

I'm only interested in women who struggle. These are the women I want to have in my films, not the others. I also offer work to as many women as possible during the time I'm shooting my films. You have to support those women who want to work with film. Up until now, we are still few in number, but if you support those women in film who are around, then slowly our numbers will grow. That's the way the men do it, as we all know. Women can work in whatever field they want. That means in film, too. The main thing is that they themselves want to do it. Men aren't likely to help women do that. Both in Africa and in Europe woman remains the slave of man. That's why she has to liberate herself.

No African country, with the exception of Algeria, has its own distribution company. In the French-speaking areas of Africa, distribution is handled by a monopoly that is in French hands. There is not one cinematheque nor even a so-called art cinema. All too often, you hear that there is no African film, or that if there is it's just Jean Rouch. That's to make it easy for those who say such things. One day, we'll come to France and shoot a film, then we'll show the African people our view of France. That will be an entertaining film.

Swedish films, Italian films and the films of other countries did not sprout up like mushrooms from the earth. In Africa there are several young people who are really talented film-makers. We have to put an end to the lack of knowledge and the utter ignorance that people have about the special problem of Africa.

Personally, I feel that Ousmane Sembène is the most talented of our directors. He's often reproached for financing his films with French capital. So what! The most important thing is that we have to develop a cultural policy that can help us – show to the world that such a thing as African film does exist. We have to teach ourselves to sell our films ourselves and then get them distributed. Today we are like small sardines surrounded by sharks. But the sardines will grow up. They'll learn how to resist the sharks.

Sarah Maldoror's most recent film is Léon G. Demas *(1994), a short documentary on Léon Demas, who along with Leopold Sedar Senghor and Aimé Césaire were founders of the Négritude movement. (Eds)*

On Inspiration

NOURI BOUZID

This is an edited version of a lecture published as *Sources of Inspiration – Lecture 5* (Amsterdam: Sources, 1994).

My approach is very original, in that most people start by writing scripts for other people and end up directing. I took the opposite road. I started writing and directing for myself, I put myself forward as author-director, and only later did I write for other people. The reasons are simple. It takes a long time to set up the financing for a film that does not fit into the normal market pattern, one or two years, especially when the film does not meet commercial requirements, such as having stars, or is not shot in a common language and has to be subtitled. During this two-year financing period I have to release my energy and express myself, hence my need to write for other people. Apart from my own films, I started with *Halfaouine* for Férid Boughedir. Then I did *La Goulette* also with Férid. With Monfida Tlatli I did the script and dialogue for *Les Silences du palais*, which was nominated for the Caméra d'Or.

I am one of a group of Tunisian film-makers all from the same generation, who, without getting together, without coming to any prior agreement, went in almost the same direction and almost all worked in a similar way. What they have in common is that they decided to make films that were like themselves. Generally, if we take Egyptian or Algerian films of the 70s, it's virtually impossible to guess who directed them. With our films, after seeing five minutes of Nacer Kémir you know it's Nacer Kémir, or five minutes of Mahmoud Ben Mahmoud, you can guess it's him, and the same with Férid, which is a quality to be welcomed. They already had a cinematic mode of discourse, and that's the only way to be a good film-maker. That's why the script is first of all a cinematic discourse, not a plot. I shall come back to this point later.

We all benefited from something without realising it. We were twenty years old during the ideological explosion of the 60s in Europe. Even if those ideas rapidly changed, it was good to have them at the time. We were then witnessing the golden age of cinema without realising it. That was the era of the best Fellinis, Bergmans, Godards, Resnais, the best Japanese, Czech, Polish, Hungarian, Swedish, Canadian and Indian films. It was also an auspicious era for the American cinema in New York, Free Cinema in England, Cinema Novo in Brazil and the Latin-American cinema. In Paris, the cultural centre of cinema in the 60s, we saw the focal point move from the Champs Elysées to the Quartier Latin, with its flourishing art and experimental cinemas. Without knowing it, we were in the golden age of cinema. Now we do know, and we are happy to have been able to benefit from it, since with television the landmarks have been lost. Television viewers don't know what a film is any more. They can't distinguish between a film, a television film, a drama and a series, all chopped up by commercial breaks. Cinema is the mode of expression associated with the best period of liberalism. This is very important: cinema does not sit well with feudal ideas, because that's a paradox. Cinema is the art of an era, of democratic and liberal ideas, and if it's not free, it dies. It needs an explosion.

So we went to war, we chose to fight using our films. But to fight what? The old cinema, in particular the Egyptian cinema which dominated the Arab market and shaped our emotions, our tastes, our morals. We were bearers of a social, cinematic and political project. We went to war against censorship, which was another thing that divided old and new. We declared war on the old emotions. Hitherto the idea had been to make people weep at fate with all the simple, melodramatic tricks. We were fed up with that cinema and wanted to go the other way. So we waged war on the aesthetic and all the models on which that cinema was based. We sometimes went so far as to reject plot and anecdote, considering that it was too easy to tell a story.

A decade earlier still, my mother used to tell me stories. Even if she was able to tell stories, that didn't mean she was the best film-maker. Making a good film is not a question of telling a story, but of bringing an audience into a discourse that's new, aesthetic, cinematic, stylistic and dramatic in its totality, and, in the second place, ideological. But never in the first place. If ideology comes first, it's not cinema.

So it was up to us to win the bet by winning over a badly educated public. Tunisian audiences were used to a different kind of cinema, so we had to challenge them too, put forward something different and accustom them to seeing new things. It was very difficult, because we had an enemy who was well ensconced and had built a very solid edifice – Egyptian cinema, which had got hold of all the Arab television stations. The few films that did not obey the laws of the market – the films of Chahine and other Egyptian film-makers who came along with him – faced the same problems as we did. Egyptian cinema had already spawned its opposite number with him and the film-makers of the 70s, but they were very soon brought back into the fold or pushed aside, marginalised.

In Tunisia, we were the only ones making films. We could not be marginalised. The great surprise was the public support we received. With *The Man of Ashes* there was a new phenomenon that we had not observed with many earlier films. For once the Tunisian audience encountered Tunisian cinema and answered 'present' in an unbelievable way. We didn't understand, because at the same time lots of critics, or rather budding journalists trying to gain favour with the public, were attacking this cinema. Instead of helping us to condition the public and teach it a new way of seeing, they went to war against this cinema. So we had yet another confrontation to deal with.

How do I see a script? For me, a script has always seemed like an urgency. I've never known in advance what script I was going to make. All the time I feel it's the only thing I want to do, the only thing I have in my head, the only thing I work for; everything else is automatically eradicated. Nothing else interests me. This urgent need that's in me is not the producer's. The producer has a different kind of urgency, the urgency of the film which is under way.

It's a new way of seeing things. To borrow an image, I would say it's the

49

urgency of a pregnant woman carrying a living being inside her who, having come to term, must give birth. If the film does not come to term it is in danger of dying. Making it is an urgent matter, and it's this urgency that stamped that group of films, some twenty or thirty by seven to ten directors. To extend the image, I would say that it's normal for a film to be like those who have carried it. It's the only way I can work. Even when I've taken scripts written by someone else, I try to get inside the skin of his character and to carry it in me. In a way, I'm like a mother carrying a child.

I become inhabited by the character – I say 'the character' because for me the germ, the gene, the genetic heritage is in a character. Everything that's to come is engendered by the character, because this is not a theoretical character but a total character who has roots which will beget needs. I want to shed light on this character, so I create one or two relationships which are necessary for him, demanded by him, with someone else. To give you an example, in the first version of *The Man of Ashes* there are two boys, Hechmi and Farfat, who have been raped by their foreman and relive the rape as a trauma as adults. To start with there was one boy, then later I said to myself, he needs someone, he can't carry both aspects by himself. He was too internal, too introverted, he needed someone who was different. I asked myself what would happen if Hechmi said to society, 'Get stuffed, I'll do what I like.' Will he make it? But he can't do it, he's not the type of character who can do that. So I had to create his double, the other side of the coin, because the germ of the double existed in the first one. That's what a script is for me. If I may use an image, making a script is like making a child, not a piece of knitting. The process is not: you make a hand, then you make one side, then you add the other; it's better if you add a scene like that, and it needs a funny scene, it needs something else, constantly adding to something that's in progress. For me, that's not a film. A film is like a child: the first page, the first idea contains the entire script, otherwise it's no good. I hate scripts that depart from the initial idea, because that means someone wants to make a script but doesn't carry it inside them, and that makes all the difference. If your job is to make a script, you can do it, computers can do it for you. Human beings can program them to do it by giving them the recipe.

You have to carry a script inside you. You have to have the courage to do the script you're carrying, whatever the problems. The character is going to be the source of everything. He is going to impose his own evolution, he is going to claim complete freedom and he is going to impose his own needs, provided he is a character with roots. But, before writing, you live with him, you get inside his skin, you talk to him, you watch him, you dream with him, you shut yourself away with him. If you find him, if you hold him, he does everything because he is real, he is authentic, because he has roots, because he settles into a strong reality. When that happens, I put this character in my own universe, and in my universe there are conscious things and unconscious things. There are things that are very conscious: those are the dramatic elements. Everything that's dramatic is very conscious. Even if you get there with the aid of go-betweens or by indirect routes, it's conscious, because drama is a science.

On the other hand, a lot of things are part of the author's universe and are not conscious. They should certainly not be made conscious. You should never say, 'My film needs this or that. I saw an image in a film, why don't I do that? It's good, I'll add that, I'll make a note of it.' That's not right. You must respect

50

your own universe. If you see him dressed in black, you must dress him in black. If someone asks you why and you don't have an answer, you just say, 'I don't know, I don't care, that's how I see him. I see him as bald, I don't know why.' Perhaps if you visit a psychoanalyst you will find explanations, but it's not up to me to provide them. I see him physically in a certain way, I look among the faces in the street for one which corresponds to my character, and when I see him I immediately pick him out from among a thousand. Why? It's unconscious. Because he carries certain things from my drama and I imagined him with a lost look and I'm searching for that look. Because I imagined him short or tall. In *The Golden Horse Shoes* I imagined him as tall. I turned down a lot of actors because they weren't tall enough, although it was almost autobiographical. People said it was autobiographical. Perhaps I wanted to be tall, I don't know, but these are things you can't explain. Perhaps I wanted the edifice to be enormous when it collapsed at the end, so that it would make a terrible din. That may be it, but these are analyses done with hindsight.

You shouldn't try to explain everything, in my opinion. You don't need to explain the dramatic elements clearly, and even in dramatic technique you're not obliged to fall back on models. You should make the effort to invent your own model, your archetype. I have no need to tell a story, but my character or characters must have a goal to aim for, the unfolding of the script must contain a *stake*. The stake is the character's. It is experienced more intensely until it becomes *vital* and is perceived by the viewer as vital to the character.

The most important thing, once I have the character, is that he absolutely must have a point of view. Up till now I have made only scripts where I adopt my character's point of view. The first two films, *The Man of Ashes* and *The Golden Horse Shoes*, were even written in the first person. This is what created the confusion and led certain people to say that it was autobiographical when it wasn't at all autobiographical. It was sincere and at the same time in the first person, which gave the impression of autobiography. Once I have chosen my character's point of view the structure decides itself, since it's my character that's going to be the structure of the film.

In *The Man of Ashes* my character is double. The structure of the film pivots on a double axis, where all the other characters revolve round the two of them. You see one or the other, then at the end I give a flick of the wrist, I don't know the technical term, and replace one with the other. I derail the main character, I abandon him and I do the end with the secondary character. People forget whether it's one or the other, and just when he is going to take revenge, to commit the act of violence, I show the two of them, one taking the other in his hands and releasing him to go and kill. The whole situation makes him a double character. This is a very special structure, a structure from the subjective point of view, but with a double axis. So it's the character who is double at the beginning who then imposes the structure on the film. You can't start from a theoretical structure, it grows out of the character.

In *The Golden Horse Shoes* this goes even further, since this character stamps his own psychological structure on the film. There isn't a single image or sound in the film that doesn't come from this character's head. This character has a scattered past. He tries to collect the broken pieces of his past and stick them together, and every time he collides with a shocking image that destroys his life even more. He sets off again to collect this life. The film is like that; it collects itself, it sticks itself together, it destroys itself with a shocking image of torture or horse-butchery, and once again the film destroys itself and once again it reconstructs itself. This is precisely the structure of the character. There must be total compatibility between the structure of the film and that of the protagonist.

I'm always talking about a film that's 'carried', but that's not the only model. I'm talking about myself. There are fifty thousand ways of making scripts, but I'm talking about my experience. I give it to you for what it's worth. In *Bezness* that changed. I made a structure with three characters, and to force the structure into threes I did the voice off three times. In other words, I have everyone's point of view, the girl, the boy and the Frenchman. The whole film is structured in threes. In *La Guerre du Golfe* there is no longer a character that is the pivot of the film. The camera has become the point of view. It's my job to bear witness, to pursue people in their defeats, and somehow I use a bit of trickery, I go beyond my technical limitations so as to escape defeat, because for me that's the only way to go beyond it.

I shall come back to this when I talk about defeat. It's not a military or political defeat. For me it's a feeling, a feeling of helplessness faced with something we're being dragged into, something we haven't chosen. That's why I called it *Le Corps défait*, the defeated body. Once the script exists (and this is why the script is a cinematic discourse), this point of view is going to be stamped at every level. It is going to justify the position of the camera, the movements that are called for, the centre of interest I am looking for. So the choice of point of view gives the film's structure precisely, even its style and aesthetic. The nature of my character, my protagonists, has always gone the other way compared with Egyptian cinema or the classic Western. The conflict is no longer between two people but in each character. There is no confrontation between good and evil with the prospect of victory for one or the other. With me good and evil are in one and the same character and the conflict becomes an internal conflict. This is what made the break with the old Egyptian cinema, with melodrama.

What are my sources of inspiration now? If I look back, I find there are some constants that recur in the eight scripts I've written and the three films I've directed (to be more precise, I've written eleven scripts, eight for other people and three and a half for myself). I've chosen six constants that I think you will find interesting. Perhaps they may give you an idea. These constants give our films an identity. When you see them with these constants, you understand the difference between a Tunisian film and a European film, since the cinematic language is the same. There is no national cinematic language. That doesn't exist. There are other things that determine the identity of the film. So I've chosen six constants, and I shall discuss them one by one.

1 Memory as Baggage

The first constant is memory – memory as almost the only baggage the characters carry, the only thing left to them as a legacy among the loss of values. We often fall back on the past, and the characters fall back on the past. I try to give each of the characters roots, a past, a life, memories. I have discovered that the word 'memory' recurs very often in our cinema since the 80s. I can quote at least four films which have the word 'memory' in the title: *La Mémoire tatouée*, *La Mémoire plâtrée*, *La Mémoire fertile*, *La Mémoire de Chahine*. We are in the presence of men and women at the crossroads of lost paths, but with a knowledge of their past. They know nothing of the future; they only have a past. They are very often searching for an identity. This question of identity keeps recurring: Are we Arabs? Are we Tunisians? What does it mean to be Arab? What is being Tunisian? Where do I come from? Why have I always been ruled? Could it be that there was a time when I was not ruled? Are we Berbers? Are we a mixture? And these films search for identity, especially cultural identity. It's not a national identity, it's very often a cultural identity. We are forced to take this step, especially coming from a francophone culture; we have gained our knowledge through the medium of a language which is not our mother tongue. We want to know what our origin is. The typical thing about my scripts is that I have always set up a violent relationship with these memories. In other words, my protagonists are in conflict with their memories and call them to account. They are not satisfied with their memories. They are ill at ease with this history and this past. I've always placed my protagonists in a situation where they are haunted by their memories, paralysed and overwhelmed even. In *The Man of Ashes* the past of Hechmi and Farfat hems in their present. They are prisoners. Hechmi cannot marry because his past stops him. Similarly with Youssef Soltane in *The Golden Horse Shoes*, who is pursued by his past. This is also the case with Alia in *Les Silences du palais*, who does not manage to rid herself of this past, which is tied to that of her mother and grandmother. Memory leads me logically to another constant which is very important for me.

2 Defeat as Destiny

It's like a destiny, a verdict, almost a feeling. One day I wrote an article on the new Arab cinema, which I called 'The New Arab Cinema, or the Cinema of Defeat'. This article was the subject of several attacks by the Arabs, by Arab critics, and this perhaps confirms that I was right. For me the word 'defeat' is not the right word; really it's decadence. It's something which is shared by everyone, but the immediate perception of people as a whole is one of defeat. At the same time, however, it's a feeling that is rejected, unrecognised, unknown. People deny defeat. They fantasise, for example, about the defeat in the Gulf War (the most recent example), where leaders drag people into a form of suicide with inflammatory speeches. People march because they are searching for anything that will get them out of this defeat; it's terrible, but it's the reality. This reality is tragic because it can beget drama and that has always been a source of inspiration for me. This idea is present in everything I've done. 'And Sheherazade killed herself for unspeakable words' is the name of the part I made for *La Guerre du Golfe*. It's the leitmotif of *The Thousand and One Nights*. At a certain point Sheherazade says, 'Whether the Iraqis win or the Saudis win, I'm still the loser.' That sums it all up. Even if there is a victory, the woman's consciousness is the consciousness of her double defeat. In other words, defeat is something which is shared by everyone except those who won't admit it. This decadence is not of the present, it has no date. If I have talked about the Gulf War, it's because these are things that are clearer to you, but this decadence is five centuries old and it resulted in the Balkanisation of the Ottoman Empire, which in turn resulted in colonisation.

With the granting of independence in the 1950s a new feeling was born, the feeling of Arab nationalism. This feeling awoke a kind of pride in the Arabs, the greatness of belonging to a power that was the centre of the world at a certain point in history. But successive defeats and the demagogy of leaders transformed this feeling of greatness into a great impotence, a kind of despondency, disarray, split, distress; and, every time they are flattered, the harder is the fall. For me this reality of extreme conflict is a pair of contradictions – greatness and impotence – which is more than tragic and is going to haunt us for a long time. It's an inexhaustible source of drama. It's where we encounter all the modern conflicts of the Arab hero up to *Bezness*, where the character is both East and West, dream and reality. He is East inside and West outside. People become double because they are looking for anything that can help them escape from this reality. There have been some extremely important films that have tried to describe this defeat. Chahine's *Le Moineau* is still a great watershed in this respect. What interests me in this business of defeat is the idea that the conflict is internal. Not only internal, the conflict is borne by every individual and it cannot be settled except by each individual. *The Man of Ashes* was a notable film in this respect, it was almost a key film, and that continued with *The Golden Horse Shoes*. The first film speaks of the destruction and rape of a child; the second speaks of another form of destruction and rape of an adult. The true defeat is in one's education and the type of relations one has with individuals; the relations between the social structure and the individual, whether the state, the family or the religious structure. This relationship is one that destroys the individual. All these things may seem bizarre to you, they may seem insane, but this is truly what I feel, what I see and what characterises my films.

3 The Filial Relationship

The third constant in my sources of inspiration, which is very strong where we come from, is the filial relationship. When I talk about the filial relationship I mean both patriarchy, the father, and machismo. This attitude that the father is sacred and the difficulty of ridding oneself of him is a constant in *The Man of Ashes* and is present in all the films I've made. Hechmi needs a father but all his fathers cause him is problems: his biological father beats him, is violent towards him; his initiation father rapes him; and his spiritual father, Levy, dies, and he remains virtually confined to the orphanage. The film tried to say that there is no longer any room for a father and you have to sort out your problems on your own. With us the problem of the father is associated not with the Oedipus complex but with the myth of Abraham, who was prepared to sacrifice his own son. The son submits to the father and serves him. In our society the individual is nothing; it's the family that counts, the group. Our cinema is trying to destroy the edifice of the family and liberate the individual. We've talked a lot about Tunisian cinema, the emergence of the subjective element, the individual. This individual has always been rebelling against the structure, the family, the patriarchy. This revolt in all the films was salutary. The issue of filial duty and machismo has inspired me in all my films and scripts. I've always tried to catch out machismo, in other words to corner man in his flaws, in his moments of machismo, even if he claims to be the opposite. Even with Youssef Soltane, who presents a liberal front, I try to corner him and catch him out. This machismo idea has sometimes even led me to have a feminine sensibility in my films, whether in *The Man of Ashes* or my films about women. I discovered that there is even an evolution in the last scripts I did. *Les Silences du palais* and *Bent Familia*, which I shall be shooting soon, were both written with a feminine eye, and perhaps this is beneficial to the way I work, since it's a form of internalisation – woman is the inside of man.

4   The Image of the Body

This brings me to a problem which has caused a lot of fuss among us, especially from the fundamentalists. This is the fourth constant, in my opinion the most important one alongside defeat – the body. The body is really the heart of the matter. For the fundamentalists the image of the body is a double prohibition, the prohibition of the image and the prohibition of the body. The body is prohibited, the image is prohibited and the image of the body is doubly prohibited. Can you make films without the body? Serge Daney says that the purpose of cinema is to show things; it's the act of showing. What are you going to show if you don't show the body? Whereas if we look back at our past and our memories the body is very much present. If you take *The Thousand and One Nights* the body is very much present there. It even inspired eroticism in the West. So why lose this extraordinary area of expression which is the body? This area ought to be reconquered; the body ought to be rehabilitated, rediscovered somehow. For me the body has always been the most important vector of dramatic technique and conflicts, dramas, characters. From this point of view the choice of actor, as regards his body and his face, is very precise and very difficult. If I take *The Man of Ashes*, for example, Hechmi needed to have a feminine beauty whose purpose is to bring out his drama still more, because he is likened to a girl, and, when a woman says that he ought to have been a girl because he has a feminine beauty, that upsets him completely. Farfat, his counterpart, needed to be volatile, androgynous, because he flies, he cannot stand roofs, he's called Farfat, and Farfat is *farfallo*, butterfly. So the choice of body is very precise; Farfat needs fragility in his body, and the camera has to caress bodies to bring them closer to the viewer. Youssef Soltane, for example, in *The Golden Horse Shoes*, needed to have a cumbersome body because he doesn't know what to do with his body – that frightened body, entirely marked by torture and his upbringing at the hands of his father. When he finally kills himself, he kills himself while purifying himself, washing himself in the detail of his body. You see his way of purifying himself; in some way his death is a purification of his body. So the body is something fundamental in cinema, as in drama.

For the fundamentalists there has always been a confusion between sex and the body, but this confusion is in me too. But while the fundamentalists think that the whole body is sex, for me sex is part of the body, everything is body. For them everything is sex, and that's the whole difference. For me showing a nude is an act of propriety. It's a propriety that reminds me of the image of a nude in a concentration camp; it's the height of propriety and emotion.

In this sense the nude can be extremely decorous, can even engender a kind of respect. In the body, the face is also fundamental, and I shall talk about the face in aesthetics shortly. In *Les Silences du palais*, the fourteen-year-old girl's drama coincides with the awakening of her body. When she has her first, traumatic period, she starts asking questions about her father, his relationship with her mother, and this will never leave her. Somehow her body has revealed her mother's body to her, with all the dramas this entails. By this process we are trying – I say 'we' meaning all our film-makers – to change the old view that

55

regards the body as something dirty and scandalous. In the Egyptian melo-dramas, for example, the only person who shows her body is the belly dancer; she is always the *femme fatale* who tries to lead a son from a good family astray; it ends up with the son escaping her clutches. The body is always as-sociated with people's moral turpitude. The only bodies shown are of people who have been morally devalued. In the end, if you want to devalue someone, you denude him, you show his body. This brings me to the emotion that the body carries with it, the emotion that has always enabled me to work.

5   Pain as Emotion

In all my films, and most of the scripts I've done, I've worked through pain. I make the character suffer in his internal dilemma. Pain, for me, is incompatible with pleasure. For example, I've never used the body for visual pleasure. When I worked on *Halfaouine*, Férid said to me, 'I leave pain to you, I don't want any.' Férid works through pleasure, but the film allowed him to, because in *Halfaouine* (and this links up with what I have said about the body) his ulti-mate aim is the sight and discovery of the body; in other words, a boy becomes a man when he has discovered the female body. He celebrates the act of becoming a man in discovering the female body. It's interesting; you could almost say that about cinema. Cinema is the art of discovering and seeing; this can be an aim in itself, and it's Férid's cinema. I work differently. That's not to say it's better; everyone works with his own emotion. I have a relationship almost of mutual respect with my audience. I try to show a mirror to the viewer, to slide it gently in front of him, trying to caress him to say that I love him. In this mirror he gradually sees his own image and discovers that it's ugly, that it's not beautiful, that this image doesn't favour him. But I am showing him him-self in pain and saying to him, 'That's your image, you have to accept it and be proud of it.' In this situation there is only the emotion of pain that enables me to respect him. Pain becomes a kind of ethic, because I am unveiling the hidden side of society and I don't want people to walk out feeling ill. I want to help them understand this side. So I share their pain with them, and, as this pain is mine too, I merge with them. Generally, the image people have in their heads is one which has to be favourable; they can't imagine anyone presenting an un-favourable image of themselves to them. So I almost rape them with my images so that they shan't be raped elsewhere. I think this refusal to be pleasing is necessary as soon as you start dealing with serious matters. Only sincerity al-lows that; it must be captivating. This is why during the whole phase, even if there are pleasant moments occasionally – it must be a show – pain is present, people's pain has to be captured.

6   The Face and the Veil

The sixth constant is concerned with aesthetics. The aesthetic is determined by the subject matter and the dramatic technique, as I have outlined. It's an aes-thetic based on prohibition. It consists in lifting the veil on society, not only on the female body, not only on the female head, but on society. Each film has to lift a flap of the veil that covers it, but always with respect for society. Anything goes as long as it's done with respect – there is no other prohibition. I see this aesthetic and I make it convulsive. It takes on the internal movement of the soul in pain, the soul subjected to multiple strains, perpetually troubled, communicating a feeling of discomfort. This aesthetic is almost there in the last ten films of Chahine, starting with *Le Moineau*. This film, by the way, is a fundamental film, in my opinion, in what I call the Cinema of Defeat. It's a fundamental film because it finds new ways of expressing this, in contrast to the aesthetic of contemplation, as in Mohamed Malas's *La Nuit*. I couldn't make a film like that. The film is a masterpiece, but it's a contemplative point of view, a contemplative aesthetic imposed on the past, and that's not my view. Few Tunisian films hide behind history, in fact; even when we make a historical film, it's made to say modern things. We are more rebellious; we don't have any self-censorship, unlike Syrian cinema, for example, which is of very good quality but rather imprisoned by self-censorship. This aesthetic somewhat recalls the aesthetic of hunger in the Brazilian Cinema Novo developed by Glober Rocha. In fact, Glauber Rocha's *Terre en transe* could have been an Arab film. The title expresses the entire aesthetic that I should like to develop. This aesthetic is going to guide the camera to find hidden things, to provide the necessities for a journey, a movement towards the interior, a detour.

In this aesthetic there is something fundamental – the face. Looking at a face is already rape, and here I need to quote a saying by the prophet Mohammed. I'm not a believer, but it is very important to understand this; it's at the root of all the misunderstandings of Islam. Mohammed says: 'If you find yourself disobeying an interdict, please do it in secret.' There are two parts to this saying. The first is tolerant: the prophet accepts that an interdict can be disobeyed, which the fundamentalists don't accept. But the second is the only one the fundamentalists have taken, doing everything in secret. In *The Golden Horse Shoes*, Sgatar, who is a small weaver, says to Youssef, who is the leftist, 'The day your father caught me singing he gave me a slap that almost blinded me.' Youssef replies, 'He wanted you to do everything, but in secret. But you can't sing in secret, you needed to find something else.' That somewhat sums up the Arab-Muslim mentality. In *Bezness* the French photographer says to Bezness, 'You're afraid of the word or the thing. The act itself isn't really serious, what's serious is showing it and talking about it.'

So what are we to do with the cinema? We'll have to make *The Invisible Man*! The problem with cinema is that it's in complete conflict with Islam, from start to finish. The problem of representation, the problem of the body, the problem of the veil, the problem of interdicts, of showing things. I showed some films and discussed them with a group of imprisoned fundamentalists, fundamentalist intellectuals, rebels who had nothing fundamentalist about them, in fact, but enrolled because it was the most radical group there was. In the 60s, for instance, they could have been Marxists. These youngsters thought we had no right to show a boy being raped or a girl being raped because it would give other people ideas. That's their theory; that's how they explain the prophet's saying: you mustn't show anything because you are giving an example; you must only show good things. So it's because of this saying, which lays down a sort of social hypocrisy, that cinema somehow becomes transgression, and, since it's total transgression, what stops us from going further? I don't understand people censoring themselves – they're already under the interdict.

To conclude, I should like to make some practical observations, which may be important for some of you. The first observation is that, for me, adult cinema, and I stress the word adult, is cinema that right from the script stage regards the viewer as an adult. There is no other adult cinema. The kind that treats the viewer like a child who has to have everything spoon-fed, explained, settled, is a cinema that despises the viewer and sets itself up as his guardian. In the film, dramatically speaking, the conflicts have to be settled at the end, obviously, the stakes must be clear at the end of the film, but the settlement of the conflict must always raise certain questions that will haunt the viewer. For me this is the only way of talking about adult cinema. It's a cinema that pursues through emotion, that pursues on behalf of the viewer in reflection. Clearly, when we are taught to make a script, if it's a detective film, the edifice has to collapse. It's built up and at the end it collapses. And for me the film reaches completion, and everything reaches completion from the point that everything collapses. You forget everything. I can't even tell the story or talk about it; I don't think there's any point in talking about it, it's a waste of time. So, especially in a society where we have so much to catch up on, it's cinema that asks questions. And a cinema that asks questions is certainly not a cinema that leaves important questions unanswered. In other words, the fundamental issues have to be clarified. But you don't have an answer to everything. It shouldn't put forward solutions. I'm against cinema that puts forward ready-made solutions. In *The Golden Horse Shoes* people said to me, 'But what's your solution? What's your programme?' The people who ask me that question are asking too much of cinema and could kill it. Cinema should not be a replacement for politics, or theory, or science.

The second observation is that you should avoid realist scripts like the plague. Let me explain. For me reality is unaesthetic. I go into a house that I want to film and I find that the plastic organisation of space, colours, tones, the style of the furniture is mediocre and unbearable. That's the reality. My duty and my purpose are to put forward a new aesthetic that's not realistic. I have to sublimate this reality, transform it, give the impression that it's true, that it's the reality. But it mustn't look like reality; you mustn't say 'That's what life is like' when you're writing a script. If you say 'That's what life is like', you revert to life and put a stop to cinema. Cinema, as Godard said, is life twenty-four times a second.

The third observation – and here I'm going to be a bit provocative towards the studios – is that I can't understand how anyone can do that; for me, the act of writing a script, the act of creation, is individual, personal and intimate. It needs privacy, and I don't understand how anyone can negotiate a script with a stranger. With a collaborator, yes. With someone from the team, yes. But not with strangers. You need a bit of privacy or else it's a throwaway script, what there is of him in the script and what there isn't. That's something I don't understand. I don't say you shouldn't do it, but my personal conviction is that people should work with professionals, but the other candidates shouldn't interfere with someone else's script. They must stay inside their script, in fact, otherwise things will get mixed up in their minds. There are theoretical courses, but practice – you can't all discuss everyone's script, it's impossible! Unless it's an exercise that is thrown away afterwards, or a remake. You can take a film that has already been made, or the script, to understand it.

The fourth observation is that you mustn't lose sight of the fact that a script and a film have a therapeutic function and that sometimes the only way of undergoing the therapy is by writing the script. You shouldn't be afraid of putting your pain on paper. Don't hesitate. That's why it's a private act, an act that demands a lot of privacy, that can't be handed over to other people while it's under way. You can't give birth in front of strangers; personally, I can't give birth in front of strangers – no one can. So I suggest you consider this question if you want to be effective.

My final remark: I should like to tell you how I start writing a script technically, because for me the actual writing of the script is the last phase. It's very short, it doesn't last more than a week, but it takes months and months to reach that stage. I can't understand how anyone can make a synopsis before making the script. As far as I'm concerned, you can talk about a character, but I don't understand making a synopsis and a résumé before the script, because it's the character that determines everything. What I do, generally – it's a bit of a fetish – is take the poster of my last film, turn it over, and on the back I try to make a plan of how the scenes follow one another, a detailed plan, and this detailed plan gets more and more detailed. Then the scenes change places and I colour in all the characters to see how they evolve on paper. And when it gets too messy, I transfer it to another sheet, but still with all the details, in a different order. I can see straight away what makes sense and what doesn't. I do that maybe ten times and then I have all the phases of the plans. Finally, when I feel it's ready, I can write the script. And when I do I have no problems, because I know that that character can't say that phrase but he can say this phrase, that he can't meet someone like that ... I know everything. I can't be mistaken because I hold all the strings, and they're inside me, because I've seen them over and over again. I've lived with a universe in a one-page structure; I can see the relationships at a glance. And I think this technique has enabled me to work very quickly and authentically.

African Cinema – Militancy or Entertainment?

Mweze Ngangura

Translated by Paul Willemen. This paper has not previously been published.

The question is to find out whether African cinema, in the context of the continent's current political, social and economic crisis, can afford the luxury of being an entertainment cinema rather than a cinema that fights against this crisis. In fact, the question should be posed in different terms because one should not assume that an entertainment cinema is necessarily incompatible with Africa's development. I would even argue that, on the contrary, it is especially the entertainment cinema which is most likely to contribute to such a development in contemporary Africa, but such a statement requires further elaboration and some explanation, which I will try to provide in this paper.

The current crisis in Africa, manifested in various forms such as malnutrition, diseases, lack of freedom of expression, corruption and the international debt, cannot be overcome just by economic growth and changes of political regimes. Today, there can no longer be any doubt that culture is one of the principal development factors for Africa, perhaps even its driving engine. And many international organisations concerned with the development of Africa do indeed include, increasingly, the cultural sector in their programmes.

If we take the term culture in its broader meaning as the manifestation in everyday life of the cohesion and the dynamism of a collective, if we understand it as the way in which each collective interprets and transforms the world, then it becomes evident that the cultural activity most likely to contribute to Africa's development is to be situated on the level of popular or so-called mass culture. Cinema, which is essentially a mass spectacle, has thus an important role to play in this respect. The huge financial as well as human resources required for the production of a film mean that it needs to be seen by a large number of people if these costs are to be amortised, and the mode in which a film is disseminated, in cinemas or on television, make it eminently suitable to reach such audiences.

For the African film-maker, the problem is to find out which would be the most efficient way for cinema to contribute to social change. The solution most commonly adopted by film-makers is to make films 'with a message' – that is to say, films which privilege the didactic aspect of their content to the detriment of their entertainment value. This option, though laudable for its generous intentions, does seem to me to be very ill suited to enable cinema to play its full role as the witness and the agent of cultural dynamism in Africa.

There are four main reasons for doubting the efficacy of this option. First, it is very difficult to control the actual impact of the message one wants the film to transmit, taking into account the distortions and the parasites that can beset the intended message. There is the often cited example of the Senegalese film which wanted to discourage people from using hemp but had the exact opposite effect on Senegal's youth. One thing is clear: promoting a message does not mean that it is perceived as such by individual viewers. Film language is as complex as life itself and its perception is more emotional than intellectual. By privileging intellectual comprehension, the message-film risks reducing its dramatic structure to an elaborate illustration of its thesis and to make the characters too much like caricatures.

Second, if a film-maker wants to push the message to its logical conclusions, he or she would inevitably end up making films that disturb the political powers that be and run up against the problem of freedom of expression, which is very limited in almost all African countries. The least that could happen is that the film-maker's work is banned in his or her own country, which means that the film will not be able to reach the very people to whom it is supposed to be addressed. Outside its country of origin, such a film would be restricted to preaching to the converted, comforting the good 'militant' conscience of a very small number of already 'aware' Africans. Consequently, such a film's efficacy would be zero. An African film-maker who at times may have official responsibilities in his or her country can only inscribe his or her message within the exceedingly narrow limits set by the prevailing political power.

Third, because the distribution mechanisms do not work very well, it is difficult to commercialise an African film within Africa. As soon as the film has a didactic character, it becomes virtually impossible to show it in mainstream cinemas, and there are no others in Africa. The only possibility to amortise such a film would then be to sell the non-theatrical rights to organisations concerned in various ways with supporting African cinema. The result would be to perpetuate the status of African cinema as a cinema 'assisted' from the outside and therefore 'underdeveloped'. How could such a cinema contribute to the development of an African mass culture?

Fourth, message-films form part of a larger sector called the 'cinéma d'auteur' in which the film-maker as the author expresses his or her personal views about film language and about society in general, disregarding the hackneyed, routinely familiar dominant conventions. In countries that have a flourishing film industry, such an elite cinema addressed to art cinema audiences does fulfil an important function, stimulating artistic creativity and reflection about society. However, in Africa, for many years now almost all film-makers have regarded themselves as authors, as people with a mission, charged with carrying a message to their people. For instance, the pioneer theoretician of African cinema, Tahar Chériaa, told film-makers: 'Your cinema shall be a militant cinema, it shall be first and foremost a cultural action with social and political value, or it will be nothing. If it eventually can also become an economic action, that will only be a by-product.'[1] Férid Boughedir tends to sound the same note when he affirms that 'African cinema, if it is to exist at all, shall be a cinema of authors'.[2]

In fact, the infatuation with 'a cinema of authors', because it did not emanate from a broad, mainstream cinematographic current (which did not exist anyway) addressed to the bulk of the audiences, has only succeeded in alienating the African audience from its own cinema, which even today it tends to regard as too 'cultural' in the pejorative sense and too didactic rather than as a spectacle. It is revealing, for instance, that comedies, a popular genre if there ever was one, in Africa just as much as elsewhere, have only been rarely attempted in the African cinema.

This situation can be explained in the light of a rather overweening European influence on African cinema from the outset. Indeed, African cinema was born in Europe with Paulin Soumanou Vieyra's *Afrique-sur-Seine* and all its pioneers were trained there. In the former French colonies, which were the first African countries to have a national cinema, production has almost always been supported by European finance and technicians, mainly through the French Ministry of Co-operation. All this happened in the early 1960s, which, for European cinema, was the time of the New Wave, militant cinema and auteur films. For a long time, the only places where African films were distributed in Africa, often free of charge, were the European cultural centres. Except for festivals where the juries consisted exclusively of European critics, the rare distribution opportunities for these films were those provided by the non-commercial and marginal circuits in Europe.

On the other hand, African television stations, which could have played a crucial role in the production of African films, are content, even today, to receive almost all their film programmes from Europe. In the last few years, at last, there have been signs that African film-makers are beginning to tackle more popular subjects. Film-makers seem to begin attaching as much importance to their audience as to their 'people'. Interestingly, this tendency manifests itself especially in the former British colonies, as Férid Boughedir noted. He went on to ask: 'Is this a sign of the often invoked difference between French colonialism, anxious to legitimate itself through cultural means, and British colonialism, exclusively concerned with "business"?'[3]

These are the main reasons for being sceptical about message-films or, more generally, about auteur films as to their ability to contribute to any genuine social change in Africa today. This leaves the question of entertainment cinema and under what conditions it could play a positive role in the development of Africa. On what grounds, and why, can we expect more from entertainment cinema?

I will answer this question starting from a little anecdote. During the last Ouagadougou Festival (FESPACO 1989), a boy of about thirteen years of age came and asked why we did not make a film with an African Rambo, because, he said, 'I really would like to see an African Rambo in the cinema.' In the context of the many screenings and earnest debates about the future of African cinema, this unexpected question at first seemed too banal to merit a response. But then I started understanding it as a challenge, a provocation. An African Rambo? Why? Well, why not? Together with a colleague, we simply gave an evasive response and politely sent the boy on his way. With hindsight, it seems to me that we should have taken that question a little more seriously, if only out of respect for a member of the audience who had paid for a ticket to watch our films and, what is more, who, because of his age, represented a future African audience.

For a film-maker interested in an African entertainment cinema, the boy's question raised three points. First, this young man, like many African spectators, consumes *Rambo*. Why? Because when he goes to the cinema he wants to be distracted and there are not enough African films able to do that. It is this absence which opens up the gap filled with imported second-rate American and European cultural products, not only ill-matched to the African realities but also carrying with them ideologies justifying or preparing the way for economic and political domination. Making good African entertainment films could thus bar the way to that kind of domination.

Second, that young man, just like any spectator in any country, feels the need to identify with the hero. It is especially at this level that the ideological responsibility of the film-maker is located: with which physical, moral or intellectual characteristics does the film-maker endow his or her positive heroes?

Finally, the point is that this boy did not manage to identify with Rambo. He sees very well that this White, American Rambo moves in a totally different world and is a totally different kind of person. That Rambo will never be able to embody the boy's most extravagant dreams and aspirations. Therefore, the African spectator expects from a film-maker a film where he or she can fully identify with the characters, the settings, the subject, and so on.

These three points constitute the necessary conditions for reconciling the African audience with its own cinema: entertaining films; African heroes embodying totally positive social values; a familiar cultural context. However, a few words of warning are in order to signal some pitfalls the film-maker must avoid if the African entertainment cinema is to be reconciled with the requirements of development.

First, there is the requirement of submission to the existing political power. As I argued earlier, it is difficult and ineffective for film-makers to attack the reigning political power. On the other hand, they can refuse to be their flag carriers. As a film-maker's national and international reputation grows, there will be more opportunity and even a greater obligation to take an increasingly independent line from the government in his or her country. This will enable the film-maker to tackle, to the greater happiness of the spectators, more and more politically 'taboo' subjects.

Second, there is the danger of making servile copies of the West's commercial cinema, unthinkingly using the ingredients of that cinema, such as sex and violence. A distinction should be made between popular and commercial cinema, the latter limiting itself to soliciting, like a pimp, the audience by flattering its basest instincts, whereas the popular cinema tries to meet the audience, including its aesthetic and ethical needs.

Lastly, there is the danger of reproducing the kind of clichés of Africa which the exoticising Western cinema has propagated. Indeed, the tendency in recent African cinema to present a mythical Africa outside any geographical or historical context could, if it were to become widespread, engender some confusions in the spectator's mind. Not to engage with these contexts would, on the part of the film-maker, be thoroughly irresponsible, if you remember that, in the Western cinema and media, the image of Africa has been all too often prostituted. Instead of helping to foster a new energy in African popular cultures which, in the face of imported cultural products, are losing out, especially in the urban milieus, the entertainment films which fall into those traps would end up strengthening the impact of the imported cultures, all the more so since they would have the justification of having been made by 'native sons and daughters'.

The reticence felt by an African film-maker vis-à-vis entertainment cinema comes no doubt from the impression that this is a cinema that has nothing to say. On the contrary, one should start from the premise that, if a spectator can remain captivated by a film for ninety minutes or more, that is because it does speak to him or her in some way. Of course, the difficulty resides in the impossibility of defining clearly and precisely what the 'some way' is, cinema being, as we noted earlier, a language far less apt at transmitting rational knowledge than emotions. Nevertheless, I am convinced that a cinema which adheres to the conditions outlined above would contribute, even without any overt message, to the reflection of African spectators' everyday dreams and aspirations and that, like a mirror, it would enable the spectator to see him or herself and to decide whether to accept the image the film-maker offers, completely or in part.

One of the numerous banners at FESPACO 87 proclaimed: 'Africa thirsts to see its own images.' The urgent need is not to make films that speak of Africa, but films for Africans. As a cultural work, a good entertainment film is already a contribution to development. To achieve that, it does not have to speak of development.

Notes

1. Tahar Chériaa. *Ecrans d'abondances ou cinémas de libération* (Tunis: Editions Sinbad, 1974).
2. Férid Boughedir, *African Cinema from A–Z*, (Brussels: Editions OCIC, 1987).
3. Ibid.

Responsibility and Freedom of Expression

ANNE MUNGAI

Translated by Alison Preston from *Cinéma et liberté, FESPACO '93* (Paris and Dakar: Présence africaine, 1993).

At present it is difficult to make films in Africa which have political connotations, because film-makers are afraid of censorship. Yet it is important that they be able to express themselves without fear, provided that this freedom of expression is accompanied by a sense of responsibility. What I mean by that is that their films must be a reflection of their own culture and not a reflection of a foreign ideology.

Africa has 170 million potential viewers. In other words a low-budget African film could make a profit without needing to get onto the European circuit. African film production companies can raise funds, create jobs, and improve the image of Africa and Africans. If they express themselves with complete freedom, but with responsibility, African film-makers can help to further ideas of national unity, African solidarity, democracy and sexual equality; they can show changes in customs and attitudes, the social injustice of apartheid – in a word films, could contribute a lot to both national and pan-African development.

Unfortunately, after political independence, most governments did not take the measures necessary to establish a national cinema industry, and did not appreciate the use of film as a means of recreation, information and education, as well as a way of alerting audiences to the problems of socio-cultural development.

Lots of African countries live on a diet of foreign films, which have no connection with the needs and aspirations of their people. It is therefore necessary that, while respecting film-makers' freedom of expression, the cinematographic industry should develop according to a clearly defined policy.

Above all, films must deal with development issues. As a woman film-maker, I want to be free to describe what affects a woman from a rural background. After all, I did grow up in a village! I was thirteen years old when my father died. I was brought up by my mother and my brother and his wife. I know what it is like when you are asked to leave school and get married because your school fees are too expensive. Many country girls have had the same experiences. I know how a widow suffers: I saw my mother suffer. When I make films, I put a lot of myself into them, a lot of my childhood. It is what I want to express because it is what I know and what I've lived. Talking about what you know demonstrates responsibility. Besides, it would be wrong to expect African film-makers to make Hollywood-style productions: it would be like wanting to run before you can walk.

Countries in the process of development don't just have a need for drinking water, food, medical care and education. They also need to develop a critical sense, and cinema can play a significant role here, if films deal with the reality of people's lives. They can be a kind of mirror to society, kindling the audience's reactions as they see their own problems and worries reflected on screen. Kenyans ought to have the right to reject the flood of Western films which have nothing to do with their own culture, and see instead films about themselves. Except that, most of the time, they are not told about Kenyan or African films. Some local papers would rather talk about films and film stars who have nothing to do with Kenya. The censor doesn't notice the way that cheaply imported foreign films and television programmes are contibuting to a feeling of cultural alienation. However, studies have shown that the majority of Kenyans, with the exception of a small minority of colonialist city dwellers, would prefer to watch African films if they had a choice.

In Kenya there is both a lack of information and a lack of professionalism – above all at the level of screenplay writing – which explains the stagnation in the cinematographic industry. A cultural policy oriented to free expression, underpinned by a keen sense of responsibility from film-makers, could contribute to the blossoming of the industry.

Cinema and Freedoms: Reflections of a Senegalese Film-Maker

MAHAMA JOHNSON TRAORÉ

Translated by Paul Willemen from *Cinéma et liberté, FESPACO '93* (Paris and Dakar: Présence africaine, 1993).

Whenever I travelled to Paris, I always went to visit Madame Diop. On one of those occasions, she addressed me with a maternal voice, saying: 'So, Johnson, could you write me a paper on cinema and freedoms?' At first, I thought she was pulling my leg. It was only a few years since I had been a victim of intolerance because I had wanted to produce the film of a young Senegalese director addressing, precisely, the question of freedom and dignity. A little later, I received a letter from Présence Africaine signed by Madame Diop, repeating and officially confirming her request. Now I find myself in an awkward position: how to deal with such a burning and topical issue as cinema and freedoms without trying to settle personal accounts? And what themes should I select, since no overall guideline was provided? After a few weeks' reflection, I arbitrarily decided to tackle the subject from two angles.

> Every film remains a necessity. It is a freedom which becomes necessity and then becomes freedom again when it is shown to others. (Joris Ivens, 1898–1989)

1 Production

Is truly sovereign cinematic creation really possible in a Southern country, for instance in Africa? In the absence of national financial structures, can the African film-maker afford to treat any subject he chooses without some money-lender – that is to say, some Northern producer – coming to fix his gaze on this or that subject, advising on which way it should best be approached, with due regard to the occidental public? Do the aid mechanisms elaborated and put into place by different African governments allow an African film-maker to create according to the consecrated canons of art – that is to say, freely? Indeed, for thirty years now, African governments have been putting money into national film production, more for reasons of prestige than to develop a genuine film industry. And they have good reason to do so, because, as they well know, the creator's economic independence necessarily goes together with the freedom to broach any theme likely to reflect the everyday conditions of African societies. In this way, by holding the strings of production, by refusing to set up genuine audiovisual enterprises, by allowing for other sources of finance to 'aid' African cinema, the political and financial powers that be retain control, by hook and by crook, over film creation in Africa.

In the absence of real, local production enterprises and production managers, the Northern money-lenders (ministries, foundations, agencies, and so on) have for a long time given money directly to African film-makers so that they could make 'their' films. This has enabled the making of many films which otherwise would never have seen the light of day. In return, this same procedure has allowed those Northern countries not only to establish the biggest African cinematheque, but also and above all to create the vocation of producers exclusively concerned with African films.

The non-existence of structures *in situ* and the absence of Africans trained to take charge of audiovisual businesses lead film-makers to look for producers in the North, especially since the traditional money-lenders require the creator to have a producer. The one who lends also controls. When the director has found his producer, the endless discussions commence:

Producer: Your subject isn't international enough. You have to rewrite it with that in mind.
Director: If I do that, the African audience will feel lost.
Producer: You have to be aware of which audience you are making the film for. There is no African audience here in Europe. So, Africa is ...
Director: Be that as it may, if I cannot work as I see it, I lose my soul.
Producer: Listen, the money-lenders are European, so your work has to meet their requirements, otherwise it won't work.

The director knows full well that even if he makes the film the way the producer wants it there still is no guarantee that he will get an international distribution. Moreover, besides losing his creative freedom, he will have to subscribe, willy nilly, to the image of Africa which Europe wants to impose. But, as he absolutely wants to make the film come what may, he will accept all the producer's suggestions. And that is why we have seen, recently, those colourless and odourless, aseptic African films. The director who ignores those suggestions and makes his film according to his own sense of ethics will pay the price. For example, Med Hondo's *Sarraounia*, produced by Soleil O Films with the participation of the French Ministry of Co-operation, was released almost secretly in France: 'they' could not forbid it, but neither did 'they' do anything to help its release.

The film's theme is the disintegration in 1899 of a French military expedition inflicted by – a woman. The film has remained virtually unseen in Africa, even though it is based on actual events and evokes a glorious moment of our heritage. In Europe, those who decide do not want this kind of product. So, in Africa, in order to avoid problems with the Northern partners, 'they' will forget to release the film to African screens.

Another example, to prove that nobody escapes: in 1985, the SNPC, of which I was the Director General at the time, was to produce *Thiaroye 44* by Ben Diogaye Beye. Knowing that the subject was likely to irritate our French partners, I decided to make it a South/South co-production. After many trips to Algeria and Tunisia, I managed to clinch what could be called the first genuine African audiovisual co-operation. An agreement was duly signed by the different parties: for Tunisia, SATPEC and Mr Akrout; for Algeria, ENAPROC and Mr Bensai; for Senegal, SNPC and myself. We three had agreed a division of labour: Senegal would take charge of the production, Algeria would be responsible for the shooting and recording equipment, and post-production would be done in Tunisia. At my request, Algeria immediately supplied an assistant director, in the person of Dahmane Ouzid.

In the end, although *Thiaroye 44* did not get made, *Camp de Thiaroye* did, directed by Ousmane Sembène together with Thierno Fati Sow. That film is now part of our film heritage and has the distinction of representing what one should never do when trying to make a film.

Since the end of the two world wars, many films have been made about Senegalese infantrymen, but none dealt with their real role, even though the blood they shed marks their participation in all the operations of war in Europe, Indo-China, Africa. All the African directors who wanted to tackle the subject heard the same refrain: 'There are so many fascinating subjects, why kick up old dust? African cinema is the future of world cinema, so look for other themes.' And if you insist, you run up against the argument that reconstructions are too expensive.

Neither can film-makers broach hot political subjects of the moment because the Northern producer does not wish to get involved in the internal affairs of an African country. This explains why, in thirty years or more, there are so few films making social and political demands. The few directors who have wanted to stray from the straight and narrow have paid for it dearly.

2 Film Policy

Since achieving independence, every African country has wanted to have its own national cinema. As the development of such an industry requires a considerable amount of resources together with coherent economic and social development policies, the authorities exploited the situation and took the opportunity to control the images that would emerge from the country. They 'aided' the directors with this in mind rather than developing a real film policy. Thirty years after the audiovisual came onto the market, African film-makers came to believe themselves to be the spokesmen for their people. So now even the smallest gathering or event has to have its meeting of African film-makers armed with motions, ringing statements, denunciations of the collusion between governments and occidental neocolonialism.

African film-makers have availed themselves of every platform, every means to point an accusing finger condemning the delays in setting up a film industry in Africa. In vain. To be sure, here and there national production houses and/or distributors did spring up, mostly completely financed by the governments. But no effort was made to get the cinema to finance itself, through a levy on the box-office receipts, nor to create a supporting fund that would incite the major African economic players to invest in the cinema. By organising an audiovisual sector in Africa, with clear and precise legislation protecting private investments, the authorities would be helping to make films able to function as foundation pillars without having to negotiate ethical twists and turns, simply facing the truth of the market.

Freedom: The Power to Say No

Jean-Marie Téno

Translated by Paul Willemen from *Cinéma et liberté*, FESPACO '93 (Paris and Dakar: Présence africaine, 1993).

In October 1988, at the Carthage Film Festival, where my film *Bikutsi Water Blues* (*L'Eau de la misère*) was premièred, I dared to mention freedom: freedom to choose the subject, the style, unfettered by the straitjacket of established definitions of and boundaries between documentary or fiction, freedom to say, loudly and clearly, what ninety years of oppression had not allowed us to say.

I was aware of the sarcastic remarks of some of my colleagues and the comment by one particular colleague: 'With those ideas and the film you have made, one can kill a career.' In the light of all the recent disturbances throughout the world, I will not dwell on these themes which today can be seen in everyday life. Instead, I will turn to the notion of freedom, a corollary of creation and growth, personal as much as collective.

Schematically speaking, the world today is divided into two blocs, North and South. In the North, as in the South, some are on top, others are underneath. Those on top live comfortably and have no wish for change. Some, underneath, exert themselves to ensure that everybody may have, at least, the vital minimum, so that the majority of the people may face daily life as something other than a nightmare. When those underneath cannot cope any longer, those on top get emotional, collect rice, pencils and paper and mobilise the media to show how generous and caring they are.

Crisis management without tackling the root causes of the evils (especially when you have the means to do so and when you are partly responsible) is a sophisticated form of cynicism. In six months, while sunbathing, they will say: 'We were there. We did what we could for them. What a tragedy, Africa!' Someone is bound to reply: 'But don't forget that we too have our homeless. Something should be done for them.'

But to those underneath who work ten, twelve hours a day, how do we explain that they cannot live decently from their work? They are told that the crisis is worldwide. The truth is that if the people on the bottom were to be better paid, the profit margins for those on top would be reduced and they would have to forgo the second car to take the kids to school. They would no longer be able to afford their flat in Paris (on the Avenue Foch) or the many villas they are in the habit of building with the taxpayers' money.

Selling off Africa's economic heritage is a game that has lasted for more than half a century and which produces, today, situations like Somalia and Liberia which threaten to spill over into many other African countries. These systems of economic exploitation have always rested on three factors: violent repression, disinformation from the public media, and a draconian censorship. The aim is always the same: to remove by any means possible the mass of Africans from the daily management of the wealth of their countries. This also implies an educational system that is unsuitable and very selective, leaving the majority of Africans by the wayside, uneducated and untrained, later to be fed images from elsewhere, rose-coloured dreams, not forgetting that they have to be taught insidiously to despise their own and their neighbour's image. Even religion is used to justify and legitimise our terrestrial misery as we are promised rivers of milk and honey in the hereafter as long as we are credulous enough and know how to say: 'Yes, boss, thank you, boss! You are right, boss, as always!'

Our cinema arrives in this troubled socio-political context. It must choose between immediate profitability, which condemns it to participate in the organised brutalisation of the continent, or making a contribution to the necessary reflection about freedom, at the risk of becoming unpopular. Each tries to solve this dilemma as he can. Even the analyses of the situation are often completely at variance. Those reflections should enrich our cinema. Unfortunately, cinema is expensive and we have entered the era of humanitarian aid which does not even spare cinema, always taking care, of course, to hide behind all sorts of well phrased concepts.

I am not going to attack those agencies which some countries in the North have set up to support African cinema. I simply want to draw both sides' attention to the elitist tendency which in the long run will not help cinema to elaborate its structures in our countries, but which will tend to develop a trend imitating the mechanisms of the European box office along with the race to obtain prizes at international festivals. What could be more pernicious than to distribute prizes, according to vague criteria, for self-promotion? And all those pithy little statements by experts, voiced in the corridors of the grand hotels where festivals take place, telling you which kind of films are most likely to be shown on the Northern televisions and which encourage you to do this or that and leave you with the words: 'Here is my card. Come and see me in Paris, Brussels, London, Milan or Montreal.'

All those people are people on top, or they work for those who are, and they are the friends of the people on top in our countries. One lot promises that we will find milk and honey at the third traffic light on the left or the right (there is no difference between them any more, as everyone knows) while the other lot lashes us with their whips if we do not go fast enough in the direction they want us to go, which happens to be the very same one.

Freedom is taking your time, choosing to take a step back, not to move at all or to advance at your own pace. Freedom is making in video 8 or super-8 documentaries or documents, especially when everyone thinks it does not add any value. It is also refusing to enter into the spiral of competition which prevents us from thinking on a longer-term scale rather than simply in terms of our next film. Freedom, for me, is the power to say no – with a smile.

Cinema and Development in Africa

JOSEPH KI-ZERBO

Translated by Robert Julian from *Afrique littéraire et artistique,* no. 49, 3rd quarter, 1978.

The cinema is a popular language. To receive its message, there is scarcely need for epic labours at the Sorbonne, or even a modest grade-school certificate. The message is received and broached directly on the screen. The cinema is a universal language. The word 'cinema' has been adopted in every African language. Every evening hundreds of thousands, perhaps even millions, of Africans enter those 'artificial paradises' called cinemas. They head for the drinking-trough, for a transport and uprooting which occur at one remove. For in Africa, unlike Europe and America, the kinds of life shown on the screen cannot be found in the reality of their settings. Instead of concrete references which bring one down to earth, here is a marvellous instant of escape and weightlessness. This is the enchanted, spell-binding universe of a mirage which is always out of reach, a dose of opium which temporarily soothes one's boredom by a dizzying leap into the abyss of the inaccessible: the glowing, dazzling, enthralling smile and lewd contortions of a starlet; the intoxicating feats of a Western lawman. Debauchery and violence are the two obsessive poles of the cinema imposed on Africa.

The continent pays an outlandish price for huge quantities of poison. Along with abundant takings at the box office, commercial effects are induced. The presentation of Western cultural models (in clothing, fashions, food, records, pharmaceutical products, furnishings, books, and so on) prepares standardised customers for the consumption of goods from wealthy countries. The cinema is an industry with ramifying effects, an industry which animates other industries. But development, if it is to occur, will be the affair of the people. It has no truck with mental escapes, the chloroforming and anaesthetising of African minds, which allows the scalpel of alienation to do its work. The most serious brain drain is not a matter of a few hundred African administrators but that of millions of African minds which exist in the 'elsewhere' of a cinema of intoxication. There are of course some excellent films. Moreover, the healthiest elements of African culture sometimes reject the poison spontaneously.

But the evil is no less present, massive and spectacular. How is it that most of our leaders, who constantly proclaim their desire to develop Africa, allow African brains to be handed over like soft wax to imperialist cultural aggression? The paradox is only apparent because the spiritual invasion is only the reflection and condition of a broader technical and economic domination.

In addition, cinema diversion is for certain leaders like the circus of the late

Roman Empire, an outlet which dissolves the potential energy of a sovereign people, turning them into sheep. This leads to the question: how can the cinema become a tool and an arm in the service of African development?

Economic Aspects

The cinema remains an important commercial, even industrial sector of African countries, even if most cannot claim, like Egypt, to have 56 million box-office entries and an infrastructure which produces over a hundred feature-length films yearly. And yet African cinema is dying of hunger! Governments are appalled by the investments needed (2 million Central African francs for ten minutes of footage), and so only a few (like Algeria) make the necessary allocations. But the cinema, like education, is a profitable investment, at least in the medium or long term. Short documentaries and educational films produce material goods and transform human resources. Like the film *Des Bras pour de l'eau* from Burkina Faso, they may deal with waterworks, agricultural or pastoral modernisation, draught donkeys or linear sowing. They educate in the service of health and hygiene. They can initiate self-taught African entrepreneurs in the mechanisms of modern economy, which often remain obscure for them and inhibit their efficiency.

An ignorant man is a blind man.
We want to make our country beautiful.
Let's fix up the house.
What interests the nose also interests the mouth.
A single hand washes itself badly: let's set up a co-operative.
Living better in my village.

Hundreds of titles can be found for this genre, which are perfectly suited for rural programmes.

Almost all of the respected film-makers of Quebec spent years producing this kind of inconspicuous film for the Canadian Film Office. Our African film-makers should not be in such a hurry to make a name for themselves with acclaimed feature films. Under the pretext that such work is belittling or will subject them to bureaucratic ministries of economy which often do little to multiply cinemas and cinema buses, they neglect a sector which concerns 80–90 per cent of our populations. But art has a role to play even in the humblest educational documentary. The poetry of film can render the audiovisual message of progress more attractive and convincing. As I have often said, there is no development but self-development. And the cinema is the best situated for persuading Africans to develop themselves. Efforts should also be made to illustrate the preconditions for African economic development, in particular the need for integration through unity.

Social Aspects

I shall not insist on this point, because this is where African film-makers have been most deserving. The cinema is a wonderful tool for description and social satire. The problems of young people, rural exodus, unemployment, émigrés, racism, intellectuals and a bourgeoisie which is national only in name – these have all been treated with more or less felicity. And doesn't the role of the

African woman in history, economy, crafts, art, and so forth, deserve to be exalted? There is almost infinite material here. The theme of mother and child in black African sculpture could provide the material for a major film, since African artists have used their creativity in a thousand ways to celebrate this exquisite tenderness.

Regarding social themes, one of the conditions of success is to flee the ethnological viewpoint like the plague. Assuming one can have an ethnological view of oneself! Certain African film-makers have indeed performed this feat; it makes for a distressing spectacle of alienation.

The African film-maker's view of society should not be headstrong and superficial, neutral as a cow's glance at a passing train, or dull as a policeman's report on a petty crime. His or her view must be perspicacious and warm. Rather than being purely descriptive, it must offer a grid which allows us to read and decode phenomena, with their internal antagonisms and dynamics. The film-maker's eye is neither photographic nor static; it follows the movement. Like radar, the eye of the camera should probe and apprehend the most hidden strata of the social fabric, detect and expose the subtlest pathological syndromes, and extirpate the most malignant tumours as with a scalpel. Only a cinema capable of problem analysis can be an instrument of development.

Tewfiq Salah, for instance, does not attempt to represent the 'good' and the 'bad' so much as to unveil social relations in action. Once the film-maker has objectively demonstrated why reality is the way it is, the African spectator and listener will make use of his or her critical faculties, which are sharper than often imagined, to deduce the moral of the story – even, or especially, when it is formulated soberly. The spectator or listener knows that he or she has nothing left to do but struggle. In this respect, one of the film-maker's arms is the African laugh. Africans laugh a great deal, perhaps to mask centuries of oppression and depression, but also because laughter is an essential part of the celebration of fraternity which is so striking in oral cultures based on personal dialogue. These smiles and laughter are more varied and meaningful than in countries where paper and bureaucracy have paralysed human relations. Yet many foreigners have reduced the African laugh to what could be adapted to their system of oppression, characterised by the dialectic of master and slave: the infantile or servile laugh, the irresponsible, gaping, blissful laugh, the 'Banania' laugh.[1]

But the film-maker who makes use of true smiles and laughter – of Africans who are hospitable, jesting, generous, sceptical, pessimistic, resigned, desperate, stoical, stubborn, provocative or seductive – will have a pedagogical tool of the highest value. The African peoples' capacity for joy is perhaps an antidote to the harshness of their history but it in no way spills over into the unbridled behaviour of many wealthy peoples, whose hypocrisy refuses the body's needs and leads directly into pornography and bestiality. African sensuality admits the body's penchants and appetite for terrestrial nourishment. Though sometimes restricted by precise sexual taboos, or rigorous social rules, the communion of the flesh is most often freed from guilt; Africans likewise refuse to view the marriage contract as a reciprocal right of private property for two isolated individuals.

The demographics problem arises within this framework and controlled growth has a specific context. The family in rural Africa is different from elsewhere, both in its conception and responsibilities. A new child who arrives too soon after its siblings is immediately entrusted to the larger family. And, if producing a child is the only great pleasure, the obsession of self-perpetuation also plays a part. Children, the only real wealth, are multiplied to fight against death, which is so familiar. A famished belly has no ears ... but it can produce children. Whence the almost metaphysical attachment to one's offspring. In Central Africa, if a man died without children, at his burial his remains were preceded by someone carrying a spent coal. But the father of a family was preceded by a live coal. Indeed there is a saying: 'Our children make us immortal.'

In short, African society is powerfully oriented towards community. Efforts to mould it into an exclusive system of private property all meet with resistance, of varying degrees. This is one of the characteristics of the social situation today.

Historical and Political Aspects

History is the ground in which African personality and its defining values are rooted (here values are the reasons for living as one does). That is why the persons who most incarnated and consecrated these values in the past appear as figureheads. Many of them are of course political leaders. But they are always associated with their subordinates, bards, and sometimes their servants.

Yusuf Ibn Tachfin the Almoravid, Sundiata, Ousman Fodio, Tchaka and Samory are not alone. In Mande country, Fakoli, Balla Fasséké and Kème Bréma are equally renowned. Such renown is more often a matter of acts than of status. The names of exceptional women, saints, scholars, healers and reputed craftsmen have been handed down over centuries. Doesn't this mean that the cult of the personality was not conceived apart from the general framework of African community? These heroes are clearly not Hollywood supermen who triumph by themselves over everyone else, at every time and in every place, by virtue of their furious individualism. Great men are not solitary, but solidary heroes.

Another historical theme to which film-makers should be attentive is African unity, omnipresent at every stage of historical development. Only the negative aspects and the sometimes bloody conflicts of ethnic divisions are usually recalled. But we should not overlook the forest of unity for the trees of ethnic groups. The inextricable map of African languages, and the numerous migrations, prove that the ethnic groups are blends of 'Africanity', and that positive exchanges between groups outweighed the destructive shocks. This crucial phenomenon can be illustrated by a thousand concrete examples, such as the migrations from the Nile basin, the Bantu diaspora from West Africa all the way to Southern Africa, the 'safari' of Nilotic populations along the rift of the great lakes, and the journey of the Mossi of central Sudan to their present location. Even Islam in Africa was not only (or especially) an epic of holy war, but a peaceful crusade of Hausa and Diola merchants, scholars and saints, who established mosques around the bend of the Niger. Prestigious or obscure, these mosques can be found in Sankore, Djemne, Kong and elsewhere. African film-makers wishing to exalt African unity in the civilisations of the past will find historians capable of providing them with proofs.

Another major theme for the cinema ought to be the liberation of the continent. In Sarah Maldoror's *Sambizanga,* a masterwork on this subject, Maria's long march (recalling the desperate quest of the mother in *Le Vent des Aurès*) will finally succeed in mobilising the people for the struggle of liberation.

Lastly, African democracy in the past and present will no doubt be another great theme for film-makers – elementary, direct democracy in the so-called segmentary societies; associative democracy in the kingdoms which colonial legends turned into brutal, bloody autocracies. Here it is worth mentioning the eminent role of the court bard in the Sudano-Sahelian region. The only person who was allowed to address the king directly and to upbraid him in public, the bard was a born negotiator, a master of speech, laughter and humour who could exorcise violence. Like the councils of elders, castes, priests and women of earlier social structures, the bard provided one of the many balances which limited the king's arbitrary will.

And what about democracy today? Social reform or revolution is characterised, especially in certain countries, by the idea of assigning manual labour to students and administrators. If this idea has become familiar elsewhere, it is worth highlighting in Africa where the Africans who replaced the colonisers so often donned the white collars and black boots of their predecessors.

Cultural Aspects

In this important domain, African film-makers must situate their problematic around two poles: science and consciousness. Socrates' immortal precept 'Know thyself' is echoed in African proverbs.

Knowledge of oneself must begin with African nature, its geography, plants and animals. Africa is beautiful, as the splendid exterior shots of *Sambizanga* prove. African men and women are among the most handsome exemplars of the human race. They do not yet suffer from the grimace of the potential heart-attack victim, or from graceless bulges due to excessive fat. In celebrating African beauty, film-makers should not look to stars who have been elevated into public idols but to the kind of beauty which is beautiful enough to be shown without make-up. Africa is beautiful, but she is too little known by her sons and daughters. Surprise is sometimes expressed at the small amount of intra-African tourism, which is of course related to problems of communication but also to ignorance. At present, as the tourism of wealthy countries risks having the effect of a cultural defoliant on our continent, African cinema must not view Africa with a thirst for exoticism or folklore but with filial, protective eyes, no longer those of the serf on the plantation or the authorised agents of foreign masters.

This is particularly the case since in the traditional African conception there is not a total dichotomy between nature and ourselves. The cosmos is not only a slave which must obey man; this mechanistic conception, beyond its spectacular material successes, is leading a polluted Western civilisation towards asphyxiation. And so one finds onself wondering if there is not something valuable in African animism and its symbiotic conception of man and nature. Nor is this a static conception. To earn money today's animists sell their masks and destroy their environment with more powerful foreign tools, which goes to show that the African conception of the world is not immobile. It was, and for many Africans still remains, based on often grandiose cosmogonies and legends of the origin of things.

As myths go, why should we not privilege our own cultural creations? They are often as sublime as the myths of Faust and Antigone. The origin of man and woman, the origin of death, the origin and duel of Good and Evil – these offer a precious source which could raise African humanism to universal heights. The same remark applies to the coexistence between magical and scientific approaches in African thought. It is well known that the Black African and Arab worlds, along with Asia, began to lay the groundworks of science thousands of years ago, which the West has developed and virtually monopolised over the last several centuries, often at great cost in human lives.

Many Africans today view Western techniques as an attribute or magical endowment of white civilisation. The cinema could reappraise the scientific discoveries of the continent's peoples. It could also demystify and rationalise the idea of progress. Another vital theme for Africa's neo-culture, which the cinema owes itself to present correctly, is technology transfer and its consequences in Africa. Technocrats in certain African countries echo the famous offer of a Brazilian minister: 'Come and pollute our country.'

Obviously the authors of such appeals are not subjected to the pollution of African shanty towns where the people too often live 'in the mire and even the urine of a hurried passer-by', as Mohammed Kheir-Eddine puts it. Space could be a luxury available to all Africans, but it is severely restricted by these same technocrats, who are no more than local trustees for the foreign world where their true roots, that is to say their interests, lie. The relations between the transfer of technical objects which are passively absorbed and foreign cultural models must be studied.

One can easily conceive of a screenplay which opens with an anecdotal sequence then gradually works its way towards the planetary structures of inequality in trade. At the same time, the positive transitions towards a 'modern' world, through an active initiation in technical creation, should be remarked and emphasised. For example, there are craftsmen who sometimes take their inspiration from abroad in order to repair, structure or invent tools adapted to their milieu. In short, African cinema must provide new roots for the creative imagination of the people, by deliberately setting its action and scenery on the African earth and by using African languages as a matter of principle.

Language is indeed the 'house of being'. And, supposing it is true that imported European languages are the bridges which connect us with the world at large, does this mean we must leave our houses and go to live on the bridge? If foreign languages are wonderful instruments we must learn to play, does this mean we have to stop singing? Shall we cut out our tongues to play the violin? The language of the people is the royal road for awakening consciousness like a lamp and, if need be (for example in the fight against racism), like an incendiary, vengeful torch. The cinema must address sick, battered consciousnesses to make them upright and militant.

Ethics and Aesthetics

The role of African film-makers in the integrated development of the continent should not be separated from that of other intellectual workers, as shown by the need for scriptwriters and especially for critics to support and improve the work of directors. Should the latter be guided most of all by ethics or aesthetics?

This debate should not even have to be aired, especially since many African languages use the same word for the good and the beautiful. But these are clearly not absolute concepts, beings of immutable reason in the heaven of metaphysics. They are relative, variable notions in time and space. If the African film-maker were forced to choose, he or she would have to opt for ethics and a social ethic, in other words a commitment to his or her people, instead of being a mandarin or mercenary of film. To be or not to be? To be a utensil or a person. That is the dilemma both for the film-maker and his or her people.

In terms of aesthetics, an uninitiated observer might be tempted to think that the screenplays of many African films are either too simplistic or too complicated and hermetic. The procedures used to dramatise the action or renew it on the springboard of suspense are not goals in themselves. But, in so far as they convey a more intense emotion, such procedures imprint their message more deeply on the minds of the public and should not be neglected. This is especially true at present, since spectators are used to the rip-roaring screenplays of the action films which have been imposed on them.

But too linear and flat a progression is unsatisfying. African eloquence is outwardly laconic and simple but it is woven of allusions, symbols and allegories which demand lengthy reflection. In the same way, with their sober lines and rough edges, African masks may at first seem like uninspired bits of sculpture. But more detailed study reveals calculated dissymmetries, breaks in the movement and symbols which enrich the meaning. African tales have likewise been shown to contain three levels of interpretation. The most obvious is like an agreeable film, a sequence of events; the second is the social significance and the third the esoteric implications or a vision of the world. African aesthetics is at home with the alloy of immediate concreteness and unfathomable depths of thought. This has lately begun to serve as inspiration, and it should continue.

It has not been easy to make the transition from participation in dance, and a dazzling art of celebration (among the Markas, for instance), to dance spectacles on stage. But the transition of African music to the moving or vibrant accents of Negro spirituals, jazz and the jerk was possible. Through the genius of European music in the 18th and 19th centuries, a transition was made from popular ballads to sumptuous symphonies. In African music a similar qualitative leap occurred in Guinea, from a linear plainsong (almost totally dominated by the rhythmic line) and music for dance to an orchestrated music with melodic arrangements around a central artistic and ideological theme, which was then developed further into concert music. Alternately dominated by harp lute, percussion, guitar and flute, this music can hold its own against so-called 'classical' music. Indeed the concert 'A Look at the Past', which retraced the life of Samory, was a red-letter date in the history of music in West Africa.[2]

African cinema is still very young (except in Egypt). But after La Voie by Mohamed Slim Riad, The Money Order by Sembène Ousmane, La Terre by Youssef Chahine, Ton Jour viendra by Salah Abou Seif, Wechma by Hamid Benani, Les Révoltés by Tewfiq Salah, Kodou by Ababacar Samb, La Momie by Chadi Abd-el-Salam, Concerto for an Exile by Désiré Ecaré, Soleil O by Med Hondo and others, there is reason for hope. On certain conditions ...

First, African film-makers need to have a real audience at their disposal, and it has been amply shown that that audience is waiting for the films. If production and distribution mutually condition each other, today they guarantee the more than copious profits of foreign firms. This situation should be altered by structural revisions which Africanise, break down barriers, and integrate markets so as to make the African cinematographical industry dynamic and profitable. These historical responsibilities of African governments and the OAU can no longer be eluded.

Regarding the question of censorship, leaders in particular must take care not to view film-makers (who must also be responsible in this regard) as systematically preventing the daily song and dance or a peaceful slumber. They should not imagine that 'art hurts more than reality' and that the film-maker is like 'a traditional bard who is allowed to eat only after having flattered the king', to use A. Kaba's words.

In this respect, there is a certain contradiction between the demands for nationalisation and for creative independence. Or at least a certain lack of realism in Africa today. Film-makers expect leaders to nationalise in conformity with their own progressive options . . .

In the field of African development, it is true, the deepest tremors result from fundamental decisions taken at the political level. But the people are present as well, displaying problems which film-makers can take as their subjects; ready to participate by offering its innate gifts to act out the dramas; and by contributing as customers and spectators. Film-makers sometimes expect that the people will also serve as a guide in the choice of their aesthetic. But mustn't the people be guided in most cases? This vicious circle will be overcome only when all intellectuals engage in constructive dialogue, to pursue the technical work of production and to put pressure on the authorities whose decisions spark the machine.

In conclusion, I think that African film-makers should not give in to the inebriation of quickly established fame. By doing so they would replace their own heroes or, rather, the only true hero, the people. Nor should they yield to the fascination of a foreign interlocutor or adversary, and gravitate towards a penchant for the foreign (or the foreigner), a frenetic rage against an enemy who provides both a target and an alibi. Masochistic ruminating and bitter dwelling on past humiliations are even less to the point.

There can be no question of taking extreme positions on the fate of unrepresentative minorities: veterans, ambivalent intellectuals, administrators involved in mixed marriages, and so on. There is no use in curling up egotistically around one's own fantasies. This would make the film-maker into an ambassador from nowhere. On the contrary, his or her role is to relay the voice of the people, to overthrow the regard directed on our continent, to act as a solidarity intellectual who occupies one branch on the great trunk of the people, determined to reconquer the cultural hegemony weighing on his or her brothers and sisters.

Film-makers who remain dilettantes and create without any concern for the exploited masses engage in a selfish intellectual masturbation – a solitary, derisive pleasure. Instead of this I hope that African film-makers will aspire to a lover's exaltation in bodily union with the people. A source of shared joy. A source of creative fervour.

Notes
1. In a well-known French advertisement from the middle of the century, a beaming African praises 'Banania', a chocolate drink, in pidgin French (translator's note).
2. 'Regard sur le Passé', the first great musical concert of Guinea by Bembeya Jazz National.

Further Readings

Armes, Roy, *Third World Film-Making and the West* (Berkeley: University of California Press, 1987).

Boughedir, Férid, *Le Cinéma africain de A à Z* (Brussels: OCIC, 1987).

Henebelle, Guy, et Ruelle, Catherine (eds), 'Cinéastes d'Afrique Noire', *Afrique littéraire et artistique* no. 49, 2ème trimestre 1978.

Pfaff, Françoise, *Twenty Five Black African Filmmakers: A Critical Study with Filmography and Bio-Bibliography* (Westport, Conn.: Greenwood Press, 1988).

Africa and the Centenary of Cinema. (Paris: Présence Africaine, 1995). A special publication of the Pan-African Federation of Film-makers (FEPACI).

Cinéma et liberté (Paris: Présence Africaine, 1993).

'Seminar on the Role of the African Filmmaker in Rousing an Awareness of Black Civilisation, Ouagadougou, 8–13 April 1974', *Présence africaine* no. 90, 2ème trimestre, 1974, pp. 3–204.

PART III
Histories and Political Economies

APARTHEID AND CINEMA

NDUGU MIKE SSALI

This is an edited version of the paper which appeared in *Ufahamu*, vol. XIII no. 1, 1983.

A cinema show was first exhibited to a special group of White South Africans on 19 April 1895 in Johannesburg.[1] That makes South Africa one of the first partakers of the 'motion picture' novelty. Cinema has since remained part of the South African social and cultural fabric, although only one scholar, Thelma Gutsche, has studied in any detail the history of the cinema in that country.

This paper proposes to discuss and analyse two major aspects of the subject that have been overlooked by film historians. The first is a historical survey of those films which the South African power structure allowed the Blacks to see and participate in. The second objective is to examine how and why those films were selected, and the social impact they were intended to have on the Black community in South Africa.

Urban Scene Setting

The Dutch East India Company's employees established a settlement at the Cape of Good Hope in 1652. After two bloody campaigns against the Khoikhoi, 1659–60 and 1763–74, the Dutch went on to defeat the Xhosa in frontier wars in 1779–81 and 1793. But in 1795 the British displaced the Dutch at the Cape. In 1803, the Dutch temporarily restored their hold over the Cape until the British reoccupied it for the second time in 1806 and subsequently declared permanent sovereignty over the Cape in 1914.[2] Hence the British began to implement their policies and establish their alien institutions in what became geopolitically known as South Africa.

From 1836 to 1838 the Boers embarked on what historians call the Great Trek. After yet another bloody war, this time against the Zulus, the Boers won the battle of Blood River and established a Boer republic in Natal. In 1867, diamonds were discovered near the confluence of the Orange and Vaal rivers. This discovery is very significant in that it became a great landmark and, perhaps more than anything else, may be responsible for shaping the history of South Africa as we know it today. The discovery of diamonds and the subsequent discovery of the first important goldfield in the Transvaal acted as a catalyst for Europeans, particularly the British, to emigrate to South Africa. It should be noted that the wars in which the indigenous Africans were defeated and the discovery of both diamonds and gold had major social and economic consequences.

With the establishment of large farms and plantations in the Transvaal and

Natal, the Zulus and Xhosas, whose pastoral mode of life depended on the availability of land, lost their cattle with the loss of their land to the European colonialists. These conditions led to the introduction of the European mass infrastructure. Roads were built, cities grew and denominational schools and churches sprang up quickly. The speedy accomplishment of these expensive projects was facilitated by the abundance of forced labour. Besides, the cost of running government projects was heavily subsidised by the arbitrary taxation of the Africans, as the following report reveals:

> Then the tax came. It was 10s. a year. Soon the Government said, that is too little, you must contribute more; you must pay £1. We did so. Then those who took more than one wife were taxed; 10s. for each additional wife. The tax is heavy, but that is not all. We are also taxed for our dogs; 5s. for a dog. Then we were told we were living on private land; the owners wanted rent in addition to the Government tax, some 10s., some £1, some £2 a year. After that we were told we had to dip our cattle and pay 1s. per head per annum.[3]

Thus the Africans were deliberately forced to participate in the new capitalist social and economic order. Given that a considerable number of the Africans could not afford to pay the levied taxes, they were faced with two unpleasant choices: either to default and go to prison to work without pay or go to work in the mines, plantations and in the urban centres. Either way, the authorities succeeded in realising their intentions. Once the Africans became established in this new environment, the authorities realised that they needed some form of entertainment or means of social control to divert the African's mind from the harsh realities he had to endure. According to a 1906 Transvaal government report, 'In 1896, there were over 90,000 male Africans working on the Rand as miners, 43,000 others employed in support services as domestics, teachers, artisans, clerks, and prisoners living around the Market Square.'[4] As the numbers of Africans continued to grow in these urban centres, social organisations evolved naturally. Night clubs sprang up, so did beer halls. For the first time Africans came into contact with Western music, mostly from the United States.[5]

It should be noted, however, that from the beginning there was an intricate set of relations between ethnic background, petty economic classes, religious affiliation and educational achievements as bases of association. The new social circumstances often came to mean closer relations between fellow workers and members of a common religious denomination and other social organisations at the expense of ethnicities. African churches and other cultural organisations multiplied around the mine centres.

As is often the case among urban dwellers, some African musicians sensed that they could benefit financially from selling entertainment; singing and band groups were started. There were dance bands as well as marabi bands like the famous Japanese Express of 1929. Although they entertained different social classes, a wide range of income, educational level and age was apparent at the famous halls of entertainment.[6] These parties, dances and concerts which the urbanised African adopted in his new cultural environment were necessary to provide a kind of communal diversion which had the appearance of making life more meaningful while also creating expressive cultural images which provided room for emerging social value systems.[7] On the subject, J. Ngubane has written:

The stratification and class oriented social networks evolving among Africans in early Johannesburg were expressed by the nature and diversity of performance styles, the places where they were staged and the social identity and aspirations of their participants. Simultaneously, the failure of white authority to acknowledge a social hierarchy among Africans reinforced levelling processes and spurred the growth of a self-conscious nationalism among the middle classes. The latter became progressively more embittered in proportion to the growth of their socio-economic and political expectations.[8]

Despite the prevailing racial barriers in every facet of life, the authorities did not turn a blind eye to the cultural activities of this emerging African urbanised class. Whites became aware that Africans might take advantage of their music and use it as a cultural political weapon. The historical lesson about the formidable role the arts can play in the struggle against fascism was not lost on the Whites, so they had to devise means to control the African music and other forms of entertainment. They stepped in and gained control of organising, programming, and making artistic decisions. Zakes Mokae, a distinguished African actor and the recipient of a 1982 Tony Award, put it this way:

> In South Africa, Whites control everything. They control our music, subject it to Western aesthetic criteria, and tell us how good or bad it is. It's preposterous. What do they know about our music if they don't even understand us as a people? It's only a matter of time. They will never succeed in interpreting our culture for us.[9]

This is proof enough of the words of the eminent African intellectual leader and theoretician, the late Amilcar Cabral:

> History teaches us that, in certain circumstances, it is very easy for the foreigner to impose his domination on a people. But it also teaches us that, whatever may be the material aspects of this domination, it can be maintained only by the permanent organised repression of the cultural life of the people concerned.[10]

In some isolated cases, however, there were progressive Whites who lent support to the African cultural groups. The Bantu Men's Social Centre in Johannesburg and the Syndicate of African Artists enjoyed a multiracial patronage. This community-based performing group was the brainchild of Ezekiel Mphalele and Khabi Mngoma. But as Mphalele points out,

> the Whites got scarcer as greater pressure was exerted by those who have taken it upon themselves to direct the lives of whole communities 'according to their own lives,' with all the cynical ambiguity the phrase possesses. The powers that be, instead of legislating against the multi-racial audiences those days, were content to wag a finger of cold war at white patrons. It worked, we retreated to our townships 'to develop along our lines'. We couldn't see the lines and footprints. They had got so mixed up with other footprints in the course of time, and the winds had been blowing away some, too.[11]

Indeed, Mphalele's Syndicate tried 'to develop along their own lines'. Left with no other option, the Syndicate became political and appealed for support from their compatriots. The message was loud and clear: 'We are beginning to create a Cultural Front in our struggle towards self-determination and we rely on you to help.'[12] Despite the banning of their cultural *Opinion* magazine following their articulated message, and the arrest of the Syndicate members, the group was the only well organised urban cultural movement to define and promote the cultural identity and socio-political aspirations of South African urban Blacks at the time.[13] Around the same period, open-air cinema shows and commercial films had increasingly become a common feature in townships and mining establishments.

The Bioscope

The name 'bioscope' originates from the first apparatuses used to project moving pictures in 1898. There was no standardisation or agreement as to which name to use. Some called it the kinetoscope, others cinematograph, and still others referred to it as the kinematograph, moving or motion pictures. The British finally settled on 'cinema', on the continent it was shortened to 'kino', in America, 'movies', but the stubborn South African conservatives retained the name 'bioscope'.[14] In South Africa people talk about going to the bioscope and not to the cinema. In this paper, for the sake of consistency, the words cinema and film will be used interchangeably. The bioscope, on the other hand, will be used to refer to a movie-house.

It should be noted that although South Africa became a Union in 1910, it remained a dominion within the British Commonwealth. Hence British culture, economic and political influence continued unabated. After the First World War, the British government did not like the idea that the American film industry had dominated their sphere of influence. The British government, business and film circles realised that the Empire's economic and political interests were both in jeopardy. The main concern was the economic aspect of the film industry[15] but there was also fear about the spread of alien ideas and philosophies. Cinema's power as a propaganda medium was believed to be incredible. Addressing a meeting of the African Society in 1931, J. Russell was very explicit: 'A successful film has a greater circulation than any newspaper and than any book except the Bible.'[16] The pioneering propagandist, Sir Stephen Tallents, added: 'Cinema is the greatest agent of international communication; its moral and emotional influence is incalculable.'[17] By the mid-1920s films were strongly regarded as the appropriate means to teach and influence the African. Commercial films, both American and British, were seen as a threat against the South African establishment because of their unpalatable image of the Whites. Some sources in the Union government believed that the success of their policies over the African depended largely on the degree of respect which they could inspire. 'Primitive' people were not supposed to be exposed to demoralising films representing criminal and immodest actions by Whites. In the eyes of the African, Whites were to be perceived as saviours, smart, intelligent, and decent. As Teshome Gabriel points out, in the United States, from the outset, films have ridiculed the minorities, particularly the Blacks, and glorifed the Whites:

from the beginning of films, the Blacks were portrayed as 'childlike' lackeys

86

meant for abuse and condescension. The earliest example of a film dealing with a wholesale stereotyped character is *Fights of Nations* (1905). In this film the Mexican was caricatured as a 'treacherous fellow', the Jew as a 'briber', the Black as a 'cake walker', 'buck dancer', and 'razor-thrower'. The White race was presented as the bringer of peace to all mankind.[18]

Of all the races on the earth none has been so deliberately and systematically slandered as people of African descent.

Colonial Films and Their Impact on Africa in General

Commercial films have traditionally exploited popular misconceptions and nearly succeeded in creating an Africa that was highly distorted and was as far removed from reality as the tales of nineteenth-century travellers. Unable to comprehend the languages, customs and other aspects of the African culture, both commercial and ethnographic film-makers refused to see Africans as a people sharing basic experiences common to all mankind. Africa is projected as a reservoir of wild animals and painted savages who play a negligible role.[19]

It is important that we understand the ideas in some feature films of major film companies. Stories of nineteenth-century naïve writers such as M. Rider Haggard have portrayed Africa as a cloak of mystery. These tales are of savage African 'tribes' behind impenetrable forests and of heathen rituals many years old. These ideas still linger in novels by Graham Greene, John Buchan, and many others. They still depict hair-raising stories about inaccessible mountains filled with ghost-guarded treasures and frightening forests that harbour enormous scorpion-swallowing baboons in troops of thousands that uproot sorghum fields and lynch lions. The two-footed animals are dramatised in banquets of uncooked meat, washed down with mead from horns and calabashes.

From the outset the cinema was quick to realise the commercial potential of these fanciful ideas. Rider Haggard's *She*, a story of a bizarre African 'tribe' with a White queen who remained ageless through the millennia, proved so irresistible to Hollywood producers that two films were made of the story. *King Solomon's Mines*, a story about unbelievable wealth amassed by a strange African ethnic group, and protected by a combination of witchcraft and savagery against four fearless British adventurers, was another box-office success. Metro-Goldwyn-Mayer (MGM) introduced yet another White queen in *Trader Horn*, equipping her with a cave furnished with human skulls and a retinue of painted Africans, brandishing spears.

The commercial cinema did not forget about the beasts of the African jungle. Ironically, these beasts were treated better than the Africans on the screen. *Tarzan of the Apes*, made in 1918, was perhaps the forerunner of an endless succession of Tarzan escapades, which have continued to the present day; and the early Martin Johnson animal epics, such as *Congorilla*, find a parallel in some of Walt Disney's African productions, such as *African Lion*.[20] It may be interesting to point out that whether Africans or animals were being portrayed in these films the style and method used by scriptwriters appear to have been similar. It is quite obvious that some ideas were superimposed upon African scenery by a bizarre form of deductive reasoning. The fact that these concepts did not reflect the African reality was of no consequence to the film magnates. For an MGM African epic, animals were flown from New York into East Africa to enliven the action, and an assortment of gaudily dressed Africans provided the decor for a melodrama between two popular American stars. In these grandiose epics, the African people play either scenery props, picturesque crowds with spears or bizarre unintelligent menials.[21]

In addition to the false exotic films, there were what can be characterised as colonial and racial films. This attitude had greater currency in Britain and South Africa. Africans were to be patronised, civilised and 'protected'. White heroes were constantly patronising. Henry Scobie, the star of Graham Greene's novel on life in Sierra Leone, *The Heart of the Matter*, is known as Scobie the Just.

'Sandy the strong, Sandy the wise, righter of wrongs, hater of lies,' sings the African chief, played by Paul Robeson, in praise of Sanders, the British district commissioner in *Sanders of the River*. In all these films, the justification of continued British presence is unmistakable: when not backward, ignorant and, therefore, in need of protection and guidance, the African was malignant, requiring the force of law from God.[22]

Given Britain's imperialist role in Africa, its film hero in Africa necessarily differed from the individualistic law-defying hunter or lover of his American counterpart. British films extolled the virtues of colonial officials, police, district commissioners, civil servants, and settlers. *Sanders of the River*, made in 1935, starred Paul Robeson in the role of Bosambo, a servile African king who saves a British district commissioner's life and secures for his people the continuance of British protection. Not surprisingly, the theme of Britain's imperial burden in Africa dominates and provides an excellent illustration of how the British cinema was a reflection of British official ideas and policies.

It is important to note that *Sanders of the River* was Robeson's first major appearance in British films. A man of his talents was betrayed and promptly put to the task of convincing the international community that Africa needed British 'protection'. The London *Daily Herald* enthusiastically noted: 'If we could only give every subject race a native king with Robeson's superb physique, dominant personality, infectious smile and noble voice, problems of native self-government might be largely solved.'[23]

Ironically, despite Robeson's passionate concern with African culture, the film turned into a glorification of British colonial rule. It should be noted, however, that the scenes in which he did not appear had been 'doctored' without the actor's knowledge, and at a special preview an angry Robeson stormed out of the cinema in protest.[24] The damage, however, had already been accomplished.

In 1943, the British released a film designed to deal with contemporary African political and social problems. *Men of Two Worlds*, supposedly a liberal film, tells of Kisenga, an African musician, composer, and pianist, who after fifteen years in Europe gives up the concert hall and returns home to the Litu people. He finds them under the spell of Magobe, the 'witch doctor', with a benevolent British officer unable to convince the people that they must escape the dreaded tsetse fly. The film revolves round the conflict between Magobe, the embodiment of darkness and evil superstition, and Klsenga, the British-trained African. As expected, Magobe is discredited, and the people save themselves by moving from the area. The film ends with Kisenga acknowledging his people's need for him and giving up his career in order to help them towards 'progress'.

Not surprisingly, the film was overwhelmingly received by the British press.

Paradoxically, *Ebony* magazine also naively praised it, claiming that *Men of Two Worlds* marked a break with tradition, and portrayed Africans with sympathy and respect.[25]

For many years small film units worked within restricted budgets, faithfully reflecting the psychology of the imperialist powers, and were anxious to appear enlightened, and able to guide their subjects along 'civilised' paths to 'progress'.

In 1935–7, the *Bantu Educational Cinema* experiment made the following observation: 'Books are of little use to a people of whom more than ninety percent are illiterate. The moving picture offers a possible substitute.'[26]

Obviously these films had the express purpose of impressing the African mind. Although some of the people behind these films had good intentions, it is quite clear today, perhaps more than ever before, what they have been able to accomplish. They succeeded, to a large extent, in selling to the African the capitalist political system as the dominant economic mode of production. These films became a medium for the commercial advertisement of European products and have also helped in imposing Western cultural values on some Africans.

Some of these films instructed the African on better methods of growing cash crops for export. Today, African countries continue to grow coffee, tea and cocoa, crops which most of their populations do not consume, while at the same time growing less food, which is the most basic item for their survival. Instead, African governments appear to find it convenient to import food from the West while some elites import drinking water from Europe despite the abundant water resources at home. This is not to imply that all this has been caused by the films discussed above, but some of these attitudes of self-hate would appear likely to be partially influenced by films.

Hollywood and Its Portrayal of Black People

We have seen how colonial cinema has been successful as a form of cultural imperialism. This cinema was not about Africans, but about what the colonialists and the imperialists thought and felt about Africans. The films in question were conceived, written and produced from either Britain or the United States, and then exported to Africa to entertain the 'natives'. Some scenes were shot in Africa by British or American film producers and used in Africa for political, economic and social propaganda. It is important here to point out that we cannot discuss the history of the African image in cinema without examining the context within which Hollywood has portrayed Black Americans. This is important in view of the Hollywood–South African connection.

We know that historically the depiction of Blacks in American films has traditionally been noted for its injustice and distortion. Hollywood has established and consolidated the stereotyped concept of Blacks as a socially inferior group: servility and laziness became the main characteristics of the Black race. In some instances Blacks are portrayed variously as subhuman and superhuman.[27] Commenting on D. W. Griffith's portrayal of Blacks in the film *Birth of a Nation*, film historian Donald Bogle observed: 'Blacks are always big, baaadd Niggers, oversexed and savage, violent and frenzied as they lust for white flesh. No greater sin hath any black man.'[28] The social critic Daniel Lead adds: 'docile but irresponsible, loyal but lazy, humble but chronically given to lying and stealing'.[29] Such caricatures in which Blacks were systematically viewed collectively as clowns, morons, and subhumans formed the stereotype of early

American cinema. Writing in the *Journal of Negro Education*, Dr Lawrence Reddick has summed it up:

> By buildlng up this unfavorable conception, the movies operate to thwart the advancement of the Negro, to humiliate him, to weaken his drive for equality and to spread indifference, contempt, and hatred for him and his cause: this great urgency for the communication of ideas and information, therefore, functions as a powerful instrument for maintaining the racial subordination of the Negro people.[30]

With more Blacks becoming film-makers, and the emergence of individual progressive White sympathisers, there have been slight improvements. But it will probably be a long time before a decent film approach to Blacks corrects the wretched record of discrimination which lasted until the Second World War, and which still continues unabated in many movies. Interestingly, up to 1915 nearly all Black parts in American films were played by Whites. Negro buffoonery supplied the theme of such films as *The Wooing and Wedding of a Coon,* and the *Rastus* and *Sambo* series, now happily buried and no longer in circulation.[31] Ironically, such films were capable at the time of being described as genuine Ethiopian comedy. All these early films portrayed Blacks either as a 'coloured clowns' with the most minute intelligence, or as devoted niggers who 'know their place'. *Uncle Tom's Cabin* was directed in 1909 by Edwin S. Porter, who used a White actor to play the part of Uncle Tom. Harriet Beecher Stowe's sincere indictment of slavery was debased in its translation to the screen.[32]

It would be safe to say that the 1909 film emerged as a melodramatic hearts-and-flowers piece, largely concerned with the dog-like devotion of Uncle Tom for the little daughter of his White master. *Uncle Tom's Cabin* was made again in 1915, this time with a Black actor, Sam Lucas, in the title role. Other adaptations were made in 1918 and 1927. Given the above role concoction, it should be no surprise that Blacks have placed the words 'Uncle Tom' on the list of gross indignity in their vocabulary.[33]

The South African Connection
Although both American and South African entrepreneurs had for years screened American-made movies, at the end of the Depression big American companies concluded deals with the South African authorities to do big business. In 1931, Colonel Edward A. Schiller, Vice President of MGM, one of the biggest and most distinguished film production corporations in the United States, opened their first super-cinema, the Metro Theatre in Johannesburg.[34] It had a capacity seating just under three thousand. In 1932, in the presence of government officials, *The Passionate Plumber,* a comedy featuring Buster Keaton, Polly Moran and Jimmy Durante, was exhibited.[35] By law Africans were not allowed to attend films in places like the Metro Theatre. Metro Theatre, owned and operated by MGM, assumed the rights to distribute the films of United Artists, British and Dominion films and London Films Production in South Africa.

The Censorship Board

By 1910, although film screening was not widespread in South Africa, the extraordinary popularity of the moving pictures had drawn attention to their social significance. They were not only regarded as a cheap means of entertainment and instruction, but also as a potential menace to public welfare. In July the same year, cinema's social menace was well exposed.

On 4 July a Black boxer by the name of Jack Johnson defeated a certain Jeffries (a White boxer) in the United States. Race riots ensued in which reportedly hundreds may have been killed and thousands injured. It was reported that prisons were filled to overflowing, and troops had to be called out. A film had been taken of the fight and, fearing that the exhibition might further disturb the public peace, the mayors of many American cities prohibited its showing. On 6 July *The Natal Times* and *The Natal Witness* urged a similar and united action on the part of all South African municipalities (in which the control of public amusements was then vested). On 7 July *The Bloemfontein Friend* endorsed this appeal, which the *Sunday Times* and *Sunday Post* also supported. Meanwhile in Europe and America, controversy had broken out. The Canadian government banned the film and movements were launched in Australia and New Zealand demanding that their governments prohibit its exhibition. On 8 July an order was issued from the government office in Pretoria instructing the police of the four provinces to prohibit the exhibition of pictures of the Johnson–Jeffries fight. On 9 July the town clerk of Johannesburg notified owners of places of entertainment, warning them not to show the film, or incur the expense of importing it (which had apparently been done) as the municipal council would definitely prohibit its screening.

This appears to have been the signal for the outbreak of a caustic controversy in which the churches also participated in a flood of correspondence to the press.[36] It was pointed out that the sole menace of the film was the inculcation of racial hatred which could instantly be prevented by prohibiting its exhibition to Coloured people. In time, the outcry died away but it had effectively demonstrated the social importance of the cinema. The public actively desired to see films that were considered destructive; however, no machinery except direct Union government action existed for censorship other than arbitrary prohibition by each separate municipal council.

The protests against the showing of the Johnson–Jefferies film on the grounds of its possible provocation of racial disturbance foreshadowed a steady stream of protests against cinema's vulgarity and suggestiveness. During 1910, 1911 and 1912, this movement gathered momentum, particularly at the Cape, where, in April 1913, it culminated in the formation of an all-White voluntary committee. It was not until 1930, however, that Dr D. F. Malan, the Minister of the Interior, introduced a Bill to the House of Assembly. The Bill sought to establish a national censorship board. It appears to have provided little consolation to the opponents of allegedly arbitrary censorship. Its provisions (which film companies opposed) were so exacting that no film was likely to escape whole or partial banning. In criticising the Bill, one of the country's influential dailies was prompted to comment:

The nature of the discretionary powers of the proposed Board may be judged from the list of prohibited films. The list is little short of amazing and if the provisions were narrowly interpreted, most of the films which come to South Africa would be liable to rejection... Surely it is a mistake to dictate beforehand and in such detail which is and what is not to be allowed.[37]

On 26 March the Bill was further considered and read for the third time. The Senate then discussed it, making various amendments, and on 26 May it was finally debated in the House of Assembly. On 3 June 1931 the Entertainments (Censorship) Act became law.[38] The select committee, chaired by Dr Malan, also included six appointed members of the Minister's choice. Specifications of censorable items included the following:

(1) Impersonations of the King
(2) Scenes holding any members of the King's military up to ridicule or contempt
(3) Treatment of death
(4) Nude human figures
(5) Scenes containing reference to controversial or international politics
(6) Passionate love scenes
(7) Scenes representing antagonistic relations between capital and labour
(8) Scenes tending to disparage public figures
(9) Scenes tending to create public alarm
(10) The drug habit, white slave traffic, vice or loose morals
(11) Scenes calculated to affect the religious convictions or feelings of any section of the public
(12) Scenes calculated to bring any section of the public into ridicule or contempt
(13) Scenes of juvenile crime and, in case of older persons, scenes of the technique of crime and criminality
(14) Scenes of brutal fighting
(15) Scenes of drunkenness and brawling
(16) Pugilistic encounters between Europeans and non-Europeans
(17) Scenes of intermingling of Europeans and non-Europeans
(18) Scenes of rough handling or ill treatment of women and children.[39]

One Afrikaner member of the House bitterly criticised the Bill, claiming that it left more doors open in that it covered public performances only. He feared that private associations could still manipulate the law and screen propaganda (especially Russian and communist) films to their members. There was nothing, he charged, to prevent natives forming themselves into such associations and thus becoming susceptible to subversive propaganda. A compromise was reached and an amendment adopted which read:

No person shall exhibit in public or in any place which admission is obtained by virtue of membership of any association of persons or for any considerations, whether direct or indirect, or by virtue of contribution towards any fund, any cinematograph film... Provided further that the minister, or a person delegated by him for the purpose, may in his discretion exempt from the preceding provisions of this section any particular class or cinematograph films or film advertisements or any cinematograph film intended for exhibition to any particular circumstances.[40]

Clearly the Amendment Act rendered private showing of uncensored films impossible, while private showings of 'beneficient' films, uncensored, was rendered possible by the minister or his designate's special sanction. In 1931 the institution of the National Board of Censors was characterised by an immediate cessation of the sensational incidents which had belonged to the provisional provincial censorships. Empowered to grant certificates prohibiting performances to Natives, Coloureds, or children, the board, obviously including no African members, was especially particular about the films 'natives' and children could see. While Europeans, their children above the age of twelve, and in some cases Coloureds were allowed to see most films, Africans, or Natives as they preferred to call them, were treated as European children under twelve years of age.[41]

The South African Board of Censors Goes to Work
Before the war against fascism injected a new liberalism into the American cinema, Hollywood had been the last place to make the South African censors and authorities uncomfortable. Therefore, the board started slowly with multi-star musical films in which Black entertainers such as Louis Armstrong, Lena Horne and the Trinidadian beauty queen Hazel Scott took their rightful places among white entertainers. Given the slightly changed 'political' and social climate, it appears that public reaction was 'cool'. Today, it is normal for Blacks and Whites to appear in films and other forms of entertainment in a single act. Although most of the films in which Blacks starred were somewhat reactionary, to the South African authorities they were despicable.[42]

William Wellman's 1943 film *The Oxbow Incident* portrayed a Black preacher, Leigh Whipper, protesting against the lynching of White men. In one scene Whipper opposes a Southern army officer. Whipper says: 'I come from a race which has always had to bear the brunt of lynch law; and lynching is no way to settle things for either black or white people.'

Several American war films showed the courage of Black soldiers. A case in point was an MGM film, *Bataan*, which was presented with an award by the NAACP. Another example was *Sahara* (1943),[43] in which Humphrey Bogart starred. Blacks were treated fairly in Stanley Krammer's *The Men*, and *Home of the Brave*, and Michael Curtiz's *Casablanca* and *Night and Day*, to name a few.

But Curtiz's *Breaking Point* (1943) may have been the most important film in which Blacks and Whites were treated alike, as human beings. The Black actor Juan Hernandez appears as an old comrade-in-arms of Harry Morgan. Never before had a White–Black friendship been splendidly brought to life on screen. Hernandez's death by a gangster's hot lead emotionally affects Morgan, and his subsequent massacre of the outlaws appears to be in direct retribution for the assassination of his companion. Nor did the director forget to end the film on a piercing note of a small Black boy, the son of Hernandez, standing lost and bewildered on the quayside, while an ambulance takes the wounded Morgan away to a hospital, where he has his arm amputated. The boy is still unaware that his father is dead. The crowd disperses, and there is a long shot of the boy on the deserted dockside. He is forgotten and ignored. That single silent scene is probably one of the strongest and most articulate in all the films featuring Blacks in the American cinema of the period.

In the United States, the social and political atmosphere was ripe for Blacks to become 'humanised' subjects of film for what Teshome Gabriel characterised as the dilemma of the 'social acceptance gap' of Black emancipation. Several reasons account for this. First, as mentioned above, Black film-makers had already emerged and started to 'correct' their image in films. Second, the effects of the Second World War, in which Blacks fought side by side against European Nazism with Whites in the name of freedom and self-determination. Third, the McCarthyism of the 50s may have encouraged White liberals in Hollywood to find allies in Blacks who, historically, had been victims of social and political injustice. The Civil Rights Movement and the NAACP's persistent struggle against injustices in all forms contributed to the new 'spirit' in cinema.

On the other hand, in South Africa the new developments taking place in the American film industry were received with characteristic disdain. As a result, political intervention in film was evidenced in the matter of the films censored. In South Africa, any film deemed to be 'political' or 'pornographic' was banned outright. Curtiz's *Breaking Point* was found to be 'inappropriate' for the South African multiracial society.[44]

There were several American films banned by the South African authorities. For the purposes of this analysis, we will examine three major films banned between 1936 and 1950. These were *Green Pastures* (1936), *Home of the Brave* (1949), and *No Way Out* (1950).

Green Pastures was an adaptation of Marc Connelly's successful Broadway play. Directed by Connelly and William Keighley, and released by Warner Bros., it was one of the best all-Black spectacles since 1929. An all-Black production, *Green Pastures* was distributed to South Africa and banned instantly because it suggested that God, Moses, Noah, the children of Israel, Abraham, Isaac, Jacob, and the Angel Gabriel were all Black. The film is a Southern piccaninny's conception of the Old Testament. God is kindly, a somewhat shabby Black preacher, and heaven is a rural resort which features choir singing and barbecue picnics. In the United States the film was acclaimed by both White and Black newspapers: 'A beautiful film – the screen version of the tender, gently pathetic, curiously touching Negro miracle play.'[45] The *New York Times* put it this way:

> That disturbance in and around the musical hall yesterday was the noise of shuffling queues in Sixth Avenue and the sound of motion picture critics dancing in the street. The occasion was the coming at least to the screen of Marc Connelly's naive, ludicrous, sublime and heartbreaking masterpiece of American folk drama ... it still has the rough beauty of home spun, the irresistible compulsion of simple faith.[46]

From a more critical position Sharifa Evans has said in an interview that *Green Pasture*'s characterisation of the religion of the Blacks was a caricature and that the only thing in it was childlike faith.[47]

The censors who banned *Little Egypt* because of its exhibition of a surfeit of bare navels promptly rejected *Home of the Brave* because they termed it seditious because of portrayals of friendship and the prospects of commercial co-operation between a Black soldier and a White marine.[48]

In *No Way Out*, the American Black was portrayed as a 'civilised' human being, capable of compassion, aware of his power, and cynical about White patronage. In this film, Sidney Poitier plays the role of a young Black doctor and saves the life of a murderous Black-hating White man (Richard Widmark). The film depicts a full-scale riot which ends in Black victory. At the end of the film the Black man stands over the wounded White man. Against the swelling clamour of the sirens of approaching police cars and ambulances, the doctor's voice says over and over in a most confident manner: 'Don't cry, White man ... No way out'. South Africa, which had legalised racism (apartheid) only two years before the release of *No Way Out*, could not stand Africans seeing such a film. It was written and directed by Joseph Mankiewicz, who also scripted and directed *All about Eve*.

It is important to note that South Africa in the 1920s was also highly influential in shaping the censorship policy of some African colonies. Films shown to the African miners on the Rand were subjected to additional and more severe censorship by Ray Phillips, a missionary, and a social worker with the American Board of Missions. At the time Northern Rhodesia (now Zambia) got its films from South Africa. In addition, it relied upon the grading of the South African censors. It became a convention that Africans were not admitted to European cinemas.[49]

D. W. Griffith in South Africa

If there was a film-maker in the world with whom South Africa fell in love, it was the American film-maker D. W. Griffith. In South Africa he was even more revered than Charlie Chaplin. If a survey on films shown in South Africa between 1914 to 1923 were conducted, there is no doubt that Griffith's works would have scored highest. In a span of nine years, he was able to show nine films in South Africa, including the infamous *Birth of a Nation*, actually screened in 1931. The rest of the films referred to here are *Judith of Bethulia* (1914), *The Battle of the Sexes* (1915), *The Avenging Conscience* (1916), *Intolerance* (1918), *Macbeth* (1919), *Broken Blossoms* (1920), *Orphans of the Storms* (1923) and *Way Down* (1922).

Among the South African viewing audience of 1916, Griffith was perceived as the most outstanding producer. According to the Johannesburg daily *The Star*, his reputation approached that of fetishism.[50] Here is a 1916 South African newspaper advertisement for D. W. Griffith's films:

THE AVENGING CONSCIENCE
BY
D.
W.
GRIFFITH
Query: Why have we billed GRIFFITH's name
in huge type and the film in very small?
Answer: Because anyone can invent a title
but there is only one GRIFFITH.[51]

Obviously, a case can be made that in his time Griffith was a film-maker of considerable repute. Indeed, some Western film historians regard him very highly and his film *Birth of a Nation* as a pioneering classic of the cinema. Less generally said, however, is that *Birth of a Nation* was perhaps the first example of a motion picture indulging in blatantly racist denigration of the Black people. The film reveals hatred, intolerance and sheer bigotry. It is on record that various scenes were banned after they had sparked serious race riots in the United States. It covers the history of the American Civil War and the reconstruction immediately following it. The major feature of this sad period (in the producer's own words) was the 'Black Stronghold' on the defeated Southern states.

Lynch, the mulatto character in the film, is portrayed as boorish and lustful. His lust extends beyond political power to embrace lascivious grimaces beamed to a White girl, Elsie Stoneman. Subsequently, the inevitable rape attempt occurs, following the Northern politician's refusal to allow his daughter to marry the mulatto. Clearly, the pathological obsession of some American Whites with the Black rape of the White woman is unmistakable, and seems to have appeared or even 'occurred' with amazing frequency in American literature of the past century. *Birth of a Nation* could well be the first film to dramatise this obsession.[52]

Griffith was a Southerner, and for a while he reacted with quintessential arrogance and stupidity to the wave of indignant criticism which greeted his film. Rabbi Stephen Wise called it an intolerable insult to Black people. *The Nation* thought it was improper, immoral, and injurious. Griffith retaliated with a pamphlet called *The Rise and Fall of Free Speech in America*, in which he reportedly said that the attacks on his beloved film were deliberately unfair. It may be interesting to note that the cast portraying mulattos and Blacks in the film were Whites painted black. Should it be surprising, then, that D. W. Griffith's films were the darling of his racist cousins in South Africa?

Canada Lee and Sidney Poitier in South Africa

On the brighter side, there were films made by liberal Whites during the 50s of whlch Alan Paton's South African epic *Cry, the Beloved Country* was perhaps the most important. The film starred Canada Lee as an old village priest journeying to Johannesburg in search of a son gone astray in the city where he is touched by poverty and filth, and bewildered by racism. He is aided in the search by a young priest played by Sidney Poitier. Considered by some African scholars to be both patronising and paternalistic, the film also attempts to plead for racial harmony and reconciliation. Lionel Ngakane, a young Black South African actor, also played a minor role in this film directed by Zoltan Korda.[53]

Zakes Mokae, who acted in David Millin's production *Legends of Fear*, commented on films in South Africa in general and more specifically on Korda's production in relation to Blacks:

Many people both in the film industry and outside have often put that question to me. First of all, the film's title says *Cry, the Beloved Country*. Whose country is it? It is the usual liberal, paternalistic stuff which in effect suggests that if only the African can be more disciplined, have faith in the White man, be patient and believe in God, the situation will improve. How long are we going to wait for the Almighty to save us from bondage? For South Africa there is only one answer. It's a people's revolution.[54]

Cry, the Beloved Country is a very decent Anglo-Saxon propaganda piece. To a large extent, however, it succeeds in diverting the blame of the repugnant White minority power structure in South Africa from the English and points an accusing finger at the Afrikaners. True, the Afrikaners control political power and they were responsible for legalising apartheid. Not only did the English lay the foundation for what the Afrikaners have accomplished, they also control the economy. The point is that both are equally guilty in the judgment of human conscience.

What is particularly interesting about the film is its timing of production. It was shot three years after the Whites of English descent had suffered political defeat in the 'democratic' elections of 1948. Given the arrogant attitude of the Afrikaners towards the English since their assumption of political control, the latter's behaviour is only natural: they appear to sympathise with the African, who has always been the victim of social injustice from both sides. As indicated above, these circumstances are not unprecedented. There are parallels in American history of the 1950s – 'the red-baiting witch hunt' – when White liberals became supporters of the Black cause. Cinema being enormously powerful as a medium of communication, *Cry, the Beloved Country* can be said to be Nadine Gordimer, Alan Paton, Sarah Gertrude Millin and William Plomer all rolled together.

Propaganda Films

A Zulu's Devotion was produced by a South African company known as the African Film Production (AFP) in 1916. Briefly, the AFP was established partly for the production of local propaganda, and partly because American fiction films became very expensive. *A Zulu's Devotion* was written and produced by Joseph Albrecht. The theme centred on a Zulu farm labourer shown frustrating the designs of two Coloured thieves and rescuing his little mistress from their clutches. The star of the film was Goba, the first African so to figure.[55] Like his American Black counterpart in the Hollywood movies of the day, Goba was portrayed as a servile brainless but faithful servant. He later became what Gutsche describes as one of the AFP stars.

The second propaganda film by the AFP was *De Voortrekkers*, a historical epic whose scenario had been written by the historian Gustav Preller in collaboration with Harold Show, the producer specially imported for the purpose. The film was a reconstruction of the Great Trek culminating in the Battle of Blood River. Goba played the role of an embattled, spear-brandishing, painted Zulu commander. Twenty thousand Africans were collected, five hundred rifles said to be of the period were used, and forty trek wagons were made to authenticate the occasion. Thousands of the Africans who were ordered to make a fanatical attack on the laager did exactly that and trouble ensued:

At a given signal, the natives charged the laager furiously, but instead of recoiling and falling 'dead' continued into the laager itself where blows with Europeans were exchanged.[56]

Mounted police intervened apparently to prevent the Africans from destroying the laager in earnest. Having been savaged by the police, the Africans ran away and retakes were rendered impossible. However, at a later date, filming of the reconstruction of the Battle of Blood River, from the African's perspective, was accomplished. When the film was released, it is said to have inspired an American counterpart in *The Covered Wagon*. Another historical reconstruction, *Symbol of Sacrifice*, in which the British claimed an easy victory over the Zulus at Isandhlwana, scene of the infamous massacre of 1879 in Zululand, was released. *King Solomon's Mines* was the second film produccd by AFP.[57]

In August 1930, *In the Land of Zulus*, another film produced by the AFP (the first sound film of African life), was released to the South African public. It was later screened in London and it seems to have had a favourable reception. The film was a documentary about the visit of the Governor-General, the Earl of Athlone. From then on, many more films were made, especially those dealing with economic production. In 1938 the AFP produced various other films, including a documentary dealing with the manganese mining industry commissioned by the department of mines.

The AFP produced *The Golden Harvest of the Witwatersrand*, which was a long documentary of over 7,000 feet on nine reels.[58] The film dealt in detail with the gold-mining industry, dubbed with natural sound, covering the entire process from the recruiting of African labour to the actual extraction of gold. But the film was not found commercially suitable for showing in South Africa because of its boring nature, so it was gainfully sold to Britain for use in mining colleges and other educational institutions.

From Red Blanket to Civilization, also produced by AFP, is a film which demeans African traditional life and glorifies Western culture. Apparently the cameraman was able to shoot the Xhosa wedding, initiation ceremonies, missionary posts, labour-recruiting depots and the African labour force on the mines. This film was shown to Africans throughout the Union of South Africa.[59] It was exhibited at Wembley and also screened in London to the Society for the Propagation of the Gospel in Foreign Parts. From *Kraal to Mine*, a series of films made in various areas by the AFP, covered Natal, Zululand, Ciskei, Northern Transvaal, and Basutoland (present day Lesotho). For many years, the use of films for propaganda purposes was practised by the government and companies, but the majority were imported from the USA and Britain.[60]

Entertainment Cinema for Africans
For many years, racial discrimination and economic factors made it impossible for Africans and non-Europeans to attend the bioscopes. Even special provisions for them to enjoy cinema were not contemplated for many years. In 1920, initial steps were taken to provide cinema as a form of entertainment to non-Europeans. It became general practice, therefore, to admit them regardless of race to the gallery of bioscopes or to the front seats in order to prohibit them from interacting with Europeans. With the passage of the Censorship Act, non-Europeans were restricted to certain types of films.[61] This move angered non-Europeans, especially the economically well-off Indians and Coloureds. When the number of Africans increased in the townships and mine industries, film companies found it expedient to exploit that market. Bioscopes catering for non-Europeans were built, especially around Cape Town.

These cinemas had a definite identity as such and their programmes consisted almost exclusively of 'wild westerns' and musicals. The 'tickey bioscope' of the suburbs soon became a popular feature among the non-European of the community.[62]

For the African miner, the Revd Ray Phillips instituted cinema shows on the mine compounds. These were severely censored films which proved extremely successful and influenced both the Chamber of Mines and the Municipal Native Affairs Department to take an interest.[63] For many years, the question of occupying the leisure time of the Rand's vast African population had been unanswered. Phillips's weekly exhibitions provided it. The Municipal Native Affairs Department arranged for shows to be given in municipal compounds and the Chamber of Mines took over the organisation and ran it through the Native Recruiting Corporation. Exhibitions were given at no charge.

Films for Education
There was an outcry from government circles that Western films could be detrimental to the relationship between Africans and Europeans. Some films, they argued, were exposing Africans to too much of the American way of life, and could ultimately influence the urbanised native to seek equality with his European boss. It was therefore agreed that most American films were unsuitable for the Africans. The Union Education Department was charged with the duty of recommending appropriate films for Africans and non-Europeans. Among other things, it recommended that propaganda films about soil erosion, overstocking, nutrition, health and child welfare were urgently required for the natives. Mobile cinema units were proposed. The department castigated what it described as cheap cinema for the natives in towns: 'Cinemas were, as a rule, only low grade undesirable films of the Wild West and gangster and thriller types are shown.'[64] The following is a list of films which were commonly shown to the Africans in the reserve: (1) *Venereal Disease*, (2) *Nutrition*, (3) *Life and Customs of the Ama Zulu*, (4) *Life and Customs of the Watusi*, (5) *Growing and Ginning of Cotton*, (6) *Life and Customs of the Pygmies*, (7) *Prevention of Blindness*, (8) *Thrift*.

These films, which were supplied by the publicity committee of the Union Education Department, were narrated by Africans.[65] The Tea Market Expansion Bureau, an advertising agency of the International Tea Growers' Association, London, operated mobile cinema units to visit reserves, locations and mines, 'educating' people to develop a taste for tea and other products.

Conclusion
In film parlance, South Africa is part of the global village. From earlier days to the present, the influence of cinema has been and remains tremendous. The films examined here clearly illustrate how cinema can create images and information which determine our beliefs, attitudes and, ultimately, our behaviour. Most of the films do not correspond to the realities of social existence. Messages and images that intentionally create a false sense of reality and thereby produce a consciousness that cannot comprehend actual conditions of life, personal or social, are manipulative propaganda. Manipulation of human minds is an instrument of conquest. The African is not only suppressed by the fascist minority regime, he or she is also taught 'self-hate' through the powerful medium of moving pictures. Films provide an excellent opportunity to divert

people's attention from their immediate problems, as Mphahlele has noted: 'We forgot our hunger, weariness, everything else, lost in the exciting movements of the movies.'[66] These films clearly reveal to us the working mind and intentions of the South African power structure. As sources of information, these films can provide excellent indications of historical, economic and sociopolitical development of Blacks in South Africa. As we saw earlier, South Africa set precedents for racial discrimination in censorship and segregation in viewing. These were later adopted in East and Central Africa. Through these films we are also able to establish the economic and sociopolitical link between the capitalist world and South Africa. A case can also be made about the unfortunate role black Americans were made, and continue, to play in the subjugation of the African through films. Witness Robeson in *Sanders of the River* and Canada Lee and Poitier in *Cry, the Beloved Country*.

I do not claim to have exhausted the subject of film as an instrument of social control in these pages. If this paper manages to invoke the critical powers of better equipped researchers, inciting them to produce better results from their investigations of the matter, my intentions will have been fulfilled.

Notes

1. Thelma Gutsche, *The History and Social Significance of Motion Pictures in South Africa, 1895–1940* (Cape Town: Howard Timins, 1972), p. 9.
2. George M. Fredrickson, *White Supremacy, a Comparative Study in American and South African History* (New York: Oxford University Press, 1981), p. 283.
3. See Margery Perham (ed.), *Ten Africans* (London: Faber, 1936), p. 74.
4. Results of a Census of the Transvaal Colony and Swaziland, 1904, Transvaal Government 1906, XVII.
5. T. Matshikiza, 'Music for Moderns', in *Drum*, July 1957.
6. Margery Perham, *African Apprenticeship* (London: Faber, 1974), p. 146.
7. A. Cohen, *Two Dimensional Man* (Berkeley: University of California Press, 1975), p. 53.
8. K. Ngubane, 'South Africa's Race Crisis: A Conflict of Minds', in H. Adam (ed.), *South Africa: Sociological Perspectives* (Oxford: Oxford University Press, 1971), p. 13.
9. An interview with Zakes Mokae, a Black South African professional actor, February 1983.
10. Amilcar Cabral, *Return to the Source*, selected speeches edited by African Information Service (New York: Monthly Review Press, 1973), p. 39.
11. Ezekiel Mphalele, *Down Second Avenue* (New York: Anchor Books, 1971), p. 154.
12. *Drum*, January/February 1952.
13. Ibid.
14. Gutsche, *History and Social Significance*, p. 27.
15. L. A. Notcutt and G. C. Latham (eds.), *The African and the Cinema* (London: Edinburgh House Press, 1937), p. 243. See also Bell, letter to *The Times*, 4 October 1926.
16. J. Russell, 'The Use of the Cinema in the Guidance of Backward Races', *Journal of the African Society*, vol. 30, July 1931, p. 238.
17. S. Tallents, *The Protection of England* (London: Faber, 1932), p. 29.
18. Teshome Gabriel, 'Images of Black People in Cinema: Historical Overview', *Ufahamu*, vol. 6, no. 2, 1976, p. 134.
19. Vaughn J. Koyinde, 'Africa and the Cinema', in Langston Hughes (ed.), *An African Treasury* (New York: Crown, 1960) p. 89.
20. *Flamingo* magazine, June 1960.
21. Ibid.
22. Donald Bogle, *Toms, Coons, Mulattoes, Mammies and Bucks: An Interpretive History of Blacks in American Films* (New York: The Viking Press, 1973), p. 97. Paul Robeson also appeared in *King Solomon's Mines* (1937) as Umbopa, the Shona Chief; in *The Proud Valley* (1941) as an African servant, and in *Song of Freedom* (1938), where he pays homage to colonial rule. See also Teshome Gabriel, 'Images of Black People in

Cinema', p. 140, and Natalie Barakas, *Thirty Thousand Miles for the Films* (Glasgow: Blackie, 1937), p. 69.

23. London *Daily Herald*, 10 December 1935.
24. See Bogle, *Toms, Coons, Mulattoes.*
25. *Ebony*, May 1946.
26. L. A. Notcutt and G. C. Latham (eds), *The African and the Cinem*a.
27. Bogle, *Toms, Coons, Mulattoes*, p. 135.
28. Ibid., p. 13.
29. Daniel J. Lead, 'From Sambo to Superspade: The Black in Film', *Film and History*, vol. 2, no. 3, September 1972. See also Gabriel, 'Images of Black People in Cinema', pp. 134–5.
30. Lawrende D. Reddick, 'Educational Programs for the Improvement of Race Relations: Motion Pictures, Radio, the Press and Libraries', *The Journal of Negro Education*, vol. 23 Summer 1944, p. 370. Dr Reddick identified some stereotypes of Blacks: the happy slave, the devoted servant, the savage African, the sexual superman, the superstitious churchgoer, the mental inferior, the super athlete, the natural musician, and the unhappy non-white, to name a few.
31. Herbert Kretzmer, 'The Negro in Films', *The Forum*, 1954.
32. Ibid.
33. Bogle, *Toms, Coons, Mulattoes*, p. 6.
34. *The Star*, November 1931.
35. Ibid.
36. *The Star*, 9 July 1910. See also *Cape Times*, 9 July 1910.
37. *The Star*, 8 March 1931.
38. Report of the Select Committee on the Entertainments (Censorship) Bill, March 1931, p. 4.
39. Ibid., p. 6.
40. Ibid., p. 24.
41. Gutsche, *History and Social Significance*, p. 303.
42. Kretzmer, 'The Negro in Films', p. 51.
43. Rex Ingram, a Black actor, appears in the film as a magnificent Sudanese soldier, engendering audience affection as he heroically kills a Nazi soldier and sacrifices his life in the name of the 'free world'.
44. Kretzmer, 'The Negro in Films' p. 55.
45. *New York World Telegram*, cited in Donald Bogle, *Toms, Coons, Mulattoes*, p. 68.
46. *New York Times*, 10 May 1937.
47. Interview with Professor Sharifa Evans, February 1983.
48. Kretzmer, 'The Negro in Films', p. 51.
49. Gutsche, *History and Social Significance*, p. 140.
50. *The Star*, 20 July 1916.
51. Ibid.
52. See Bogle, *Toms, Coons, Mulattoes*, p. 135, and Gabriel, 'Images of Black People in Cinema', p. 135.
53. See Sidney Poitier's autobiography, *This Life* (New York: Alfred A. Knopf, 1980) p. 136; *Drum*, December 1951.
54. Interview with Zakes Mokae. See also *Theater Magazine*, Spring 1982.
55. Gutsche, *History and Social Significance*, p. 313.
56. Ibid.
57. Barakas, *Thirty Thousand Miles*, p. 151.
58. George M. Fredrickson, *White Supremacy*, p. 313.
59. S. Kirkland, *The Forum*, December 1930.
60. *The Star*, February 1935.
61. Gutsche, *History and Social Significance*, p. 356.
62. Ibid.
63. Ibid.
64. R. Phillips, 'The African and the Cinema', *Race Relations*, vol. 2, June 1936, p. 42.
65. Adult Education in South Africa, Report by a Committee of Enquiry appointed by the Minister of Education, Pretoria, 1945, p. 118.
66. Mphahlele, *Down Second Avenue*, p. 40.

The Present Situation of the Film Industry in Anglophone Africa

Manthia Diawara

Reprinted from *African Cinema: Politics and Culture* (Bloomington, Ind.: Indiana University Press, 1992).

Recently, some anglophone states have begun to encourage film production by nationalising distribution and raising subsidies from the exhibition of foreign films to finance national productions through state-sponsored agencies. In Zimbabwe, for example, the government set up a production and training centre with the help of the Federal Republic of Germany, which was also responsible for the National Film and Television Institute in Ghana and the Kenya Institute of Mass Communication. The production centre in Zimbabwe has trained film-makers and technicians who, so far, have made newsreels, documentaries and short fiction films. In Tanzania, the Audio-Visual Institute has been in existence since 1974, donated by the government of Denmark. It contains facilities for processing, printing, and mixing narrative and sound effects. The Institute trains film-makers and technicians and produces educational, publicity and documentary films. The Institute has participated in international film festivals in Mogadishu (Somalia) and Ouagadougou (Burkina Faso), presenting docudramas on the teaching of the *Ujamaa*. In 1985, a Tanzanian co-production, *Arusi ya Mariamu (The Wedding of Mariamu,* 1985), directed by Nanga Yoma Ngoge and Ron Mulvihill of the USA, was awarded the prize for the best short film at the Festival Panafricain du Cinéma de Ouagadougou (FESPACO). *Arusi ya Mariamu* is about the traditional science of healing and the conflict between tradition and modernity.

Like Tanzania, Kenya has just begun its interest in feature-film production. Two government branches, the Kenya Film Corporation (KFC) and the Kenya Institute of Mass Communication (KIMC), handle film activities. The KFC deals primarily with distribution, which it has monopolised since 1972. In Kenya, as in other anglophone countries, US films dominate the market, challenged only by Indian melodrama and kung fu movies. Since its creation, the KFC has distributed a few African films from Cameroon and Ghana, one of which, *Love...Brewed in the African Pot* (Kwaw Ansah, 1980), is the third most popular film in the country, grossing 1,022,443 Kenyan shillings.[1] The KFC has also distributed American films in Tanzania, Somalia, Ethiopia, Zambia and Uganda.

Other functions of the KFC involve the development of a mobile cinema system in the rural areas and video centres on the outskirts of Nairobi. According to Sharad Patel, 'These films on wheels can reach 500 semi-urban and rural centres a month, attracting audiences of over 40,000 every evening. And thanks to advertising, not a single one of these moviegoers pays even a cent for this entertainment.'[2] Therefore, the KFC limits its film production to videotaping urban products for advertisement in rural areas and for television commercials.

The KIMC, on the other hand, has facilities in 16mm production and laboratories where film-makers train for the Kenyan television. So far the KIMC has produced tourist-attraction films (*Waters of Mombasa, Passport to Adventure, Immashoi of Massai*, directed by Sao Gamba), educational documentaries, and other information films. In 1985, Sao Gamba directed *Kolormask*, a didactic film about a Kenyan student who returns home with a White wife. The marriage is threatened by social and cultural differences between Kenya and England. Presented at the 1987 FESPACO, *Kolormask* was criticised for being too exotic in its emphasis on documenting African cultures. The real promise in Kenyan cinema may come from creative writers such as Ngugi Wa Thiong'o and Meja Mwangi, who are now turning to cinema as did Ousmane Sembène in Senegal and Wole Soyinka in Nigeria, for a more direct way of communication with their audiences. Ngugi participated in the 1986 Edinburgh Film Festival, where he presented a short video about South Africa and discussed the film course he had taught in Sweden. As for Meja Mwangi, he was listed as assistant director in *Out of Africa* (1986), and his novel *Carcass for Hounds*, was adapted into film by Ola Balogun.

The only countries in anglophone Africa to have gone beyond the government productions to create an independent cinema are Ghana and Nigeria. Film production continues to progress in these countries despite the lack of strong support from their governments. In Ghana, independent directors such as King Ampaw and Kwaw Ansah have replaced the old documentary tradition with feature films that blend comedy and melodrama and draw their themes from popular culture and the meeting between Western and African civilisations. In Nigeria, a Yoruba cinema has emerged since the early 1970s to become an original expression of directors such as Ola Balogun and Bankole Bello and popular Yoruba theatre stars such as Chief Hubert Ogunde, Ade 'Love' Folayan, and Moses Olaiya Adejumo.

The government branches that handle the film industry in Ghana are the Ghana Film Industry Corporation (GFIC), the Ghana Broadcasting Corporation (GBC), and the National Film and Television Institute (NAFTI). Like similar government agencies in Kenya and Tanzania, the GFIC, the GBC and the NAFTI manage distribution, censorship, the training of technicians, and the production of documentary and information films. The GFIC inherited the facilities of the Gold Coast Colonial Film Unit, which specialised in the documentary genre in the tradition of John Grierson. It is still possible to find in the archives of the GFIC pre-independence classics like *The Boy Kumasenu* (1952), a film about city life, as well as post-independence Nkrumah-era classics like *Tongo Hamile* (1965), which is a screen adaptation of Shakespeare's *Hamlet*.

The GFIC has 16mm and 35mm production equipment with laboratory facilities. With GFIC alone, Ghana is better equipped than all of the other West African states, and it is capable of turning out more than twelve features a year. Ghanaian film-makers trained at NAFTI and abroad find their first employment at GFIC and GBC. In this sense one can find the influence of GFIC's documentary style on such well-known Ghanaian directors as Sam Aryetey (*No Tears* for Ananse, 1968), Egbert Adjesu (*I Told You So*, 1970), Kwate Nii Owoo (*You Hide Me*, 1971; *Struggle for Zimbabwe*, 1974; *Angela Davis*, 1976), King Ampaw (*They Call It Love*, 1972; *Kukurantumi*, 1983; *Juju*, 1986), and Kwaw Ansah (*Love... Brewed in the African Pot*).

The GFIC manages distribution and censorship in such a manner that national and Third World films are shown in the movie theatres in Ghana. It is pushing the government, for example, to put a quota on film import and to encourage film exchange between Third World countries. It is in this vein that 'Cuba and Ghana have run seasons of each other's films and the Havana festival had a retrospective of African cinema in 1986.'[3] The GFIC has had to deal with video piracy, too, because the shortage of foreign currency in Ghana makes the import of films expensive. Since 1982, video centres have opened everywhere in the big cities, and the most recent films are shown on video monitors in violation of the copyright and cinematography laws in Ghana. More important, the pirated videos contribute to the economic crisis through the evasion of exhibition taxes and the uncensored showing of pornographic films that affect the patrons negatively.[4]

Unlike the case in Kenya and Tanzania, where film production is in the hands of the government, Ghanaian cinema is not limited to the productions of GFIC, GBC and NAFTI. Ghana's best-known directors, King Ampaw and Kwaw Ansah, are independent directors who produce their films by raising funds locally and internationally. Ansah's latest film, *Heritage Africa* (1988), for example, is funded by the Social Security Bank, the Ghana Commercial Bank, the National Investment Bank, and the Cooperative Bank.[5] The relative freedom that the independent directors acquire in being their own producers enables them to make popular films that are not burdened by didactic and propagandistic precepts imposed by the government. This is not to say, however, that independent directors do not need governments and their agencies. On the contrary, both Ansah and Ampaw use the equipment and personnel of the GFIC and the facilities provided by such government departments as the army. Furthermore, film-makers need the government to set quotas on film import and reduce entertainment tax for local films so that their films can compete with foreign products.

The significance of producing independently is seen in the fact that Ansah and Ampaw choose their films on an artistic and financial basis, not on the basis that the government wants this or that type of film made. It is the artistic freedom that enables them to go beyond the documentary tradition fostered by the GFIC and to look to popular culture as a source of fictional inspiration. As Jim Pines points out, their 'films draw on local culture and experience'[6] and thus ensure a box-office return both in Ghana and in other African countries. The films of Ampaw and Ansah blend comedy and melodrama, ridiculing eccentric paternal figures and emphasising the tragic clash between tradition and modernity. A look at the films reveals the contradictions between the values of the city and those of the village; they denounce acculturation and attempt to raise the consciousness of the characters in the end.

In *Love ... Brewed in the African Pot*, for example, Ansah draws upon elements from Ghanaian cultural experience to construct a narrative with the themes of repression and class difference. The story is about a love affair between Aba, educated in a posh Cape Coast school and trained as a dressmaker, and Joe Quansah, a semiliterate car mechanic (fitter) and son of a fisherman. Aba's father, Koffi Appiah, who is a civil servant, wants her to marry a lawyer, Bensah, instead of Joe.[7] The film thematises repression by putting into play two of the most effective dream sequences in African cinema.

The first dream shows Koffi Appiah's repressed origin returning to haunt him. Ansah positions the spectator in this dream sequence by describing the fishermen's tradition as a source of pride and authenticity, which has a deeper influence on Koffi Appiah's mind than the surface appearance of Western civilisation among Ghanaian elites. The silent cinematic message satisfies the unconscious expectation of African audiences, the majority of whom come from traditions similar to those of the fishermen in the film. The violence with which Koffi Appiah is punished by his unconscious serves not only to vindicate the fishermen who are humiliated by him, and with whom the spectator identifies, but also to awaken the elitists like Koffi Appiah who run away from tradition and mimic the West.

The other dream sequence concerns the return of Aba's worst repressed fears in the shape of a witch. Aba's desire to marry Joe, a 'fitter' beneath her class, is in violation of class differences and of her father's interdiction of such a transgression. Aba overlooks these obstacles by simplifying and dismissing her father's Westernised ideas as irrational, grotesque and superficial. On the other hand, she romanticises the fishermen's tradition, which Joe represents, as strong, natural, music-loving, and authentic. However, when the forces of class difference turn Joe against her, she is no longer able to dismiss them as irrational and grotesque. In Aba's dream, her unconscious thematises all the obstacles into the shape of a witch, dressed in a white dress. Aba succumbs to a powerful monster that, while awake, she dismisses as superficial and grotesque. Ansah has been criticised by Françoise Pfaff for failing to construct a more 'realistic' face mask for the witch. What captivates the spectator, however, is less the realism of the form of the film than the content. In other words, the spectator accepts the dream because of its content, which is consistent with other rational elements that are presented in the story as obstacles to Joe marrying Aba. It is because the representation of the dream satisfied the collective psychic need of the spectator that *Love ... Brewed in the African Pot* beat record attendances in Kenya, Liberia and Sirra Leone, where it was screened for three months. Ansah ensures the popularity of the film with African spectators by drawing from other popular experiences such as wedding ceremonies, wrestling matches, and musical performances.

The government of Nigeria manages the film industry through three agencies: the Film Unit, the Nigerian Film Corporation and the National Film Distribution Company. The Film Unit, which was inherited from the colonial administration, produces educational documentaries and trains film-makers for other government departments. As an office of the federal government, it functions to satisfy the country's need for documentaries in agriculture, health and housing. Between 1979 and 1983, the Film Unit produced 25 documentaries, 65 newsreels, and 390 short information films. However, according to Françoise Balogun, who is the foremost authority on Nigerian film, the productions of the Film Unit do not reach a wide audience: 'Nigerian television is bombarded by foreign productions and it has no link with the Film Unit. Furthermore, there are no rules which require the theatre owners to show a short documentary of the Film Unit before showing the feature films.'[8]

The Nigerian Film Corporation (NFC) and the National Film Distribution Company (NFDC) are outgrowths of the 1972 Indigenisation Act, which gave exclusive monopoly for distribution and exhibition of feature films to Nigerians with the capital and business contracts. The NFC was set up in 1979, but did not begin operating until 1982. According to Adamu Halilu, a film-maker and former secretary of the NFC, its purpose was to promote production and to chart the course of the film industry complex. In view of the fact that films produced in Nigeria faced marketing difficulties, the NFC's role was to review distribution and to implement a quota system that would force theatre owners to run one Nigerian film for every ten foreign films that they showed. The duties of the NFC also involved talking to merchant banks and businessmen on behalf of film-makers and reviewing the entertainment tax with regard to Nigerian film.[9]

As for the NFDC, it has been in existence since 1981, replacing the American Motion Picture Export Association ten years after the Indigenisation Act. Its functions include film importation, distribution and exhibition. The NFDC own theatres around Lagos and shows some of its films in the National Theatre, which is equipped with 16mm, 35mm, and 70mm projectors. The National Theatre contains two projection rooms with 676 seats each, and the main hall with 5,000 seats. In 1982, forty-two films were shown there, including *Orun Mooru* and *Money Power* by Ola Balogun and *Love...Brewed in the African Pot* by Ansah.[10]

The NFDC also imports films for other national distribution agencies such as the Nigerian Motion Picture Corporation and the West African Pictures Corporation. All these companies show Nigerian films in their theatres; however, they charge more for them in order to make the same amount of profit they make for running less expensive foreign films that have already recouped their cost of production before reaching Nigeria. Nigerian film-makers have pleaded with the government to reduce or completely eliminate the entertainment tax for local films so that they can compete with American and kung fu films, which flood the market. As Ola Balogun puts it, 'The most that the government can do and should do is to help regulate film distribution and exhibition in such a way as would permit an individual Nigerian filmmaker to progress.'[11]

The most important state participation in feature film production involves Adamu Halilu's *Shaihu Umar* (1976), which was totally financed by the government for the Nigerian entry in the 1977 FESTAC. The film, which tells the epic story of a Hausa religious leader, is based on a novel in Hausa by the first Prime Minister of Nigeria, Sir Abubakar Tafawa Balewa. Even though *Shaihu Umar* is important because of its use of Hausa tradition and historiography and its glorification of Islam and the Hausa past, it risks letting the spectator down because of its length (140 minutes) and the repetitious scenes.

Independent production continues to progress in Nigeria, despite the difficulties mentioned above, because of the Indigenisation Act, which enables the film-makers to distribute their films and recoup the cost of production. Since 1972, for example, Ola Balogun has become the most prolific director in sub-Saharan Africa, producing at least one feature film a year. Balogun's films enjoy a big success in Nigeria, which lets him recoup his money each time and make new films. In 1978, he made *Black Goddess*, a film about Afro-Brazilians who returned to Nigeria after gaining freedom from slavery. It traces the roots of Babatunde, whose ancestor, Prince Oluyole, was captured in a tribal war and sent to Brazil as a slave two centuries ago. Babatunde travels from Lagos to Rio de Janeiro with the sculpture of the goddess Yemanja, which he hopes will be recognised by the part of the family that remained in Brazil. During a religious ceremony in Rio, Elisa, daughter of a priestess, reveals to Babatunde that what he is looking for is is the Bahia region. The mythico-poetic and historical aspects of *Black Goddess* are appealing to film critics. Even though the film did not meet the same success in Nigeria as the films based on popular Yoruba theatre, it was internationally acclaimed, winning the award of the Office Catholique International du Cinéma. It also won an award for the best musical score at Carthage (1980). In fact, Balogun's international reputation is no longer in doubt, with such features as *Cry Freedom* (1981), a film about liberation movements and based on the novel *Carcass for Hounds* by Meja Mwangi (Kenya), and *Money Power* (1982), which have more universal themes that would appeal to audiences beyond the frontiers of Nigeria.

Eddie Ugbomah comes after Balogun with more than eight feature films produced since 1976. Ugbomah's films are inspired by contemporary events and politics in Nigeria. His first feature, *The Rise and the Fall of Dr Oyenusi* (1977), is based on a true story about a Lagos gangster in the 1970s who was arrested and executed publicly. *The Mask* (1979) shows how a fictitious Nigerian president sent a secret agent to retrieve the famous mask of Queen Adesua of Benin, which was stolen by British colonisers and put in a London museum. The film, starring Ugbomah himself, uses the Manichaean aesthetics from James Bond films, thematising the Nigerian hero as super-clever and the British police as stupid. *Death of a Black President* (1983) is based on the events leading to the assassination of General Murtala Mohamed, who was head of state of Nigeria between 1975 and 1976.

More important, the Idigenisation Act has attracted the stars of popular Yoruba theatre to film. In 1976, Ola Balogun made *Ajani Ogun* with Ade 'Love' Folayan, who is a star in the Yoruba popular theatre. The film tells the story of a young man who has to fight an evil rich man to get his fiancée and his inheritance back. Long screen times are devoted to Ade Love in the title role, as he sings long romantic songs or fights with his opponents. Balogun directed the film with the help of Duro Lapido, who had long experience of directing his own plays for Nigerian television. The success of *Ajani Ogun* and the public's request for a sequel was such that Balogun and Ade Love teamed up again in 1977 to film *Ija Ominira* (Fight for Freedom), a popular story about a tyrannical king who was chased out of his kingdom. *Ija Ominira* is the first Nigerian film to have recouped its cost of production within one year.

The success of *Ajani Ogun* and *Ija Ominira* at the box office led other popular figures of the Yoruba theatre, such as Chief Hubert Ogunde and Moses Olaiya Adejumo (alias Baba Sala), to seek out Balogun to adapt their plays to film. In 1979, Balogun and Chief Ogunde produced *Aiye*, based on a play written by Ogunde. *Aiye* is a story about a struggle between a traditional medicine man and an evil magician. The film is full of special effects that produce a sense of magic. The popularity of *Aiye* was also assured by the presence in the film of Chief Ogunde, whose name would bring loyal admirers of his theatre to the movies. In 1982, another pioneer of Yoruba theatre, Baba Sala, produced *Orun Mooru* with Balogun. Presented to the Pan-African Film Festival at Ougadougou in 1987, *Orun Mooru* was one of the most popular films for the spectators in Burkina Faso. Baba Sala plays Lamidi, the hero, who decides to commit suicide after having been robbed by swindlers. As Lamidi undertakes his journey to the Kingdom of the Dead, he realises that Death, Iku, is not ready for him. Iku sends him to Ayo, the spirit of Joy. Ayo gives Lamidi two eggs without telling him that the first contains wealth and the second, death. Ayo sends Lamidi back to earth, advising him to break the first egg immediately upon his return home and the second egg fifty years later. Following Ayo's recommendation, Lamidi breaks the first egg and becomes instantly wealthy. Led by greed, he thinks that he will become even richer by breaking the second egg. Yet, as Lamidi breaks it open he finds himself confronted by Death.

Other stars of popular theatre have come to cinema as a result of the commercial success of *Ajani Ogun*, *Ija Ominira* and *Orun Mooru*. In 1982, Akinwauni Isola teamed with Bankole Bello, who assisted Balogun in the production of *Ajani Ogun*, to produce *Efunsetan Aniwaura*. Furthermore, Baba Sala, Ade Love, and Chief Ogunde have left Balogun to fly on their own wings as producers, directors and actors of their own films. They believe that they owe their popularity at the movies less to the cinematic form that Balogun was giving to their films and more to their own performances as stars and the illusion of reality and magic provided by film.

After this brief survey of Yoruba theatre on film, what kind of evaluation can one make of it? For her part, Françoise Balogun believes that Yoruba cinema is limited to Yoruba audiences because it stresses the interior aspects of Yoruba tradition, instead of the universal aspects. 'Outside of the Yoruba country, the Yoruba cinema constitutes an exotic curiosity instead of an artistic expression.'[12] She also states that Ola Balogun, her husband, is tired of directing 'these fairy-tales' for Yoruba theatre companies and is more inclined to direct films that communicate with the public at a deeper and more intellectual level.

Other critics believe, on the contrary, that the future of Nigerian cinema is in Yoruba popular theatre. The question becomes, then, how to operate within the social conditions of cinema and popular theatre in Nigeria and to create great works of art. In the words of Luky Isawode, 'Today, there are countless numbers of actors, dramatists, playwrights, singers, martial artists, etc., in this country. What the Indians and Chinese did, Nigerians can also do.'[13]

Wole Soyinka also thinks that the Yoruba popular theatre can provide Nigeria with a new art form, as well as an economically viable industry for the producers and the businessmen. The stars of popular theatre have, over many years, already shaped the taste of audiences in Nigeria. The new Yoruba cinema can make this audience its own by carefully appropriating the elements of popular theatre (stars, magic, dance and music) that appeal to the spectators and mixing them with that which cinema offers (photography, close-ups, illusion of reality and magic produced by editing and putting together images). For Soyinka, what film-makers need in Nigeria is an 'intermutual interrelation' between theatre and cinema, keeping in mind all the time that the two media are not exactly the same.[14]

Soyinka believes that the Yoruba cinema is economically viable because it does not resort to the aesthetic precepts that are moulded by Western cinema and that are expensive to produce in an African film. The least expensive cameras, 16mm and super-8, can be used in the production of Yoruba cinema without a loss of quality. Because the Yoruba theatre comes to cinema already equipped with its own actors, costumes, stories and props, all the film-maker has to do is to put the theatre in a cinematic time. It is in this sense that Soyinka states his preference for cinéma vérité as a model for Yoruba cinema. This cinema is not only relevant to the social conditions of Nigeria because it reflects stories and spectacles based on everyday life and on the collective myths, but it also provides an aesthetic and economic alternative to the Western superproduction. For Soyinka, the Yoruba cinema can manipulate the technology provided by film to evolve a new art form for the masses, as opposed to an elitist art form open only to the intellectual.[15]

Soyinka's interest in the interrelation between theatre and film is not, however, limited to these written statements. In 1971, Ossie Davis adapted his play *Kongi's Harvest* on film, in which the role of Kongi, a totalitarian leader, was played by Soyinka himself. The Nobel-Prize-winning playwright has since denounced the film version of *Kongi's Harvest* as unfaithful to the script he wrote for the screen adaptation.[16] In 1984, Soyinka directed his first feature film, *Blues for a Prodigal*.

Considering the success of Yoruba cinema in Nigeria and the fact that the best Yoruba films like *Orun Mooru* are also popular in other African countries, it may be that the film-makers in other parts of Africa should generate a more popular form of cinema looking at existing popular spectacles such as theatre, wrestling matches, song and dance. Both Nigerian and Ghanaian cinema can learn from the mistakes and innovations of the francophone cinema that preceded them and that is world-famous, with such directors as Ousmane Sembène and Souleymane Cissé. The movement towards popular culture constitutes a step toward giving African cinema its own identity.

It is obvious from this survey that there were enough resources in anglophone Africa to enable the emergence of a regional and international film industry. Since the early 1970s, film distribution has been nationalised in such countries as Tanzania, Kenya, Nigeria, Ghana and Ethiopia. The Indigenisation Act has enabled private Nigerians with the business contracts to take control of film distribution and exhibition. Not only does this create new jobs for Nigerians but it also stimulates the economy because the revenues from distribution and exhibition remain in the country instead of being evacuated to banks in London, Bombay or New York, which was the case when foreigners controlled the industry. A regional system of film distribution can also come from the nationalisation of the industry. The cost of foreign films can be reduced by acquiring films through a co-operative constituted by different countries in a region. It was in this way that Kenya used to distribute films in the 70s to Zambia, Ethiopia and Uganda. Such a regional distribution network has been in existence in francophone Africa since 1973, even though it has to fight foreign distribution for control of the market.

Distribution is also the key to national film production. Because of import quotas, France and Germany, Europe's two most important film producers, have survived the bombardment of their film market by the US Motion Picture Export Association of America (MPEAA). Similarly, a quota on the import of foreign films in anglophone Africa can liberate more screen space for African and Third World films. For example, audiences in anglophone Africa should be given the opportunity to see the independent Afro-American and Black British cinemas. Like France and West Germany, anglophone countries in Africa can also raise taxes on the distribution of foreign films to subsidise national film production. At the same time, the governments can lower entertainment taxes for national films to make it easier for them to compete with the imported films.

Like film distribution, film production can also be regionalised in anglophone Africa. So far, co-production of films has yet to take place between Africa and the West. The landscape and the people in Africa are often used as a backdrop for stories about Westerners: *King Solomon's Mines,* shot in Zimbabwe, *Out of Africa,* in Kenya; *Dogs of War,* in Ghana, and so on. With the number of film-makers available in Africa today, it is ironic that some anglophone African countries call upon Westerners to direct documentaries and educational films intended for Africans. Co-productions are desirable but, if possible, they should be between African nations. There are many reasons why I assert this principle. First, by using Africans, the producers will spend less. Second, the film, by its double or triple nationality, increases the chances that it will recoup its cost among an African audience. Co-production among Africans may also put to full use the equipment in such countries such as Ghana, Kenya and Zimbabwe, where all the production facilities exist but feature films are rare. Most important, aesthetic films run far less risk of misinterpreting African cultures and reifying African people when made by African directors. Ghana has opened the way for such co-production on the African level. In 1980, Ola Balogun shot *Cry Freedom* in Ghana with the co-operation of NAFTI. More recently John Akomfrah of the Black Audio Film Collective and director of *Handsworth Songs* (winner of the first Paul Robeson Prize at FESPACO) has turned to Ghana for the location as well as subject of his second film. Haile Gerima also looked to Ghana for possible locations for his latest film (*Sankofa,* 1993).

Notes

1. Paul Lazarus, 'Film Production in Kenya', unpublished report to ICDC and KFC, May 1983.
2. Sharad Patel, 'The Communications Gap', unpublished paper presented to the Kenya Film Week, December 1986.
3. Janice Turner and Jai Kumar, 'Shooting it out with Rambo', *South*, November 1977, p. 93.
4. 'Video Piracy in Ghana', *West Africa*, no. 3463, 2 January 1985, p. 22.
5. Nanabanyin Dadson, 'The Bad Old Days', *West Africa*, no. 3655, 31 August 1987, p. 1694.
6. Turner and Kumar, 'Shooting it out with Rambo', p. 93
7. Françoise Pfaff, *Twenty-Five African Film-Makers* (Westport, Conn.: Greenwood Press, 1988).
8. Françoise Balogun, *Le Cinéma au Nigeria* (Paris: Editions OCIC/L'Harmattan, 1983), p. 20.
9. Saddik Balewa, 'Nigerian Film Industry', *West Africa*, no. 3513, December 1984, p. 2584.
10. Balogun, *Le Cinéma au Nigeria,* p. 25
11. Richard Ikeibe, 'Nigeria Film Industry Get More Attention', *Daily Times,* 24 May 1980, p. 7.
12. Françoise Balogun, *Le Cinéma au Nigeria,* p. 87

13. 'Filmmaking in Nigeria: Problems Inherent', *Nigerian Standard*, 13 May 1985, p. 3.
14. Wole Soyinka, 'Theatre and the Emergence of the Nigerian Film Industry', in Alfred E. Opubor and Onuora E. Nwuneli (eds), *The Development of the Film Industry in Nigeria* (Lagos: Third International, 1979), pp. 102–3.
15. Ibid., p. 101.
16. Ibid., p. 97.

France's Bureau of Cinema – Financial and Technical Assistance 1961–1977

Operations and Implications for African Cinema

CLAIRE ANDRADE-WATKINS

Reprinted from *Society for Visual Anthropology Review*, vol. 6 no. 2, Fall 1990.

Introduction

Independence throughout francophone Africa in 1960 ushered in an era of transition for France and her former colonies. Development assistance and technical expertise to francophone African colonies was provided by France through the Ministry of Co-operation, created expressly for the newly independent countries.[1] In cinema, financial and technical assistance was provided through the Ministry of Co-operation on two levels. First the Consortium Audiovisuel International (CAI), the private sector arm of the Ministry of Co-operation, established in 1961, produced newsreels, educational documentaries and other special projects for the former colonies; second, the Bureau of Cinema provided financial and technical assistance to African film-makers.

The Bureau of Cinema, from its creation in 1963 until the 1979 restructuring of the Ministry of Co-operation, provided the technical and financial assistance which made francophone Africa the most prolific centre of Black African cinema. Prior to independence from France, not a single feature had been made by an African, yet by 1975 over 185 shorts and features were produced and realised with the technical and financial assistance of the Bureau of Cinema, with four out of five of all Black African films being made by francophone Africans.[2]

Why did France supply financial and technical assistance to African cinema through the Ministry of Co-operation? Was it neocolonialism, paternalism, or a genuine effort to assist in the development of an autonomous and self-sufficient African cinema? As Black African cinema moves into its third decade, many of the obstacles for financial and technical self-sufficiency in production, distribution and exhibition have remained largely unresolved. Efforts to establish national film structures, or regional centres for distribution, exhibition and production, have not resulted in viable, stable and profitable ventures capable of supporting an independent African cinema. Film-makers must still piece together the financial and technical package from largely foreign sources to produce their films, which in many instances are still shut off from the African audiences because of the continued monopoly by European companies of commercial theatres throughout francophone Africa. This does not imply that there is no hope for African cinema without French assistance, yet it reaffirms the piecemeal, displaced and disembodied process of production.

In retrospect, the primary objective of France's post-colonial support of

African cinema between 1961 and 1977 was to maintain the colonial legacy of assimilation, perpetuating and strengthening a Franco-African cultural connection through newsreels, educational documentaries and films of cultural expression produced by Africans and distributed and shown in non-commercial venues such as cine-clubs, cinematheques and French embassies throughout francophone Africa.

France's financial and technical assistance to francophone African cinema between 1961 and 1977 illustrates the means through which post-colonial cultural dominance was maintained by the CAI through its newsreels and other special projects. Furthermore, clear limitations and constraints are evident in the Bureau's assistance to films of *cultural expression* by individual African film-makers. A close look at the financial and technical resources provided to the CAI and the Bureau of Cinema supports the perception that France's development initiatives toward African cinema – particularly the work of the Bureau of Cinema – were undercapitalised and, indeed, that France's primary objective was not directed toward the development of an African cinema.

What distinguishes and supports this perspective is the kind of information on the resources and projects of the CAI in general and the Bureau in particular, which describes the administrative policies, terms, conditions and amounts of assistance provided. Reconstructed accounts by French administrators and technical personnel and the written documentation provide a kind of information on the production of African cinema which is unique.[3] Combined, these materials present a consistent and solid database that makes it possible to examine the terms as well as the shifts in the technical and financial assistance provided to African cinema between 1961 and 1977.

Historical Overview 1961–1977

Although *de jure* independence was granted in francophone Africa, *de facto* political, economic and cultural ties to the former French colonies remained a priority for the French government. Unlike the English, who preferred to maintain a distance between themselves and their African subjects, the French pulled their subjects into francophone culture. France's colonial policy of direct rule and assimilation perpetuated the idea that France and the colonies were a family, bound by the French language and culture. Through a process of education and immersion in French culture, francophone Africans, particularly the African elite and their children, were indoctrinated to view France as the mother country and the Gauls as their ancestors. For France, the emphasis on cultural assimilation was the dominant colonial policy, and it was from this context that economic and political relationships with the colonies were determined. It was a bond the French were unwilling to relinquish at the end of the colonial era.

The importance attached by France to maintaining post-colonial cultural, economic and political ties can be seen through the creation of the Ministry of Co-operation in 1961 by the de Gaulle government. Through the Ministry critical and significant financial and technical resources to the former colonies were provided, which also preserved France's dominance in the region – culturally, linguistically and economically. The Ministry remained a dominant vehicle for economic, cultural and technical assistance to the former colonies in areas such as agronomy, diplomacy, film-making and other areas requiring technical specialisation and expertise.[4]

Sub-Saharan francophone Africa – with Senegal at the epicentre of the activity – dominated African cinema ideologically, quantitatively and qualitatively. Three factors account for this dominance. First, there was the creation of the CAI and the Bureau of Cinema. Second, francophone Africa was home to major pioneers of African cinema – including the Senegalese film-maker/historian Paulin Vieyra and Ousmane Sembène, the internationally renowned author, film-maker and creator of the first feature made by an African, *La noire de ...* (*Black Girl*, 1966). Sembène is also known as the leading exponent of *cinéma engagé*, or militant cinema. Widely acclaimed as the father of African cinema, Sembène was a notable exception on several fronts, the most significant being that he did not produce his films through the Bureau of Cinema.

Lastly, it was francophone Africa which provided much of the leadership for FEPACI (Fédération Panafricaine de Cinéastes), the 33-member-country organisation of African film-makers which was established in 1969.

Administration of the Bureau of Cinema
Created in 1963 within the Ministry itself, the Bureau in turn worked with the CAI on the educational documentary series for francophone Africa. The major mission of the Bureau, however, as the largest producer of African cinema during the era, was to provide technical and financial resources to individual African film-makers to create works of *cultural expression.*

The creation of the Bureau of Cinema was actually preceded by a general cinema service within the Ministry. Lucien Patry, the creator of the Section Technique within what became the Bureau of Cinema, was recruited in early 1962 to organise a cinema service to address, in some logical fashion, the technical needs of the films or projects by film-makers – Africans as well as French – sociologists, ethnologists, geographers, and associates of the Ministry, who made films in the newly independent African states. Patry rapidly went about setting up a small 16mm production centre, with editing tables and sound transfer equipment, the basic minimum needed to provide technical support to the work coming in. The administrative entity which was built on that small technical section set up by Patry came into being several months later in 1963 as the Bureau of Cinema.[5]

Surprisingly for an organisation which became the largest producer of African cinema, the actual full-time staff at the Bureau of Cinema was rather small at the beginning, with only five or six people. The key personnel involved with African cinema were the director, Jean-René Debrix; Lucien Gohy, who worked at the Bureau from 1966 to 1976, first with the educational documentaries done by the CAI and the Bureau, then as Debrix's assistant; and Patry, who was in charge of the Section Technique of the Bureau. In addition to supervising the technical end of the Bureau's operations, Patry was also responsible for hiring the freelance technicians. At the height of the Bureau's activities the number of full-time people never exceeded a dozen. Not all worked directly with African cinema; others worked on projects or tasks associated with the 16mm educational and documentary projects of the CAI which were edited at the Bureau of Cinema.[6]

Gohy classifies the early years, up until the late 60s, as the experimental period of the Bureau – one in which it was thought possible for the state to work directly with individuals. This approach became increasingly problematic; and, as Gohy notes, in what he terms the second period, which ended with the Ministry phasing out the Bureau by 1979, the state began to distance itself from the policy which it had embraced in the preceding years:

In the second period, it was necessary to concede that the prior policy could no longer be permitted. The [Ministry of] Co-operation was no longer there to implement a policy with individuals. It was there to implement a policy with states to the exclusion of any co-operation having an individualistic characteristic. When one speaks of co-operation with a country, one is not saying to assist a particular farmer, but all farmers. When one says train engineers, one is not saying train Mr X or Mr Y; rather we're saying to the governments that we can give scholarships to study in France to those who wish to pursue those studies. It is not for us to determine the recipient of the scholarship, that is for the countries to do. All of the operations that the Co-operation made were state to state. Similarly for newspapers and publishing, the assistance was for national societies, not for individual editors. Cinema escaped this rule during an experimental period which lasted fifteen years.[7]

Gohy notes that individual aid to African film-makers became the critical weakness of the Bureau. The crux of the issue arose when the technical and financial support provided by the Bureau in exchange for France's cultural products became a liability for France's politics of cultural development. Perhaps not during the early years of the Bureau's operations but by the early 70s the Bureau was becoming a costly political liability. It is clear that in giving assistance to cultural expression the Bureau did not foresee the inevitable conflicts which were going to arise from the its policies.

The lack of foresight did not protect the Bureau from coming under increasing attack – on one side from African film-makers, who as well as condemning the Bureau's non-commercial distribution of their work began pushing for better services and greater financial and technical assistance to enable them to make features; and, on the other side, by the Ministry of Co-operation and some of the African governments for providing support to films which they felt were critical of or detrimental to their respective governments.

That the Bureau of Cinema provided financial and technical assistance to African film-makers in exchange for the non-commercial rights to their films is a well-known fact.[8] What is not so apparent are the criteria used and formulas applied in determining the financial and technical support. In the actual operations of the Bureau there were concrete checks and balances within the administrative process, as well as established procedures for providing technical and financial assistance which were logical and had a bottom-line accountability.

There were two major policy precautions at the Bureau which were used to minimise the economic and, particularly for the Bureau, political risk factors involved in the technical and financial assistance provided to the African film-makers. First, funds for individual projects were rarely released directly to the film-makers; rather, the allocated amount remained within the Bureau and was applied directly to the costs of the technical services, labs, editors and sound mixing of a project which was billed to the Bureau.[9] The second major policy

115

precaution at the Bureau was a strong preference for completed films or works in progress, meaning those which the film-maker had already shot.

Areas of financial and technical assistance have been separated so that different perspectives could be highlighted. In actuality, however, the purchase of the non-commercial rights, the project selection and the assistance package were integrally related. The scenario or project selection was actually very casual, as we shall see from the observations of the editors in the discussion of the technical operations of the Bureau. A major administrative objective (which differs from the political considerations noted earlier) was looking at the work or project to determine if there was a reasonable possibility from a technical perspective that it could be finished. If the assessment made was that the assistance needed was reasonable and within the means of the Bureau, a package was put together and a contract was drawn up between the Bureau of Cinema and the producer, who could be either the film-maker or a third party acting on behalf of the film-maker. The type of assistance package varied: a combination of money or materials and services. The preference at the Bureau was for the latter two provisions.

Though contractual arrangements were made with the African film-makers, the assistance covered only the costs of technical support (salaries of editors, laboratory costs, and so on). It did not include a salary for the African film-makers, which was particularly difficult when they came to Paris to edit. While the film-maker was in Paris, the Bureau would sometimes provide a small daily allowance.[10] It was only in extreme emergencies – either personal or technical – that extra costs associated with travel or reshooting were picked up. Even in those cases, however, those costs were charged to the CAI, which paid the bills.

Although cost overruns in post-production were expected, the Bureau tried to keep overruns from exceeding 50 per cent of the assistance assessed in the original agreement. Yet, even with the Bureau's assistance, only part of the total costs of the project were covered. The Bureau avoided the problems attached to providing up-front funds for the actual productions, preferring to intervene at the stage of the post-production. While this safeguarded the Bureau's investment, it denied the film-maker the production flexibility that an advance cash flow would provide in terms of production stability or predictability. Therefore the film-maker was forced to raise the funds somehow or find the means to get the work filmed.

This strain on the individual film-maker becomes part of the problem in the long-range viability, success and productivity of the Bureau; for the immediate reality of the African cinema, it narrowed the field to those Africans who had either pre-existing access to resources for production, influential friends, or personal resources. The Bureau's administrative procedures for technical and financial assistance in return for non-commercial rights were also somewhat penurious.

Much attention is focused on the point that Debrix and the Bureau paid significantly more for the rights of African films than for the rights to French or foreign films, using as an argument that with African films there was a much greater cultural significance for African audiences of the cinematheques.[11] While a French feature film received what appeared to be a significantly smaller amount for rights at 7,000 or 8,000 francs, the 30,000 figure for non-commercial rights of an African feature at face value is deceptive, since that figure included the cost of the technical services and materials and was actually retained within the Bureau.

To understand the limitation of the system, we must first explain the payment scale for non-commercial rights purchase, and how it was applied to African cinema:

> In the 1967–1968 period 30,000 francs were given for a feature film, 5,000–10,000 francs for a short and 15,000 francs for medium length. A little extra might be added, but that was the base. When assistance was given in the form of materials, the amount was much higher. Most of the time, when the rights of the film were bought and the funds turned over to the film-maker, he had already paid for the film in one way or another.[12]

This basic formula determined the purchase terms for the non-commercial rights of features (90 minutes), mid-length films (under an hour) and shorts (under a half hour). That this policy was followed with some regularity is evident in the contracts between the Bureau of Cinema and the African film-makers which delineated the terms of the assistance and the length of time for which the rights were purchased.

It is difficult to determine the exact total cost of a finished work, particularly the production costs, which would include the donated services and time from resources pulled together by the film-maker. In the rare instances that the film-makers received money – which for the African film-maker was when they delivered or sold a finished film to the Bureau – it only defrayed part of the costs of the production which had been absorbed or paid by the film-maker. The amounts allocated by the Bureau were modest even for that period, and, as Gohy says: 'Even for that period, not that much could be done with 30,000 francs.'[13] A review of the actual allocation and administration of technical and financial resources to films made in Senegal – the most prolific country during this period – illustrates with some specificity major trends and patterns within the Bureau of Cinema and the correlation to the kinds of films produced.

The Bureau of Cinema's Golden Years: 1969–1977

If in the first period between 1961 and 1969, the Bureau's activities leaned more heavily towards the educational, bilateral projects of the CAI. The second period, from 1969 to 1977, is characterised by a steady and consistent increase in the works originated or realised by the young African film-makers through the Bureau of Cinema. In this section, the trends in the types of films assisted will be examined as well as the amounts allocated to the different types of films through the data collected from contracts and other written materials on African films produced through the Bureau of Cinema.

In contrast to the wide range of cinema projects supported by the CAI, the Bureau of Cinema appears to have operated from a much narrower mandate, concentrating on assistance to African film-makers.

The discussion of the Bureau's particular mandate draws on materials on the films produced between 1969 and 1977 in Senegal, the region's most prolific production centre. By no means do the works referred to represent the full total of works produced in Senegal; yet, among the films for which documentation exists as to terms of their technical and financial package, there is a surprising degree of similarity with the package for technical and financial assistance described earlier by Gohy.[14]

Seeing the actual terms of the financial and technical assistance to individual African film-makers in Senegal from 1969 reinforces the notion that, in spite of the ambitiousness of the experiment of African cinema, there was a bottom-line budget accountability for the films which was reinforced by administrative procedures that kept the financial and technical assistance offered within prescribed limits. Beginning in 1969, the cluster of African films produced heralds the most prolific period of African films which are also distinguished by the consistency of the terms and amounts given for financial and technical assistance.

With six notable exceptions – Yves Diagne, Ababacar Samb, Ousmane Sembène, Blaise Senghor, Momar Thiam and Paulin Vieyra – the works of the other thirty-one film-makers listed did not begin before 1969. For those six cited above who were actually producing work before 1969, the means through which they were financed or received technical assistance changed after 1969 only in that the ties and connections were even more highly personalised.

From examination of the contracts for these films, administrative tendencies and historical trends within the Bureau after 1969 become apparent. First, there is clearly a dramatic decrease in the number of CAI-initiated documentaries or projects after 1969, although the CAI continued its long-standing role as the administrative and fiscal regulatory agent for the Ministry of Co-operation. There is a concomitant rise in the work directly with African film-makers coming through the Bureau of Cinema. Yet a more important point is raised. With a few exceptions, if one looks closely at Senegalese cinema, films made by Senegalese film-makers do not really appear before 1969. Additionally, most of those works are short to medium-length films. Assistance from the Bureau for feature-length films by Senegalese did not begin until 1971. Subsequently, one could conclude that over all the years of cinematic activity by the Bureau true cultural expression by African film-makers did not begin until 1969, and that expression did not take the form of feature-length productions until 1971, scarcely six years before the Bureau was phased out in the restructured Ministry of Co-operation.

The financial and technical assistance provided between 1969 and 1977 indicates an apparently consistent, if not stable, administrative and fiscal structure through which clearly established procedures and limits are applied to the allocation of resources to African film-makers in exchange for non-commercial rights to the films. The rate scale and the established assistance package remained consistent throughout the period. However, it is clear that assistance in exchange for non-commercial rights for distribution was primarily provided after production or upon completion of a work. The administrative consistency of this procedure, which applied to the majority of the African films produced in this era, could also be construed to be rigid or inflexible.

Perspectives from the technical staff and personnel – especially the editors who worked at the Bureau of Cinema – provide a rich purview of the processes, problems and obstacles encountered in the period discussed above. Drawing on interviews with technical personnel, issues of post-production operation procedures and training and the implications of that assistance for African cinema, particularly between 1969 and 1977, will be explored.

It's very experimental because there are so many problems which have yet to be tackled. But it is not intentionally experimental. It is a result of circumstance.[15]

This comment by Andrée Daventure, one of the key editors at the Bureau, gracefully and diplomatically addresses the contradictions within the Bureau of Cinema. The Bureau and the work were experimental, in part because of having to grope ahead while carrying the unresolved problems along. Mme Daventure, beginning in 1974, worked extensively on African films through the Bureau, including some of the most internationally acclaimed films in African cinema.

Her perceptions of the Bureau, particularly in the latter years, and those of Bernard Lefèvre and Danièle Tessier, also editors during the early years and mentioned as major figures in the literature on African cinema, form the foundation of a discussion of the internal workings of the Bureau – its early history, ambience and working conditions, experience and training of African film-makers, administrative procedures for employment and technical services, film selection, and finally the problems, obstacles and issues that arise during the editing process.

The editors worked at the Bureau on a freelance basis; they were called in when there was work. As noted by the editors, and Patry, as well as in the documentation, the average editing time allotted for a short film was from three to four weeks. The editors note that there was not a great deal of time to do the work, especially given some of the major technical problems which had to be addressed. The conditions and terms of the editors' work at the Bureau were set by the CAI, which issued their contracts and paid social security contributions. Unlike editors at French production companies, the editors at the Bureau were not paid overtime.[16] This meant that it was often the commitment of the editor to a particular film, project or film-maker that led them to put in hours of time for which they were not compensated. Bureau work was not as a rule the principal employment activity of the editors.

Daventure notes that many of the early African film-makers who came to the Bureau with their work were from administrative or ministerial cadres within their governments. Their attitude to the work was not as committed as that of some of the others such as Souleymane Cissé, Ousmane Sembène or Jean-Pierre Dikongue-Pipa, to name a few of the more ardent African film-makers. Many of the Africans who came to the Bureau during this era would make one or two short films, then forgo further film-making – either because of the extreme hardship or because they were pressed into service by their governments in various ministries and agencies.

Danièle Tessier, another veteran editor of the early years of the Bureau, goes even further in detailing the major limitations in the film-makers' preparation that she encountered:

Each case was different, but generally, it was like this. Those who brought their materials to the Bureau were people just getting started, and they had no idea how to make a film.

There were problems in structuring the films, connecting the sequences and even the shots. Often the film was really difficult to recover because it didn't make any sense. It's like taking hundreds of photographs and trying to assemble them... Further, the shots were often very short because the means for filming were not there.[17]

The issue really is not just the lack of training or professional experience; it is readily apparent that for many African film-makers this was their debut. What is really striking is Mme Tessier's professional assessment of what those constraints imposed by lack of training translate into in the film-making process, which is totally distinct from analysis of the aesthetics of a given work. She cites difficulties in basic film construction, ordering sequences or even the shots themselves. If the film-maker had only a vague idea of how to put the pieces together before the production, it becomes excruciatingly difficult in post-production to make sense out of the work. What she touches on is an important cognitive distinction for film-making: being able to make a transition – intellectually and aesthetically – from thinking that a film is made from a series of snapshots to being able to integrate the visuals into a realisable and coherent whole. One of the pivotal components in constructing a film is the ability to integrate the narrative structure with the visual elements. Some broader questions on the differing perspective between the African film-makers and the (European) editors – particularly in language and the integration of language with the visual elements of film – will be discussed later. However, it is difficult to pursue, except in the broadest sense, some of the cognitive and aesthetic issues touched on in Tessier's observations, because of some of the real and concrete obstacles and problems created by the training and the technical problems in African cinema to which we now turn.

Although film-making is a very individualistic process, as Tessier indicates, and varies from situation to situation, the actual process is made more difficult because the production means and materials were often lacking, resulting in not having enough material to edit or the shots being too short to use, which is one of the endemic problems which plagued African cinema during those years.

Daventure basically concurs with Tessier's assessment, but emphasises that the Bureau experience actually was an important vehicle for the training and education of the African film-makers:

> ... work began at 9.30 a.m. and continued until 3 a.m. The film-maker couldn't go straight from beginning to end, if it was a film with many problems, a long film with difficulties with *mise-en-scène* or technical problems. It was very difficult. Then you had to talk to Monsieur Debrix... It was necessary to do the work, to edit the film, in order to complete the film-maker's training. A great deal of money could not be spent on a film which would never be sent out. Training would cost more money than editing a film, and training programmes are very expensive. Therefore, we edited the work with the view of finishing a project – so that the film-maker could draw as many lessons as possible from the process.[18]

Although Daventure echoes the frustration of Tessier, she raises several key additional points. First, how problems were resolved within the Bureau, particularly addressing a film or work that was almost uneditable, or even with the greatest amount of effort ended up with discernible technical flaws. The resolution would be to complete the work so that the film-maker could learn, or draw as much as possible from the experience, which made the process more of a teaching and training programme.

Actually, the professional French production houses wouldn't touch most of the work that came into the Bureau and would say point blank: 'Listen, it's not professional enough, and we have no time to waste.'[19] Many of the problems, however, were beyond the control of the African film-makers, or in fact were exacerbated by the milieu through which they were exposed to professional training. The film training on the newsreels was really very weak, yet many of the young Senegalese film-makers received a great deal of their professional experience and exposure from working on the newsreels. As Lefèvre notes, the newsreels were basically short minute-and-a-half segments, with maybe 20 to 30 seconds per subject, which is read voice-over a visual of a flag or something similar – very sketchy – yet that was the extent of newsreel production.[20] Of course, there were film-makers such as Vieyra, Sembène, Cissé, Mahama Johnson Traoré, Mustapha Alassane and others who received professional film training either in France or elsewhere, but they were the exception, not the norm.

From discussions with the editors and administrators, it appears that the review of work occurred on a relatively ad hoc basis. Debrix would, of course, be the first person consulted, along with Patry, who was his technical consultant, and they assessed the work. According to Daventure, Debrix always said that one never said no to an African film.[21] Of course, Debrix's rejection of Sembène's work is a cause célèbre in African cinema; however, from material available at this time, there is no way to determine if there were other situations like Sembène's that occurred at the Bureau. Technically, Debrix, as head of the Bureau (which was part of the Ministry of Co-operation and therefore directly accountable to the Director of Cultural Affairs), had to submit work to his superior for approval. But that was not normally the case because, in general, if Debrix approved of a work, the Director went along with it.[22] The Sembène case aside, the process really appears to have been rather informal.

Patry indicates that he, Debrix and Gohy met as the need dictated, read the scenario, if there was one, and proceeded accordingly.[23] It appears, however, that formal presentations of a written scenario, or treatment, were the exception rather than the norm. Film-makers would turn up with work in all stages of production – rushes (film just shot and developed) for a whole film, or part of a film, with or without complete sound. It was a very eclectic process.

Lefèvre's recollections indicate an even more laissez-faire process. He would come to the Bureau, meet the film-maker who had some film, look at it, and then the film-maker would indicate what he wanted to do, and as Lefèvre simply states, 'We would go to the editing table and the boy [garçon] would explain what he wanted and I would help him.'[24] Ideally, as Lefèvre suggests, the film-maker directs the editor. One could speculate on whether Lefèvre's appellation 'garçon' is a familiar or pejorative title for the film-makers. In either case, and particularly the latter, it becomes one of the many complex dynamics and interrelationships between the key personnel – the film-maker and the editor. Ideally, the editing process reflects a balance between points of view, either similar or opposing. Depending on how equally matched and compatible the team is, there is a certain amount of give and take in editorial decision making, but there is also a balance of power. If the team is imbalanced it is possible for the resulting work to reflect the strengths or preferences of the stronger element. Personal editorial preferences aside, the actual state of African production exacerbated any normal working post-production relationship.

The undercapitalised state of African film production, however, resulted in major irregularities and disruptions in normal working relationships, such as that between the editor and the film-maker, as well as the problems which ensued from having materials from the original production which often did not meet minimum audio or visual specifications. It is worth reiterating a major point discussed earlier – the administrative and financial preference of the Bureau to intervene in African films after production was started and, ideally, completed. The consequence of this was that a disproportionate amount of attention, effort and resources of the Bureau at the post-production stage were directed at rectifying technical problems, some of which could have been avoided with adequate production funds and/or better equipped and better trained personnel. This piecemeal production process precipitated a chain reaction that affected every subsequent stage of production. We now turn to concrete examples of acclaimed Bureau of Cinema successes and challenges.

As indicated earlier, the Bureau was unable to pick up extra expenses. Although the CAI would step in, it was done only in extraordinary situations, as we shall see, such as with Dikongue-Pipa's *Muna Moto* (1979). The result was that the post-production was a very choppy, discontinuous process. Although three or four weeks was the norm allotted to editing a work, the reality was that the editing process stretched over a much longer period and was not continuous. Considerations such as loss of concentration and continuity created by such interruptions, as well as the cost factors involved in doing pick-up shooting or audio work, often placed the film-maker in the untenable position of having to use what he had, in spite of obvious flaws, errors or omissions.[25]

Editing was more difficult because of the low budget for the productions, which meant in many cases that all the pieces necessary for going smoothly into post-production editing were lacking. Very often camera reports, basically a listing or log of the shots and sequences taken on each roll, were lacking. Often the sound was not synchronised to the picture.[26] Poor camera reports doubled the work for the editor: he or she would have to spend a great deal of time with the film-maker viewing, reviewing and determining exactly what material there was.[27]

Besides the lack of required support material to do a really smooth professional editing job, Tessier adds: 'It was really film for reporting – it was more that than directing. It did not have the vision of a director, except in certain cases.'[28] Beyond the fact that film-makers often did not or could not provide adequate material to realise a technically coherent and logical film, Tessier touches a more amorphous issue, the conceptualisation process, or vision of the total work, which really transcends the rudimentary mechanics of process and editing. Some of the African film-makers who were highly regarded for their acumen in this area by Tessier and others included Oumarou Ganda, Dikongue-Pipa, Souleymane Cissé, Djim M. Kola, Daniel Kamwa, Ousmane

122

Sembène and Désiré Ecaré. Across the board, comments were made about these film-makers' incredible memory, skill and vision, by which they were able to overcome or compensate for tremendous production obstacles.

Perhaps the crux of the editing process, particularly in regard to African cinema, revolves around the issues and problems of technically dealing with African languages – the translation, the editing and the differing perceptions of use of language between the film-makers and the editors. All editors concur on the significance of this component and present their insights on how they approached the process in general, or, in the case of Daventure, the historic saving of the film *Muna Moto*.

The Camerounian film-maker Dikongue-Pipa's film *Muna Moto* encountered a full range of problems created by an underfinanced production. First, he had no money to pay his crew, and he fished for their food. He had a small camera, and black-and-white film. The audio equipment fell and broke, leaving him with sound for only a third of the film. To compound the problems, part of the film when processed was unusable because it was fogged, which happens when old film stock is used. When he presented the work at the Bureau, Daventure was called in to look at it because the consensus was that it was not salvage-able. However, she felt it was and indicated as much. Subsequently, Dikongue-Pipa was given more film to go back and re-shoot and to re-record the audio. This is an instance where the CAI assumed the costs associated with doing the pick-up work (including the air fares) of a film.

The issue of language in *Muna Moto* was complicated by the fact that, first, only a third of the original sound was recorded; six months later, Dikongue-Pipa had to re-record the sound of the silent part absolutely verbatim so that it would match with the film which had already been shot, as well as the ad-ditional pick-up work. This required an incredibly lucid recall, given that there was no written scenario.

He and the editor, Daventure, cut the audio in word by word. It was such an exact job that it is almost impossible to tell that it was shot and edited sep-arately. However, the cost in labour was tremendous. Daventure notes that she worked up to eleven hours a day on the film, while her contract with the CAI only paid for eight hours.[29] *Muna Moto* is now recognised as one of the most acclaimed African films.

Tessier indicates the difficulty in editing African languages, which also touches on the different cultural perceptions between the editor and the film-maker, and the difficulty and strain in coming to a common understanding and in finding a technical and effective way of translating the work:

The translation of [Oumarou] Ganda's films was one of the interesting things I had worked on with him ... A great deal of attention was devoted to the translation. Once the film had been edited, he gave me, word by word, what the people were saying in the shots. And it was really word for word. Besides causing many problems between us, it became exhausting for him. He couldn't translate word for word because a thought was so different, or a manner of expression so different, that he had many difficulties translating word for word for me. From then on, we tried constructing phrases in French which best expressed the African thought, keeping as much of the colour of the African language as possible, for the most realistic impression on film of

123

African life ... which reflected the best possible perspective ... and the thought.[30]

Tessier notes the difficulty of trying to translate the film literally word for word. It was inordinately draining for Ganda, and they disagreed on how to proceed. They found it more effective to build phrases in French, which preserved with more integrity the African thought as well as the colour of the language.

Lefèvre had a different approach, which really reflects his editing style. First, as with Daventure and Tessier, he notes that he rarely had any support materials from the production or even a single piece of paper, with notable exceptions, one of them being Djim Kola of Upper Volta.[31] Interestingly, his approach was to look at the rushes and visually see how the film played, the reactions between subject A and subject B, and what the best takes were. As he told the film-maker: 'I know that you wrote your script differently, but look at the film. That way you can really see and understand what you shot.'[32] Basically, his preference, which is a standard one, is to look at the visuals to determine the strengths of the material actually shot. He explains very nicely the internal thought process engaged when looking at film. An editor absorbs the sensations of the images and the sounds, and the plan is really a reference point, but not the critical tool for the initial assessment. He reads the script or the plan afterwards. Of course, it is ultimately up to the film-maker to decide; however, the critical interaction and rapport between the film-maker and the editor are essential.

The preference of francophone African film-makers for dialogue clashed with Lefèvre's sense of cinema:

I often reproached those young people, for their cinema was a cinema of dialogue; for me cinema is not dialogue – cinema is images. Really! But for them it was dialogue. Even Sembène. I believe that dialogue is part of the African *mentalité*.[33]

Lefèvre touches on a critical asethetic difference which goes beyond the technical translation of African languages into French, into the cognitive, traditional variables which determine communication and language. One could argue that the preference of the African film-makers for dialogue indicated by Lefèvre is in fact part of the reality of oral traditions and the significance accorded to the historical recording and transmission of information orally.

By delineating specific technical limitations created during production and the ensuing problems in post-production editing, Tessier and Lefèvre's comments open the way to look beyond the technical shortcomings to broader issues of cognitive, or cultural and aesthetic differences between the perspectives of the European film professionals and the African film-makers. The issue of aesthetic perspective – African or European – is a central issue in the ongoing debates in the critical analysis of Third Cinema in general and African cinema in particular. The question of an African aesthetic, both in terms of definition and context for analysis, continues to be a critical issue in the scholarship on African cinema.

Tessier and Lefèvre's methods of approaching editing reflect both their training and their individual aesthetic preferences in regard to assessing material and building the structure of a particular film. Aside from those individual preferences, Tessier's, Lefèvre's and also Daventure's observations all overlap in noting – to a greater or lesser degree – the difference between them and the African film-maker in the integration of language or narrative structure with the visual image. Although their insights do not conclusively separate a Eurocentric aesthetic from an African aesthetic, it appears that a significant difference, aesthetic if not cultural, between the European film professionals and the African hinges on the struggle between them in the integration of the narrative structure with the visual elements of the film. This is over and beyond the technical impediments detailed by Tessier, Lefèvre, Daventure and others.

Given the eclectic, unpredictable and underfinanced state of much of African cinema, the technical obstacles must be identified before it is possible to continue to some of the broader issues and questions raised by the editors' observations. The perception of the editor provides a different but by no means conclusive insight into the operations and obstacles faced by African cinema and film-makers within the Bureau of Cinema. What is clear is that low budgets, underfinanced productions and poor training made the post-production process an arduous undertaking. The non-commercial work environment of the Bureau did not contribute to a more qualitative, technically refined product. Not paying overtime meant that work that might need to be done – particularly given the difficulty of production – would not get done, unless it was an instance where an editor was committed to a project. In his very frank manner, Lefèvre wonders aloud if there ever really was a plan to develop African cinema: 'I had the impression that much more could have been done, but the means were not provided; and that France really did not have a great interest in developing African cinema.[34]

The limitations notwithstanding, the Bureau did fill a niche during the era. There is validity in Debrix's often quoted observation that African film-makers were particularly prolific between 1963 and 1975, and that 80 per cent of the films produced were done with Bureau assistance. This claim is corroborated by Gohy, who indicates that there was a concomitant and consistent increase in the budget allocated to the Bureau between 1963 and 1974. The budget increase each year during this period reflected the overall importance accorded by the state to the cultural aspects of development.

After 1974 the budget allocation to African cinema began to taper off, followed by a sharp decline which ended in 1980 when the Bureau ceased to exist as a separate entity under the restructured Ministry of Co-operation. Although cinema was still supported, it was not concentrated on individual film-makers; rather, it was transferred to regional efforts and initiatives in francophone Africa.

Conclusion

Although forceful political and ideological pressure was brought to bear on the Ministry of Co-operation and its Bureau of Cinema from Africa and France against the assistance to African cinema, the material dependence of African cinema at the end of the era under consideration was as great as at the beginning. Was France's assistance through the Ministry of Co-operation neocolonialist or paternalistic? Or, to return to a query from Guy Hennebelle: 'Why did France concern itself with the birth of African cinema?'[35]

As noted by many of the editors, the Bureau served as an on-the-job training programme where the emphasis was on the educational experience accruing to the African film-maker rather than on the commercial viability of the final product. Although there was a shift in support by the Ministry of Co-operation from the educational documentaries of the CAI between 1961 and 1969 to an emphasis on individual assistance to African film-makers at the Bureau of Cinema between 1969 and 1977, the objective remained the same – a continuation of Franco-African cultural hegemony, no more, no less.

Pressure on the French government and the Ministry of Co-operation by the African film-makers, particularly after the creation in 1969 of FEPACI, and aggressive lobbying efforts for more assistance to African film-makers and access to the lucrative commercial market for their films, as well as internal ministerial criticism, forced the French to re-evaluate the policies towards cinema in particular and the overall co-operative programmes of the Ministry of Co-operation.

Some interesting perspectives do emerge about cognitive and aesthetic differences between the Africans and the European technical personnel. A major ongoing effort in Third Cinema in general and African cinema in particular is the identification and definition of a structure for critical analysis which is not Eurocentric in origin. As scholars have begun to look increasingly to traditional African oral narrative structures, the roots of this direction in critical inquiry can perhaps also be traced back to some conflicts or differences that resulted from the various interactions between the African film-makers and the French technical personnel regarding matters of aesthetics, film language and narrative structure.

In the area of cinema, at least, it appears that *de jure* independence for the African states in 1960 did not bring economic, technical and cultural independence from France. Instead it appears that the colonial practice of assimilation was rearticulated, reappearing under the guise of *cultural expression*.

Notes

1. Consortium Audiovisuel International Final Report, 10 May 1979.
2. Guy Hennebelle, 'Entretien avec Jean-René Debrix', *L'Afrique litteraire et artistique*, no. 43, 1977, pp. 77–89.
3. The literature on francophone African cinema widely acknowledges the anomalous and irregular characteristics of African cinema, and the lack of economic or technical infrastructures necessary for a self-sufficient or autonomous industry. Yet the scholarship of the era emphasises the ideological and political movements within Third World cinema in general and African cinema in particular. Although both scholars and film-makers acknowledge and deplore the material dependence of African cinema on France, and recognise the lack of extensive research on production, those needs – either in material autonomy or the gaps in the scholarship on production and the means of production – have not been met. For a fuller discussion of the scholarship and literature on this period of African cinema, see Claire Andrade-Watkins, 'Francophone African Cinema: French Financial and Technical Assistance 1961 to 1977', unpublished dissertation, Boston University, 1989, pp. 41–100.
4. Lucien Patry, Paris, unpubished interview, 9 July 1987.
5. Ibid
6. Ibid.
7. Lucien Gohy, Paris, unpublished interview, 16 July 1987.
8. Paulin Vieyra, *Le Cinéma au Sénégal* (Belgium: Organisation Catholique Internationale du Cinéma et de l'Audiovisuel, 1988), p. 38.
9. Gohy, interview 1987.

10. Ibid.
11. Roy Armes, *Third World Film-Making and the West* (Berkeley: University of California Press, 1987) p. 223; Gohy, interview 1987.
12. Gohy, interview 1987.
13. Ibid.
14. The films produced in Senegal before 1969 were few and far between and were evidence of a wide-ranging financial base for the means of realising production: *Grand Magal à Touba* (Blaise Senghor) 35mm 20/21 minutes, *Marche de gré à gré*, no. 73, 18 June 1962, CNC/UCINA and Les Films Pierre Remont – 10,000 (new francs) for rights (Foreign Ministry and Ministry of Co-operation); *Sarzan* (Momar Thiam), *Marche de gré a gré*, no. 27, 1 March 1965, rights for 8 years (29 minutes, 35mm) – 5,000F; *Les Chemins de l'Afrique* (Delou Thiossane), Yves Diagnes/Lovichi, Actualités Françaises, *March de gré à gré*, no. 11, 22 February 1966.
15. Andrée Daventure, unpublished interview, Paris, 25 August 1987.
16. Unpublished interviews with Gohy, Patry and Daventure, Paris, 1987.
17. Danièle Tessier, unpublished interview, Paris, 28 August 1987.
18. Daventure, Paris, 1987.
19. Ibid.
20. Bernard Lefèvre, Paris, 1987.
21. Daventure, Paris, 1987.
22. Ibid.
23. Patry, Paris, 1987.
24. Lefèvre, Paris, 1987.
25. Ibid.
26. Patry, Paris, 1987.
27. Daventure, Paris, 1987.
28. Tessier, Paris, 1987.
29. Daventure, Paris, 1987.
30. Tessier, Paris, 1987.
31. Lefèvre, Paris, 1987.
32. Ibid.
33. Ibid.
34. Ibid.
35. Guy Hennebelle, unpublished interview, Paris, 13 July 1987.

State Initiatives and Encouragement in the Development of National Cinema: Mozambique

CAMILLO DE SOUZA

Reprinted from Keith Shiri (ed.), *Africa at the Pictures* (London: National Film Theatre, BFI, 1990).

Images of Mozambique appeared in the Portuguese cinema from the early 1940s. Portugal began to make films in an attempt to legitimise its colonial role at a time when the first signs were detectable of the effervescence that was to lead to the Afro-Asian conferences, crucial in the broad process of decolonisation of Africa. It was the signal for the production of a series of documentaries by teams coming from Portugal for the purpose, or by Portuguese settlers in Mozambique. These documentaries were highly propagandist and had the primary aim of illustrating the justness of colonialism's 'civilising mission'.

The first newsreels of the 1950s came within a similar ideological perspective although (latterly) with a clearly commercial aim. The common aspect of all these documentaries was the settler's point of view: how he perceived Mozambique. No attempt was made to portray Mozambican reality or how its particular social and cultural character could be distinguished. Nor was any attempt made by the producers of these images to go deeply into the geographical context, except for its curiosity value. Hence the 'Negro' and 'traditional African society' were also portrayed as something exotic and hidebound by folklore.

Along with capitalist penetration in the 1960s the commerical side saw expansion. Advertising films were made, and under South African influence some features ventured into the field of pornography, giving rise to low-quality films. At the same time, film clubs active in the cities of Lourenço Marques and Beira played a part in the anticolonial movement. One consequence was the growth of amateur cinema on 8mm stock, marked by a more studious and honest search for Mozambican reality, but still within the Portuguese perspective of Mozambique. In the same context came the first 16mm productions, including some feature material, most of which was severely cut or banned by Portuguse colonial censorship.

These well-meaning efforts fell far short of showing Mozambicans their own reflection. A hunger for identity and identification by their authors, mostly born in Mozambique and therefore considered second-class Portuguese, led them only as far as formulae of 'good neighbourliness' and 'possible understanding' between the settler and the 'native'. The 'Negro' appeared on the screen to illustrate these notions. The fundamental causes of social stratification were never tackled. Colonialism was never questioned, and its full impact never considered.

128

But by then the national liberation struggle was already opening up new cultural scope. As more and more areas were liberated from cultural domination, this scope also widened. A culture that had been deliberately forgotten and pushed aside began to re-emerge. The scope became wide open when national independence was proclaimed in 1975. It was the culmination of a cultural movement that could then take firm root in a land where interchange of various manifestations of this culture became a matter of course. Each manifestation could play its full part in the search for identity in a young and complex nation.

Clearly the cinema was important in the process. The first cultural action by the Mozambican government after independence was to establish the National Cinema Service, with the dual role of ensuring distribution of films – even to parts of the country where cinema was hitherto unknown – and of producing an image of Mozambique.

I shall give an illustration of the nature of the task that included the establishment of a new coding of images appropriate to Mozambican cultural reality.

In the early years of independence, Mozambique's Ministry of Health included in its environmental health policy a priority concern for the building of latrines in the suburbs and in the countryside. It launched a publicity campaign that included a poster using a diagonal red cross over practices to be avoided. Follow-up surveys showed that these were precisely the examples that were followed, as the red cross had been interpreted as an indication of what should be done. The response was almost spontaneous: reality lay between eye and hand, and sensibility and knowledge was deployed to dig deep for what it could bring of novelty, grandeur and vivacity.

There was intense day-to-day activity of a political, social and cultural character. Its manifestations must be brought to the whole country. Newsreel was the answer. None of the Mozambican languages had a word for this, as the very idea of cinema was restricted to large-scale commercial output, often of gratuitous violence, shown in the colonial era. That was cinema; that was the Western stereotype the public in the large towns were used to swallowing whole.

In contrast to this model and on the principle that the genuine image of Mozambique had still to emerge and would emerge from a close liaison between the new film-maker and the new reality, it was decided to call the Mozambican newsreel *Kuxa Kanema*, meaning the birth of the image.

The newsreel was produced on a weekly basis and soon became familiar throughout the country, even in places where mobile cinema was introducing the medium for the first time. The expression 'Kuxa Kanema' was adopted by nearly all the Mozambican vernaculars to mean any kind of documentary, and became the Mozambican expression for the moving image. The spontaneity was the incentive for a movement that gave rise to what we might call Mozambican cinema. It was the enthusiastic discovery of a new country and the essential pre-condition for this new kind of cinema.

It was not enough, however, to meet the needs of a growing market for exhibition. Nor could it meet the information needs of a country where only 6 per cent could read and write in a population speaking dozens of languages with distinct structural forms. Along with radio, cinema was the only means of communication that reached every part of the country.

129

All these factors contributed to the classic concept of 'Cinema – A Cultural Weapon' and enhanced its role in the prevailing social and political context. It was time to transform it into an industry capable of meeting the needs. Hence the reorganisation of the National Cinema Institute. New methods of planning and control were introduced, equipment upgraded, retraining and training provided for technicians.

Film distribution for enlightenment rather than pure gain still provided enough income to keep the infrastructure operational and to finance the local currency costs of the production sector. A period of gradual and significant growth followed when film production was at its highest rate and where in addition to the *Kuxa Kunema* newsreels, documentaries of the most varied kinds were produced and technical and aesthetic values were outstanding. The process of enlightenment over several years bore fruit. The spectator had been exposed to all genres of films, and was familiar with foreign and domestic production. The spectator was no longer satisfied with seeing the country portrayed only in documentaries. A combination of major international films and the great tradition of popular storytelling engendered a wish to see feature treatment of everyday life.

In the same way the arrival of colour television in the capital meant that films in black-and-white were not enough. There was a demand for colour production, not only from the public but also from the international film market. Human resources were available but faced serious bottlenecks. At the very moment when an advance seemed possible, and the Mozambican state would within a few years have the financial means to invest in a new system of film production, the war in Mozambique escalated alarmingly. Terror was almost constant and hunger widespread; more than half the population displaced and agriculture (the vital source of the country's earnings) was brought to a virtual standstill. The consequence was that a promising economy fell into crisis and all the state's resources were channelled to emergency needs.

This explains why a policy of a co-production was adopted in 1985 for feature films, which have been made at the rate of one a year. With the exception of José Cardoso's *O Vento sopra do norte* (*The Wind Blows from the North*, 1987), made in black-and-white by the National Cinema Institute as sole producer, all the feature films have been produced under this system of co-participation from various countries, namely Yugoslavia, Austria and France, and various official and unofficial bodies.

The National Cinema Institute has provided most of the equipment, nearly all the technicians and all the local currency production costs. The co-producer has financed the purchase of film stock, laboratory processing and the engineering of the soundtrack. The practice has proved viable, although it has some disadvantages in regard to the screenplay of the film, as there are always two distinct perceptions addressing one reality.

Mozambican cinema has a strongly patriotic component, but it also draws on its inherent links with other peoples and other countries, especially with those who are closest in geography, history, politics and culture. We have sought to integrate our cinema in the regional context. It was soon seen that the link was not only possible but also inevitable for the development of the various filmographies of southern Africa. It was brought out in the first co-production between Mozambique, Angola and Zimbabwe of the film *Pamberi ne Zimbabwe*

(*Let's Fight for Zimbabwe*, Jono Costa, 1981). It was followed by a series of agreements on production and distribution of films through reciprocal use of national infrastructure between Tanzania, Angola, Mozambique and Zimbabwe.

Of all these intitatives the most significant is undoubtedly the preparation under way for a Frontline States Cinema Festival to be held in Zimbabwe's capital, Harare.[1] The holding of a film festival in southern Africa is a reflection of the need to extend regional co-operation into culture as reinforcement of the economic co-operation launched by the Southern African Development Coordination Conference (SADCC) action programme. In conjunction with the festival, a workshop is proposed to examine such matters as co-production in the region, regional distribution of the region's films, international sales, exchange of equipment and personnel in the film industries of the SADCC countries and the establishment of a regional vocational training institute or centre. As well as providing a showcase for films, the festival will highlight the struggle against apartheid, a recurring theme of many of the films and the shadow under which they were made.[2]

I have tried to point to the effort being made to develop cinema in our country and in the other states of southern Africa; and the vital role of regional co-operation. It is the only path we can follow in a region devastated by a war that is forced upon us. It is the way forward for the effort we began at independence to transform colonial models into something that answered our needs. Step by step we shape a cinema that is our own in the new situation, in a process that is already national and increasingly regional. We seek the co-operation of all film-making bodies, not only in our own continent of Africa, but also above all from the most technologically advanced countries.

Notes
1. The First Frontline Film Festival and Workshop was held in Zimbabwe, 15–21 July 1990.
2. See Final Communiqué, pp. 31–4, above.

Portuguese African Cinema: Historical and Contemporary Perspectives 1969–1993

CLAIRE ANDRADE-WATKINS

Reprinted from *Research in African Literatures*, vol. 26 no. 3, Fall 1995.

Introduction

The history of film production in sub-Saharan Africa, and of films by African film-makers in general, must be considered in the context of an acute shortage of technical and financial resources, as well as a lack of viable circuits of distribution and exhibition. These difficulties, in turn, have been compounded by colonial and post-colonial traditions and policies regarding cinema: first, cinema targeted for Africans during the colonial period, where it existed, was integrally linked to administrative, military, religious, or educational objectives; second, post-colonial film policies (either European or African), and film-makers' initiatives aimed at ameliorating colonial conditions have not led to an economically viable and stable film industry in the region.

A major stumbling-block continues to be the bottleneck created by European and American conglomerates who own and operate the lucrative distribution mechanisms for cinema throughout Africa. For these companies, the continent is merely a commercial market, a dumping-ground for foreign films of dubious merit. The continued lack of control by Africans and their governments over the distribution process means that revenues are being drained from the continent, rather than redirected to building and supporting cinema production and its related industries.[1]

Given this scenario, the context of film production and distribution – specifically, the manner in which financial and technical structures of film production have had a major impact on the ideological perspective, form, content, and purpose of cinema in post-colonial Africa – assumes added significance in the history of cinema in Africa. Historically, the dominance of francophone Africa in film production was due in large measure to France's two-pronged post-colonial film policy. Financial and technical assistance was provided to African governments for production newsreels and documentaries, and to aspiring African film-makers to explore and expand their 'cultural expression in film'.[2] Technical facilities, however, were not created within Africa, perpetuating the need for African governments and film-makers to go to Paris to complete the film production process. This underdevelopment was arguably tied to the primary purpose of France's post-colonial aid to its former colonies: a continuation of cultural, linguistic, and economic dependency on France.

Mozambique, on the other hand, insisted on merging ideology with form and content, pioneering a successful model of 'guerrilla' cinema that embraced a

132

Marxist conception of the engagement between film and society. More important, the film industry was nationalised, so that infrastructures of production, distribution and exhibition were created and supported by a government that viewed cinema as a vital force in post-colonial development and education. Mozambique and the other Portuguese colonies spread around the continent – Angola, Cape Verde, Guinea-Bissau, Sao Tome and Principe – shared the legacy of a harsh and impoverished colonial reign. Galvanised by the revolutionary movement for independence, a distinguished vanguard of senior African statesmen and revolutionaries – Agostinho Neto in Angola, Eduardo Mondlane followed by Samora Machel in Mozambique, and Amilcar Cabral in Cape Verde and Guinea-Bissau – provided the intellectual, political, and ideological leadership that challenged, fought, and overturned colonial rule throughout Africa.

Conceived ideologically and thematically in the spirit of the liberation struggle against the Portuguese during the 1960s and the 1970s, films from lusophone countries – particularly Mozambique and Angola – comprise an important chapter in the history of African cinema in general and the genre of 'guerrilla', or liberation cinema in particular. For the purposes of this study, the period of liberation cinema begins in 1969 with 'Towards a Third Cinema', a pivotal manifesto written by Argentinian film-makers Octavio Gettino and Fernando Solanas. The subsequent development of 'guerrilla', or liberation cinema in Mozambique during the 60s and 70s is examined in the context of film production in sub-Saharan Africa, and the study concludes with the transition in Mozambique in the late 1980s from state to private-sector production, international co-productions, and financing. The discussion of change in Mozambique and Portuguese-speaking Africa is placed in the wider context of film production in sub-Saharan Africa, while the historic and contemporary participation of Cape Verde, Angola, and Guinea-Bissau is also highlighted.

The Origins and Development of Liberation Cinema, 1969–1978

The 1960s witnessed an explosion in cinema that cut a swath through the 'Third World. Fuelled by the Argentinian film-makers Gettino and Solanas's pivotal 1969 manifesto 'Towards a Third Cinema', and further encouraged by leaders of African independence movements, waves of revolutionary ideology swept across Latin America and Africa, leaving in their wake a cinema that confronted dominant historical, colonial, cultural and ideological norms in society and cinema. Latin America, Cuba, North Africa and French-speaking and Portuguese-speaking Africa – especially Mozambique – became major centres for the theoretical and practical development of cinema. Only Ghana in English-speaking Africa and Guinea Conakry in French-speaking Africa came close to the production potential of post-independent Mozambique. The government of Guinea Conakry shared Mozambique's commitment to a functional and educational Third Cinema, going so far as to nationalise part of the distribution and exhibition film sectors in the country.[3] However, the British had no interest in the post-colonial development of cinema, although a colonial legacy of documentary traditions in English-speaking Africa is visible in the strong television and government networks in Ghana and Nigeria.[4] While Ghana inherited full 16mm and 35mm capabilities from John Grierson's Colonial Film Unit, the government unfortunately neither espoused the

133

ideological significance of cinema nor entertained the vision of Ghana becoming a regional centre for production.[5]

In contrast, vestiges of colonial cinema were extremely faint in Portuguese-speaking Africa.[6] In the decade preceding independence from the Portuguese – 1974 for Guinea-Bissau and 1975 for the other colonies – film production was galvanised by two revolutionary forces. The first was an internal, newly awakened sense of unity, purpose and collaboration among the colonies, and the second was external support from the international community for the revolutionary war efforts and governments that included FRELIMO (Frente de Libertaçao de Mozambique, 1962); the MPLA (Movimento Popular de Libertaçao de Angola, 1965); and the PAIGC (Partido Africano Pela Independencia de Guinea e Cape Verde, 1956).[7]

Both forces – the African liberation movements and their foreign supporters – viewed cinema as a powerful force in the liberation struggle and a vital component in the documentation, education and dissemination of information about the war. Consequently, films produced both informed the international community of the armed struggle against the Portuguese and contributed internal information and education and cultural programming for the African populations.

The revolutionary governments of Mozambique and Angola, the most active centres for film production, supported landmark films made by pioneering film-makers in the nascent African cinema. Sarah Maldoror was a major contributor to both the cinema emerging from within the lusophone region and the revolutionary cinema of the era. Maldoror received her training in Moscow and became a long-time supporter of the independence struggle. *Sambizanga* (1972), her first feature-length film, was also the first and thus far only fiction film devoted to the liberation struggle in Angola.[8] The film's story-line was based on the Angolan novelist Luandino Vieira's *The Real Life of Domingos Xavier* and adapted to the screen by Marion de Andrade. Set in the 60s during the war for independence from the Portuguese, the narrative follows Maria in her search through the prisons of the capital for her husband, an organiser for the MPLA independence movement. The film celebrates the comrade and his wife's sacrifice and loss while exhorting supporters to continue the struggle. The last line of dialogue is a call to arms for 4 February 1961, the day hundreds of Africans attacked the police and military in Luanda and launched the armed struggle in Angola. This ending clearly reflects the political tone, theme and focus of films made during this period.

Prior to filming *Sambizanga*, Maldoror directed a short film of 18 minutes, entitled *Monangambee*. Filmed in 1970 and financed by the Comité de Coordination des Organisations Nationalistes des Colonies Portugaises, *Monangambee* illustrates the total lack of understanding between Portuguese and Africans through a dramatic confrontation between an African prisoner, whose comment about a national dish made during a visit by his wife is totally misconstrued by the Portuguese officer, who orders the prisoner beaten. While not distinguished by its cinematic quality, this production reaffirms the themes of revolutionary struggle.

Films made by an eminent group of international film-makers and activists from countries as diverse as France, Sweden, Yugoslavia and Cuba comprise the second, congruent movement of revolutionary cinema. Efforts from the United

States were spearheaded by the Afro-American Robert Van Lierop, a lawyer turned film-maker. These films chronicled the struggle against Portuguese domination, and were shown extensively abroad, resulting in a ground swell of international support for the liberation struggle.[9]

Neither Cape Verde nor Guinea-Bissau were engaged in production. Rather, growing political and revolutionary stirrings against Portuguese colonialism were felt in the Cape Verde islands, a tiny archipelago of drought-stricken islands lying 200 nautical miles off the coast of Senegal. A modest yet significant intellectual movement stimulated by the cinematic and revolutionary ideals of the period began as early as the late 1950s.

Cape Verdean intellectuals studying at the lycée on the island of Sao Vicente were profoundly affected by the fervour radiating from the intellectuals and young revolutionary leaders studying in Lisbon, as well as the Negritude writers like Léopold Senghor, and Aimé Césaire, pan-Africanists like W. E. B. DuBois, and Afro-American literary giants such as Richard Wright, author of *Native Son*. Imbued with the spirit of African nationalism through books clandestinely brought into Cape Verde from Senegal, the young intellectuals of the 50s were closely attuned to the activities on mainland Africa and throughout the diaspora. Encouraged by the emergence of leftist protest in Lisbon against the fascist government of Antonio Oliveira Salazar, a small group of Cape Verdean intellectuals formed a cine-club in the capital city of Praia, on the island of Sao Tiago, following the example of the cine-clubs in Lisbon that served as forums for intellectual dialogue, debate and artistic exhibitions.[10]

The first meeting of the cine-club was held in 1960 at the Cine-teatro Municipal da Praia. Open to the public, this cultural programme featured Cape Verdean poetry. Plans were made to develop and continue a range of cultural programming, including cinema, music and poetry. A list of possible films was proposed for future exhibitions, although the only concrete activity in cinema was a regular radio commentary, presented by the president of the cine-club, on social and cultural issues raised in commercial films being shown at the theatres.[11] However, by April 1961, the PIDE (Policia Internacional de Defesa do Estado, the Portuguese political police), fearing collusion or support for anticolonial revolutionary movements, brought the activities of the fledgling cine-club to a halt with the arrest and imprisonment of two leaders of the association, Anastacio Filinto Correia e Silva and Alcides Barros, and the deportation of others from Sao Tiago.[12] No further efforts were made to revitalise the cine-club until independence.

Immediately following the coup in Lisbon, Portugal, which overthrew the fascist government of Salazar, colonial rule ended in 1974 for Guinea-Bissau with a defiant, unilateral declaration of independence. Angola, Mozambique, Cape Verde, Sao Tome and Principe followed suit in 1975. Independence coincided with the crowning moment of cinematic endeavour in lusophone Africa: the creation of the Institute of Cinema in Mozambique. The architect of that reality was a legend in the history of world cinema, Ruy Guerra.

A Mozambican by birth, Guerra was the leading figure in Brazil's Cinema Novo movement. His return to Mozambique after independence to head the Institute of Cinema was a major factor in the cultural ascendance of Mozambique in southern Africa, sub-Saharan Africa, and the lusophone diaspora.

This early national period of cinematic activity was a time of experimentation in the form and direction taken for cinema and television in Africa – a harbinger of subsequent developments in lusophone Africa. In a rare convergence of ego and talent, progenitors of three major movements – Ruy Guerra (Cinéma Novo), Jean Rouch (cinéma vérité) and Jean-Luc Godard (*nouvelle vague*) – converged on Mozambique in 1978. The Institute had invited Rouch to explore the possibilities of super-8mm film, and Godard had a contract with the government to do a study about the possibilities for television and video in Mozambique.[13] The connection between the critical and even acrimonious interactions among these cinematic giants and the forces that shaped the formal, social and technical development of Mozambique's cinema illuminates a dilemma intrinsic to African cinema in general, and merits a digression in the narrative of the region.

The experimental phase of Mozambican cinema was preceded by the postcolonial initiative in cinema launched by France. While lacking the revolutionary fervour of Portuguese-speaking Africa, the French shared a spirit of adventure and experimentation and were optimistic about the prospects of cinema within Africa. In 1961, France created the Ministry of Co-operation with the express purpose of providing financial and technical assistance to her former colonies. The Bureau of Cinema, created within the Ministry in 1963 under the direction of Jean-René Debrix, provided technical and financial assistance to Africans to foster cultural expression through cinema, allowing Africans from francophone Africa to launch the embryonic movement of sub-Saharan African cinema.

In retrospect, African cinema as envisaged by Debrix through the Bureau of Cinema was flawed, if not doomed, from the outset. Government bureaucracy hampered rapid deployment of resources or technical support. Administrative and operational procedures imposed by the Ministry on the Bureau were unwieldy, impractical, and ill suited for production. For example, instead of a lab order taking one call in a non-governmental production centre, technicians at the Bureau had to wait days for the processing of a request for the same service through the Ministry.[14]

The French film professionals looked askance at the Bureau, viewing the whole operation as unprofessional and financially and technically inadequate. The inability of the Ministry to provide effective and appropriate administrative mechanisms for production exacerbated increasing tensions between the film-makers and the Bureau, on one hand, and the upper echelons of the Ministry and African governments on the other over a range of issues involving the films, their content, form and distribution.[15]

Jean Rouch, a pioneering ethnographer and film-maker, and a controversial figure in African cinema, clashed both with African film-makers and with Debrix on techniques and themes. Rouch and the African film-makers had distinctly different philosophies: he dreamed small, 8mm or 16mm, and the Africans dreamed large, 35mm format, the standard for professional, commercial cinema.[16] Rouch was reproached by the film-makers for trying to institutionalise a level of technical underdevelopment by advocating the use of the small formats. In Rouch's view, however, the 35mm format was neither pragmatic nor cost-efficient and the Africans' emphasis on it amounted to a mystification of technology, where 'the tripod was the beginning of a temple, an altar'.[17] In Rouch's capacity as Director of Research at the Centre National de Recherches Scientifiques in Paris, he was involved in innovative experiments with the super-8mm format, which he applied to the 1978 experimental pilot project in Mozambique, supported in part by France's Ministry of Co-operation. Rouch believed that super-8mm was an expedient, cost-effective format which would help developing countries catch up with the more technologically advanced countries. Furthermore, Rouch felt that the super-8mm format demystified the process of film-making and was a format that was accessible for use by more people since the cameras and editing equipment were cheaper, lighter, and smaller than 16mm or 35mm.[18]

While Rouch argued for super-8mm, Godard, on the other hand, was fascinated with the possibilities of video and television, and the creation of the images for that medium. For both men, Mozambique was in some ways a laboratory – an opportunity to identify or select the tools of production to build and shape a national cinema and television. Neither Rouch nor Godard's experiments came to fruition. Both were perceived as too costly and were cancelled.[19] Although unproductive, these efforts in Mozambique revealed the ideological and theoretical implications of production methods and technological choices. Had either Rouch or Godard's vision been sustained, the unique convergence of Marxism with viable structures of production, distribution and exhibition achieved under Guerra's direction might never have occurred. While Godard and Rouch were arguing the merits of their vision for Mozambique, Guerra was actually realising his vision in the documentary, educational and feature film projects launched at the Institute of Cinema. Closely modelled after Cuba's acclaimed ICAIC (the Cuban Institute of Cinematographic Art and Industry) where many of the Mozambican personnel were trained, Mozambique's Institute of Cinema became the most powerful centre of politically engaged and economically innovative indigenous cinema on the continent of Africa.

These differing perceptions among the Europeans, on the one hand, and the Africans, on the other, also underscored a wider struggle in post-colonial Africa between indigenous cultural, political and economic autonomy and neocolonial control. In this instance, the locus of the struggle was the context of production. Guerra's success ensured that the Institute of Cinema produced a viable, prolific, engaged cinema – integrally connected to the issues and realities of achieving military, psychological, educational and cultural independence in Mozambique in particular, and southern Africa in general. In short, the effective and triumphant creation of a functional 'guerrilla', or liberation, cinema.

Transition from Revolutionary to Free Market Film Production, 1978–1991
Cinema production in Mozambique after 1976 was on the ascendant, due in large measure to the activity of the Institute of Cinema. Launched in 1975 and officially established in 1976 by the revolutionary government of Samora Machel, the Institute of Cinema was the first cultural institution to be set up after independence. By 1978, an ambitious and sustained vision was created in Mozambique that addressed the cultural, educational, and informational needs of a people engaged in armed struggle and a socialist reconstruction of society and government.

137

Despite the internal battles with the South African-backed opposition forces of RENAMO, the Mozambique government continued to support the Institute and its efforts to articulate, document, educate and disseminate cogent and germane films about the crisis in the region and the ongoing destabilisation efforts by South Africa against the Marxist governments in Mozambique and Angola. In Angola, on the other hand, film production after independence dropped off markedly – the result of non-existent production infrastructures and ongoing internecine warfare between the Marxist MPLA and the opposing FNLA and UNITA factions.

The Angolan Sarah Maldoror, a pioneering film-maker of the previous decade, continued to produce within the intraregional lusophone community, making two short films in 1979 for the government of Cape Verde, *Fogo, l'Ile de feu*, a profile of the environment and culture of the island of Fogo, and *Un Carnaval dans le Sahel*, which includes feast-day celebrations and a PAIGC rally.[20]

Unlike Mozambique, Angola, which lies parallel to Mozambique on Africa's west coast, never developed a national centre or infrastructure for cinema. However, television was established in 1975, and after independence senior Angolan film-makers, including Ruy Duarte de Carvalho and Antonio Ole, produced many documentaries for that medium. Portuguese by birth and Angolan by declaration, Duarte produced five sections of *Sou Angolano trabalho com força*, a major eleven-part 1975 documentary series on the workforce. He collaborated on this series with Ole, who went on to make *Apprendre pour mieux servir* (1976), *Le Rythme du N'Gola Ritmos* (1977), and *Pathway to the Stars* (1980). Although Duarte produced mostly for television, he also produced the feature film *Nelista* in 1982, an elegantly crafted film based on two tales from south-eastern Angola. *Nelista* is the story of two families escaping from a great famine and their efforts to overcome their situation. Nelista, the hero of the film, fights against evil spirits and, with the help of animals and his friends, delivers his people.[21]

Television (TNCV) came to Cape Verde after independence in 1974, including productions by local film-makers on the stories and folklore of their islands. Independence also brought a revival of the cine-club movement and renewed participation in the dialogue of the nascent African cinema. On 7 May 1975, the Cineclub Popular de Praia was established, including many of the members of the earlier thwarted cine movement of the late 50s and early 60s. The objectives of the cine-club, as delineated in their former charter, stressed the support of the cine-club for cinema and TV as vehicles for informing the population about current and foreign events through documentaries, encouraging active participation in national history, contributing to national arts, popular culture, the education of the population – politically and socially – as well as for creating a national cinema.[22]

Supported and encouraged by the PAIGC, the club resumed the exhibition of films which were rented through the cine-clubs in Lisbon, and then shown on a weekly basis. Fortunately, the artistic films were much cheaper to rent than the commercial ones, giving the members of the cine-club exposure to many different genres, ranging from Italian neo-realism and American classics to Cuban, Brazilian and Japanese films. Picking up the slack from the new revolutionary government, which was busy organising the first elections and facilitating other critical transitions of independence, the cine-club organised the filming of the first elections and other independence activities. This highly visible, informed and engaged community of intellectuals was committed to the development of cinema and television in Cape Verde and helped disseminate a wider vision of cinematic development throughout mainland Africa.

A delegation from the cine-club in Cape Verde joined representatives from nine other revolutionary African countries for a historic meeting in Maputo, Mozambique, between 21 and 24 February 1977, when the Conferencia Africana de Cooperação Cinematografica, or Association Africaine de Coopération Cinématographique (AACC) was formed. The primary objective was to displace the foreign distribution monopoly and create regional, intra-African circuits of distribution for cinema. This initiative failed, due in large measure to a lack of political commitment by the majority of the participating countries.[23] During these halcyon days, the Institute in Mozambique was already recognised as the centre for cinema, as evidenced by their convening and hosting this ambitious but flawed attempt to address the distribution problems within the continent. Fortunately, the internal successes of the Institute were more tangible and long-lived.

The Institute was empowered by its mission and mandate to restructure all sectors of cinema, including distribution, exhibition and production. The Institute grew to include a lab, a cinematheque and a training programme. Additionally, the significance accorded to cinema in the revolutionary process was apparent in the Institute's allocation of resources and manpower. During the peak years of the Institute, from 1976 to 1986, three shifts worked twenty-four hours a day to produce, process and edit the newsreels, documentaries and, eventually, dramatic productions distributed within Mozambique and abroad.[24] Films such as the African-American film-maker Robert Van Lierop's O Povo organizado (1976), a documentary on the challenges facing the reconstruction and development of the newly independent country, helped foster continued support for Mozambique and bolstered the high international visibility of the fledgling Institute.[25]

The jewel in the crown of the Institute was the Kuxa Kanema. Conceived in 1981, this project was created to answer specific needs of the population for information about the country, and it provided the first step in the technical training of the staff of the Institute. As the major centre for documentary production, Kuxa Kanema produced 395 weekly editions, 119 short documentaries and 13 long documentary and/or dramas before the decline and ultimate collapse of the Institute in 1990.[26]

The military engagement with South Africa, the corrosive influence of the West, internal criticism of Mozambican political structures, the battles against illiteracy, disease and poverty, historical and cultural self-determination – these were the themes that dominated the productions of the Institute.[27] As a result, Mozambique's ability to quickly respond, reflect, document, produce and disseminate documentaries and programmes on current events established the country as the ombudsman of the region. Vertically integrated infrastructures of production, a cadre of trained personnel and the Institute's innovative horizontal systems of distribution and exhibition (which included mobile cinema units reaching out to rural areas and urban audiences with little or no previous exposure to cinema) were the marks of a self-sustaining, healthy national cinema, capable of recouping its production costs through distribution and exhibition. In short, inspired by the vision of an ideologically engaged, alternative cinema with appropriate vehicles of distribution and exhibition and the development of trained African technicians, the ultimate objectives of the Institute were achieved. Mozambique, already assured a leadership role in the cinematic development of the region, was poised to become the model for the future of African cinema.[28]

That vision, however, was not to be realised. The revolutionary transformation of the 1960s and 1970s reversed direction in the 1980s. No longer were the ideological demands of liberation struggles the determining force in the form, content and purpose of cinema. A series of external and internal crises accelerated the decline of the Institute and the future prospects of cinema from Portuguese-speaking Africa. First, the assassination of Amilcar Cabral in 1973 and the death of Samora Machel in 1986 weakened the ideological, intellectual and political leadership of lusophone Africa. Second, the unity of the lusophone community began to fray after the split in 1980 of the PAIGC (the political party under which Guinea-Bissau and Cape Verde fought for independence) into two separate parties: the PAICV for Cape Verde, and the PAIGC remaining in Guinea-Bissau. Third, independence for Angola and Mozambique from the Portuguese provided a pyrrhic victory – a lull before the plunge into protracted internal guerrilla warfare and the destablising manoeuvres of what was Rhodesia and of South Africa.

Activity and production at the Institute began to taper off, especially after the death of Machel in 1986. However, before its demise, four major large-scale productions were realised between 1986 and 1991. Zdravko Velimrovic's *Time of the Leopards* (1987), a Yugoslavia/Mozambique/Zimbabwe 90-minute feature co-production, recounts a fictional episode in the armed struggle for the liberation of Mozambique. The primary action of the film takes place during the turbulent early 1970s when the war-weariness of the Portuguese was apparent, and victory was imminent. The story unfolds in the northern plateau's rich and protective cover for guerrilla fighters. A hunt is organised for Pedro, the commander of a FRELIMO detachment, whose courageous actions begin to worry the Portuguese military in the area. Pedro becomes the object of a manhunt, is captured and killed. His memory inspires the new generation, who continue the struggle and attack the barracks where Pedro had been imprisoned.

Jose Cardoso's *O Vento sopra do norte* (*The Wind Blows from the North*, 1987), a 16mm 90-minute feature, opens in the north of Mozambique in 1968, where the liberation was has been going on for four years. Colonial settlers, unable to comprehend the reality of the slaves' revolt, exhibit an arrogant boldness along with a sense of uncertainty. Rumours of the changes sweeping through the rest of the country create widespread terror and guilt among the colonialists, who fear the vengeance of the Blacks, *mainatos*, coming to reclaim the land taken from them five centuries earlier.

The third film, *Borders of Blood* by Mario Borgneth, a 16mm colour 90-minute documentary, was shot in 1985 and completed in 1986. This feature film examines South Africa's destabilisation tactics and subsequent impact on Mozambique's reconstruction. Finally, *Devil's Harvest*, a 1988 Institute of Cinema co-production with France, Belgium, Channel Four in England and Denmark, directed by the Brazilian Licinio Azevedo and Brigitte Bagnol from France, weaves fiction and fact to tell the story of a drought-stricken

Mozambican village which is defended by five veterans of the war for independence who struggle against the daily menace of harassment by bandits hidden in the surrounding forest. These productions illustrate the capacity of the Institute to produce feature-length fiction and documentary films while incorporating the themes of armed struggle, regional destabilisation, internal cultural and historical change and post-colonial turmoil. Ironically, the Institute halted at the peak of its financial and technical capability to produce, distribute and exhibit politically and ideologically engaged cinema. Unfortunately, instead of being harbingers of a powerful voice within the region and of African cinema in general, these films were public symbols of the end of an era.

The death-knell for the Institute was an electrical fire on 12 February 1991. The Institute and its technical facilities were badly damaged; the film equipment depot, sound studio, editing rooms, and processing labs were destroyed. As a result, all documentary production halted, training of personnel ceased and distribution ground to a halt, since all the prints were destroyed in the fire.[29] This devastating loss, compounded by the death of President Samora Machel, changes of leadership within the Institute, the economic toll of protracted internal guerrilla warfare and the declining support and influence of Marxist regimes for Mozambique, effectively brought a close to the fifteen-year history of the Film Institute.

Private Sector Production, 1991–1993

The democratic changes sweeping through Africa in the late 1980s were accelerated by the crumbling of the Soviet and Eastern bloc's ideological and financial support to Marxist governments. The ascension of a conservative, Western-leaning government in 1990 in Cape Verde and movements toward negotiated peace settlements with Angola and Mozambique in 1991 and 1992 presage subsequent changes in cinema. In Mozambique the bureaucratic and administrative transition from state-controlled production to a free market was already under way, as evidenced by numerous seminars held on 'the democratisation of television' for film and television producers. The changes became more concrete after the fire in 1991.

The subsequent shift in Mozambique was both geopolitical and economic. Mozambique's geographical, political and economic relationship within the southern African region superseded to a large degree the earlier cultural and political links with the wider lusophone community. The regional realignment of Mozambique with Angola, Botswana, Lesotho, Namibia, South Africa, Swaziland, Zambia and Zimbabwe, however, creates new challenges, exacerbated by diverse historical, political and cultural experiences and differing expectations and traditions for cinema and television.[30]

Hypothetically, the financial and technical potential for regional film production, backed by the resources of a stable South Africa, are enormous. Producers from the region are collaborating on a range of ventures, including the production in 1992 of *The Southern Africa Film Television and Video Yearbook and Catalogue*, which lists the regional production companies and films available for distribution. Economically, Mozambique is increasingly linked to the international, competitive, commercial film marketplace. Close on the heels of the Partenariat in 1989 and 1991, four privately owned production companies emerged in Mozambique. A leading force is Ebano Multimedia Lda, an independent production and distribution company established in 1991 by experienced film professionals, including many senior producers and administrators from the former Institute of Cinema. Ebano is the first of the private companies to venture into feature film production with *The Child from the South*, a 1991 co-production with Channel Four in England. Set in war-torn Maputo, Nadia, a South African woman journalist, meets a committed but weary Mozambican doctor. The elegant contemporary love story addresses Nadia's feelings of loss and alienation created by her forced exile as a child from South Africa. *Marracuene*, a 43-minute 1991 Ebano co-production with German television (ZDF) and Channel Four in England, is a dramatic documentary about a village situated in a heavy war zone. Once a bustling stop on the railway line, the village has become a veritable shadow. Every night, the remaining villagers flee to the other side of the river to avoid the terror of nightly raids, returning the next morning to the sight of devastated homes and businesses.[31]

Both films – *The Child from the South* and *Marracuene* – modify the treatment of the prevalent war theme of the earlier didactic/revolutionary films of the regions, and are stories that appeal to non-African television audiences. In *The Child from the South* especially, war becomes a backdrop for an intense personal drama. *Marracuene*, while actually set in the village, includes stylised visual cut-aways and dramatised personal accounts of the nightly sieges. Arguably, in both instances, forces of international financing and marketing have resulted in shifts in content and form. A similar trend to lighter, or stylised, touches is also apparent in contemporary Angolan productions.

A North/South co-production between Belgium and Angola yielded *Mopiopio* a 52-minute documentary on music and everyday life in Angola made in 1990 by Angolan-born Zeze Gamboa, a veteran of Angolan television. Another recent Angolan co-production between Italian and Portuguese television is *Moia – O recado das Ilhas*, a 1989 35mm feature film by the veteran Angola producer Ruy Duarte de Carvalho. A poetic drama, taking place in both the present and an eighteenth-century set adapted from Shakespeare's *The Tempest*, *Moia* is the story of an Angolan woman of Cape Verdean descent whose return to Cape Verde forces her to confront and question her existence and identity as someone who is neither totally European nor African. Always strong in television, Angola remains relatively quiescent in film production. Unlike Mozambique, Angola did not develop production facilities. Furthermore, the uneasy peace in the country inhibits further television production or wider participation in regional activities. However, interest and hope remain strong among Angolan film-makers for their future participation.

In West Africa, Guinea-Bissau, the tiny mainland neighbour of the Cape Verde islands, has emerged as a major presence in African cinema. The 1989 film *Mortu nega* catapulted the native-born director Flora Gomes and Guinea-Bissau to international acclaim. The narration is focused through the eyes of Dominga, the wife of a guerrilla fighter, and the viewer witnesses the commitment, tenacity and will for independence that sustains the morale of the soldiers. Dominga follows her husband through the bush as he and his unit engage the Portuguese in unequally matched warfare, providing encouragement, love and unswerving support to her husband and friends. Unparalleled in its drama and realism, *Mortu nega* offers an unprecedented and distinct dramatic and highly realistic portrayal of the high human cost of the war against the Portuguese.

Produced solely by the government of Guinea-Bissau, *Mortu nega* affirms the priority of cinema in the country's development plans. Although there are six film-makers in the country at the moment, the National Centre of Cinema is collaborating with the Ministry of Education and the government to improve commercial importation and exhibition in the country; produce and co-produce films by Guinea-Bissau film-makers; and train personnel for all levels of film production. To reinforce these goals, film-maker trainees are attached to all productions occurring in Guinea-Bissau.

Flora Gomes's second feature, *The Blue Eyes of Yonta* (1991), again brought critical acclaim to the director and his country. The government of Guinea-Bissau participated in the production, along with the Institute of Cinema in Portugal, Vermedia Productions, and Portuguese television. Set in the capital city of Bissau after the war, the film involves a beautiful girl, Yonta, who falls in love with a war hero. He never learns of her infatuation, nor in turn does Yonta recognise the passion that a young man from the waterfront, Ze, harbours for her. More important, the film shows a post-war reality for Guinea-Bissau, its people, and their sense of loss, psychological displacement, love, conviction, and hope for the future.

The contemporary movement in Guinea-Bissau is similar to the former Institute of Cinema in Mozambique in the effort to develop stories germane to the historical and political reality of the people of Guinea-Bissau. Similarly, Guinea-Bissau's National Centre of Cinema and the government are developing strong production, distribution and exhibition structures. The key difference between the contemporary initiatives of Guinea-Bissau and the former Institute of Cinema in Mozambique is the shifting focus from Soviet bloc financing to free market economies, international financing, and/or collaborations.

International television is an increasingly important production partner in African cinema. The credits for *The Blue Eyes of Yonta* include Portuguese and English Channel Four television as well as the Institute of Cinema in Portugal. The experienced Lisbon-based producer Paulo de Sousa and his company, Vermedia, have been instrumental in securing international financing for film-makers from the nascent lusophone sector. Vermedia produced *Yonta* and served in the same capacity for the 1993 production of *Ilheu de contenda*, the feature debut of the Cape Verdean director Leao Lopes. Based on a novel by the noted Cape Verdean author Teixeira de Sousa, the story takes place in the 1960s on the island of Fogo. Two brothers, united to settle a family estate, struggle with conflicting values and perspectives on emigration and Cape Verdean identity, dominant themes in Cape Verdean literature, history and culture. Financing for the production was raised from advance television sales and the Institute of Cinema in Portugal. The experience gained in the location shooting of *Yonta* in Guinea-Bissau and now Cape Verde establishes Vermedia as a leading production partner in Portuguese-speaking Africa.

Cape Verde is an increasingly popular location for feature film productions, a development encouraged by the revitalised Cape Verdean Institute of Cinema. Founded in 1977, the primary function of the Institute was the distribution and exhibition of foreign films. Since 1988, under the direction of Daniel Spencer Brito, the Institute has been successfully broadening its scope to attract foreign productions and train local personnel. Prior to 1988, most productions in Cape Verde were documentaries produced or co-produced for Cape Verdean television. Brito is cautiously optimistic about the future of cinema by and for Cape Verde. He hopes to bring more African films to the screens in Cape Verdean. Language, however, presents a daunting challenge for both production and distribution. Portuguese is the administrative language; Cape Verdean, however, is the spoken language of the people, the music and the literature. Furthermore, it varies from island to island, creating difficulties for the local distribution of indigenously produced films as well as imported films.[32]

It is clear that Portuguese-speaking Africa – Mozambique, Angola, Cape Verde, and Guinea-Bissau – is in step with changing trends and influences in the production and distribution of cinema in sub-Saharan Africa. How their participation affects, modifies, changes, or encourages the development of African cinema remains to be seen.

Conclusion

Mozambique in particular and lusophone Africa in general represent a small but vital contribution to the extant history of sub-Saharan and world cinema. This unique purview has contextualised the instrumental if not pivotal role of Mozambique and lusophone Africa within historic movements and events that shaped these first decades of African cinema. More specifically, the strongest influences on cinema in Portuguese-speaking Africa between 1969 and 1975 were: the internal and external movements and productions in support of liberation struggles; the launching of the Institute of Cinema in Mozambique; and broad issues and debates within African cinema – as evinced by the experimental period with Rouch and Godard of the Bureau of Cinema.

Without question, the pinnacle of the cinematic achievement of lusophone Africa was the Institute of Cinema. Prior to its demise and destruction in 1991, the Institute had evolved into a mature, successful production centre combining theory, practice and implementation – a monument, a testament and, finally, a solitary beacon of sub-Saharan Africa's revolutionary cinema. Historically, the Institute symbolised the optimism, euphoria and expectations for cinema throughout the lusophone diaspora in the years immediately following independence where early initiatives such as internal and foreign lusophone collaborations or the cine-club movement in Cape Verde continued, or in the case of the Institute of Cinema, flourished. Those dreams died, in large measure because of the constant instability of film production and distribution in sub-Saharan Africa.

Lusophone film-makers are today joined in a common, competitive pursuit of a global audience. As southern Africa begins to pull together under the aegis of democratisation, the lusophone producers in the region, Mozambique and Angola, prepare to re-enter the global film market on a new footing. The nascent commercial sector is expanding with private production companies developing projects and exploring co-production and collaborative ventures with other African countries and Europe. Cape Verde and Guinea-Bissau are also part of this scenario. In short, film-makers from the sector are employing increasingly sophisticated marketing and economic strategies to meet the growing demands of an increasingly appreciative international audience. Always susceptible to shifting external and internal political and economic trends, sub-

Saharan African cinema is a microcosm, or barometer, of the shifting priorities in sociopolitical, historical, ideological and economic trends occurring within a broader, continent-wide context. As indicated in the three areas of this study – liberation cinema, the transition from state to free market production, and private sector productions – each shift brought new directions, trends, themes, and participants in African cinema.

Although the 1990s have brought increased visibility and acclaim to African cinema, the sector moves towards the future like the sankofa bird from Akan mythology that flies ahead while looking to the past. African cinema marches backwards into the future, searching for an aesthetically, economically and culturally 'liberated' voice, while shackled to a past and present encumbered by perennial problems in distribution, exhibition, and financing.

Notes

1. Some African countries have successfully nationalised their film sector completely or in part. However, the lack of inter- and intra-regional co-ordination impedes the possibility of creating comprehensive, alternative, continent-wide distribution circuits, creating a void that exceeds the capabilities of individual African states in general or film-makers in particular.
2. The argument advanced in my 'France's Bureau of Cinema' (pp. 112–27, above) is that the cinematic development supported by the French in the newly independent French-speaking West African countries was undercapitalised, creating a neocolonial economic and technical dependence on France that reinforced colonial policies of assimilation through French language, culture and finance.
3. While capable of 16mm production, the 35mm facilities were never completed, and the lack of laboratory processing facilities made them dependent on technical supports in Europe. Furthermore, the unmitigated anger unleashed by de Gaulle and France at Guinea Conakry's dramatic declaration of independence in 1958 resulted in a brutal economic and political backlash that hobbled Guinea Conakry's potential in all sectors.
4. Ghana has the most sophisticated 16mm and 35mm facilities and laboratories in West Africa. Unfortunately, it has never been fully and effectively used within Ghana or for the rest of sub-Saharan Africa. The Bantu Educational Cinema Experiment (1937–9) and the British Film Unit (1939–45) were, in the first instance, short-lived programmes aimed at rural education of the Africans and, in the second, propaganda films to mobilise Africans to fight during the Second World War. Other noted ventures in colonial cinema include films made by Catholic missionaries in the Belgian Congo's Congolese Centre for Catholic Action Cinema (CCAC). Finally, in French Conakry Guinea, Sily Cinema was created in 1958 and made documentary and education films and newsreels. Basic 16mm production was established, but 35mm facilities remained incomplete.
5. Anglophone Africa has pioneering film-makers in African cinema, including the Nigerian Ola Balogun, the Ghanaians Kwaw Ansah, King Ampaw, Kwate Nii Owoo, and others. However, although they might receive some government assistance, most of the work is produced in the private sector. As noted earlier, dramatic and documentary television programming to date is the main activity in anglophone Africa.
6. Clyde Taylor, 'Film Reborn in Mozambique', *Jumpcut*, vol. 28, 1983, pp. 30–1.
7. See Lars Rudebeek, *Guinea-Bissau: A Study of Political Mobilisation* (Uppsala: Scandinavian Institute of African Studies, 1974); Hilary Anderson, *Mozambique – A War against the People* (New York: St Martin's, 1992); Daniel Kempton, *Soviet Strategy towards Southern Africa* (New York: Praeger, 1989); Barry Munslow, *Mozambique: The Revolution and its Origins* (New York: Longman, 1983).
8. Guy Hennebelle, *Guide des films anti-impérialistes* (Paris: Centre d'Information sur les Luttes Anti-Impérialistes (CILA), 1975), p. 110.
9. See Hennebelle, *Guide des films*. Maldoror also made two short films after independence for the government of the Republic of Cape Verde in 1979, *Fogo, l'Ile de feu* and *Un Carnaval dans le Sahel*.
10. Anastacio Filinto Correia e Silva, interview, Sao Tiago, 22 August 1993.
11. Ibid.

12. Ibid.
13. See Manthia Diawara, *African Cinema* (Bloomington: Indiana University Press, 1992), p. 97.
14. Andrée Daventure, interview, Paris 9 and 10 August 1987.
15. For a fuller discussion of this issue see Andrade-Watkins, 'France's Bureau of Cinema'. For Mozambique, films include: *Viva Frelimo* (1969, Dutch), a report on Frelimo and an interview with Samora Machel; *A Luta continua* (1971, American), by Robert Van Lierop, on Frelimo with historical analysis of the country; *Dans notre pays les balles commencent à fleurir* (Sweden); *Etudier, produire, combattre*, a film on a Frelimo school in Tanzania; *No pincha* (1971, Guinea-Bissau), 70-minute documentary on PIAGC; *Madina boe* (1968, Cuba); *Nostra terra* (1966); *Labanta negro* (1966, Italy); *Le Cancer de la trahison, Une nation est née* (1974, Sweden); *Free People in Portuguese Guinea* (1970, Sweden).
16. This is despite the fact that the productions through the Bureau of Cinema were 16mm, an issue which became a source of contention between the film-makers and the Bureau.
17. Jean Rouch, unpublished interview.
18. See 'Jean Rouch, un griot gaulois', in *CinemaAction*, vol. 17, 1981, special issue ed. by René Predal, pp. 20–36.
19. Television came to Mozambique in 1979 without any particular benefit of Godard's participation.
20. See Françoise Pfaff, *Twenty-five Black African Filmmakers* (Westport, Conn.: Greenwood Press, 1988), p. 212.
21. Duarte's films include, chronologically: *Sou Angolana, trabalho com força* (1975), a five-part documentary; *Uma Festa para viver* (1976, TV); *Angola 76 e a vez da voz do povo* – three documentaries for TV (1977); a 1977 feature film, *Faz la coragem, camarada*; *Presente angolano, temp mumuila* (ten-part documentary series, 1979, TV); *O Balanco do tempo na cena de Angola* (documentary, 1982); *Nelista*, feature (1982); *Moia – O recado das ilhas*, feature (1989).
22. In late 1976–7 the cine-club of Praia suspended its activities. Lack of financial support and internal struggles over direction of the cine-club contributed to its demise.
23. See 'Estuato', document of the Cineclub Popular de Praia, May 1975, 'B.O.' 19, 10 May 1975.
24 Pedro Pimenta, interviewed New York, 11 November 1992.
25. For example, the first major benefit in the US for the Institute was a historic national tour in 1981, organised by Positive Productions, Inc., in Washington DC, and spearheaded by the Ethiopian film-maker Haile Gerima. The success of that tour resulted in the purchase of an optical printer and other materials for the Institute of Cinema. Gerima, an early supporter of the Institute, contributed his films to the library and archives of the Institute and encouraged other film-makers to do likewise. Haile Gerima, interviewed 21 January 1993.
26. Pedro Pimenta, letter to author, 27 January 1993.
27. Early landmark films of the Institute include: *They Dare Cross Our Borders* (1981, BW 25 min., 16 or 35mm), on South Africa's attacks on Mozambique and the reaction of the government and people; *The Offensive* (1980, BW, 30 min., 16mm), an internal offensive against inefficiency and incompetence; and *Unity in Feast* (1980, colour, 10 min., 16mm), a film on Mozambican culture, with a particular objective of valorising and preserving the rich traditions scorned by colonialism. A prime example of regional collaboration is the documentary *Let's Fight for Zimbabwe* (1981, 60 min.), a documentary, co-produced by Mozambique and Angola, dealing with Zimbabwe's independence and with questions about the political stability and future of the region. The first feature-length documentary was *These Are the Weapons* (1979, BW, 50 min., 16mm), a chronicle of the fight for independence, the internal struggles facing the people of Mozambique, and South Africa's strategies of disruption. Bringing the touch of Cinema Novo to Mozambique, Ruy Guerra's *MUEDA: Memorial and Massacre* (1979, BW, 35mm) was the first feature by a Mozambican; it is a blend of theatre and reality. A small village in northern Mozambique, Mueda, was decimated by a massacre by the Portuguese in 1960. The theatre play, created in 1968, is an annual re-enactment staged by the survivors to commemorate the massacre.
28. Although Angola had a National Film Institute and shared the commitment of Mozambique, their lack of infrastructures limited their production capabilities to collaborations or co-productions. A growing cadre of trained African technicians and administrators such as Pedro Pimenta, who joined the Institute in 1976, found their way to the

Institute. As the Assistant Director/General Production Manager of the Institute, Pimenta played a pivotal role in the emergence of Mozambique. Born in the Central African Republic, he studied Economics in Portugal and taught in Maputo before joining the National Film Institute.

29. Pedro Pimenta, fax to Rod Stoneman at Channel Four Television, London, February 1991.
30. Some films were caught in the transition from the Institute to the free market sector. Two young Mozambican film-makers, Joao Ribeiro and Jose Passe, were finishing their film training in Cuba during the upheavals at the Institute. Ribeiro's *Fogata* (1992, 20 min., 16mm) is a drama based on a novel by the Mozambican writer Mia Couto, in which a peasant couple struggles with assuring each other's proper burial. Passe's *Solidao* (1991, 30 min., 16 mm) is a drama set on the eve of independence and revolves round the despair of a white Portuguese settler over his marriage to a Black woman, and the subsequent inevitable changes coming with independence.
31. Jean-Pierre Garcia and Caroline Helburg, 'Cinéma et télévision au Mozambique, rencontre avec Pedro Pimenta', *Le Film africain*, vol. 9, 1993, pp. 11–12.
32. Jean-Pierre Garcia, 'Le cinéma au Cap-Vert', *Le Film africain*, vol. 12, 1993, pp. 24–5; Daniel S. Brito, interviewed 12 August 1993.

African Films are Foreigners in their Own Countries

EMMANUEL SAMA

Reprinted from *Ecrans d'Afrique*, no. 4, 2nd quarter, 1993.

From the wholesale plunder carried out by the colonial distribution companies to nationalisation, from the invasion of the American majors to the monopoly of the CFAA, via numerous national experiences, this is the adventurous story of film distribution in Africa.

African film-makers are desperate: they continue to face problems regarding production and distribution. Production conditions are often so derisory that the acrobatics they have to perform to finish shooting a film deserve any number of medals. But of what value is the finished product if it has no circuit for distribution? African films are foreigners in their own countries; they are making a bashful entry in exactly the same way as a stranger entering another land. The irresponsibility of governments towards culture, and the cinema in particular, is an addition to the burden of the colonial past.

In 1966 Tahar Chériaa wrote: 'Those who control distribution control the cinema.' Some countries in the African continent have tried to control distribution but the general observation is that we are far from mastering it. Import and distribution are still under the authority of yesterday's masters who have been ruling over the same 'evening classes' virtually ever since the invention of the cinema by the Lumière brothers in 1895.

In the same year, the city of Algiers applauded *L'Arroseur arrosé*, which was shown in 1897 at the Royal Palace in Fez, Morocco. Travelling cinemas began to prosper on the continent and very soon the Compagnie Marocaine du Cinéma Commercial (COMACICO) was set up. *L'Arroseur arrosé* was shown in Dakar, the capital of French West Africa, in 1900 and twenty-six years later Comacico was established there. And, ever since, Africa has been under the deluge of films coming from abroad.

Game Reserves

The Balkanisation of Africa has its effects in all fields. Thus, in the cinema, from the colonial period onwards the masters remained such in their area of domination – until the 1960s, when the American majors took the continent by assault. We will deal in greater detail with the French-speaking countries due to the relative advance they have over the English-speaking countries on the level of both production and distribution in relation to the policies of their respective colonisers. The British, apart from educational documentaries, did not

148

place great importance on the cinema. The best example is that of the giant Nigeria with its 100 million inhabitants. Today film distribution in Nigeria is in the hands of foreign companies (from the USA and the Lebanon). Since American, English and Indian films are economically advantageous to distributors, their policy has been to discourage any attempts at national film production.

In the particular case of French West Africa, the two main importing and distribution companies were COMACICO and SECMA (Société d'Exploitation Cinématographique Africaine). In actual fact, these represented two companies based in Monaco, IMPORTEX and COGECI (Compagnie Générale Cinématographique), with the aim of getting round French taxation. IMPORTEX supplied COMACICO and SECMA was supplied by COGECI. Controlling the dual monopoly of distribution and commercialisation, they sent back each year to Monaco about 40–50 per cent of their turnover. 'This is in fact nothing less than misappropriation of income.' In 1960, COMACICO reigned over 85 cinemas and SECMA over 65 in the fourteen French-speaking countries of West and Equatorial Africa. To date no complete assessment can be made of the systematic plundering these cinemas underwent. Hundreds of billions of francs were stolen from the continent without any substantial compensation. The cinema managers were given a mere trifle and they in turn threw crumbs to the employees and paid the low local taxes. For example, in Burkina Faso, in 1969, a year before nationalisation, the income declared by the two companies was 70 million CFA francs. Taxes, paid on a lump sum basis, only amounted to 10 million francs, that is 14.50 per cent of earnings, whilst the companies pocketed the remaining 85.50 per cent, some 60 million francs. And we are far from the true figures as the box offices in all the different countries were under their control. It was wholesale plundering until some countries woke up and dared to nationalise their cinemas and place the import and distribution of films under the management of national companies.

In Guinea, nationalisation took place *de facto* when it boldly became independent in 1958. The cinemas were nationalised and returned to private control in Algeria in 1969, in Burkina Faso in 1970, in Mali in 1970, in Senegal and in Benin in 1974, and in Zaire in 1973. The Madagascar revolution followed in 1975. Tunisia had been the first to try out this experiment. But from the moment when the first hints at nationalism were manifested, COMACICO-SECMA on the one hand and the American majors grouped together in the Motion Pictures Export Association of America (MPEAA) on the other, through the intermediary of its subsidiaries AFRAM and AMMPEC, responded by a boycott. The MPEAA dominated the Maghreb. In Algeria the National Board for the Film Trade and Industry (ONCIC), founded in 1967 and granted the monopoly for production and distribution in 1969, ended up by signing agreements with MPEAA. South of the Sahara, in the first country to rebel, Burkina Faso, the National Film Company (SONAVOCI, today SONACIB) was forced, according to its Director General at the time, after vainly looking for sources of supply, to accept a contract of exclusive film scheduling at his cinemas with COMACICO-SECMA; but this contract of film rental has become considerably flexible. There is no longer the obligation to give priority to one production or another as long as it respects the conditions of the rental contract fees.

Alongside the case of Burkina Faso, the situation was completely different in the neighbouring Ivory Coast. Victor Bachy relates (in his 1970 report of a mission to the Ivory Coast, unpublished) that the whole of distribution and two-thirds of commercial cinema management were in the hands of two companies, SECMA and COMACICO. The only 'freedom' the independent cinema owners had was to request successful films for a second showing.

Until 1969, COMACICO and SECMA rented out the ordinary cinemas at a fixed rate and the first-run cinemas, where the African elite and expatriates went, on a percentage basis. Since 1970, the American majors have encouraged the generalisation of the percentage system for a general Americanisation of cinema screens.

The executives of MPEAA declared in 1961 that 'the time has come to strike a blow in this Africa that is beginning to emerge. A co-ordinated invasion of the continent is on the agenda' (*Variety*, 17 May 1961). After North Africa and the British colonies, ten years later, French-speaking Africa was in their sights. The West Africa Import Co. Inc. was founded in 1969 and established in Dakar in 1970 under the name AMFRAM Inc., reflecting the American Motion Pictures Export Company of Africa (AMPECA), created in 1961 for the English-speaking countries. The Dakar office was to become fully operational in January 1972. The new system made it compulsory for COMACICO and SECMA to pay a guaranteed minimum before any films could be supplied and to transfer between 40 and 50 per cent of the net takings.

The Explosion of the Markets

The consequences of this remodelling of the system were not long in coming. COMACICO and SECMA sold their distributing shares at the end of 1972 to the French group UGC (Union Générale Cinématographique). Drawing a lesson from the nationalisations and in the face of the head-on advance of the Americans, the UGC, for strategic reasons, wanted to become an associate of the national companies to form a Société de Participation Cinématographie Africaine (SOPACIA), thus protecting its interests on the circuits it had bought. Senegal, a dual bridgehead for the French and the Americans and the engine of African cinema at the time, refused to sell the cinemas that COMACICO and SECMA had resold to the UGC. SIDEC (Société d'Importation de Distribution et d'Exploitation Cinématographique) was founded on 1 January 1974, with a capital of 750 million from the partial contribution of the assets from the former COMACICO and SECMA, and has two partners. The Senegalese state has 80 per cent and SOPACIA 20 per cent.

Neverthless, with its theoretical 20 per cent the UGC (SOPACIA) continued to control the monopoly of distribution in Senegal. This means that one country alone, because of its small size and the tiny number of its cinemas, is incapable of guaranteeing profitability and facing up to these giants. SOPACIA had a network of 110 cinemas at its disposal in West Africa, as well as 130 private independent clients, and covered 75 per cent of the market. AFRAM had 22 per cent and the other distributors shared the rest of the cake. Following the incessant appeals of the African film-makers for greater control of the cinema structures, the states of the Common African and Madagascar Organisation (OCAM) set up an Inter-African Consortium of Cinema Distribution (CIDC) in Ouagadougou in 1979. In the logic of its creators, the CIDC was to function as

150

a 'common market', a purchasing co-operative grouping together some fifteen countries which would be a leading force in promoting the production of films through a twin structure, CIPROFILMS (Inter-African Consortium of Film Production).

This was a step towards what African film-makers have called 'the decolonialisation of our screens'. Unfortunately, CIDC turned out to be a mere flash in the pan.

In view of the determination of the different countries, UGC, in 1980, sold its cinemas and portfolio of films to CIDC while remaining a member of the purchasing bureau in Paris. Through a subtle legal ploy, the UGC remained in control of this bureau, the nerve centre of the whole system. In 1980, the capital of CIDC was 70 million CFA francs; the UGC had sold its business for 550 million in the form of accounts payable.

In 1984, Mr Inoussa Ousséni, the first Director General of CIDC, was alarmed: 'We undertook these commitments because the States had undertaken to negotiate a loan of 600 million. Since then, nothing has been done and we are not paying.... We owe them 405 million.[1] Today, the main part of our capital consists of 50 per cent of debts.' The Africanisation of CIDC-France has never taken place in this legal imbroglio with strong whiffs of embezzlement in various forms. CIDC met a dramatic end against a background of court cases, unpaid salaries and compensation, not to mention discordances between states. Nevertheless, CIDC did exist briefly and its experience may enlighten other approaches in the efforts to form groups which alone can save African cinema from total asphyxia.

Even looking at the panorama of African film distribution in Africa through a magnifying glass, no structures capable at the moment of coping with the invader can be found. There are several countries that have never had national cinema companies, whether for production or projection, let alone for distribution. Those countries that did have them in the western subregion or in the Maghreb saw the keys being put under the mat when these same companies did not undergo great changes.

In English-speaking Africa, the idea of each man for himself has always been the rule and the film-makers are their own distributors. Some self-made men have been able to rise above the crowd in their own countries and even take their films further afield to the English-speaking countries in eastern and southern Africa. One example is Kwaw Ansah from Ghana with *Love ... Brewed in the African Pot* and *Heritage Africa*. In Nigeria, mention can be made of Ola Balogun and Adejumu Folayan.

A Desolate Panorama
The Nigerian Film Distribution Company only exists in theory since the Indians and the Lebanese have control of the cinemas. In the English-speaking countries of eastern and southern Africa, the situation is even more dramatic.

The United States and South Africa dictate their law. In the excellent dossier on the cinema in Zimbabwe, we learn that 'the great majority of films shown on Zimbabwean cinema screens are distributed by multinationals based in South Africa'.[2] In this part of the continent the majority of films come from the United States. Is it really necessary to mention here the case of two other countries, Namibia and Ethiopia? Everything remains to be organised on the level of production and distribution. In Namibia, there are only seven cinemas (1992 figure). Sub-Saharan francophone Africa, despite its attempts, is far from seeing the end of its troubles. In Mali, a National Film Office (OCINAM) was created but has long since fizzled out. This structure is being reorganised with many difficulties.

The Benin Cinema Board (OBECI), created after the 1974 nationalisation, no longer exists. The same goes for the Côte d'Ivoire: the Ivorian Cinema Company (SIC) which came into being in 1962 in the form of a commercial company breathed its last in 1975. In Niger, SONIDEC (Société Nigérienne d'Exploitation et de Distribution Cinématographique) was a creation of Inoussa Ousséni, former Director General of Cidc-Ciprofilms, in partnership with private individuals in order to act as an agency for the consortium. The disappearance of CIDC took SONIDEC with it. A little further away from the Sahel, in Cameroon, the Fonds de Développement de l'Industrie Cinématographique (FODIC), created in 1980, had raised many hopes. Set up at a cost of billions, it became entangled in a web of political and financial intrigue until it was completely suffocated. In North Africa, Morocco has always practised an open market (we may recall that COMACICO was set up there in the 1900s). In Tunisia and Algeria, SATPEC and ONCIC were transformed into private structures.

In the Maghreb, the question is rather that of changes dictated by the universalisation of economic liberalism which the whole world is experiencing. The states no longer have a formal commitment but they set up forms of aid. Private distributors, in practice subcontractors, especially Syrian-Lebanese, have appeared here and there. New transnationals have been born out of this hotchpotch.

SOCOFILM, for example, which had its head office in Geneva and supplied francophone West Africa, was sold to the Compagnie Franco-Africaine de l'Audiovisuel (CFAA) in 1989. This company took over the former COMACICO-SECMA circuits. CFAA is in fact a large holding company made up of banks including the Crédit Lyonnais and the Caisse Populaire. It controls the French 'game reserve'. In Senegal, CFAA is the shareholder of a new national company created on 1 August 1991, SIMPEC (Société d'Importation, de Promotion et d'Exploitation Cinématographique). SIDEC controls 8 per cent of the capital, the French 30 per cent and the nationals 62 per cent. Isn't there matter for concern in consideration of the experience of the UGC which, with 5 per cent of the capital of SIDEC, had 'kept the control of programming and therefore greatly maintained its ideological influence'?

Today, the share reserved for foreigners in SIMPEC is said to 'represent only 30 per cent of the capital'. Although he signed a 'standard agreement' and not a contract of exclusivity with CFAA, the Director of SIMPEC acknowledges that there is perhaps an implicit clause of first preference at the same price. Concerning the eastern area, covering the countries of Central Africa, no nation has shown concern over establishing a real film policy. In Cameroon, FODIC has never really worked.

In Gabon, out of an average of, for example, 350 films shown in the country's fourteen cinemas, including three in Libreville, the capital, 65 per cent are American, 25 per cent French and 10 per cent from other countries. One of the grand old figures of the Gabonese cinema, Charles Mensah, states that 'distribution today is almost completely carried out by CFAA, which acts as planner'. And, of course, without any legislation, the state has no control over distribution and cinema ownership.

Lastly, in the central area, with Abidjan (Côte d'Ivoire) as its epicentre, the situation is no different. CFAA has gobbled up CODIFILM, the main supplier of this subregion, destabilising the supply market. And let's not mention sub-distributors such as Jader or Mallouh films! The French company supplies the various companies with about 52 films a month for a monthly fee of some 7 million CFA francs. These films arrive in a group circuit. They are usually shown for about three weeks in each of the countries of the pool (Côte d'Ivoire, Burkina Faso, Niger, Togo and Benin). The Director General of SONACIB, Mr François Vokouma, remarks that with CFAA

The whole of distribution has changed its formula ... and since the destabilisation of the market, buying films really means increasing the costs for the company. We buy five big films a month. And since the beginning of this year [1992] we haven't bought any more. We have had to start renting them. Between 750 and 800 non-African films are shown each year on Burkina's screens, which goes to show all the financial difficulties that the company faces. It is the only one in the subregion today to continue with three showings (6.30 p.m; 8.30 p.m; 10.30 p.m.) but for how much longer?

The Problem of Audience

After this picture, where the lack of structures is blatant, it is completely logical that African films are a rare commodity for consumers of the continent's images. It is also a fact that the continent's screens are polluted by mind-numbing and alienating films of karate, filmed Hindu plays, old Westerns, war films and ideologically intoxicating films where the 'Rambos' and partners have a leading role. Very few well-made important films are shown to the mass of African cinemagoers.

Serge Galanky, a former executive of CIDC and manager of the Société Béninoise d'Exploitation de Loisirs et Commerce (BELCO), speaking of the place of African films in Benin admits: 'We do not have the possibility of showing African films ... We mainly show Nigerian films due to the fact of the common language. We have a Nigerian film a month. As far as French-language African cinema is concerned, it is hard to get copies.'

In Niger, the situation is hardly better. Here, in addition to the difficulties of supply and language, there is the problem of profitability, a very important question which is often the object of camouflage attempts. For Mr Mounkaïla Hassane of Anashua Distribution, it is clear that 'at the present time, it is not very clever to show an African film. It is a total loss'. The problematic situation of African films and their audiences is thus raised. Are African audiences, after being injected with foreign products for over a century, now rejecting the works of their own film-makers?

We don't think so. The quality of production certainly has something to do with it. Everywhere in Africa, African films are well received by audiences who are becoming more demanding as their awareness grows.

Two other closely linked major problems face African films – the age and small number of the cinemas and the small quantity of films, a consequence of

153

the difficulties of production. We must not delude ourselves. No African country today left to itself can cover its own market, except perhaps for Egypt, but there the problems of the public's taste must be raised. This is underlined by Mr François Vokouma of SONACIB, which has the reputation of being the most advanced distribution and cinema operating company regarding African films:

> In Burkina Faso, there are continuous efforts to encourage the consumption of films. But we also have to accept the evidence that there are not enough African films to meet the public's needs. Burkina consumes more than 700 films a year whilst there are only 50 films available. African films that have a certain audience have been bought by SONACIB but they have been shown so many times that people are fed up of them.

Distribution and cinema management must be capable of generating new resources for production. If one link is missing the whole system comes to a halt 'because the money that can be re-invested in the cinema can only be that of the cinemagoer', says Gaston Kaboré.

The Case of SONACIB

Burkina Faso's cinema and its national distribution and cinema management company (SONACIB) offer an example that still has to be perfected. Created out of the nationalisation in 1970, SONACIB started off with an initial capital of 20 million, 52 per cent of which belonged to the State, 29.65 per cent to its agencies and 17.83 per cent to private individuals, including film-makers. A mixed economy company, SONACIB, is therefore dominated by the state, making the cinema a domain of relatively national sovereignty. The fund for promotion and, by extension, cinematographic activity, which was created at the same time, was financed by a tax of 15 per cent of annual net takings. Over the past few years the company has made an effort to help film-makers. The management of the company states that there is not a single Burkina film-maker whose film has not been bought by the company. The Film Production Department (DIPROCI) is given a copy when SONACIB buys a film that has been co-produced by the state. At the level of box-office earnings, when a Burkina film goes on to the circuit, 40 per cent is returned to the company and the remaining 60 per cent is the production's share, and vice versa in the case of African productions. SONACIB also buys copies of these films. Its portfolio of African films has about fifty productions, including all those that have been awarded the FESPACO Etalon de Yennenga. For some films, the company has charged an advance on takings. On the inter-African level, Burkina Faso has removed tax on African films and SONACIB has taken some significant steps. From as early as the time of CIDC, it chose to get its films solely from this organisation. This structure would perhaps still be alive today if the other thirteen member countries had followed this course of action. SONACIB has also taken a number of initiatives for the distribution of various Burkina films abroad. In the subregion, apart from SIDEC in Senegal for a certain period, there is no company that has taken similar risks as the control of the box office and the fragility of the partners pose greater problems, as do the high cost of such operations (transport, hotels and other expenses). Nonetheless, at the pre-

154

sent time SONACIB is facing enormous financial difficulties which it will have to overcome to preserve this important instrument for national cinematographic development in Burkina Faso.

Almost everywhere on the continent film-makers know that it is urgent to act and to shake up the authorities, which often fail to take action, as well as economic operators. With privatisation becoming generalised from north to south, it is time that the states and the private sector understood that culture is not 'unproductive'. A representative of the American majors said in 1971: 'The cinema industry sold America to the whole world.'

We are witness to a slow but encouraging redefinition of the audiovisual landscape. In North Africa, Tunisia is already well ahead and over the past five years films of excellent quality such as *Halfaouine* and *L'Homme de cendres* (*Man of Ashes*) have met with enormous success, both with audiences in Tunisia and elsewhere.

A Shock Is Needed

In sub-Saharan Africa, structures are being re-created where they had perished. In Senegal it is SIMPEC, whose Director General, Mr Boubacar Hane, is determined to promote the seventh art on the keynote of quality: 'We fight to sell their [the film-makers'] films at conditions which, of course, are the best for us, as we are a commercial business concerned about profitability.'

In the Côte d'Ivoire, the Fonds Ivoirien d'Aide à la Création (FIAC) has been established; a film centre still remains to be created. The Compagnie Ivoirienne du Cinéma et de l'Audiovisuel (CIVCA) is studying a number of projects, including that of a box-office system in this country where private cinema owners are legion. In Mali a Cinema Code, which summarises the Burkinabe (1991) and the French codes, is yet to be adopted by the National Assembly. For the time being, individually or in collectives such as Kora Films (*Nyamanton, Ta Dona* ...), film-makers tuck their films under their arms and films are soon to be privatised. In Gabon, following the first Week of Gabonese Cinema (7–12 September 1990 in Libreville), on the occasion of the creation of the National Council of Communication, audiovisual producers and technicians formed a collective.

The shock wave provoked by African film-makers has been felt as far away as Zimbabwe where the first full-length film, *Jit,* by Michael Raeburn, was produced ... in 1990! The Zimbabwe Film and Video Association (ZFVA) created in 1982 is 'concerned about the total absence of African films and television productions ... and is trying its utmost to give Africa its cinema'.

A series of measures that are essential if production, distribution and cinema management are to develop to the full must be implemented with the greatest urgency – in particular, a substantial reduction of taxes on production, which should benefit from various forms of subsidies.

The distribution of African films must have the benefit of tax exemption or rebates. In some countries, such as Niger, taxes and duty are excessive, while in Tunisia a rebate equal to 3 per cent of the gross takings is granted to cinema managers who show Tunisian films; value added tax on production and distribution has been abolished in this country. Production material and raw materials are exempt. With the existence of adequate structures, the system of pre-sale and advances on takings should be generalised as well as the control of national ticket sales.

A policy of extension of cinemas and the involvement of television in production will enlarge the potential market represented by the 850 million inhabitants of the African continent. Today, we have to think of cinema and television at the same time. Experience has shown that television, the cinema's younger sister and rival, is today its natural partner and its 'safety exit', due to decreasing cinema audiences, the threat of images from the sky and the explosion of video, which nevertheless remains an alternative (the cases of Niger and Ghana).

Finally, only the grouping together of African countries in purchasing and distribution centres similar to the late CIDC-CIPROFILMS will enable distribution to be organised and become profitable. At the 5th FEPACI Conference in February 1993 it was decided to set up an executive secretariat for distribution and production co-ordinated by the Tunisian producer Ahmed Attia. Is this the beginning of getting a firm grip on this knotty dossier? The urgency of the situation does not leave much of an alternative.

Note
1. This refers to fees payable at 31 December 1983.
2. See 'Cinema in Zimbabwe', *Ecrans d'Afrique*, no. 3, 1st Quarter 1993.

African Cinema in the Tempest of Minor Festivals

SAMBOLGO BANGRÉ

Reprinted from *Ecrans d'Afrique*, no. 7, 1st quarter, 1994.

'To become known, African cinema has gone towards international festivals,' said the father of African critics, Paulin Soumanou Vieyra, at the beginning of the 1970s. Kept at a distance from the continent's screens monopolised by the former distribution structures of COMACICO and SECMA, the first films by African film-makers produced from the early 1960s onwards were revealed to the public only after having negotiated their recognition at festivals organised outside the continent.

The 1961 Berlin Festival was the first to select African films, which were by Senegalese film-makers: Blaise Senghor's *Grand Magal de Touba* (1960), which received a Silver Bear for the best short film, and Paulin Soumanou Vieyra's *Une Nation est née* (1961), which received a special mention. Between 1961 and 1975 numerous festivals in Europe and America followed Berlin's example, thus contributing very early on to the recognition of African cinema. Films shown to the public at Moscow, Leipzig, San Francisco, New York, Venice and Locarno included *Borom Sarret* (1961), Ousmane Sembène's first short film, and *The Mummy* (1970) by the Egyptian Chadi Abd-el-Salam. But there can be no doubt whatsoever that it was the prestigious Cannes Festival, by awarding prizes to Sembène's *La Noire de ...* and *Le Vent des Aures* by the Algerian Lakhdar Hamina, in 1966 and 1969 respectively, that definitely marked the recognition of African cinema. Since then, it has continued to arouse increasing popular and critical interest at Western festivals.

In Africa itself, the idea of creating film festivals on the continent came about with the birth of African cinema as a solution that would enable the cinema to go forth and meet its public. The first Festival des Arts Nègres at Dakar, organised in 1966, responded in part to this spirit. It was to open up the way for the Journées Cinématographiques de Carthage, created in 1966 in Tunis, and the Pan-African Festival of Cinema and Television in Ougadougou in 1969.

For twenty years, with a production having its fair share of ups and downs, African cinema thus went out towards the festivals to find credibility that neither the monopolised African market nor the local cinema authorities could guarantee. For about ten years it has now been the festivals that have been going towards African cinema. The number of international festivals and events has been growing and, with them, the number of seminars and professional meetings. The window that was opened in the past to African films in the festivals has now been opened much wider and festivals devoted exclusively to

African cinema have been established almost everywhere in the course of the years. European countries now have a total of more than 500 film events. The record belongs to France, where more than 160 film events are held each year. Here, three major festivals are exclusively or partially devoted to African cinema, namely the Amiens Festival, created in 1980, the Cinemas of Africa Festival of Angers, first held in 1987, and the Festival of Three Continents, held in Nantes since 1982.

Whatever the 'obsessions' behind them, the other events in Europe or in America (women's film festivals, festivals of films for children, and the like) all or nearly all grant a place to African cinema. The flourishing of festivals was noticeable especially in the years between 1983 and 1990, a period during which very different types of festivals were established in the majority of European cities. In France again, more than 150 towns are concerned. In the film industry, the disappearance of film clubs in the 1960s and of art theatres in the 1970s left a void that the festivals have filled, thus continuing to satisfy the desire of cinema lovers for images. In 1992, the French public interested in festivals was estimated to be about a million, that is, 1 per cent of cinemagoers.

When they are being created, all the festivals declare the same objectives: to distribute and promote films; to enable film-makers, critics, the public and producers to meet; to offer an opportunity to get to know the realities of the different film-makers and of their countries – noble objectives, which may at times hide other ambitions behind certain festivals.

An Attempt at Classification

Three categories of festivals can be distinguished. The first concerns festivals which are devoted to discovering films that have never been shown before, to the satisfaction of lovers of the seventh art. The second category uses the cinema as a support for a market. Cinema becomes business. Finally, the third category of festivals is that of 'public relations festivals'. The cinema becomes an instrument to promote a city or a product. The proliferation of festivals gives the unpleasant sensation that this category of festivals is the only one that applies. And African cinema is the ideal excuse to fill this role of promotion that the majority of cities need against a background of drums celebrating cultural dialogue and the promotion of marginalised films.

In France, thanks to a law passed in 1901 authorising subsidies for events of a cultural nature organised by non-profit making associations, any city or any mayor can take advantage of the subsidies to create a film festival to promote the image of the city. Most years, the municipalities, the departments, the regions and also state institutions and private partners contribute to the budget of cultural events, of which film festivals are the main beneficiaries. Festivals that are financed essentially by their own takings are few and far between. The budget for an average festival held in Europe is estimated at between 5 and 12 million French francs. Cannes or Berlin go way beyond this figure with budgets of more than 27 and 41 million francs respectively. As well as the promotion of the cities holding the festivals, it is not impossible that, in the current situation of economic crisis, a festival represents a solution for a temporary reduction of unemployment.

All African film-makers are unanimous in recognising that festivals are useful. The best-known film-makers in fact owe their careers to the opportunities to meet people, and the presentation of their films at festivals have often led to their winning awards. The 'cultural expectations' of African film-makers vis-à-vis the festivals have always been fulfilled. The large audiences created by international festivals have always extended a warm welcome to the film-makers' work. These cultural expectations are met to an even greater extent when the African film-maker has the opportunity to meet the public at festivals in Africa itself. The economic expectations – distribution in cinemas or sale to televisions – are less obvious. The addition of a film market to a festival has not always led to improved distribution or to the creation of viable conditions for co-production.

Few festivals, even amongst the most serious organised both in Africa and outside the continent, have had this driving force. However, original ideas are being increasingly developed regarding the funding of film-makers' projects or training in the sectors of distribution, production, and so on. It is therefore not surprising that many film-makers increasingly have the ambition of knocking at the doors of the major festivals, such as Cannes or Venice. *Chronique des années de braise* (1975), by Lakhdar Hamina (the only Golden Palm – awarded in 1975 – granted to an African film), *Yeelen* (1987), by the Malian film-maker Souleymane Cissé, awarded a prize at the 1987 Cannes Festival, and Idrissa Ouédraogo's *Tilai* (1990), which was also awarded a prize at the same festival three years later, only began their commercial careers after this festival. Mohamed Camara (*Denko* (1993), prize for the best short film at FESPACO 93) and Burkina Faso's Regina Fanta Nacro (*Un Certain matin* (1992)), who were able to sell their films to several televisions after having won awards at Ouagadougou and Carthage, are examples which do not yet allow a definite degree of optimism for the career of the majority of young film-makers.

Their dream of ascending the steps of the theatre on the Croisette comes to a halt more often than not at the markets of the minor festivals, more inclined to awarding accommodating prizes to the young film-makers invited. Between accepting an invitation from some city or another in Europe and the refusal to play at puppets, many do not hesitate and choose the first solution. Henri Duparc, the film-maker from Côte d'Ivoire (*Bal poussière*, 1988, *Le Sixième doigt*, 1991, *Rue princesse*, 1993), who took a clear stance several years ago, choosing only to go to festivals which guarantee the sale of his films, has few, if any, followers.

A real discomfort has existed for some time with African film-makers regarding the proliferation of festivals and their consequences. The frequency of the festivals (festivals are often only a week or even less apart) has as one consequence the overexploitation of the films. Between May 1993, the date his short film *Octobre* was released, and April 1994, Abderrahmane Sissako, the Mauritian film-maker, received at least thirty invitations to attend festivals all over the world. The same applies to Mohamed Tazi, the Moroccan film-maker whose recent film *A la recherche du mari de ma femme* (1993) has aroused a similar frenzy. On the other hand, many festivals graciously exploit the films entered in the competition without any particular beneficial consequence for those concerned. Taking as their argument the insufficiency of their budgets and their prime concern in promoting the films, many festivals are unaware of or pretend to be unaware of the principle of the payment of a fee (between 1,000 French francs for short films and 3,000 French francs for features, according to the rates currently in force) for the rental of the films shown. Worse, and that's where the shoe pinches, it is not infrequent for festivals to send invitations to film-makers who live in Africa with the condition that their travel expenses are paid from Paris.

The film-makers' ill-ease is also the feeling of *déjà entendu* with regard to what is being said at the various seminars organised by the festivals on the problems of African cinema. On this topic, one film-maker says:

> When I go to festivals, I know that the same things are going to be repeated again and again. I have the impression of being a record that's played at each festival. Why don't they stop asking us to speak about our problems? We've had enough of speeches; we want more money to make films.

FEPACI's Initiatives

Well aware that the only solution lies in the organisation of a market based on South/South co-operation and conquering the market of the North, for many years film-makers have contributed to working out different strategies for the development of their cinema. The festivals of Ouagadougou and Carthage and the meetings at Maputo in 1974, Mogadishu in 1981 and Niamey in 1982 have provided a framework for reflection on the question of the film market. The first realisation of these reflections had been the creation in 1974 of CIDC (Inter-African Consortium of Film Distribution). Its aim was to regulate the market of fourteen countries in Western and Central Africa. The failure of CIDC in 1984 again left African cinema like 'a head without a body', according to the phrase coined by Tahar Chériaa.

The absence of an internal market and the increasing desire by the continent's population to see their own images led to voices being raised to demand the creation of other festivals in Africa apart from FESPACO and Carthage. The recent birth of the Southern African Film Festival, which materialised in October 1993, is a response to this request. Several initiatives encouraged by FEPACI tend towards the organisation of weeks of cinema in the majority of countries. The urgency of the question of festivals open to African cinema led FEPACI, in conjunction with FESPACO, to organise a seminar on the subject on the occasion of the 25th anniversary of FESPACO held in Ouagadougou from 20 to 25 February 1994. The conclusions of this meeting noted the historic role played by the festivals of Ouagadougou and Carthage in the promotion of African cinema, the diffusion of images of the continent's film-makers, the strengthening of the bonds of solidarity between the peoples of Africa and the assertion of African cinemas in the face of that of the North.

The intensification of dialogue between these festivals was seen as a pressing need. The real risk for the film festivals held on the continent can be stated in terms of the interest of the film-makers in their own festivals because the economic expectations of the film-makers who are satisfied by the large international festivals remain stronger in appeal than the cultural expectations. The laudable initiatives taken by the Ouagadougou, Carthage and Harare festivals to organise the film market respectively through MICA, the project market and Input Africa are to be encouraged. African cinema still has a lot to do if it wants to continue to exist first and foremost for its audiences.

Further Readings

Blignaut, J., and Botha, M., *Movies, Moguls and Mavericks: South African Cinema 1979–1991* (Capetown: Showdata, 1992).

Cheriaa, Tahar, *Ecrans d'abondances ou Cinéma de liberation en Afrique?* (Tunis: Laplume, 1978).

Diawara, Manthia, *African Cinema: Politics and Culture* (Bloomington, Ind.: Indiana University Press), 1992.

Ekwuai, Hyginus, Okome, Onokoome, *et al.* (eds), *Studies in Film and Television* (Nigeria) (Jos: Nigerian Film Corporation, 1993).

Ilboudo, Patrick, *Le FESPACO 1969–1989: Les Cinéastes africains et leurs oeuvres* (Ouagadougou: Editions La Mante, 1989).

Martin, Angela, *African Cinema: The Context of Production* (London: BFI (Dossier no. 6, 1982).

Notcutt, L. A., and Latham, G. C., *The African and the Cinema* (London: The Edinburgh House Press, 1937).

Opubor, Alfred, and Nwuneli, Onuora (eds), *The Development and Growth of the Film Industry in Nigeria* (Lagos and New York: Smyrna Press, 1988).

Tomaselli, Keyan, *The Cinema of Apartheid* (New York: Smyrna Press, 1988).

Ukadike, Nwachukwu Frank, *Black African Cinema* (Berkeley: University of California Press, 1994).

Vieyra, Paulin, *Le Cinéma africain, des origines à 1973* (Paris: Présence Africaine, 1976).

Critical Arts, vol. 7, no. 1/2, 1993.

Ecrans d'Afrique (all issues).

The OCIC (Office Catholique International de Cinéma) series on cinema in various selected African countries: *Cinémas d'Afrique noire* (Brussels, Belgium).

PART IV
Issues of Representation

'African' Cinema: Theoretical Perspectives on Some Unresolved Questions

KEYAN G. TOMASELLI

This is a revised version of the paper published in *Critical Arts*, vol. 7 no. 1, 1993.[1]

For a South African reader a slightly disconcerting feature of Manthia Diawara's book on African cinema is the total exclusion of South Africa (except for a few passing references) from the discussion. There are clear historical reasons for this, of course, not the least important of which are the facts that South Africa was not colonised and decolonised in precisely the way that the rest of Africa was.[2]

Publications on African cinema – or, more correctly, cinema in Africa – began to appear with considerable regularity in the 1980s. The end of apartheid in South Africa significantly altered both the terrain and scope of debates about cinema in Africa. In the paper that follows, I discuss the nature of the shift, and examine questions on what attributes might be applied when discussing definitions of 'African' and 'Black' cinema.

Questions of Geography, Questions of Identity

Questions not easily resolved on the issue of what is African cinema concern, for example, what constitutes Africa. Is Arab film and South African production part of African cinema? Is 'Black' cinema necessarily 'African' in origin? Is there such an identity as 'the African personality'?[3] Should African cinema necessarily be linked to its Black diasporic equivalents in the United States, France and England?[4]

South Africa, which has produced more films than the rest of the continent put together, was, during the apartheid years, generally excluded from the category of an African state by film scholars. Nancy Schmidt, for example, considers South Africa as part of 'Sub-Saharan African Filmmaking'. However, South Africa was excluded from another commentary of hers, 'Culture and Nationalism in Sub-Saharan *African* Filmmaking' (my italics).[5] Southern Africa is not mentioned in Victor Bachy's panorama of sub-Saharan cinema, while Frank Ukadike, and A. Gardies and Pierre Haffner narrow their focus to 'Black' films only. Although considered part of Africa-the-continent, it appears that these authors, writing prior to the defeat of apartheid, may have, if ambivalently, denied White South African film-makers an identity as Africans.[6]

Schmidt's most recent bibliography, however, specifically omits South Africa because, she states, 'the development of mainstream filmmaking there excludes the black population and follows a European pattern markedly different from that of the rest of Sub-Saharan Africa'.[7] The most recent reference I could find in Schmidt's work was 1993. However, a distinct anti-apartheid feature cinema drawing on ideas on Third Cinema[8] and neo-realist forms had begun as early as 1973 with Ross Devenish and Athol Fugard's *Boesman and Lena*.

Domestic anti-apartheid documentary film-making had begun as early as 1970.[9] Films like *African Jim* (1949) and *Magic Garden* (1961), dealing with the urban Black experience in South Africa, though made by the White director Donald Swanson, reclaimed serious critical attention in the late 1980s as a legitimate form which speaks empathetically to Black African audiences. As Lewis Nkosi remarks of comments recorded by two Black South Africans in Peter Davis and Dan Reisenfeld's *In Darkest Hollywood* (1994):

... the immense popular success of *Jim Comes to Jo'burg* [the alternative title] pointed to one important fact: the enormous hunger in the townships for images within which the black victims of apartheid could identify. As [John] Kani puts it ... 'We saw black people in this movie. We saw black people talking.' And Maimane adds that: 'The plot didn't matter. A film shot with people you recognised, on the streets you knew ... sometimes it was difficult to hear the dialogue because people were shouting, "Hey, that's my street, I live on that street ...!" You know, they sort of became like home movies'.[10]

Even though Jamie Uys's *The Gods Must Be Crazy* (1980, 1989) films have been mercilessly attacked by anti-apartheid campaigners, a contextual reading of Uys's earlier film, *Dingaka* (1964), strengthens the argument of audience recognition of themselves as a measure of a film's cultural integrity.[11] *Dingaka*, made in Panavision Technicolor with American audiences in mind, negotiates its conflicted Black and White characters through the discrete discourses and consequences of 'civilised' versus tribal legal traditions. The following comment, by the Black writer and cultural activist Mtutuzeli Matshoba, puts this argument in perspective:

[*Dingaka* is] an honest attempt to represent the controversial traditional theme. A picture may not be especially intended for a particular population group, but because that group recognizes itself authentically represented within the theme, it will respond positively to it.[12]

Afrikaans (meaning 'African') language film genres too, even when made by Whites, have their own cultural qualities not always easily or even appropriately tied to European genres and conditions.[13]

Few commentators mention the prolific Black South African director and actor Simon Sabela, who belatedly found out that his films were being financed by the South African government as part of its propaganda.[14] Contemporary scholars refer to the White director Oliver Schmitz's *Mapantsula* (1988) as the country's first 'Black' film, a catchphrase also used by the film's American distributor. Chinua Achebe *et al.* include *Mapantsula* under the heading 'African'.[15] Soweto Musician/playwright Gibson Kente was, in fact, the first Black South African to make an anti-apartheid film, *How Long ...*, in 1976. Unfortunately, this film is untraceable.

166

Ideologically very revealing is the White South African Volker Hooyberg's *exclusion* of South Africa from the category of African cinema industries.[16] He writes in a South African textbook: 'In the 1960s only two African nations, Egypt and Tunisia, were producing films on a regular basis.' This startling sentence evidences two prime assumptions. The first is that South Africa is *not* part of Africa, an exclusion which Hooyberg fails to explain or develop. The second is Hooyberg's totally inaccurate, incomplete and extremely dated description of film industries in only three countries on the continent. He references only a single little-known source on African film industries. Hooyberg takes for granted the Western assumption that there is no cinema of note in Africa despite clear evidence to the contrary, and many seminal studies, which contradict his biased description.[17]

Indigenous production and distribution tend to follow neocolonial language contiguities – Arabic, French, Portuguese and English. Many films have nevertheless been made using African languages only. Arising out of these neocolonial relations, what kinds of relationship have developed between the metropolitan states and their former colonies?[18] How do these international relationships impact on definitions of 'African cinema'?

Ali Mazrui offers four definitions of Africa in terms of different criteria.[19] These are based on 'racial', 'continental' and 'power' considerations. The 'racial' definition excludes non-Blacks. The 'continental' definition is self-explanatory. The power criterion excludes those parts of Africa under 'non-African' control, such as apartheid South Africa and Rhodesia. In the fourth perspective, some scholars argue that North Africa is more like Arabia, and is really part of the Islamic Middle East.[20] A case could also be made that parts of South Africa could be part of Europe, not Africa, in view of its close economic and historical and cultural ties to the metropolitan states.

Discourses of Resistance

'Culture' is another problematic term in identifying African societies. A seminal scholar appropriated by African revolutionaries in this regard is Frantz Fanon. A Westernised West Indian and French citizen who worked as a psychiatrist for the French army in Algeria, Fanon's experiences led him to cross sides. He then moved into Algerian politics and resistance. Fanon argues for the idea of 'national cultures' rather than 'African cultures'.[21] This definitional imperative emerged from the nation-building attempts which underpinned the continent's independence movements of the 1960s. Fanon argues that culture takes concrete shape around the struggle of the people, not solely around signs, poems or folklore, which supposedly disconnect leisure time from work periods. Culture is not for him a predetermined model offered by the past. It is not a state of being, but a state of becoming.

The Cape Verdean Amilcar Cabral offers a different emphasis of the term 'culture'. Like Fanon, he invests it with a strategic component in the offensive against imperialism and neocolonialism. But Cabral's strategies differed from Fanon in that he drew on cultural sites through which the colonised were able to mobilise the bulwark of residual traditional cultural forms and rituals to preserve their precolonial identities, traditions and dignity.[22]

Cabral opposed the Portuguese and French forms of colonisation, which attempted partial assimilation of the Other into the metropolitan society. He

was a cultural conservative who called for a return to precolonial social and cultural formations. In his role as 'revolutionary' within the Cape Verde liberation movement, Cabral's writings were rhetorically appropriated by African Marxists, who quote him as their theoretical guru.

Where Cabral identified sites of resistance in pre-modern traditions and identity, Fanon argues that Black petty bourgeois politicians often call on the idea of nationalism and 'culture' to disguise their own opportunistic political agendas. 'Culture', as a discursive romantic mobilising agent, is common to both nationalist and popular struggles in Africa. In this way the strategies of these African interior bourgeoisies are similar to those offered by Cabral, though with different ends in mind. Their political articulations are also calling for a recuperation of a romantic past, as well as bygone 'traditional' values and some forever lost sense of original community. Through 'culture', the colonised would remake their common-sense humanity, diminished and distorted by the colonial experience.

Cultural occupation rather than assimilation was the experience of the British colonised territories. This contrasts sharply with the early Dutch settlement of the Cape (1642–1806), which followed basic assimilation policies. However, the subsequent South African Afrikaner rulers from 1948 on, who derived from the Dutch, took their cue from the British model of separation. They established 'princely states' based on the British Indian model. This is where the term 'bantustan' came from. Afrikaner Nationalists developed discursive strategies to inhabit reconstructed indigenous cultures and discourses, aimed at encouraging cultural (or 'tribal') difference. They thereby forced idealised ideological content onto 'tribal' groups to sustain and even reconstruct tribal 'identities' and territories through apartheid. In India these spaces were called 'compounds', while in South Africa they were known as 'group areas'. The term 'bantustan' derives from the British Indian model also using the term 'stan'. But 'bantustan' was dropped from the official apartheid lexicon once it had been appropriated as a sign of derision by the international anti-apartheid movement.

How does the appellation 'Africa' then fit against this background of differing colonial policies and indigenous experiences? What does the term 'culture' mean in each of these instances? I address these questions below.

African Cinema?

Are the ideas of a 'single African cinema' and 'continental culture' too limiting in terms of regional differences, historical forms of resistance, discursive strategies and definitions of Africa as described above? Can there be a single African aesthetic or personality? What is the relationship between African aesthetics and partnered representations of African cultures in different kinds of films – feature, documentary, ethnographic? Do each of these forms expose different levels and dimensions of culture, history and cosmology?

What about partnerships which have developed between groups indigenous to Africa and foreign film-makers? The French anthropologist Jean Rouch is often referred to, for example, in the Western film literature as the 'Father' of African cinema. Numerous ethnographic film-makers who have developed Rouch's practices of 'shared anthropology' have produced films which speak reflexively from 'inside' the African communities imaged.[23] How do such interpellations gel with each of Mazrui's definitions of who and what constitutes

Africa and Africans, or what might constitute African film contents, form, language and aesthetics?[24]

Questioning Assumptions

Africans are diverse: culturally (ways of life), ethnically, ideologically, gender-wise, in terms of gnosis, family and lineage structures, kinship patterns, ethnicity, cosmology and so on. The wisdom of racially essentialising the category of Africans to designate exclusion of certain 'settler' groups from Africa rather than inclusion into its peoples has, of course, been the driving discourse of most liberation struggles.

Migrations and Discourses

The slogan of 'White settler' governments, amongst others, however, masks often violent and imperialist pre-(Western) colonial migrations between Black African societies themselves, not to mention the enforced Islamicisation of vast tracts of North Africa. Nearly all African peoples are settlers of one sort or another, having forcibly displaced earlier inhabitants.[25] Ousmane Sembène's *Ceddo* (1976), for example, is a critique of both Catholicism and Islam. But where *Ceddo* shows Catholicism to be impotent, the Islamic imposition is depicted as dominant, pervasive and ruthless.

Other than the San in Namibia and Botswana, now known as the 'First People', and what remains of the Copts in Egypt, there are few exceptions among current African peoples who are not also settlers in one sense or another – who have not themselves displaced others in often violent intra-continental migrations. Different sets of significations have developed to indicate exogenous from indigenous population movements. Historically, the Islamicisation and Arabisation of North Africa was and is no less an 'invasion', implicating both economic colonisation and religious hegemonisation.

Romanticisation

Much writing on African film tends towards romanticisation of all things African. In one effort to contest Western 'cultural brainwashing', P. M. Bouteba applies functionalist analysis to recuperate 'African cultural heritage'.[26] Original traditions, however, are not necessarily beneficial for everyone. As with most societies, the currently subordinate status of women in modern Africa, for example, was not always 'traditional'. In many cases, customary and neocolonial laws have combined to trap women especially in double-binds. Contemporary women's struggles are documented in feature, documentary and ethnographic films made by both Africans themselves and in partnership with foreign film-makers. One such feature is Cheick Oumar Sissoko's *Finzan* (1990), 'an impassioned cry for the emancipation of African women'.[27] Sissoko's narrative criticises wife inheritance and female circumcision. But, as Frank Ukadike's discussion of the film suggests, residual discourses of 'tradition' still permeate often emotional debates on the controversial issue of enforced female circumcision.[28]

African nationalist ideologies blind some scholars and ideologues to the fact that female circumcision was always an unacceptable form of the oppression of women. But then so too, perhaps, are practices forced on male initiates, such as piercing of ears, scarification, removal of teeth and adolescent circumcision.

Commentators critical of the 'colonised mind' ought also to attribute similar ideological workings around gender and cosmology as sites of oppression and control. With regard to the imaging of women in African cinema, Amie Williams comments that she deflects the colonial gaze, that she is the 'engendering symbol for the new aesthetic', the outsider who liberates her people (as in Sembène's Ceddo).[29] Expressions of the sacred have been less well documented, an omission largely characterising Western-authored analysis which fails to understand the influence of orality and spirituality in African expression.[30]

Culture is not some fixed state of being or age-old way of life. Rather, culture describes networks of meaning and how individuals encounter these and articulate them in relation to existing and new social practices. The sense of community and tradition symbolically recuperated by scholars like Ukadike and Bouteba is found in the practices that exist for a given community within which these signifying practices (film, TV, and so on) are distributed and exhibited.[31] This remembrance phase is socially constructed rather than being a concrete historical fact, and is therefore subject to romanticisation by both film-makers and film critics.

Locations

The foreign locations of the majority of African scholars and directors of African films are rarely interrogated in the analytical literature. Their location elsewhere has often been a political and financial necessity, also resulting in the publication of works on African cinema which may not otherwise have occurred.[32]

The inappropriateness of Western film theories in discussing African films, African film-making and African spectatorship was first identified through this largely exile and expatriate community of African film scholars and film-makers.[33]

Psychoanalysis and Subjectivities

Increasingly, scholars and film-makers in Africa itself are attacking unproblematised importations of screen theories developed in other contexts. They are especially critical of the assumptions of theory developed to explain Westernised subjectivities applied to societies which can by no stretch of the imagination be understood solely within deconstruction and the parameters of Freudian/Lacanian perspectives.[34]

How can the Metzian mirror phase apply to communities of spectators who may only recently have begun to use mirrors, such as those who live in, and travel over, the vast tracts of Africa. Yet the paradox is clear: African and many Fourth World spectators don't 'see' the screen as a mirror, but sometimes as the reality itself.[35] Often they interact with the screen as if the characters on it actually exist in one form or another. The absence of the spectators' body from the image and soundtracks is replaced by their interaction with these two tracks during the viewing experience. The analogy of film being like a dream can only come from a Western psychocentric epistemology which imposes metaphors and Cartesian dualisms where analogical connections may exist for other cultures.

In some African gnoses, discussion of unknown forces and the supernatural considered to be part of concrete reality – such as found in the films of Jean Rouch and some ethnographic films – are rarely evident in Western discussions on African cinema. First and Second World theoretical frames have largely excluded discourses of religiosity and spirituality, dimensions which remain real and influential in Black African cosmologies. These cosmologies draw on orality and collective imagery and largely shape rural, and aspects of urban, African subjectivities. The characteristics of orality question the idea of the individual as the centre of signification. The central protagonist of African cinemas is usually the context of the film; the characters only provide the punctuation within it.[36]

The Western Theoretical Gaze

Another problem relates to the Western gaze at Africa. Africans are painfully aware of foreign scholars who write about them without drawing on their studies or debates. Apart from Hooyberg, another glaring example is Roy Armes's *Third World Filmmaking and the West,* which fails to cite a single source published in Africa itself.[37] The result is that Armes writes about African cinema as individual artistic expression rather than from the perspectives of African gnosis and its emphasis on group cohesion.[38] Interaction between African and Western scholars is largely restricted to the buzz of the annual Ouagadougou Film Festival in Burkina Faso. As crucially important as this event and others like it in Tunisia and Ghana have become, it is insufficient to stimulate sustained critical debate.[39] Such debate requires intense academic activity in Africa as well as in the United States and Europe, the two foreign continents where it has been largely incubated.

African Counter-Gaze

The insistence that the problems disastrously confronting Africa today stem purely and only from the machinations of neocolonialism and Western imperialism, rather than also from some of the problems originating from within Africa itself, is another issue that needs critical assessment. The notion that Africa is a helpless mass at the mercy of international capital and superpowers' foreign policies is partly of the making of African governments themselves.

As the continent repositions itself politically and economically following the collapse of the Soviet Union and apartheid at the end of the 1980s, it also needs to develop new conceptions of itself as capable of addressing both inherited problems and those of its own making. Cinema has a crucial role to play in this task. Certainly, more and more academic interest is being shown in African and South African cinema, and on the way the continent is imaged, than ever before.[40] The issue is to examine critically the nature of theoretical frameworks being applied to the kinds of question outlined above. This task is especially necessary in the light of the two major developments in South Africa facilitating its reintegration into Africa.

The first was the opening up in 1993 of the Annual M-NET Film Awards to products emanating from the continent as a whole. Related to this initiative is M-NET's commitment to exposing South Africans to African cinema and its film directors through the awards and the screening of African films both on its pay station, which reaches throughout Africa, and through film and cultural organisations, and universities.[41]

The second development concerns the agreements reached between the SA Broadcasting Corporation and African film-makers on the screening of African films on public TV. This will involve the dubbing and/or subtitling of non-English-language (both indigenous and French) films into English. This kind of synergetic co-operation could well facilitate the increased availability of such films in the English-speaking world generally.

Conclusion

History and discursive negotiations will be the ultimate arbiter as to who think of themselves as living in Africa. While a general discourse of the individual-in-the-community might typify most African film narratives, if not always their societies, it is doubtful whether a homogeneous African personality exists. An African identity may exist in terms of the other (the West), but this too is shaped by interacting global processes rather than existing in an essentialising form. The reintegration of South Africa into the notion that is Africa, however, may well boost both Western and African film industries, as well as massively increasing their viewership in Africa itself through television.

Notes

1. This paper is developed from the article of the same title in *Critical Arts*, vol. 7 nos 1/2, 1993, and Tomaselli, 'Theoretical Perspectives on Cinema in Africa: Culture, Identity and Diaspora', *Visual Anthropology*, vol. 7, 1995; Tomaselli, 'Some Theoretical Perspectives on African Cinema: Culture, Identity, Diaspora', in FEPACI, *L'Afrique et le centenaire du cinéma/Africa and the Centenary of Cinema* (Dakar and Paris: Présence Africaine, 1995). I am indebted to P. Eric Louw, Ntongela Masilela and Jeanne Prinsloo for their comments on earlier drafts on this paper.
2. Edwin Hees, 'Film in Africa and South Africa', *Critical Arts*, vol. 7 nos 1/2, 1993), p. 127.
3. Gaston Kabore, 'L'Image de soi, un besoin vital', in FEPACI, *L'Afrique et le centenaire*, p. 23.
4. See Mark A. Reid, 'African and Black Diaspora Film/Video', *Jump Cut* 36, 1991; Tomaselli, 'Theoretical Perspectives on Cinema in Africa'.
5. *Visual Anthropology*, vol. 2 no. 1, 1989.
6. V. Bachy, 'Panoramique sur les cinéastes africaines', *CinémAction*, vol. 26, 1983; F. Ukadike, *Black African cinema* (Berkeley: University of California Press, 1993); Gardies and Haffner, *Regards sur le cinéma négro-africain* (Brussels: Editions OCIC, 1987).
7. Nancy Schmidt, *SubSaharan African Films and Filmmakers, 1987–1992; An Annotated Bibliography* (London: Hans Zell, 1994, p. 4).
8. First Cinema describes Hollywood films; Second Cinema accounts for art and auteur films; and Third Cinema is a cinema of resistance and emancipation, emanating primarily from progressive Third World film-makers; see Octavio Gettino and Fernando Solanas, 'Towards a Third Cinema', in Bill Nichols (ed.), *Movies and Methods* (Berkeley: University of California Press, 1976).
9. See Tomaselli, *The Cinema of Apartheid: Race and Class in South African Film* (Chicago: Lake View Press, 1988); H. Gavshon, ' "Bearing Witness": Ten Years Towards an Oppositional Film Movement in South Africa', *Radical History Review*, vol. 46 no. 7, 1990; Lynette Steenveld 'Reclaiming History: Anti-Apartheid Documentaries', in Johan Blignaut and Martin Botha (eds), *Movies – Moguls – Mavericks: South African Cinema 1989–1991* (Cape Town: Showdata, 1992).
10. Lewis Nkosi, 'US Diary', *Southern African Review of Books*, January/February 1994.
11. See Tony Volkman, ' "Out of Africa": The Gods Must Be Crazy', in Larry Gross, J. S. Katz and Jay Ruby (eds), *Image Ethics: The Moral Rights of Subjects in Photographs, Film and TV* (New York: Oxford University Press, 1988); Rob Gordon, *Bushman Myth: The Making of the Namibian Underclass* (Boulder, Col.: Westview, 1992); Tomaselli and Mikki Van Zyl, 'Themes, Myths and Cultural Indicators: Structuring Popular Memory', in Blignaut and Botha, *Movies – Moguls – Mavericks*.

12. Mtutuzeli Matshoba, an unpublished essay, 1979.
13. See Tomaselli, *The Cinema of Apartheid*; Tomaselli and Van Zyl, 'Themes, Myths...'.
14. Tomaselli, *The Cinema of Apartheid*, pp. 53–83.
15. Chinua Achebe (ed.), *Library of African Cinema* (San Francisco: California Newsreel, 1990).
16. Volker Hooyberg, 'From Distant Drums to Satellite', in Arrie S. De Beer (ed.), *Mass Media in the Nineties* (Pretoria: Van Schaik, 1993).
17. See Schmidt, *Bibliography*.
18. Much has been written on extensive French financial and technical assistance on African cinema – see Claire Andrade-Watkins, 'France's Bureau of Cinema', above, pp. 112–127. The French government, through its centres for Direct Cinema located in Johannesburg, Maputo and Kenya, has also influenced style – see R. Aronstam and S. De Waal, 'Une Expérience: le Centre du Cinéma Directe', in *CinémAction*, vol. 23, 1986, which critically discusses the cultural implications of these centres with regard to the Johannesburg case. See also Pierre Haffner and Jean Rouch, 'Comment filmer la liberté?', *CinémAction*, vol. 17, 1983; Louis Marcorelles, '16 et Super 8: de Boston au Mozambique', ibid.
    Histories of British and Portuguese efforts, in contrast, have been negligible. On the British connection see Menthe Diawara, *African Cinema: Politics and Culture* (Bloomington: Indiana University Press, 1992); Diawara, 'Film in Anglophone Africa', in Andrade-Watkins and Mbye Cham (eds), *Critical Perspectives on Black Independent Cinema* (Cambridge, Mass.: MIT Press, 1988). Diawara's discussion is restricted to Ghana and Nigeria. Zimbabwe gets a back-handed mention in passing. See also David Kerr, 'The Best of Both Worlds? Colonial Film Policy and Practice in Northern Rhodesia and Nyasaland', *Critical Arts*, vol. 7 nos 1/2, 1993, which discusses how the British used film to facilitate their colonial policies. For information on the Portuguese influence see Diawara, *African Cinema*; Andrade-Watkins, 'Portuguese African Cinema', above, pp. 132–47.
19. Ali Mazrui, *The Africans: A Triple Heritage* (Boston, Mass.: Little Brown, 1986).
20. Ibid., pp. 28–30.
21. Frantz Fanon, *A Dying Colonialism* (New York: Grove Press, 1965); *Black Skin, White Masks* (New York: Grove Press, 1967); *The Wretched of the Earth* (Harmondsworth: Penguin, 1967).
22. See Amilcar Cabral, *Revolution in Guinea* (New York: Monthly Review Press, 1969).
23. See Peter Loizos, *Innovation in Ethnographic Film: From Innocence to Self-Consciousness* (Manchester: Manchester University Press, 1993), on the work of John Marshall with the !Kung, David and Judith MacDougall in East Africa and Rouch amongst the Songhay in Niger. See also Paul Stoller, *The Cinematic Griot: The Ethnography of Jean Rouch* (Chicago: Chicago University Press, 1992); Jay Ruby, 'The Cinema of Jean Rouch', in *Visual Anthropology*, vol. 2 nos 3/4, 1989; Ruby (ed.) *The films of John Marshall* (New York: Harwood, 1992).
24. These questions are dealt with in various ways by Haffner, 'L'Esthétique des films', *CinémAction*, vol. 26, 1983; Gardies and Haffner, *Regards sur le cinema négro-africain*; Brendan Shehu, 'Cinema and Culture in Africa', in FEPACI, *L'Afrique et le Centenaire*.
25. One example of this process concerns Sotho groups (the Fokeng and Kwena) who used to occupy the South African high veld. In the 1820s the Difagane devastated their area. Some of the Sotho groups fled into the Lesotho mountains. Others, such as the Fokeng, fled north in 1822 into western Zambia and the Caprivi strip. Having captured and colonised the Caprivi, they renamed themselves the Kololo, and called their new state Lozi. Today, western Zambia and the Caprivi are, as a result, Sotho-speaking. The area the Fokeng evacuated (between Bloemfontein and Pretoria) was, in turn, colonised by the Ndebele (Matebele). In 1837, the Boers defeated the Matebele, who fled north into western Zimbabwe, which they, in turn, colonised by displacing the Shona. The Boers then occupied the high veld areas previously inhabited by the Fokeng and the Matebele. See Paul Maylam, *A History of the African People of Southern Africa* (Cape Town: David Philip, 1986).
26. P. M. Bouteba, 'Cultural Heritage in African Films', *Ufahamu: Journal of the African Activist Association*, vol. 17 no. 3, 1989.
27. Cornelius Moore, 'Finzan: A Dance of Heroes', in Achebe (ed.), *Library of African Cinema*.
28. Frank Ukadike, 'African Films: A Retrospective and a Vision of the Future', in *Critical Arts*, vol. 7 nos 1/2,. 1992.

29. Amie Williams, 'Dancing with Absences: The Impossible Presence of Third World Women in Films', in *Ufahamu*, vol. 27 no. 3, 1995.

30. See P. J. Vast, 'L'Évocation du sacré dans le cinéma africain', in FEPACI, *L'Afrique et le centenaire*; P. N. Pokam, 'L'Evocation due sacré', in *CinémAction*, vol. 26, 1983. Exceptions are Stoller, *The Cinematic Griot*, and the films of Rouch.

31. Teshome Gabriel in 'Third Cinema as the Guardian of Popular Memory: Towards a Third Aesthetics', in Jim Pines and Paul Willemen (eds), *Questions of Third Cinema* (London: BFI, 1989), calls this 'the phase of Remembrance' or 'cultural reapportion' (pp. 32–3).

32. For example Diawara, 'Film in Anglophone Africa'; Ukadike, *Black African Cinema*.

33. See Gabriel, 'Third Cinema as the Guardian of Popular Memory'; Haile Gerima, 'Triangular Cinema, Breaking Toys and Dinkish vs Lucy', in Pines and Willemen (eds), *Questions of Third Cinema*; Cham and Andrade-Watkins (eds), *Critical Perspectives*; Nixon Kariithi, 'Misreading Culture and Tradition: Western Critical appreciation of African Films', in FEPACI, *L'Afrique et le centenaire*.

34. See Pines and Willemen (eds), *Questions of Third Cinema*; Jane Gaines, 'White Privilege and Looking Relations', in *Screen*, vol. 29 no. 4, 1988; Gaines, 'White Theory/Black Film', paper presented at the Modern Language Association, December 1992; Tomaselli and Greg Smith, 'Sign Wars: The Battlegrounds of Semiotics of Cinema in Anglo-Saxonia', in *Degrés – Revue de synthèse à semiologique*, cc1–26; Tomaselli, Arnold Shepperson and Maureen Eke, 'Towards a Theory of Orality in African Cinema', in *Research in African Literatures*, vol. 26 no. 3, Fall 1995; Sheila Petty, 'Whose Nation Is it Anyhow? The Politics of Reading African Cinema in the West', in FEPACI, *L'Afrique et le centenaire*.

35. See Kulick and M. Wilson, 'Rambo's Wife Saves the Day: Subjugating the Gaze and Subverting the Narrative in New Guinea Swamp' (mimeo, 1993); Dwight Conquergood, ' "Is it Real?" Watching Television With Laotian Refugees', *PCDS Directions*, vol. 2 no. 2, 1986.

36. See Gabriel, 'Third Cinema as the Guardian of Popular Memory'.

37. Roy Armes, *Third World Filmmaking and the West* (Berkeley: University of California Press, 1987). This omission has been rectified by Armes in Roy Armes and Lizbeth Malkmus, *Arab and African Film Making* (London: Zed, 1991).

38. See also Schmidt, 'Review of Six books on African Cinema', in *Africa Today*, 2nd Quarter 1989.

39. See FEPACI, *L'Afrique et le centenaire*, as an example of the critical work fostered by the Federation. Significantly, this volume contains a chapter by a White South African, which may be indicative of South Africa's inclusion after apartheid under the rubric of Africa. An exiled South African, Lionel Ngakane, was a founder member of FEPACI and is active on its executive.

40. See, for example, Jeanne Prinsloo, 'Beyond Propp and Oedipus: Towards Expanding Narrative Theory', *Literator*, vol. 13 no. 3, 1992; John Higgins, 'Documentary Realism and Film Pleasure; Two Moments from Euzhan Palcy's *A Dry White Season*', ibid.; Blignaut and Botha (eds), *Movies – Moguls – Mavericks*; Botha and Adri Van Aswegan, *Images of South Africa: The Rise of Alternative Film* (Pretoria: Human Sciences Research Council, 1992); Schmidt, *Bibliography*; Ruby, *The Films of John Marshall*; Ukadike, 'African Films'; Achebe (ed.), *Library of African Cinema*; FEPACI, *L'Afrique et le centenaire*; Gardies and Haffner, *Regards sur le cinéma négro-africain*.

41. The first M-NET/University of Natal Festival of African Cinema occurred in October 1995. This co-operation for the first time makes African films systematically available to the university for study purposes.

South/South Axis: For a Cinema Built by, with and for Africans

ROD STONEMAN

A version of this paper was published in *Ecrans d'Afrique*, nos 5/6, 3rd/4th quarter, 1993.

Thirty years after Sembène's pioneering *Borom Sarret*, this is a moment of celebration but also of self-assessment for emergent African cinema – an opportunity to think through questions of funding, the bases of production, and the way that various African films address their different audiences.

Pieces of Identity

In Europe and North America a nebulous, imaginary unity is projected onto Africa. This lazily assumed misconception continues to underpin the distorting insularity and ignorance of the North. It is precisely an imaginary, implicit unity and not to be confused with the distinct political unity proposed by the project of pan-Africanism, built from conscious political and cultural alliances. One does not have to be too familiar with the continent to understand that there are also many Africas – culturally, politically, socially. Indeed more than a thousand languages are spoken in Africa and there are as many complex social systems, cultures and organisations of community life.

In the past African cinema has been depicted with a broad brush stroke, mapping its productions onto wide geographic categorisations: Northern, Western and Southern African cinemas. These cultural divisions are overlaid by colonial boundaries – strange and arbitrary groupings – but they constitute a set of relations which separate some countries and connect others. More attention could be devoted to articulating the complex categories of similarity and difference in Africa; indeed, all this can be said about Europe too. Any attempts to edge the tectonic plates of a continent together that does not recognise the diversity and hybridity of its cultures is unlikely to succeed.

African cinema makes connections between such separations, drawing out correspondence and indicating differences. Films offer unexpected recognitions, bringing images into focus and debate. One thinks of the Tunisian film *Halfaouine*'s success in Morocco and other Muslim countries and the young South African who spoke movingly of being startled half way through Cissé's *Yeleen*, suddenly realising that he had never before watched thirty minutes of any film without white faces.

Most approaches to cultural and national difference in African cinema are made without reference to the questions of class and gender. It seems necessary to stress the shameful fact that over 90 per cent of African cinema is still produced by men and that inevitably most of those that get to make films come from the urbanised, educated elites of their respective countries.

175

Ultra-Auteurism

African cinema has developed largely on auteurist lines with a predominance of directors who are also, at one and the same time, the producers of their own films. The same people conceive, write, raise the finance for, direct and produce most African movies – and then they organise the festivals and run the magazines. While this represents a welcome dissolution of the strict demarcations between roles in industrial cinema, at some point the lack of complementary specialisation may also be a disadvantage. A body of professional, entrepreneurial, cultural producers is badly needed to articulate potential funding sources and, it can also be argued, to strengthen individual production processes.

This artisanal basis condemns many directors to long gaps between their films, as the Senegalese film maker Gai Ramaka indicates: 'they have always gone on the long, solitary and laboured quest for international aid, accepting all its criteria and demands, making one film every four to ten years'. Then, when production eventually commences the directorial id has no productorial superego to keep an eye on the budget. This leads to questions about the way in which different production modes provide different bases for films to address their audiences. The scores of scriptwriters and a heavily hierarchical structure that industrial production brings to bear on every film produces a high degree of formula production – versions of this can be seen in Indian and Hong Kong, and even Egyptian, cinema. This is not to pose a reductionist dichotomy – either 'industrial' or 'individual' – for African cinema, but to propose an examination of the spaces available. To win a cultural war with guerrilla tactics it is necessary to navigate this terrain, and think through the way any mode of production affects what appears on the screen.

Footnotes in Dependence

As a result of the cultural and political conservatism of virtually all African television, in many countries the most vigorous production sector has come into being around feature film-making. The complete lack of space for intelligent or imaginative work within television has increased the isolation and financial constraints of cinema on the continent. To some extent this also accounts for the concentration of feature production and the lack of creative documentary work in Africa, in comparison with Latin America and Asia, for instance.

Although only available to a small, urban fraction of most populations, the constraints of terrestrial television in Africa are serious. Unlike the foreign domination of cinema exhibition, at this point the problems of television are more a matter of internal political blockage than external imposition. It is not entirely a question of financial resources although the constant and reliable supply of cheap Western product has made real challenge more difficult. But, as democratic movements in various countries demand air space for the contending dynamics of a society as part of its transformation, gradually the first multinational versions of foreign television intervention across the continent via satellite are making their appearance on the horizon.

Although one of the benefits of a concentration on features for cinema release has been an avoidance of governmental interference, the considerable budgetary and human resources involved in any cinematic enterprise inevitably place economic pressures on the independence of the producer. The major outside force at play in African cinema is French government finance in its several forms. The Ministry of Co-operation often provides 20–25 per cent of production budgets, while the recently created Ecrans du Sud supports development, distribution and training. The effect of this sustained funding centred on francophone Africa can be seen in comparison with the uneven and debilitated development of other, say anglophone and lusophone, cinemas; although there may be other geographical and cultural factors in this.

In response to the field of force exerted by French funding and longer-term strategic aims, it is imperative to extend and consolidate an interactive mosaic of funding. A range of financial sources should come into play in different, specific configurations. For each African film the funding source should be a balanced combination of monies from several disparate directions (indigenous and Northern, television and cinema, commercial and state). Although considerable effort is necessary to draw these different sources of finance together, when achieved it guarantees a level of independence and wide dissemination. In this context the connection and co-operation of different African states in production and in supporting distribution and exhibition is still imperative. Ousmane Sembène's *Camp de Thiaroye*, made in 1987 with financial backing from Senegal, Tunisia and Algeria, is exemplary in this regard.

One of the dangers of a fixed dependency on a few limited sources of external finance is perhaps indicated by the French Ministry of Co-operation's recent, short-lived and inappropriate attempt to place a precredit sequence and logo 'The Minister of Co-operation presents' (plus a new version of Pathé's gallic cockerel?) on the films it part-funded. Nothing should be taken for granted. Any source of funding can fade away as quickly as it arrived for distant and irrelevant reasons. Much of the current Northern funding network was set up for other logics and motives, and operates within different dynamics, not necessarily relating to the needs of development of Southern cinema. Last year TVE in Spain completely cut its $20 million budget for co-production with Latin America, and Channel Four has made severe reductions in the budgets for Third World feature work over the last two years.

Film-makers are now addressing the complex and pertinent issue of how money coming from the North affects or modifies the overall range of cinema in the South. Is there an unconscious predilection for certain kinds of product, a selective prioritisation of certain types of films? What kinds of African films are more difficult, or even impossible, for European television? Do specific interventions change particular films? No commutation test exists when asking how these relations may affect the organic development of African cinema – it is not possible to know those films which have never been made! But perhaps it would be worth carrying out some research to produce an exact analysis of the proportion and typology of African films made with little or no Northern funding.

It would be inappropriate to seek to dictate, or impose a 'modelisation' – in this context it is essential for Northern funders to maintain a pluralistic, open attitude and develop their support for a wide range of forms and tendencies in film. It is the free contention of those varied tendencies that creates a healthy cinema culture. In Mao Tse Tung's elegant formulation: 'Letting a hundred flowers blossom and a hundred schools of thought contend is the policy for promoting the progress of the arts.' But such formulations are all too often merely rhetorical; as the sad example of the artistic regime in China itself indicates, governments habitually prefer more constrained policies.

In and Out of History

In trying to track the influence of foreign funding a tentative typology of texts might be useful. One can approach the diversity and specificity of recent production through three (somewhat reductive) categories:

Village Films

This anthropological and folkloristic genre is generally imprecisely located in the precolonial epoch. *Wend Kuuni* is an exquisite and early example. More recently, *Yaaba, Layla, ma raison* and *Tilai* have been very successful.

Modern Social Films

In contrast, these are marked by an engagement, in some form or another, with contemporary social reality: *The Blue Eyes of Yonta, Bezness, Guelwaar*. They may still be set in the village but they generally deal with some aspect of the effect of the city on that rural economy. *Zan Boko, Ta Dona, Sango Malo, Finzan, Disha, After the Storm* and *Tinpis Run* are equivalent examples from other parts of the world (India, Argentina and Papua New Guinea).

Magic Realist Films

These involve more of a formal departure from the constraints of the dominant mode of representation, the language and grammar of the classical narrative cinema which evolved in America and Europe in the first twenty years of this century. The term 'realist' signifies the modern setting into which magic, the Other, erupts; connecting that reality with forms of specifically African culture and religion: *Touki Bouki* and *Hyenas, Laada* and *Saaraba*. Even though they are set in Europe, *Africa am Rhein* and *Ama*, and *African Voyage of Discovery*, in their invocation of the power of ancestors and contemporary manifestations of animism, can be seen as part of this genre.

There is a danger that the anthropological genre of 'village films', more attractive to European cinema and television, potentially allows the magnetic pull of foreign audiences and foreign finance to affect the range and emphasis of African cinemas. The North's desire for 'village films' can be connected with an underlying humanist ideology traceable to (at least) 'The Family of Man', a photographic exhibition organised and published by *Life* magazine just after the Second World War. It comprised images of humanity in all its diversity, juxtaposing photos of, say, an Inuit hunter from Canada with an Italian child, a Peruvian peasant with a Hong Kong taxi driver. In the context of the immediately post-colonial era this exhibition was a well-intentioned assertion of an underlying 'common' humanity at a specific historical moment when the recently liberated nations were placing themselves on new and more equal terms internationally. The photographs of the myriad individuals seemed to say 'different, but the same' – a meaning encased within strong connotations of the exotic produced by the extreme unfamiliarity and distance of the signified. But today at quite a different historical moment this same humanist enterprise effaces other sets of differences which underlie the new world order, differences around the relative distribution of power, money and resources, for instance. For how long can the richest 20 per cent of the world continue to consume 80 per cent of the world's goods and resources?

'Village films' also disavow the relations of history – one of their defining characteristics is that they position their narratives outside history and outside time. It is this historical and social imprecision that allows them to fall more easily within the penumbra of humanism. 'Modern social films' confront the society in which they are made, as do specific historical explorations like Med Hondo's *Sarraounia* and Haile Gerima's recent *Sankofa*, which represent a purposeful invocation of a historical moment in the face of the present. The West African bird which looks both forwards and backwards, in the title of Gerima's film, specifically invokes the role of the past in affecting the present and changing the future.

The recent genre of 'village films' seem to inhabit the same humanist ideology as 'The Family of Man': they may be read in their countries of origin as a reclamation of an image of precolonial history, sometimes engaging in a polemic with traditional values in contemporary society. But a Western audience watching *Yaaba* recognises the adultery, the closeness between small children and a 'grandparent' as asserting that humanity is the same here and there...

This is not to condemn or dismiss a whole genre. Some examples, such as *Wend Kuuni*, *Yaaba* and *Layla, ma raison*, are strong pieces of cinema that have found wide resonance at home as well as abroad, but their success should be related to the complex questions of audience, reception and finance. A cinema which is not based on productive interaction with its own social context is displaced, adrift. The dangers of cultural production for export are also touched on by Adewale Maja-Pearce, echoing Ngugi wa Thiong'o, in his polemical critique of the Nigerian novel – 'continuing to write in "European" languages perpetuates the colonial dependency that has brought the continent to its present point of collapse'. The initial equilibrium between artistic aspirations and political aims in the founding declarations of the film-makers' organisation FEPACI seems to be less evident at this time, but anyone who is interested in the social role of cinema must always ask: How do these films function and for whom?

The Question of an Audience

Given the problems of distribution and exhibition in Africa, perhaps it is not surprising that many film-makers do not consciously connect themselves with the notion of specific audiences or think through the way that their films work with different publics at home and abroad. The high proportion of finance coming to productions from Europe exacerbates the problem and abstracts film production from its felt relationship with audiences. The proliferation of festivals of African cinema, many of them outside Africa, displace the moment of the film's reception, leading to a deeper confusion and the spurious notion of a 'universal' audience.

The more urgent and concrete problems of distribution and exhibition in Africa have always been a serious infrastructural deficiency. As Flora Gomes put it, 'Nowadays film-makers must think about African audiences ... we must be able to produce and distribute in Africa to be closer to our public.' It is to be hoped that gradually forms of South/South distribution will grow up alongside the North/South axis. The problems of American cultural hegemony are considerable and they have become a global phenomenon (of all the films

179

shown in British cinemas in 1990, 93 per cent were American). In this sense the pretensions and aspirations which English and Italian cinema, say, had to being 'industries' are almost over – European cinema also exists at an artisanal level now.

A film means different things to different audiences. It may be located very differently in separate cultural contexts – in the country of its production and abroad. A film like Férid Boughedir's *Halfaouine* shifts cultural space quite dramatically. It is a strong example of popular cinema in Tunisia, breaking all box-office records and out-grossing all American production in the year of its release. It made back one-third of its production cost (£600,000) in its home market, although it was cheaply sold to a distributor in sub-Saharan Africa (a return of only £5,000). But it is relocated in the space of 'art cinema' when shown in Europe or America. Everything from the use of subtitles, the style of publicity, to the type of buildings it is shown in confines it to a socially limited audience. To some extent this is also true of the television spaces available; both Channel Four and BBC2 have specific young/male/middle-class audience profiles – part of the British speciality for anachronistic class distinctions.

Desire for Diversity

One of the real strengths of African cinema in recent years has been its sustaining interaction with the fast-changing ferment of African culture and society, where, for example, many countries are starting to question the idea of the one-party state. There are intense debates about models and forms of democratisation; meanwhile urbanisation and the rapid transformation of rural communities continues apace. At the same time the relations between men and women, the open affirmation of other forms of sexuality, are changing fast. A whole range of fresh possibilities and problems are developing at unprecedented speed.

The turbulence of this social maelstrom has its effect on cultural production and on different cinematic strategies. Cinema has had a relevant role in relation to the development of emancipatory, democratic desires on the continent – as a means of exploring a contradictory process, provoking openings, challenging constraints and testing limits from *Le Vent* and *Zan Boko* to, more recently, *Allah Tantou* or *Thomas Sankara*. Feature work has provided a space to restate fearlessly desires for free media as one way of countering corruption and tyranny. As Souleymane Cissé recently suggested, 'Cinema should have a disruptive influence even in a democracy – the new constitutions should include creative freedom and not only freedom of the press.' In the long term the African cinema that is going to sustain its 'disruptive influence' is not going to be built outside Africa. For it to have an effective social, cultural interaction it has to be built inside Africa by, with and for Africans.

Images of Women

FARIDA AYARI

Translated by Paul Willemen from *CinémAction*, no. 26, 1983.

On our continent, the seventh art is still mainly men's business. We lack actresses because in African societies this activity is still not regarded as a profession. Women technicians are even scarcer because it is assumed that technical matters are part of the male preserve. We are especially short of women producers and directors. (Farida Ayari, Mogadishu Symposium, 1981)

Of course, there are exceptions, though few and far between. In Black Africa, only the West Indian Sarah Maldoror has cast a woman's eye on African women. Her *Sambizanga* celebrates the Angolan liberation struggle through the film's heroine. As for the second exception, the ethnographer and only women director in Black Africa Safi Faye, she addresses the rural milieu. While stressing the difficulties peasants have to survive as their conditions of life are completely overturned by the introduction of industrial cultures, she nevertheless insists on bringing to the fore the role of women within traditional village societies, as in *Lettre paysanne* and *Fad Jal*.

But for these two exceptions, the image of African women in African cinema remains essentially that created by men. Of course, African films, however modest, do present us with a fairly representative kaleidoscope of female figures. However, these are women fabricated within the imaginary of the men who make the films, regardless of how close to reality this imaginary at times may be, since, apart from a few surrealist beacons like Ousmane Sembène's *Emitai* and *Ceddo* or Diop Mambety's *Touki-Bouki*, African cinema is realist, socially oriented, didactic and linear.

Consequently, it is no surprise that the stories and the characters in these films, primarily derived from observation, bear the signs, like all creative works, of having been worked over by the imagination or of being the products of projection. The image of women in African cinema is the result of a male gaze at a mostly male society, in spite of a film such as *Kodou* by the Senegalese director Ababacar Samb, which is based on a story by Annette Mbaye d'Erneville and features a heroine. The point is that there is a whole universe which escapes this male gaze – the world of women, as confirmed by Peuhl proverb that says: 'A man cannot imagine what a woman can do.' At times, this inexplorable jungle is deftly circumvented by the complicity, in the best sense of the term, that grows between a director and an

181

actress. In such cases, when the imagination of the director combines with the female mentality of the actress, a result even truer than reality may be achieved.

All this does not mean that the image of women in African films is utterly false; only that regardless of the degree of realism, veracity or sensitivity, the representation remains a male one. In this respect, the work of the Malian film-maker Souleymane Cissé is noteworthy because this director has addressed the condition of women like none of his male colleagues. In *Den Musso* he paints a portrait of rejected women. Why rejected? Because they are denied the right to speak as well as the right to be heard. To emphasise the point, the director constructed the character of a mute: 'To make the public understand the utter isolation experienced by these unfortunate young women, I chose to make my heroine a mute.' Cissé is a director who deals mainly with what he knows best and he focused his powers of observation on the Bamako society to which he belongs. Neither a city nor a village, Bamako is typical of the Sahel capital towns with their whitewashed walls right next to the concrete façades of the administrative buildings. In between them, a whole world circulates, a world all too quickly coming up against the edges of the countryside and in which shards of Occidental society, the tattiest and most superficial aspects of a foreign culture, have become surreptitiously insinuated. In that microcosm which can be found in all the metropolises of the continent, there is but little to choose between a hand-to-mouth job and unemployment.

In Cissé's film, a man from that lumpenproletariat fathers the heroine's child. This unwanted child is heaven's punishment, a living proof that a sin was committed. Being a single mother is the worst sin a Muslim woman can commit. The sin is indelible and unforgivable, and the family tries to deny it by rejecting their sinful daughter. To 'make amends' for the misfortune, there is only one conceivable course of action: throw the daughter into the street. This story which may seem antediluvian to a Westerner is repeated every day, thousands of times, in Africa. Because in this story many women recognised themselves, their friends or relations, and many men too recognised their peers, *Den Muso* achieved an immense popular success in Mali. And, even if the heroine had not been a mute, her fate would have been the same. Imprisoned in the solitude generated by the total lack of understanding that surrounds her, she has no way out other than suicide.

Oumarou Ganda broaches a similar problem in his *The Polygamous Wazzu*. Satu isn't even consulted over her marriage to the old polygamist. After passively resisting, the heroine flees to the city, where, of course, she has no option but to 'sell ass'. What distinguishes the heroines of Souleymane Cissé and Oumarou Ganda is a question of sensitivity. If the heroine of *Den Muso* is tragic, that is because Cissé animated her with all his feelings of rebellion. Ganda's character remains superficial and so becomes a stereotype, a cliché. Satu's downfall and degeneration is never explained; it isn't even shown. Ganda is content simply to inform us that 'she got entangled in the maelstrom of the city'.

Such a tendency to deploy clichés is even more pronounced in the Cameroonian cinema. In *Muna Moto*, Jean-Pierre Dikongue-Pipa also tackles the issue of forced marriages. Again, it is the richest suitor who gets the young woman. The force of this first feature made in flashback is due to the impact of its black-and-white imagery in which gesture wins out over speech. With this story, Dikongue-Pipa denounces his society, the values of which have been destroyed by the money introduced by the colonialists. The encounter between traditional culture and European culture has created in many minds a confusion about values. This is the subject of his second film, *The Price of Freedom*, where he describes the journey of a young woman who wants to escape her traditional milieu and goes to the city. There, she will pay a heavy price to achieve the freedom she craves: prostitution. One could object that Dikongue-Pipa's characters are one-dimensional and lack complexity. True, the film is clichéd and deploys stereotypes: the Westernisation of young African women is by no means as crude as the director makes out.

It is worth noting that nine times out of ten, female characters in African films meet a sorry fate. No doubt because the film-makers feel they have a pedagogic and moral mission, the screen presents characters who cannot overcome. There are almost no positive heroines. Film-makers are quick to show us the examples that must not be followed, but rarely do they show women with all their qualities as well as faults without judging them. And yet, there are exceptions.

In *Baara*, Souleymane Cissé gives us two portraits of women. The university-educated wife of the engineer stays at home because her husband forbids her to go out to work. Here, male attitudes are critiqued: no matter how 'modern' he fancies himself to be, he remains attached to traditional values which are fast becoming anachronistic in today's Africa. Such incomprehension threatens to destroy the couple, but Cissé is more concerned with something else and he doesn't dwell on the matter, merely suggesting it. More interesting is the wife of the factory boss. I see her as typical of a whole category of women who, without the benefit of a formal education, mobilised their own natural aptitudes and learnt the ins and outs of the business world. Djeneba has been raised according to the tradition that regards women as merchandise to be sold at the highest possible price. She has understood the system perfectly and sold herself to the rich industrialist, while reserving her heart for her lovers. In this way, she achieves a kind of personal equilibrium. At first sight, one might think her a bad woman. In fact, her behaviour is dictated by the need to survive. She has no choice: in order to support her horrible husband, she needs an escape, which she grasps whenever she can. If she had been an intellectual, perhaps she might have had recourse to nobler activities. I regard Djeneba as one of the most engaging female characters in African cinema. Intelligent, she is also capable of emotion. Beautiful, she also has a strong personality.

Before Cissé, Ousmane Sembène tackled the neocolonial bourgeoisie in his *Xala*. There, too, traditional and modern women come face to face, but the most interesting character is the young daughter of the Hadj Abdu Kadr Bey. She is a cultivated student who speaks to her father only in Wolof. She symbolises a certain kind of modern Africa. She is 'a positive heroine' in the sense that she does not allow herself to be suffocated by the weight of tradition nor does she get carried away by the intoxicating mirages of modernity. On the other hand, the character of Fanta in *Djeli* by the Ivorian director Fadika Kramo-Lancine is a little tarnished by her suicide attempt. Fanta is a modern young woman who is very close to her father, a man attached to traditional values who nevertheless accepts that his daughter studies and chooses her own husband. But Fanta will break because of an old custom which forbids a member of her own noble caste to marry someone from a lower caste, to which her fiancé happens to belong.

African film-makers seem to regard the issue of women's emancipation as a favourite subject. Polygamy, liberation, emancipation, the shock between cultures and values are, and will no doubt long remain, their principal sources of inspiration.

Black African Feminist Film-Making?

SHEILA PETTY

Reprinted from *Society for Visual Anthropology Review*, vol. 6 no. 1, Spring 1990.

In an article published on the occasion of the 5th Journées du Cinema Africain in Montreal, 24–30 April 1989, Harold Weaver outlines certain 'observable trends' in current African film production. Two of these trends involve the 'proliferation of complementary African Diaspora films', of which '*Sarraounia* and *Testament* join the earlier *Harvest 3000 Years* as revisionist cinematic products challenging the traditional Eurocentric interpretations of African history ... a common denominator of these African Diasporic films, no matter the birthplace of the film-maker, is an Afrocentric sensitivity', and 'a deeply feminist – not always female – commitment to human and equal rights for both genders'.[1] Mbye Cham has argued that the pan-African spirit of recent productions works to recover an African past and contextualise it within present-day Africa.[2] The references to pan-Africanism, Afrocentricity and feminism raise interesting yet problematic issues for examining women's representation and the processes of reception that provoke a multiplicity of readings in African film.

While feminist theory has been largely concerned with gender-specific issues (women's position as 'other', and so on), the question of race and class being sublimated into other discourses, a phallocentric pan-Africanism validates racial differences, conflating those of gender and class. This latter type of thought structure privileges Black nationalism over specifically feminist concerns. To what degree, then, are African films 'feminist' or 'pan-African'? Ideally, an African feminist film should strive not simply to synthesise feminist and pan-African ideas but to balance concerns in an attempt to understand the interconnectedness of race, gender and class oppression, so that binary oppositions are not created wherein one term takes precedence over another.

It is the purpose of this paper to analyse certain systems of strategies employed by African film-makers which could lead to claims of feminism when perhaps the film-makers have other more urgent agendas. In pursuing such an analysis, I shall explore the implications of Africans' and women's shared views of experiences of oppression on the processes of production and reception of Black African film.

It has been argued that the African 'world view' and the feminine 'world view' share certain similarities. Each 'group' has suffered a common experience; a shared history of oppression through slavery, colonialism and apartheid has encouraged an 'Afrocentric' consciousness among Black societies and a shared history of patriarchal oppression has led to a 'feminist' consciousness among women.

The varying material conditions of oppression from group to group may lead to the valorisation of certain issues at the expense of others. Thus, each group may create its own hierarchy of priorities. Both groups, however, have been 'assigned' similar perceptions of the self: the individual as insignificant in the face of the group, as dependent on and defined through relationships with others, the continuity and inseparability of nature and culture, and so on. Thus, 'to Africans and women are attributed ethics that emphasize responsibilities to increasing the welfare of social complexes through contextual, inductive and tentative decision processes; and epistemologies that conceptualize the knower as a part of the known, the known as affected by the process of coming to know, and that process as one which unites hand, brain, and heart'.[3]

Since these commonalities are sketched out and produced within projects of social domination, it could be argued that both African film-makers and feminist film-makers are reacting to a mainstream aesthetic. The issue, however, is much more complex considering that, although both feminist and African cinematic practices are deconstructive on the levels of ideology and style, 'those who argue for a women's culture are electing to value, rather than denigrate, those traits associated with females in white patriarchal societies'.[4]

Thus, feminist discourse is created in the context of and produced by oppression whereas an Afrocentric discourse, rather than defining itself in relation to the 'dominant', identifies itself with an independent, historic culture associated with a society.[5] Determining what might constitute the 'feminist' or the 'pan-African' in production and reception processes necessitates an examination of how discourses present themselves in given texts. Focusing on *Sarraounia* (Med Hondo, Burkina Faso/France, 1986), I shall argue that, although the film presents certain positive directions for the representation of African women, the film-maker's chief concern does not lie in the delineation of a specifically feminist African aesthetic.

The film *Sarraounia* depicts the encounter in the 19th century between the French colonial troops and the Aznas of Niger led by their warrior queen, Sarraounia. Sarraounia's desire for a 'pan-African' kingdom free from colonial rule and Muslim conquest is conjured up in the code of conduct she continually evokes as she rallies her people: solidarity, love, honour, dignity, death rather than shame and slavery. The film-maker's adoption of the epic genre to create a larger-than-life portrayal of Sarraounia and her quest is logical given the subject matter, but Hondo also calls into question the hegemony of dominant modes in the industry by investing the film with his own political and aesthetic project. Not surprisingly, Sarraounia's code of conduct becomes the film's subject, subsequently informing the film's structure and use of cinematic codes.

The film conforms to a classical narrative ordering in its linear and chronological presentation of events. The departure from the model occurs, however, on two levels and this reordering of certain elements upon which the classic text depends helps forge the film's aesthetic project. Although the film is bounded at both ends by the assertion of synchronic order, the narrative itself does not effect a return to the *original* synchronic order. A conventional text depends upon movement towards a denouement and its economy dictates that no events be superfluous to this purpose. But in *Sarraounia* subject rather than plot lends unity to the film.

Not all images necessarily function to advance the narrative. In fact, there are precise moments of shifting away from a presentation of the 'dramatic' events of the narrative in order to foreground discourse centring on the efficacy of solidarity in the preservation of a menaced society. This form of presentation necessitates the subordination of the visual image to spoken dialogue and of action to space. Not surprisingly, Sarraounia's power, courage and exploits are expressed through speech rather than dramatic actions.

The fact that narrative events revolve round conflicting attitudes and behaviour towards a code of conduct, rather than interior or interpersonal conflicts, may account for (but not justify) some European critics' rejection of the film as poorly constructed and unnecessarily didactic. This rejection lies, perhaps, in the film's inability to mirror a desired image of the European as omnipotent and omnipresent in Africa. Furthermore, these critics have failed to understand that it is the binary opposition African space to European space that is the central organising principle of the film, not the dramatic events themselves. The centrality of this dualism to the filmic structure is characteristic of many other African films.

In *Zan Boko* (Gaston Kaboré, Burkina Faso, 1988), Tinga and Nopoko witness the 'confiscation' of traditional space as city boundaries continue to expand and eventually absorb their village. The continual clashing of the two cultures forces a progression in the narrative and renders a highly elliptical structure in which key narrative events are de-emphasised. This structuring was regarded as 'disconcerting' by some critics (once again, European) at FESPACO in Ouagadougou, Burkina Faso, 1989. Are these critics inferring that the narrative's treatment is naïve?[6] According to Kaboré, no elements of the script were eliminated during the shooting. *Zan Boko*'s structure, however, conjures up the film-maker's philosophy that certain events occur in life without a premise. The result of these events' collision raises questions about modern African society. For example, will the collision of traditional African and modern European values and space allow Tinga to remain faithful to his Zan Boko.[7] The resolution is left for the viewer to sort out.

In *Sarraounia*, identification with European space involves the adoption of the 'master' language as the only valid means of communication. Yet the subscription to the dominating power means the loss of one's African identity; the young African woman's propositioning in French of the army doctor conjures up a sort of pathos because of its lack of spontaneity. *Sarraounia*'s (Hondo's) proposed project of pan-Africanism involves the recovery of an African space in which Africans from all ethnic groups join forces to fight European imperialism. This project is realised in the film's resolution as Sarraounia welcomes the women and men from neighbouring kingdoms who join her forces and return with her to her kingdom. Recovery as well as rehabilitation of traditional space is made apparent as Sarraounia returns to her City of Lougou all the while urging each new member to retain her or his language and spiritual beliefs.

To identify with Sarraounia offers a stake in a 'feminist' claim to the body and its image. A woman is cast as the heroine of the film and, according to the encoding of dominant cinema, she should be present in almost every shot from the beginning of the film to its end. This does not occur in *Sarraounia*. The person of Sarraounia is not always shown on the screen; her presence is more often psychical than physical and images of her body are never constructed in ways which are accessible to the male gaze. In fact, the film demystifies the phallic idea that all women are reproductive apparatuses in waiting. Quite the opposite discourse is at work in another 1986 production focusing on African life in Paris. In *Black Mic-Mac* (Thomas Gilou, France, 1986), original cinematic content and forms are not being generated to probe African realities. The young Congolese woman, Anisette, is eroticised and objectified on the screen. During a dance sequence, a series of medium and close-up shots of her undulating hips is the focus of her 'cousin's' and the French inspector's attention. As she becomes the object of their gaze, the 'cousin' exclaims, 'Look at those curves!' This male gaze carries with it the power of action and possession, for the 'cousin' promptly proceeds to 'sell' Anisette to the inspector: 'She can cook, she can clean ... go ahead, dance with her ... go on ... attack, ATTACK!'

The assessment of Anisette's domestic talents momentarily directs attention away from 'woman as ornament' to 'woman as object of exchange and as producer of producers'. But women's hips are not fetishised as such in African societies; they are considered part of a whole 'sacred vessel' carrying life and strength. By refusing to consider Anisette's body in its totality, the film-maker is rejecting her as a whole person and is resorting to the clichéd practice of fragmenting woman's body for male pleasure.[8]

Safi Faye's feature work offers a much more positive direction for women's representation and identification in film. In *Peasant Letter* (Senegal, 1975) and *Fad Jal* (Senegal, 1979), Faye creates an invisible heroine of cultural identity and collective consciousness and then proceeds to position this heroine outside the frame space and in the extra-diegetic, thus challenging the construction of the female subject 'as body'.

Sarraounia, who is described by Manthia Diawara in his essay as 'an African woman taking the hero position of Western films and becoming larger than life',[9] may appear as an individual heroine at first. Yet rarely is her screen presence divorced from that of her people. Her presence transcends the diegetic so that she is read through the actions of her people. Her desire for solidarity and dignity and her promise of eternity to the loyal (by association with her name when griots sing her praises) ensures that cultural identity becomes the collective heroine of the film. The curious process whereby cultural identity becomes subject and heroine leads one to question just how subjectivity is inscribed in the film.

By what process is subjectivity displaced from producer of discourse to receiver of discourse? How are the 'I' and the 'You' of discourse 'collapsed in the figure of the spectator'?[10] Here the term spectator should not be understood as a direct reference to a social subject, but to a psychical subject. If identification is a process and not a state, then spectatorial positions are processes of construction. Mary Ann Doane argues that both women and men spectators alternate between feminine and masculine positions but 'men will be more likely to occupy the positions delineated as masculine, women those specified as feminine'. Finally, she hopes that spectatorship can one day be theorised outside the pincers of sexual difference as a binary opposition. 'On the other hand, the shift in focus from the male spectator to the female spectator in contemporary film theory is a political gesture of some significance in itself.'[11]

The concept of female spectatorship, however, still invokes the female/male dualism and assumes that all women share equal experiences and histories. This form of phallic reasoning denies women of colour their various histories. The independent film-maker Alile Sharon Larkin explains that 'historically, Black men have abused us, but they have never held the kind of power that white women hold in this culture. Both historically and currently, white women participate in and reap the benefits of white supremacy. Feminism must address these issues, otherwise its ahistorical approach towards Black women can and does maintain institutional racism.'[12]

Sarraounia challenges the textual operations of dominant cinema by imposing a transformation in spectator–text relations from passive receptivity to a more active, questioning position. The film-maker's project recalls the political objectives of Brechtian epic theatre's anti-illusionist strategies. Epic theatre refuses psychologically rounded character representations in order to discourage passive identification with characters. *Sarraounia*'s process of subjectivity inscription operates in a relatively more complex manner. The film's refusal of psychologically rounded characters in fact encourages spectator identification. Various devices that would traditionally encourage cinematic address are disrupted so that the stitching-in of the spectator is performed in the name of Afrocentricity as opposed to Euro-homo-centricity. The film's very use of the shot/countershot pattern defies the traditional function of this edit.

Conflictual encounters between two individuals stemming from purely personal motives are rare in African cinema. Rather, this type of edit is used to present conflicts of opinion of a more collective nature. For example, Sarraounia's confrontation with her lover Baka is not a lovers' quarrel or a declaration of Sarraounia's emancipation (when Sarraounia is still a child, her protector describes her future relationships with men: 'The male will be an object of pleasure for you, not an arrogant, egotistical master'). It is quite simply an affirmation of the queen's desire to lead the attack against the enemy in the way she feels will best ensure the preservation of her kingdom's identity. When Baka rejoins her army towards the end of the film, Sarraounia welcomes him not as a lover but as a warrior identifying with the struggle. Both encounters are presented in shot/reverse shot structures in which Sarraounia is always accorded the reverse-angle view.

During this process of suture, the spectator 'stands in' for Sarraounia and becomes the subject-in-the-text. Spectator/subject as centre and origin of meaning is further reinforced through point-of-view shots involving a relay of looks in a series of shots at the beginning of the film between Sarraounia, her griot and the spectator. As the griot sings her praises, he addresses Sarraounia/the camera/the spectator. The next shot frames Sarraounia, whose look coincides with the look of the griot. As the viewer looks at her or his own process of looking, she or he is hailed by the text and is required to address consciously the process of identification itself.

Med Hondo's presentation of the griot conforms to his own political project. Although other African film-makers have chosen to denounce the griot's prostitution of his new status in neocolonial Africa, Hondo 'recovers' the person of the griot in his film because of his belief in the griot's ability to offset the loss of cultural identity in post-colonial Africa. All the aspects of his past status are compiled in the griot's final song. He is teacher, witness and judge as he implies that Sarraounia has taught her people that death is preferable to shame and that the struggle will continue until all Africans are free. He immortalises her name and her exploits in proclaiming that words live on after deeds.

As a discursive device, the griot ensures that subject, heroine and spectator become one so that collective consciousness, cultural identity and an eternal African memory are called into concrete being. This specific recovery of African history foregrounds Hondo's projected desire for the solidarity of liberation struggles in contemporary Africa. Interestingly, the film's denouement defies Kitia Touré's conjecture that an overwhelming number of African films end in death or in a failure of some sort, leading one to question whether a 'philosophy of failure and self-denial runs through the film-makers' heads'.[13] Is Touré referring specifically to the first two decades of African film-making, for besides *Sarraounia,* other current African productions (*Heritage Africa,* Kwaw Ansah, Ghana, 1988, and *Mortu Nega,* Flora Gomes, Guinea-Bissau, 1988) portray victorious outcomes in the struggle against structures of alienation or (*Dunia,* Pierre Yameogo, Burkina Faso, 1987, and *Finzan,* Cheick Oumar Sissoko, Mali, 1989) compel the audience to create resolution?

Meanings constructed from Hondo's projected Utopia at the end of the film are based on viewers' various histories and experiences, social class, race, gender, sexual preference, and so on. The African feminist spectator searching for a critique of race, gender and class oppression in *Sarraounia* may enter into the polemics of negotiation.[14] Sarraounia's/Hondo's Utopia certainly maintains a Black communal solidarity but the critique of sexism is sublimated into various portrayals of White male behaviour toward African women and the subsequent appropriation of these models by African men during colonialism. At no point in the film does the film-maker effect a critique of those specific mores of traditional African society that oppressed women. Although the creation of a new Utopia involves displacement of original synchronic order (a monolithic kingdom replaced by a pan-African kingdom), the extent to which gender relations will be revised is not made clear.

Unlike Negritude, Med Hondo's project certainly does not encourage a romantic nostalgia that glosses over contemporary problems and promotes the essential 'goodness' of all Africans despite their behaviour. The glorification of African civilisation became almost narcissistic during certain moments of the Negritude movement as verbal majesty and highly refined human values directly opposed the European label of 'savages in need of civilising'. The 'verbal majesty' of Sarraounia and her griot is less an attempt to restore a mythical, mystical Africa than a device to contextualise the past in present-day Africa. This device together with other cinematic codes form a cohesive unit to organise filmic enunciation around the discourse of pan-Africanism. Although feminist discourse is present in Hondo's project, it does not occupy the primary rank in Hondo's hierarchy of priorities.

What directions have other current African productions taken in relating gender inequality to other structures of social and political inequality? If *Sarraounia* does not necessarily challenge women's prescribed roles in traditional society, Idrissa Ouédraogo's *Yaaba* (Burkina Faso, 1988) seemingly takes a step in that direction. 'Yaaba' signifies grandmother in the More language and is the name the young twelve-year-old Bila gives to Sana, an old woman considered a witch and forced to live on the fringes of society since she has no family and no children. Sana adopts Bila as the grandson she never had, gradually wins his confidence and provides him with a valuable education. Drawing on her personal experiences, she teaches him not to judge others on the basis of dominant public reaction but to search for each individual's inner qualities. In this way she is portrayed working from the fringes of society, transgressing the boundaries defined by belonging/not belonging and encouraging spiritual and moral superiority in Africa's hope for the future, the children.

The film's idealisation of motherhood, however, defies a rigorous examination of alternative paths to success or happiness for barren African women. Motherhood functions in the end to repress and deny Sana equality, for once she has 'mothered' Bila and thus been 'reintegrated' into societal order she must die. Diawara argues that 'Sana dies at the end without alerting the spectator to the plight of other outcast women like her. Her history as a particular type of African woman is made transparent while the spectator thinks of her as Bila's friend.'[15] In portraying Sana as the barren African woman who is incomplete without Bila, the film-maker not only resorts to stereotyping but he also locks her into a posture of dependence where she can only be 'humanized through the eyes of the young boy who defies the village tradition of staying away from outcasts'.[16] Sana is presented as what she represents for patriarchy and treated more as a symbol than as a living, suffering individual.[17] The meanings she might construct vis-à-vis her societal roles are suppressed in favour of a discourse structured by and perpetuated through patriarchy (Bila).

Certainly, it would seem that for Ouédraogo women exist only in relationship to men. This type of thought structure is further evident in the portrayal of the character of Nopoko. Her creation and maintenance of relations with Sana can only be established through Bila – for example, Sana's gift of the bracelet and her words of wisdom transmitted through Bila, 'Don't judge others, they have their own reasons.'

This relationship is reminiscent of certain male and female relational models in *Wend Kuuni* (Gaston Kaboré, Burkina Faso, 1983), where Pongnere wishes she were a boy so she could always be with Wend Kuuni. But why the insistence on masculinity? Why must Pongnere's 'emancipation' be conceptualised within masculine parameters? It is as though the film-makers of both *Wend Kuuni* and *Yaaba* view masculinity as a self-sufficient position with access to agency, and femininity as 'the non-subjective sub-jectum'.[18] If the two films fail to achieve portrayals of women in traditional societies with existences for themselves, *Finzan* attempts to bring a feminist consciousness to the narrative by providing the other half of the story.

Nanyuma fights for the right to choose her own destiny, map out her own future by refusing her impending marriage to her dead husband's brother. Her situation is not resolved at the end of the film, but she makes it clear as she takes her child and leaves the village that her fate is in her own hands. Nanyuma embodies Steady's definition of African feminism as 'an abnegation of male protection and a determination to be resourceful and self-reliant'.[19] Furthermore, the film-maker is attempting to reveal, rather than gloss over, structures which deny women equality.

Finzan joins the earlier work of Safi Faye in setting out to define an African feminist film aesthetic. Both *Peasant Letter* and *Fad Jal* effect critiques of sociocultural and political realities of a rural community in Senegal. The films recognise African women's and men's common struggle against imperialism but also acknowledge that, while modernism may have introduced new structures of oppression for women, certain inequalities which existed in traditional societies may have been reinforced by colonialism. For example, both films condemn the introduction of peanut monoculture as the source of all the community's problems and carefully delineate how this type of farming has increased women's oppression in modern rural Africa.

Françoise Pfaff writes that 'Safi Faye is today the only independent African-born woman director of Black African film-making'. Of Sarah Maldoror, she claims that 'although she is not an African by birth, because of her ethnic origins, her work, and her dedication to the cause of Africa, Sarah Maldoror is commonly given a privileged place in comprehensive analysis of Black African cinema'.[20] Maldoror's *Sambizanga* (Angola, 1972) along with *Peasant Letter* and *Fad Jal* attempt to discover for women a voice and a subjectivity that are of paramount importance to the film narrative.

In this paper I have referred to various African films as presenting certain positive directions for 'feminist' expression. One cannot, however, single out any one text as the 'first African feminist film'. Analysis of what constitutes feminist discourse in African cinema necessitates a continuous, rigorous investigation of how both female and male-authored texts expose and examine the interconnectedness of race, gender and class oppression.

Notes

1. Harold Weaver, 'Vues d'Afrique: The New African Cinema in Canada', in *Cinema Canada*, 161, March/April 1989, pp. 22–3.
2. Mbye Cham, 'Issues and Trends in African Cinema – 1989', *African Journal*, vol. 13 nos 1–4, 1982 (three essays from the 9th Annual Atlanta Third World Film Festival and forum, 2–5 November 1989), p. 3.
3. Sandra Harding, *The Science Question in Feminism* (Ithaca, NY: Cornell University Press, 1986), p. 171.
4. Patricia Hill Collins, 'The Social Construction of Black Feminist Thought', *Signs,* vol. 14 no. 4, 1989, p. 756.
5. Ibid.
6. *Zan Boko* won a prize for the best script at FESPACO 89.
7. Among the rites practised by the Mossi of West Africa is the burial of the placenta. This act consecrates the first bond between the newborn child and the nourishing earth. It is also the home of the ancestors and of the spirits which protect the family and the social group. The place where the placenta is buried is called Zan Boko.
8. See Sheila Petty, '*Black Mic-Mac* and Colonial Discourse', in *Cineaction*, no. 18, Fall 1989.
9. Manthia Diawara, *African Cinema – Politics and Culture* (Bloomington: Indiana University Press, 1992), p. 154.
10. Mary Ann Doane, *The Desire to Desire: The Woman's Film of the 1940s* (Bloomington: Indiana University Press), 1987, p. 10.
11. Ibid., p. 8.
12. Alile Sharon Larkin, 'Black Women Filmmakers Defining Ourselves: Feminism in Our Own Voice', in E. Deidre Pribram (ed.), *Female Spectators: Looking at Film and Television* (New York: Verso, 1988), p. 159.
13. Kitia Touré, 'Une Dramaturgie dominée par une volonté de didactisme', in *Cinémas noirs d'Afrique: CinémAction*, 26, 1983.
14. See Stuart Hall, 'Encoding/Decoding', in Hall *et al.* (eds), *Culture, Media, Language* (London: Hutchinson, 1980).
15. Diawara, *African Cinema*, p. 163
16. Ibid., p. 162. See also Carol Boyce Davies, 'Motherhood in the works of Male and Female Igbo Writers: Achebe, Emecheta, Nwapa, Nzekwu', in C. Boyce Davies and A. Adama Graves (eds), *Ngambika; Studies of Women in African Literature* (Trenton, NJ: Africa World Press, 1985), p. 244.
17. Luce Irigaray, *Speculum of the Other Woman*, trans. Gillian C. Gill (Ithaca, NY: Cornell University Press, 1985), p. 165.

18. Filomina Chioma Steady (ed.), *The Black Woman Cross-Culturally* (Cambridge, Mass.: Schenkman Publishing, 1981), p. 736.
19. Françoise Pfaff, *Twenty-five Black African Filmmakers: A Critical Study, with Filmography and Bio-Bibliography* (Westport, Conn.: Greenwood Press, 1988), p. 118.
20. Ibid., p. 205.

Reclaiming Images of Women in Films from Africa and the Black Diaspora

NWACHUKWU FRANK UKADIKE

This is an edited version of the paper published in *Frontiers*, vol. 15 no. 1, 1994.

Female subjectivity in Africa, as elsewhere, has often been defined by men rather than by women. Black women have fallen victim to a tendency to 'de-womanise Black womanhood' – to paraphrase the Nigerian playwright Zulu Sofola.[1] Consequently, films made by African women and men are attempting to rehumanise portrayals of women and to reassert their identities. Furthermore, African women film-makers are facing the challenge of regaining for women the power of self-definition and self-representation. Toward the accomplishment of such goals, new social and political currents in Africa and the Black diaspora involve new levels of critical awareness and new challenges to Western intellectual hierarchies.

The hegemony of colonialist ideologies and Hollywood domination cannot be excluded from a historical investigation that seeks to provide a nuanced portrait of complex ethnic and cultural questions. For a long time questions of cultural difference have been neglected by the dominant cinema and by dominant media practices, thus discouraging the articulation of an accurate and whole-some Black identity. Given the heritage of distorted images, some critics under-standably regard the docile ancillary African woman seen in much international cinema today as a media creation.[2] Partly for this reason, the calling into question of the 'native informant', in Gayatri Spivak's term, is the *sine qua non* of the Black woman's film project. As Maureen Blackwood and Martina Attille have noted, Black women 'must be the ones who define the areas of importance in [their] lives: work toward the breakdown of "mainstream" conventions and popular assumptions perpetuated by existing forms of cinema and television'.[3]

Because of the ways Black subjectivity has been constantly abused in films, a new sensitivity to Black women's concerns indicates a concerted effort to move questions of the 'other' toward the centre. This stance also represents a movement toward thoroughgoing cinematic decolonisation; in other words, the need for a 'theory that takes into account the economic history of [Black] (mis)representation and ensuing stereotyping, as well as the interaction between social realities (whole lives) and cinematic fictions (fragmentation), and ... Black women need to give that theory [and practice] its direction'.[4] Hence, Black women must take the lead in a revisionist dialogue, an alternative dis-course that requires culture-based interpretation around questions of ethnic identity and representation. In support of such efforts, I will examine alternative film practices of male as well as female film-makers who seek to redefine and reclaim Black/African female subjectivity from a history of filmic (mis)representation.

The Diasporic Experience: Some Shared Features

Traditionally denied access to the medium of film, Black women throughout the world have been taking more control of the camera and the cinematic apparatus in recent years. Seeking to advance the process of looking at themselves from within, these women film-makers, including Julie Dash in the United States, Tracey Moffatt in Australia, and Sarah Maldoror, Safi Faye, and Salem Mekuria in Africa, have been exploring cultural directions and innovative strategies that challenge Eurocentric assumptions and readings of Black female subjectivity in films and in other areas of culture. A number of Black male film-makers, including the Africans Ousmane Sembène, Désiré Ecaré and Med Hondo, have been contributing to this challenge. This paper will focus primarily on the changing inscription of female identity and subjectivity in African films made by both men and women, but will first briefly consider aspects of the diasporic context in which African cinema has been evolving.

The efforts of Black cultural producers to forge a distinct identity and to implement a positive representation of Black people have been a struggle almost as fierce as the battles waged by the various African liberation movements to gain their independence. Throughout the history of film, film-makers have relentlessly attempted to force a psychic transformation of Afrocentric mores, traditions and values into roles exemplified by Western definitions of culture.[5]

Western exclusionist ideologies relegate Black film practice to marginal status. Hollywood's monopoly of processes of production and exhibition, for example, has stifled Black-directed films. In Britain, as in the United States, economic deprivation has fostered the death of early, sporadic Black productions. Africa's late entry as film producer, accurately dubbed by the film scholar Clyde Taylor the 'last cinema',[6] is a sad case. It was not until the middle of the 1960s, when African countries started freeing themselves from the yoke of colonialism, that indigenous African film practice emerged. Only recently has Black film practice begun to expand in the United States, with women joining their male counterparts in constructing authentic images of Black people. Here we remember Kathleen Collins for her film *Losing Ground* (1982), which was never theatrically released but is on record as the first independent feature film by an African-American woman director. Julie Dash's *Daughters of the Dust* (1991) is the first feature film by an African-American female film-maker to gain wide theatrical release. (Africa's first feature by a woman, *Kaddu Beykat*, was made in Senegal by Safi Faye in 1975.) The struggle by Black people everywhere has diasporic significance because they all share and articulate protest against colonialist exploitation and deculturation. In terms of cultural production, Black film-makers aspire to portray the truth about their lives partly by producing works that exemplify a communal sensibility. Significant to this sensibility is the invocation of Afrocentricity as a profound cultural hermeneutic.

Daughters of the Dust, a tapestry of cultural history, is influenced aesthetically by African cinema more than by any other tradition. The film eschews the conventions of dominant Western practices and instead deploys Afrocentric visual conventions, cultural symbolism and codes that privilege Black people. This African mode of address, as the author/director has stated in the press kit

195

and in various newspaper interviews, originates particularly in Igbo cultural symbols and traditions of Eastern Nigeria. Zeinabu Irene Davis's films, like Dash's, suggest meditations about the historical truths of Black women's lives. *Cycles* (1989), for example, which illustrates moments of waiting for a woman's menstrual period to begin, is a simple story, but the multilayered cultural motifs and symbolism employed render it complex. Moreover, these motifs exemplify the film-maker's 'growing knowledge of spirituality' and, as she puts it, 'connections with my Yoruba ancestors and with Yoruba-derived new-world religions such as Santeria (Spanish-speaking America), Vodun (Haiti and southern United States), and Candomble (Brazil)'.[7] As in *Daughters of the Dust*, the elevation of woman's position in *Cycles* is part of a filmic process that derives empowerment from decoding and recoding. Cinema here becomes a contested terrain, where conventional representations are challenged and the Black woman's subjectivity reclaimed.

It is from Australia that Tracey Moffatt's *Nice Coloured Girls* (1987) emerges, presenting us with a distinctive view of Black women under the yoke of colonialism – the exploitation of aboriginal women by White men. Moffatt's film links the violent colonial past to intolerable urban encounters in the present. The slave ship functions as an obtrusive reminder of the persistent truths of racial inequality.

In a similar fashion, Ngozi Onwurah's *Coffee-Coloured Children* (1988) becomes a self-reflexive autobiographical essay on internalised British racism. The film presents us with the depths of sociological conflict and trauma through the experiences and memories of children of a mixed marriage of a White mother to an absent Nigerian father as the children grow up in a predominantly White British community.

All of these films succeed in deconstructing or at least challenging the traditional norms of film-making and film-viewing experience. It is not necessarily their innovative stylistic strategies alone that make them regenerative, however; rather, it is the full variety of ways in which they seek to counter the subliminal racist and negative images that continue to define the Black image in dominant practice. Such challenges to dominant practice throughout the Black diaspora are strongly linked to the counter-hegemonic impulses within African film practice to which we now turn. I will examine the construction of Black female subjectivity in four African fiction films. The first three are directed by men; the last one by a woman. These films are *Ceddo* (Ousmane Sembène, Senegal, 1977), *Faces of Women* (*Visages de femmes*), Désiré Ecaré, Côte d'Ivoire, 1985), *Sarraounia* (Med Hondo, Mauritania, 1987), and *Sambizanga* (Sarah Maldoror, Angola, 1972). Then I will discuss two African documentaries by women – Safi Faye's *Selbe: One among Many* (Senegal, 1982) and Salem Mekuria's *Sidet: Forced Exile* (Ethiopia, 1991).

Women in African Films

A cursory look at the image of Black women in American films proves, as critics have indicated, that 'movies have not been a humanistic medium for black women'.[8] In these films the important contributions made by all Black people are downplayed or relegated to the sidelines. Often women in particular appear ineffectual and incapable of standing on their own. Of course, such a depiction of women would be as misleading in African films as it is in

196

American. As Senegal's Ousmane Sembène has noted, 'Africa can't develop [and has never developed] without the participation of women'.[9] The grand prize of the Pan-African Festival of Film and Television (FESPACO), awarded every other year to the best competing film at the festival, is the bronze statuette of Princess Yennenga, an African warrior riding a stallion and brandishing a sword. Hopefully, this figure will bear witness to the recognition of more African/Black women in the expanding history of African experience.

Africa's eminent novelist, Ama Ata Aidou, comments as follows on the unfortunate European view of African female subjectivity:

This is a sorry pass the daughters of the continent have come to – especially when we remember that they are descended from some of the bravest, most independent and innovative women this world has ever known ... the Lady Try of Nubia (ca. 1415–1340 BCE) the wife of Amenhotep III and the mother of Tutankhamen ... is credited with, among other achievements, leading the women of her court to discover make-up and other beauty enhancing processes. Her daughter-in-law was the incomparable Nefertiti, a black beauty whose complexion was nowhere near the alabaster she was now wilfully painted with. Again from the pharaonic era, we evoke Cleopatra, about whom [quoting John Henrik Clarke, whose work Aidou says stems from 'the impatience of painstaking scholarship'] more nonsense has been written ... than about any African queen ... mainly because of many writers' desire to paint her white. She was not a white woman. She was not a Greek.[10]

In many African countries, women remain, at best, sexual objects enveloped in a culture of chauvinism; and, in the words of Ousmane Sembène, they are 'still refused the right of speech'. Some African films, especially those by Sembène, suggest that the problem in colonial times was compounded by Islamic/Arab and Christian/European imperialism, which created hierarchical divisions that favoured men at the expense of women.[11] Zulu Sofola contends that the 'dewomanization of African womanhood' has been a direct result of colonial brainwashing: 'She [African woman] has been most viciously attacked through the cosmology of the alien cultures of the European and Arab that has left her stripped bare of all that made her existence worthwhile in the traditional African system of sociopolitical order of governance.'[12]

Sembène's *Ceddo*, a film highly critical of colonising religions, depicts the Ceddo resistance to Islamic patriarchy. An Arab-looking imam embarks on neutralising the African resistance by conquering the men and forcing them to declare allegiance to Islam. This forced conversion makes it easier for the imam to marry Princess Dior. The king (Dior's father) dies a mysterious death, probably murdered by the imam. The village men then debate the authority of the princess. They refuse to recognise her as a legitimate heir to the throne because her sexuality automatically signifies ineffectiveness and the inability to lead.

The film suggests that before the direct assault on African traditions by alien cultures 'most African societies were matrilineages lasting millennia, from the prepharaonic period all the way down to the micronation like the Akans of Ghana. What changed the pattern in some areas were, first, Islam and, later, Christianity, since both religions were obviously patriarchal in orientation.'[13] As the representative of such a patriarchal tradition, the imam underestimates

Princess Dior and never suspects that she is capable of killing him. He is wrong of course, and dies. This woman brings dignity and pride to her people at a crucial moment when the men have been subdued and enslaved and have renounced their traditional ways of worship. As an articulation of national struggle, a model social change is hereby constructed for Africa. Princess Dior not only rekindles her people's spirit and commitment to self-determination but also projects a sense of direction in which capable and trustworthy women are leaders. The image of Princess Dior after her triumph is mythic; the camera privileges her, making her a prominent figure whose image is indeed larger than life. The final frame is emblematic of this assertion: she stands freeze-framed like a warrior, her eyes permanently fixed on her people.

Other African male directors besides Sembène have forcefully delineated woman's image in terms of her involvement with the independence movement and the resistance to colonial aggression. Med Hondo in *Sarraounia* vividly constructs a positive image of an African queen (Sarraounia), a warrior who successfully mobilised her forces and waged a stiff resistance to the invading French colonial army of occupation. Like *Ceddo*, this film dispels the myth, often propagated by traditionalist as well as colonialist assumptions, that women are not born to rule or that they are simply sexual objects or exotic clichés. Sarraounia is elegant; her imposing figure, magnificent. However, she becomes heroic not by using her beautiful body to seduce and kill, as might occur in Western movies, but by her tactical manoeuvring to substantiate her role as commander-in-chief. When we see her in her war attire addressing her subjects, we identify her not as a woman but as a warrior, a liberator. None of her soldiers are diverted by her sexuality. The preparatory war sequences are inundated by panegyric voices of community – a griot sings to her and to everyone about her people's loyalty, citing the common ground that upholds their movement toward national unity and transformation. Sarraounia's example perhaps supports the contention that 'women have got a capacity which men have got to learn',[14] or, the slogan might as well read, 'What a man can do a woman can do better.' It is interesting, though, that Sofola relates the latter slogan to African women of intellect, whereas her non-literate counterpart would say, 'What a woman can do, a man cannot do'[15] – suggesting that militant feminism is even stronger among the peasants, a thesis reminiscent of Frantz Fanon's and Amilcar Cabral's emphasis on the peasantry and on cultural emancipation.

Désiré Ecaré's *Faces of Women* suggests a feminist ethic that the contemporary African might well embrace.[16] Questioning Africa's cultural patrimony and the strategies of patriarchal subordination of women, the film suggests paths women can follow to liberate themselves from men. The film constructs a revolutionary ideology with a central focus that addresses feminine perspectives. The main emphases involve the refusal of women to succumb to the machinations of male domination and women's efforts to share control in the new market economies.

The central female character in the second of two parallel stories is Bernadette (Eugene Cisse Roland), a middle-aged industrialist who owns a fish-smoking business. Bernadette is deprived of a bank loan to expand her business by a male manager who later flirts with her daughters when they come to intervene on their mother's behalf. When he meets the girls, the manager becomes very accommodating, apparently dazzled by their good looks. Although he does not approve the loan at first, his broad smiles and the manner in which he ask for a date with any of the girls ('when you are passing by') suggest that it is possible to bend the rules. Through Bernadette's assertive articulation of Senegal's socioeconomic decadence, she demonstrates an intense understanding of African women. In a conversation with her daughter, Bernadette, still fuming about the bank's refusal to grant her a loan, lambasts the system, claiming that if everyone tried to own a business Senegal would be relieved of unemployment. Although this might seem a simplistic solution to Africa's complex economic quagmire, her actions demonstrate a motivation that is not evident in any of the parasites around her – the men in her family who depend on her for subsistence. Her strong desire to end male repression of progressive ideals and to install formidable and progressive change provokes her to counsel her daughter to go to the military academy after her high school examination to train and get tough like men.

Bernadette's position is diametrically opposed to her daughter T'Cheley's acerbic proclamation that as a beautiful woman she is well equipped to confront the problematics of social transformation:

> Our bank is our thighs, our breasts and our ass; with these we have got all the power; with my backside, mother, I can get the government toppled tomorrow if I want. I can get a new Ambassador appointed to Paris, to Peking and even to the Vatican. The Pope won't twig, God and women always see eye to eye. For that you've got to be twenty and good-looking.

This statement, of course, reflects T'Cheley's youthful exuberance and her myopic view of contemporary life, which her mother shrugs off in disbelief as she continues to emphasise her progressive agenda. Yes, female sexual power exists in Africa as in other countries; however, the above picture of T'Cheley cannot be dismissed as a stereotypical image of African woman. Rather, Ecaré is reflecting on elements of social realities and blends fiction with satire, sometimes metaphorically, to criticise contemporary inefficiencies and decadence. These problems are symptomatic of African society's effort to grapple with the changes wrought in chaos and conflicting ideologies. Moreover, *Faces*' narrative points to the potential of future sociocultural revolution and challenges the viewer to reflect upon Black sexuality. It contains what has been described as Africa's steamiest erotica, a controversial lovemaking sequence, which, arguably, is a manifestation of Western influence. Showered with favourable reviews in the West, the film is proscribed in Côte d'Ivoire. From a traditionalist/ Africanist perspective, it is understandable that the film is considered lurid, since nudity and indecent exposure are generally taboo. Yet the controversial sequence has a positive aspect, in that sexual intimacy between African people is seldom depicted in Hollywood films.[17]

Thus, *Faces of Women* also enables us to use African aesthetics to repostulate the notions of feminism and feminist film theory exemplified by Laura Mulvey's seminal article 'Visual Pleasure and Narrative Cinema'. In this regard, I have argued elsewhere that:

> It is possible to interpret the nude sequence as a feminist squeal or phallocentric construction in which the woman's body no longer 'holds the look'

nor 'plays to and signifies male desire' since the social and cultural implications bounce against the two characters. [Kouassi's and Affoue's bodies as shown in the nude sequence can be read as] sexual objects coded *for erotic* spectacle and the gaze of both male and female spectators – she for her body and he for his penis.[18]

The black body in this nude sequence is beautifully shot, provoking a series of harmonious images.

Sarah Maldoror's celebrated film *Sambizanga* (1972) gives female subjectivity special attention as it pertains to revolutionary struggles. Here, the coloniser/colonised syndrome is poignantly depicted as tension between exploiters and the exploited through a deliberately didactic revolutionary aesthetic. *Sambizanga* was shot in the People's Republic of Congo and depicts the armed struggle by the militant freedom fighters of PAIGC (African Party for the Independence of Guinea and the Cape Verde Islands) and MPLA (the Popular Movement for the Liberation of Angola). The film is not necessarily about the war, but it delineates the spirit of solidarity existing among individuals pursuing the same goals. While the camera follows Maria (Elisa de Andrade), who frantically searches for Domingo, her husband (who was abducted and tortured to death by the agents of the Portuguese colonialists), the feminist aspect of the film's structure becomes apparent. As in *Sarraounia*, it is aimed at giving credibility to women's active participation and involvement in the dangerous business of revolutionary struggle. The character of Maria is exemplary and suggests the spirit of solidarity existing among the women. When Maria learns that her husband has been murdered, the women, in the typical African gesture of communality, rally around her. They share the sadness of her loss, the joy of caring for an aggrieved neighbour, the comfort in wearing the traditional black mourning clothes and in taking care of her infant, who accompanied her all the while she confronted the intransigent colonial officers. This sense of collectivity and femininity is acutely captured with a lingering camera that pans almost endlessly on the women's emotion-laden faces. In challenging the traditional role of women, *Sambizanga*'s structure is markedly different from any of the above-mentioned films in two respects. First, its text, language and form derive specifically from a woman's emotional experience. Second, it demonstrates distinctly economical as well as intelligent choices concerning profilmic elements – using what is available in terms of light, existing colours, and so forth.

Cultural critics contend that it is almost impossible to understand the concern in Black film practice with the social construction of reality and of women without recognising the influence of former styles of realism that Black film practice rejects. Referring specifically to Black British practice, though his remarks are relevant to the broad diasporan connection emphasised here as well, the critic Kobena Mercer opines that the desire to rehumanise the distorted Black image, reclaiming and revealing it vividly 'like it is – should be understood as the prevailing mode in which counter-discourse ... [is being] constructed against the dominant versions of reality'.[19] This statement indicates the rebellious stance of feminist aesthetics – challenging norms of representation and established traditions of film-making, both dominant and (at times) oppositional. If 'the focus is activism within the socio-political power game of contemporary world order', as Sofola argues, 'there is no doubt that today's international feminist militancy could not have by-passed Africa'.[20]

Two African Feminist-Oriented Films

It has been my intention to use the previous discussion to reinforce the argument I want to present for the rest of the paper. I am arguing here that although African film practice in general is alternative and counter-hegemonic, within this structure African women's films can be read as constructing a paradigm. First and foremost, this paradigm consists of speaking from within and attempting to compose a rich and varied portrait of the African woman via canonical modification and revisionism – something that male-dominated narratives have not completely grasped. From this perspective, two documentary films by women film-makers are extremely significant: *Selbe: One Among Many*, by Safi Faye, and *Sidet: Forced Exile*, by Salem Mekuria. Both are significant in their examination of female characters with regard to the social and cultural parameters that define the spaces they occupy or seek to inhabit. Also significant are the ways in which the critical emphasis on re-imaging and revisioning the African woman permeates the films' structure, thus rendering it far more than a mere appendage to male-oriented narrative.

As already stated, African film practice to this day is male-dominated. Since 1963, a number of African women have ventured into the profession, including the Cameroon journalist Therese Sita Bella (*Tam Tam à Paris*, 1963), Ghana's Efua Sutherland (*Araba: The Village Story*, 1967), Tanzania's Flora M'Mbugu-Schelling (*Sun Sunup*, 1985) and Kenya's Anne G. Mungai (*Productive Farmlands*, 1990; *Wakesa at Crossroads*, 1986; and *Saikati*, 1992). Others include Burkina Faso's Fanta Regina Nacro, whose film *Un Certain Matin* (1992) was the winner of the 1992 Carthage Film Festival gold medal award for short films, and Kenya's Wanjiru Kinyanjui, a bright and promising young student in Berlin who has made two critically acclaimed shorts, *Black in the Western World* (1992) and *The Sick Bird* (1991). There are also a host of other women professionals working in television across Africa. However, Safi Faye remains the dominant figure in film production, and just recently, with the release of *Sidet*, Ethiopia's Salem Mekuria has been gaining visibility.

Selbe is a thirty-minute documentary that portrays the lives of women in a contemporary Senegalese village. As the men leave temporarily for the urban centre in search of jobs, the women bear the economic and social burden of caring for their families. Safi Faye reflects on the personal struggle of one woman whose story has collective significance. The film's structure is marked by an ethnographic perspective as well as an African sensibility. Faye was trained as an ethnologist and as a film-maker. In this film she works both to delineate the socio-political and economic problems of Senegal and to lend support to the oppressed Serer peasantry.

In all Faye's films, the characters participate in the film-making process itself – doing their everyday chores and expressing themselves as though oblivious of the camera's presence. The conversation between Selbe and the film-maker is intimate at times, as there is no omniscient voice pushing or directing what the woman is saying or what the viewer should see – a technique that we might well trace to the heyday of cinéma vérité. I must point out, however, that in the American print there is an irritating and often distracting voice-over narration.

Subtitles would have worked best for me, as extra narration was not necessary to convey action that was quite explicit. (The most powerfully indoctrinating sequences in the film, arguably, are the ones in which there is silence.) From the visuals, the viewer is provided with specific insights into the villagers; the historical, cultural, and socio-political milieu; and the culturally bound male–female relationships. Thus, when we see the women potters in action, we also know why the men are absent: it is the dry season, when there is no work for them to do at home. What is left are the familiar everyday chores – cooking, caring for the children and providing food for the family. The film criticises the village men who will eat without asking where the ingredients come from or how much they cost and who do not help the women who are working ceaselessly. The men are portrayed as parasites and, as Selbe puts it, 'scroungers'. Providing the family with everyday nourishment, in most cases, has traditionally been the burden of women. At one point, Selbe, with a baby strapped to her back, has three other kids pester her as she draws water from the well while the men sit idle – one smoking a cigarette – without providing any help. In another sequence in which the camera plays a discerning role, an ox-driven cart loaded with firewood arrives carrying Mamadou's wife, with her infant sitting on her lap. The cart stops in front of their house, and the woman is seen struggling to hold her child as she manages to alight from the cart, after which she starts to unload the firewood. A slow pan to the left reveals Mamadou, sitting, completely nonchalant. When his wife asks for help, he responds with impudence, saying, 'I helped you yesterday.' His indifference to the reality confronting him only reminds the viewer of the deprivation and indignation expressed earlier in the film when Selbe states, 'The strength of my arm is all I can rely on.' When she is not cooking, she is collecting mussels to sell, the proceeds from which she uses to buy fish and rice to feed her family.

Selbe depicts the men as village parasites – totally indifferent toward familial bonds. There is no question of who is in charge here in the filmic process; this is a woman's story told with utmost realism. The development of female subjectivity here echoes the central characters in certain Black literary works that explore the self. As Alexis De Veaux writes, 'It's the self in relationships with an intimate other, with the community, the nation and the world. Self is universal in this context because it has an understanding of the one as the beginning one and then moves beyond that.'[21] As Faye's title indicates, the film focuses on one woman's life (Selbe's), but as the subtitle, 'One Among Many', implies, there are many other Selbes – African women straddling the same pedestal trying to change their lives. The filmic mode employed, which juxtaposes fictional and documentary elements, draws attention to the national dimensions of the individual problems posed here. The film privileges women – people restricted by the community and by immense social, political and economic forces. The legacy of monoculturism imposed by colonialism and the neglect of rural life due to the entrenched economic impotence of Senegal and of virtually all African states are shown to be sources of the contemporary quagmire.

However, *Selbe* deviates from traditional constraints by reversing the syncretic (Islamic/African) code of conduct forced on woman by Islamic patriarchy. The film-maker herself is a devout Muslim and under a strict Islamic code would not, as a woman, interact publicly with men or put forward a representative and communal vision, as is foregrounded in this film. *Selbe*'s narrative and documentary codes in the control of women criticise and revise traditional criteria of filmic content and conventions. (Regarding traditional filmic criteria, I am comparing *Selbe* with earlier films that deal with women and Islam, such as *Xala* and *Ceddo*, which depict women as symbols of tradition – as taciturn figures whom critics have dubbed 'silent revolutionaries'.)[22]

Faye's narratives have a tendency to foreground communal concerns and to invite spectator identification with these concerns. Faye states that her films 'are not primarily focusing on women',[23] because she is concerned with the plight of all Senegalese peasants, men as well as women. An examination of her narrative strategy, however, suggests that it is through female eyes, either hers or those of female characters, that this collective dimension emerges. Nonetheless, the quest for identity, community and history as a collective enterprise does strongly emerge. Although *Selbe* foregrounds individuality, it uses individuality as a metaphor for the people. Moreover, national problems take on continental dimensions in this film; all visual evidence suggests the pan-African nature of Selbe's experience.

The strength of the film lies in the powerful images that convey female subjectivity from the point of view of the film-maker as she directs the viewer to witness African women's situation as a relentless struggle for survival. However, it is also from the details in these images that the viewer familiar with Africa's contemporary socio-economic affairs begins to notice the obfuscation of important societal problems, which the film alludes to but does not address. For example, at the beginning of the film we are told that Selbe is thirty-nine years old and that she has lost one child and now has eight. Although one would admit that *Selbe* is not a United Nations or Planned Parenthood commercial, one still wonders why in the face of the abject poverty afflicting all African countries there is such a tolerant attitude towards overproduction of children. In another scene, the film presents the case of a mother whose husband left the village to seek a job in the city only two days before his child died. It is worth noting that infant mortality is a perennial problem in Africa. Perhaps this is the reason Selbe is so industrious. Her children look healthy, but does the need for all this toil by Selbe reflect a lack of vision or courage on the part of the leadership in the contemporary period? 'Leadership in this context', as Ama Ata Aidou puts it, 'does not refer to the political leadership exclusively.'[24] There was not any real enforcement of family planning in Africa until the late 1980s, when the continent's economic stagnation, in conjunction with IMF's Structural Adjustment Programmes, imposed inhumane austerity measures and hyperinflation on the people. These are topics that Safi Faye does not expand upon, but they are there in the film's structure; despite the brevity of the film, just thirty minutes, it still manages to acknowledge their existence. The most pathetic issue of the villagers' plight is elicited when, towards the end, a little girl asks her mother why she has not been sent to school. The mother's reply is that she has to stay at home to help with domestic work. Again, one of the causes of Africa's illiteracy problems is identified but not elaborated upon or presented as an issue that demands urgent attention. What seems to be the film's central theme is woman's aspirations for family cohesiveness with a husband who is constantly present but completely irresponsible. In addition, by using a female character to hint at the problem of illiteracy, Faye indicates that in African societies women are less likely to be educated than men. Her narrative mirrors her anti-establishment stance and her critique of female marginalisation. *Selbe* ends on an optimistic, albeit ironic, note with the women asking for God's help to provide food and a better life for the children. But how – since God cannot descend, feed, clothe and educate the teeming African population?

Optimism is also a theme in *Sidet*, which takes place amid dreams of faraway Australia, the possible future home of Ethiopian refugees fleeing the ravages of war and destruction. *Sidet* documents the life stories of three Ethiopian women refugees driven from their homes to the Um Gulga Settlement Camp in Sudan. The film highlights their miserable living conditions in exile and the women's efforts to cope with their families. The life stories of the three women inform the film's narrative, and it is from their point of view that the viewer understands the drama of their daily lives, their struggle for subsistence, and the collective mobilisation that keeps the life of the refugees resilient. Camp life is submerged in scarcity; even as the women struggle to create life in exile, water is not free. It is also from the women that we learn about the international relief operations that have failed to meet the needs of the refugees. Equally pathetic are the diminishing health care resources resulting from budget cuts and the consequent drastic decline in children's health care and nutrition.

The most prevalent cause of death for women and children in the camp is shown to be malnutrition. One sequence replays images of the famine victims of Ethiopia in the 1980s. As the screen is filled with skeletons in human skin, the narrator tells the audience that malnutrition is the greatest problem for children and that 150 out of 1,000 die before they are five years old. Worse still, 55 out of 1,000 mothers die when giving birth. The film clearly blames Ethiopia's civil strife and the annexation of Eritrea, which institutionalised some of the most blatant human rights abuses in modern history.

Mekuria's camera captures with utmost intensity the refugees' difficulties under arbitrarily imposed conditions and their struggle to survive while maintaining a strong commitment to their traditions. Thus, in the camp, a woman sustains her family by making and selling injera, a staple for most Ethiopians; others sell an illegal locally brewed Ethiopian alcoholic drink, which must be hidden from Islamic Sudan's law enforcement agencies. The most painful moments are sequences dealing with refugees' reminiscences about their loved ones. Significantly emotional and especially haunting is the scene that dramatises the pain of separation between Abeba Tsegaye and one of her little sons who has been left behind in Ethiopia. After a separation of five years, mother and child are aurally and spiritually reconnected through the replay of a recorded message that speaks of memory and longing. As Abeba listens, the little boy's voice sings, telling his mother how he would want to liberate his people from abject poverty through education. And this quest for knowledge is strongly reinforced following the emotionally charged poem he has written and sung to Abeba:

To be strong and expand your mind
There is no way except education.
To develop our land, to find solutions to unlock
the wealth of our earth it is not by miracle,
but through education.
To reclaim our countrys' wealth to benefit ourselves and to
help others it is through education.

Let us quickly mention in passing that this liberationist and progressive message echoes the yearning of the little girl in *Selbe* who wants to be educated but is deprived of the opportunity. Similarly, the women in *Sidet* are continuously looking for the opportunity to break away from exile and, in some cases, to resume their education and normal life in Ethiopia when the fighting ends. It is from the perspective of the women's struggle in Selbe that the ending, which involves the wait for manna from heaven, seems problematic. Such a solution is unsatisfying because hard-working Selbe and the other women require not a miracle but the assistance that an informed and capable government should provide to improve the living conditions of its people. One wishes the women would call pragmatically for basic improvements related to economic infrastructure, for example, and to a safe and ample water supply. Nevertheless, Selbe's self-motivation during most of the film epitomises a major aspect of African feminism, which, in Filomina Chioma's terms, is 'an abnegation of male protection and a determination to be resourceful and self-reliant'.[25] Selbe addresses the issue of equality poignantly, unafraid to question the gender restrictions imposed upon women in her society.

Following the little boy's thought-provoking message in *Sidet* is a sequence that projects the question of survival – an abiding concern of the majority of marginalised people in continental Africa. Particularly disturbing is the scene in which Abeba meets with representatives of the United Nations High Commission for Refugees and the Christian Council of Churches, who help to arrange for the permanent emigration of Ethiopians to Western countries that will accept them. Isn't this the worst form of degradation and denigration of African and Third World peoples, who, after the euphoria of independence, find that the neocolonial structure has created such unprecedented poverty that they now aspire to get out to any place other than Africa? When Abeba learns that her visa to Australia is approved, she laughs, and initially a look of total relief and satisfaction can be seen on her face. Although she is delighted, she laughs reservedly, knowing that Australia is only a temporary refuge because her spirit will never leave her motherland, Ethiopia. If, as Sofola contends, 'the world view of the African is rooted in the philosophy of holistic harmony and communalism rather than in the individualistic isolationism of Europe',[26] Abeba's asylum in Australia negates the 'principle of relatedness' that is indispensable to the African socio-cultural fabric; as O. Ehusani states, 'Relatedness characterizes the African experience of the living person [and] if one is cut off from his/her community, one is considered dead'.[27]

In appreciating her new status, Abeba talks about giving her little boy a good education. But it is also clear that she and her little boy are joining millions of other 'lost' Africans driven into exile by Africa's menacing economic problems. They are in the United States, Australia, Europe, the Middle East, and Asia – wherever they can lead 'normal' lives. But the 'lands of milk and honey' they aspire to reach are also 'deterritorialised', where Blacks as 'niggers' are constantly reminded that they should go back to Africa. For me, as someone in temporary exile living in the United States, Mekuria's film is symbolic as an exilic text that can be used to formulate a discourse of exile. This sweet/sour feeling is echoed in Hamid Naficy's notion of 'exile as liminality':

This compound sense of pain and paralysis is not due solely to the displacing

205

conditions one finds in exile, but also often it is related to the dire circumstances one has left behind. Tragedy at home, which often drives people out of their countries, looms larger, even larger in exile.[28]

It is interesting that *Sidet*'s message is so pointed and yet the women depicted cannot be said to be simply illustrating a point but rather initiating a dialogue in a process of mutual exploration that includes the film-maker, the filmed and the audience. The propriety and naturalness of this exploration are supported by the subtle cinematography, including the long takes and unobtrusive camera, and by culturally specific signifiers such as the lyrics and the music of stringed instruments. One can hardly ignore the emotional resonances of the song from the opening sequence:

I'm thirsty my sister
I'm hungry, my mother.
Who can I tell this to?
I'm in exile
Oh me, oh my ...
In silence all seasons
I have nothing at all
except old age and poverty
I am crying about poverty
give me injera
I will eat it standing
Since there is no respect for one in exile.
Exiles don't raise their heads to look straight
People in trouble never have enough.
Poor people don't give injera to other people

The woman who sings this song appears melancholic. Her mood and her song reflect the vast cultural and political problem the film attacks. The song is 'infectious', because the structure of the film enables the lyrics to keep reverberating in the viewer's mind, serving not only as a voice of female experience but as one that invites the audience to share that experience. As the song instructs us, 'In silence all seasons' parallels the experience of many African women, and it is indeed rejuvenating to see, once again, this doubly marginalised group – African women film-makers – taking control in an exceptional manner, eloquently confronting the 'silence' that has eclipsed their lives.

Mekuria and Faye can also be seen as having developed methods of externalising this silence – through their inquiring lenses and other devices related to the masterful integration of cinematic and cultural codes. Like *Selbe*, *Sidet* is deliberate in its dramatic rendering of feminine encounters. These perspectives, like diasporic Black feminist discourse, are conveyed vividly and are devoid of fetishisation and stereotype. Judicious use of the film medium and careful character delineation work toward a counter-hegemonic conclusion. Both films speak for diverse audiences and marginal groups, but this captivating power is very specific in terms of choice of images, composition, camera movement, lighting, editing, and the overall narrative rhythm. Coupled with these features is a natural portrayal of mannerisms. Together, these characteristics dignify

Africanness, autonomy, and non-compliance, which tend to be deconstructive in terms of ideology and style.

African cinema has done considerable work in privileging women's issues, particularly the re-creation of female subjectivity. However, there obviously is much still to be done. On a global level, women film-makers in the diaspora are 'fixed on the same pedestal' – in Fanonian terms, trying to confront the hegemony inherent in mainstream production and distribution practices. In the films *Sidet* and *Selbe*, and in many other films made by women, it is clear that thematic and aesthetic prerogatives are determined by specific social, political and gender objectives rather than by conventional spectacle and commercial success. In sum, the tension between the manifold identities of Third World and other marginalised peoples, on the one hand, and the pressures of colonialism and imperialism, on the other, marks the point of convergence for 'alternative' cinema, which, understandably, female film practice embraces.

Notes

1. Zulu Sofola is a Professor of Performing Arts as well as a playwright. Her paper 'Feminism and the Psyche of African Womanhood', delivered at the first international conference on 'Women in Africa and the African Diaspora: Bridges Across Activism and Academy' at the University of Nigeria, Nsukka, June 1992, is invaluable to the dialogue presented in this paper.
2. See, for example, Ama Ata Aidou, 'The African Woman Today', *Dissent* 39, Summer 1992, p. 320.
3. Martina Attile and Maureen Blackwood, 'Black Women and Representation', in Charlotte Brunsdon (ed.), *Films for Women* (London: BFI, 1986) p. 203.
4. Ibid., p. 204.
5. I am referring to the hegemonic definitions of races – in this case when *non-white* people arbitrarily connote 'primitivity', 'underdevelopment', 'Third World', the 'other' in contradistinction to whiteness, which automatically translates to 'First World', 'advanced', 'developed', 'industrialised'.
6. Clyde Taylor, 'Africa, the Last Cinema', in Renee Tajima (ed.), *Journey Across Three Continents: Film and Lecture Series* (New York: Third World Newsreel, 1985), pp. 50–8.
7. Zeinabu Irene Davis, 'Woman with a Mission: Zeinabu Irene Davis on Filmmaking', *Voices of the African Diaspora*, University of Michigan's *Centre for Afroamerican and African Studies Research Review*, vol. 7 no. 3, Fall 1991, p. 38.
8. Pearl Bowsser, 'Sexual Imagery and the Black Woman in American Cinema', in Gladstone L. Yearwood (ed.), *Black Cinema Aesthetics: Issues in Independent Black Filmmaking* (Athens, Ohio: Ohio University Centre for Afro-American Studies, 1982), pp. 41–51.
9. Ousmane Sembène has conveyed this important fact on several occasions to his audience. It was also been cited in Françoise Pfaff's *The Cinema of Ousmane Sembène* (Westport, Conn.: Greenwood Press, 1984) and in Ulric Gregor's interview with Sembène, *Framework*, Spring 1978, pp. 35–7.
10. Aido, 'African Woman'. See also footnote number 2 of her article.
11. Some African women have made progress in recent years. There are instances since 1975 of women becoming university leaders, government ministers, and members of parliament. In Mozambique, a country almost obliterated by Russian and American ammunition during its protracted civil war, women account for 16 per cent of the representatives of the House of Parliament (a higher percentage than in comparable institutions in Britain, the United States or France). Sylviane Diouf Kamara's comparative analysis, 'Changing Roles? African Women at the Turn of the Century', *West Africa*, no. 3837, 18–24 March 1991, p. 403, is a stimulating commentary on women in African society.
12. Sofola, 'Feminism and the Psyche'.
13. Aidou, 'African Woman'.
14. C. L. R. James, 'Towards the Seventh: The Pan-African Congress – Past, Present and Future', *At the Rendezvous of Victory* (London: Allison & Busby, 1984), p. 250.

15. Sofola, 'Feminism and the Psyche', p. 24.
16. The film supports women's empowerment. However, African viewers find the portrayal of women misleading, at best, and downright false and compromising at other times. For example, an African woman would not call her husband stupid in public, while N'Guessan does.
17. The 'rereading' of the lovemaking sequence stems from the discussion of the film in my 'Cultural Issues in Cinema' class when one of my African-American female students made reference to this interesting analogy.
18. See N. F. Ukadike, *Black African Cinema* (Berkeley: University of California Press, 1994), p. 222.
19. Kobena Mercer, 'Recoding Narratives of Race and Nation', in *Black Film British Cinema* (London: BFI/ICA Documents 7, 1988), p. 9.
20. Sofola, 'Feminism and the Psyche'.
21. As quoted in Gloria J. Gibson-Hudson's article, 'African American Literary Criticism as a Model for the Analysis of Films by African American Women', *Wide Angle,* vol. 13 nos 3 and 4, pp. 44–54. See Claudia Tate, *Black Women Writers at Work* (New York: Continuum, 1988), p. 54.
22. See David Uru Iyam, 'The Silent Revolutionaries: Ousmane Sembène's *Emitai, Xala,* and *Ceddo*', *African Studies Review,* vol. 29 no. 4, December 1986, pp. 79–87.
23. This statement was made at the 1982 ASA conference and cited in Françoise Pfaff's *Twenty-Five Black African Filmmakers* (Westport, Conn.: Greenwood Press, 1988), p. 118.
24. Aidou, 'African Woman' p. 320.
25. Filomina Chioma, *The Black Woman Cross Culturally* (Cambridge, Mass.: Schenkman, 1991), p. 35.
26. Sofola, 'Feminism and the Psyche', p. 8.
27. O. Ehusani, *An Afro-Christian Vision 'Ozovehe'* (New York: University Press of America, 1991), p. 86.
28. Hamid Naficy, 'Exile Discourse and Television Fetishization', *Quarterly Review of Film and Video,* vol. 13 no. 1–3, p. 85; also in Naficy and Teshome Gabriel (eds), *Otherness and Media* (Chur, Switzerland: Harwood Academic Publishers, 1993).

Popular Culture and Oral Traditions in African Film

MANTHIA DIAWARA

Reprinted from *Film Quarterly*, vol. 41 no. 3, Spring 1988, by permission.

In spite of the increasing number of African films released in the course of the last twenty years (from *Borom Sarret* in 1963 to *Nyamanton* (The Garbage Boys) in 1986), there has been no African film criticism as enlightening and provocative as the criticism generated by the Brazilian Cinema Novo, the theories of Imperfect Cinema, and the recent debates around Third Cinema.[1] This gap must be filled to overcome the repetitious nature of criticism which has addressed itself to African film in the last twenty-five years and to make possible the definition of a dynamic aesthetic proper to Africa. The lack of African critics who know African traditions is at fault, as well as the critical practice of the West, where the ethnocentrism of European and American film critics has limited them to evaluating African cinema through the prism of Western film language. Thus, they refuse to look at African cinema 'straight in the eyes'. They think that that cinema is in the process of finding its individuality, that the film-makers have not yet mastered the film medium, that the camera style is still primitive in African films.

European critics are afraid to look at African cinema in the same manner that Africans used to be afraid to watch the first movies from Europe. According to Amadou Hampate Ba, the wise man of Bandiangara, when film was introduced to his village in 1935, the imam and the head of the village accused it of being loaded with lies, tricks and anti-lslamic goals. In order to protect the village against this diabolical invention imposed upon them by the colonial administrator, the imam commanded women and children to stay at home. Only men came to the projection and they closed their eyes for the entire length of the film. At the end, the men told the administrator that women and children could not come because they were afraid of the images in motion on the screen.[2]

Today, African cinema must combat this resistance to foreign images. Europeans close their eyes in order not to see the questioning of Western values, the reaffirmation of cultures repressed by the West, and anti-neocolonialist discourses. European critics sent to view these films, in another form of the reactions like those of Amadou Hampate Ba's village chief, bring back inevitably indulgent and non-analytical comments on African cinema.

To analyse African cinema, one must first understand that twenty-five years of film production has necessarily created an aesthetic tradition which African film-makers use as a point of reference which they either follow or contest. An African aesthetic does not come merely from European cinema. To avoid making

African cinema into an imperfect appendix to European cinema, one must question Africa itself, and African traditions, to discover the originality of its films. In his article, 'Sur les formes traditionnelles du roman africain',[3] Mahamadou Kane wrote that 'the originality of the African novel must be found more precisely in its relation with the forms of oral literature from "Black Africa"'.[3] In the same article, Kane compared the oral storyteller to the novelist, exploring the themes, the narrative devices and other features of the novel which also form the basis of the oral tale. He also showed that the novelist, as well as the storyteller, uses realism as a means of expression, resorting to a linear story with one action which unfolds around three units of time (departure, arrival, and return). Like the traditional storyteller, the novelist opts for a didactic enunciation and, consequently, reproduces in the text the apprenticeship of life as well as moral and social codes.

In this paper, I will try to bring out the relations between the oral tradition and African cinema in the same manner that Kane does for the novel. I will compare the griot (the bard) to the film-maker, looking particularly at their reproduction of traditional modes of being, so as to show the similarities and the differences between their works.

First of all, it seems logical to underline the fundamental difference between oral literature and cinema. The means put into play in the construction of a film – the camera movement, close-ups, and shot/reverse-shots – are not the same as those used by the storyteller. Indeed, the latter enunciates by incarnating characters one by one, dominating the narrative by his or her presence. The griot depends on spoken language as well as on music to actualise the story. The film-maker, on the contrary, uses the means of mechanical reproduction to give shape to the story. Whereas oral literature speaks of life, cinema reproduces an impression of life.[4]

Putting this difference aside, can one say that the originality of African cinema must be found in the oral tradition? Can one also overlook the notion that African cinema had nothing to inherit when it started its development?[5] According to this postulate, there would exist only one film language, the one to which the West has given birth and which it has perfected. The Black film-maker would then only have to place the content of his or her work in a framework that takes its condition of possibility from the rules and precepts already elaborated by Western masters.

However, when African films are examined, one sees that all the directors resort in different ways to oral storytelling forms. As Kane noted in regard to the novelist, the film-maker too is influenced, consciously or unconsciously, by the storyteller's techniques of narrating. 'At night, he/she used to be fed with oral tales, historical or cosmogonical legends... very often, he/she grew up in a milieu which had a specific mentality as regards the forms of discourse, a sensibility which expressed itself in particular ways.'[6]

First, it is important to look at the manner in which popular cultures are filmed in African cinema, because such popular practices as song and dance, the performance of the griot and the representation of African social systems such as polygamy are often used to create the effect of the real in the films. In *Xala* (Ousmane Sembène's 1974 film about independence and the impotence of the new leaders), for example, after the Africans have taken control of the Chamber of Commerce, song and dance are represented to accentuate the transition of power in the story as a return to authenticity. The dance occurring at the beginning of the film, instead of having a fixed exotic meaning as in anthropological films about Africa, is a spectacle open to several interpretations. First, one can see in it the desire of the new public employees to be considered traditional, and therefore authentic. But one soon realises that the dance and music outside are used as masks to hide the incompetence of the new leaders inside, who accept bribes from the very Frenchmen they had kicked out.

Finally, the dance connotes in an ironic manner the representation of half-naked Africans who are always dancing in European and American films. At the level of the signified, song and dance in *Xala* position the spectators to criticise the superficial use of tradition by politicians. The opening scene helps the audience build a revolutionary attitude relative to the regressive behaviour of the characters in the film.

In *Visages de femmes (Faces of Women,* a 1985 film by Désiré Ecaré, which tells two different stories about two women in Côte d'Ivoire), song and dance are narrative processes which move the story forwards. In this film song and dance, at the beginning and end of the river love scene, constitute a mini-narrative with a beginning, middle and end. Through their performance, the women tell the story of how a boy and a girl deceived everybody and met in the river to make love. In *Xala* Sembène negates the Hollywood stereotypes of exotic Africans and gives a contextual interpretation to song and dance, but in *Visages de femmes* Ecaré emphasises the manner in which song and dance in Africa are used to inform people of what is taking place behind their backs. This balletic cinema, or a cinema that dances in order to tell its story, has its parallel in at least one West African popular theatre, the Koteba, which also can imitate all forms of representation through dance.

As the dancers of *Visages de femmes,* in their colourful attire, move to the beat of the music in harmony with the rhythm of the editing and the camera movements, one cannot help but think that Ecaré has invented a new language for African cinema. But how is this aesthetisation of an African popular culture, which pushes the spectator to identify with the dancing women, different from the old tradition of constructing the body of women as the site of desire in Western cinema? Furthermore, it seems that the dance scene, through the use of medium close-ups of women's feet, arms and heads, is addressed to the desire of the male spectator, and thus contradicts the lovemaking in the river which seems to proclaim the sexual freedom of African women. In other words, as Ecaré places song and dance in African cinema, away from anthropological and Hollywood films, he surrenders to the sexist codes of African popular culture which undermine his very attempt to keep alive in *Visages de femmes* the political commitment of African directors.

This brief analysis of the representation of song and dance in *Xala* and *Visages de femmes* reveals that the appropriation of popular culture by the fiction film in Africa creates a movement away from Western film language, toward a predominance of traditional narrative codes. Sembène leads this movement by first negating European stereotypes of song and dance in Africa, and by putting into question the African elite's attempt to exploit these popular forms for its own gains. Ecaré's desire to let African dance and song speak in a cinematic language coincides with a phallocentric construction of the characters which turns them into objects of desire for the spectator. *Visages de femmes* teaches us, thus, the necessity for the film-maker to interrogate popular culture in order to divest it of its manifest and/or repressed phallocentrism.

As regards social practices such as polygamy in African film, two examples suffice to illustrate its cinematic representation. In *Sey Seyeti (One Man, Several Women,* 1980), Ben Diogaye Bèye puts polygamy and modernity into play in order to bring to light the contradictions in a contemporary African society. Bèye constructs polygamy as the common denominator of the problems of several men in the film, and ends by focusing on the freedom of a young woman who is forced to marry an older man. There is no central story in *Sey Seyeti,* which tells one anecdote after another, using polygamy as the over-determining factor. This complex film, which runs the risk of confusing the spectator in the West about the relationships among many characters, or of being dismissed as an example of African avant-garde, shocked the inhabitants of Senegal. When it was released, the film provoked an unprecedented reaction in the press from sociologists, ethnologists and politicians.

Bèye was accused by some for looking at polygamy, an African custom, with European eyes, and praised by others for boldly exposing a regressive practice which no longer finds its justification in modern Senegal. The fact that *Sey Seyeti* shocked African audiences, while its message remains opaque or confusing to the spectator in the West, indicates that Bèye simultaneously fashioned an African film language while attempting to shed light on the repressiveness of a popular practice such as polygamy.

In *Finyé (The Wind,* Souleymane Cissé, 1983), polygamy is a principal theme. One of the scenes in this film debunks polygamy by exposing its internal contradictions. Indeed, the youngest of the governor's wives takes the initiative in the quest for a lover by expressing her desire for a young man of her own age. The man this young woman chases also happens to be the lover of the governor's daughter. Symbolically, therefore, both women have become the governor's daughters and/or wives because they have the same object of desire. What becomes an issue in this scene is polygamy's inability to answer to the emerging needs of sexual freedom in Africa. But the tradition of polygamy is more seriously questioned in the film by the belittling of its social and economic meaning. Women play the role of respectful spouses, who submit to their husbands in order to cheat on them even better and to get from them what they want.

For example, in another scene the oldest and the youngest wives stage a mock fight to distract the husband from his commitment to punish a disloyal daughter. As for the governor/husband marrying three wives, which in the past would have served to emphasise his prestige, this now appears as a movement toward the weakening of moral and social values. The youngest wife squanders his money, drinks whisky, and smokes in front of him. These signs of depravity in a traditional Islamic society are ascribed to modernity and the persistence of polygamy. An understanding of local culture (anthropological signs) is necessary to appreciate the play of the actors as authoritative and phallocentric husband, or oldest and youngest wives. One has to go beyond the simplistic conception of art as functional in Africa and see, for example, the aesthetics over-determined by polygamy in the comic scene of the mock fight between the wives.

The figure of the griot, symbol of the oral tradition, has also often been represented in African films. Historians of African cinema have already studied the griot's presence in Sembène's films. In a pioneering article on the subject, Mbye Cham argues that Sembène sees himself as 'the mouth and ears of his people' and in his role as a film-maker, he 'prefers to amalgamate, adapt, develop, and enhance certain features of the *gewel* [griot] and the Lekbat [storyteller]'.[7] In her book *The Cinema of Sembène Ousmane*, Françoise Pfaff compares Sembène's cinematic techniques with the griot's narrative techniques. She also analyses the representation of the griot in films by Sembène such as *Niaye* (1964), *Borom Sarret, Xala,* and *Ceddo* (1976). I will limit myself to the figure of the griot seen in a scene of *Borom Sarret*: fat, well-dressed, and even with a gold tooth. By contrast the borom sarret (cart driver) is skinny, poorly dressed, and tired from his work. The opposition between these two characters is so striking that it reminds one of an earlier scene where Sembène uses high and low angle shots to contrast the cart driver with a crippled beggar who crawls on all fours.

As money is transferred from the cart driver to the griot, one sees tradition as tainted with obvious corruption. The griot turns tradition into a tool of exploitation when he evokes the cart driver's past nobility in order to take away all the money he has earned for the morning labour. The griot's narrative about the cart driver, which would have been authoritative in oral tradition, is debunked here as exploitative and not inclusive of the contemporary realities that oppress the cart driver. Sembène transcends the griot, therefore, and surrounds him and his old narrative with a new vision which traces the mechanism by which people such as the cart driver are exploited. It is important to notice that in the same scene, as the griot goes on taking the cart driver's money, one young boy shines the shoes of another who is stronger and who leaves without paying. Here again Sembène uses high- and low-angle shots, as he does throughout the length of the film to maintain this hierarchy of power not only between people but also between the two sides of the city.

The richness of this scene is such that it shows the spectator that a return to tradition, to authenticity, does not always bring about solutions to the problems of Africans such as the cart driver. While criticising the inhuman Westernisation of the inhabitants of the Europeanised side of the city, the 'Plateau', *Borom Sarret* questions the unconditional return to tradition. Sembène creates a distance between spectators and the characters in the film which enables the spectators to criticise themselves in their tradition. This cinematic language takes its form and content from the figure of the griot, symbol of the oral tradition which Sembène uses as his point of departure. The difference between this first film by Africa's leading director and Western films resides in Sembène's ability to transform Western cinema's exotic characters like the griot and the cart driver into thematic as well as structural elements for the content and the form of his film language.

In *Djeli (The Griot,* 1981), on the contrary, Lancine Fadika-Kramo resists this transcendence of the griot's art form. He posits the griot as the point of departure and the master of narrative. *Djeli* starts with a flashback retracing the griot's mythic origin in order to put into question the hierarchies of the caste system. According to this rhetoric, the griot was originally a hunter who changed trades to become a singer, storyteller and musician. Interestingly enough, another West African myth of origins, 'Gassire's Lute', states that the griot was a brave warrior who, tired of killing, turned into a musician to follow and entertain the warriors.[8] *Djeli* blames the caste system for the contemporary negative image of griots as inferior to other social groups. To show that this definition of griots is opposed to any revolution of ideas, to love and life, Fadika creates a love story between a man from the griot caste and a woman from another social group so as to reveal the regressiveness of caste systems which suppress such a possibility. The aesthetic in *Djeli* defines itself as a movement out of the stagnation of caste hierarchies, towards a transformation of tradition into an egalitarian system. It is in this sense that the film valorises 'Djeli-ya' – the state of being a griot – through beautiful images of the griottes (female artists), slow-motion shots of griottes singing and dancing, and the flashback which shows that griots were originally equal to other groups. The film positions the spectator to get rid of hierarchical notions, to enjoy the art of the griot and to see a coincidence between the rehabilitation of griots and progress in Africa.

Finally, in *Jom* (1981), Ababakar Samb paints a romantic figure of griots. According to Samb, they are the historians, the educators and the guardians of people's conscience. In *Jom* the griot is the main character, the omniscient narrator of the different sketches that form the film, and the immortal persona who travels through time and space. He remains unchanged by age and by the weapons used by the enemies of tradition. Neither money nor fear can corrupt him. He is the griot of the poor as well as of the rich. Samb's griot, like Sembène's narrator in *Borom Sarret*, is a committed activist who fights for the right of the oppressed. He provides leadership and moral support to the factory workers who are on strike, ridicules the eccentricities of the *nouveaux riches* in Africa, and praises the courage and dignity of the migrant workers who had to leave their villages because of the drought.

Samb's construction of the griot and his narrative as master and model respectively for African cinema has for a consequence the subordination of the film-maker's narrative to that of the griot and the creation of a nostalgic mood to serve as a refuge for the spectator. The figure of the griot is used to reinvent a beautiful image of the past. Unlike Sembène, who puts the griot's narrative within a larger narrative, Samb surrenders to the narrative authority of the griot. This romanticisation of the griot defines Samb's film language which valorises tradition as characterised in the film by authenticity, dignity and truth, and negates modernism as characterised by alienation, colonialism and exploitation. *Jom* positions the spectator to identify with tradition without any attempt at self-criticism: everything positive is pushed on the side of tradition and everything negative on the side of modernism.

Up to now, I have shown the manner in which elements of popular culture have been incorporated into cinema. I will show now how the structure of oral literature has helped to shape the originality of African cinema. At the beginning of this paper, I pointed out that film-makers, like novelists, are infuenced, consciously or not, by the narrative forms of the oral storyteller. They have been initiated into oral tradition before going to Western schools. The way the storytellers narrate becomes their point of reference when they take their first steps at a film school. During the rest of their careers, they are bound to be dealing with oral tradition, to move it sometimes, contrasting it with the modern forms of the novel and of cinema, or even to repress it. One can see the influence of oral tradition in all African films, including Sembène's *Xala, The Money Order* (1968), *Finyé* and *Baara (The Porter*, 1978), even where the narrative forms of the classic novel and cinema dominate.

Elsewhere, I have shown how Gaston Kaboré's *Wend Kuuni (The Gift of God*, 1983) makes orality its subject and questions the hermetic and conservative structure of tradition in oral literature.[9] One can also mention Sembène's *Ceddo* as another film which takes the oral tradition for a principal subject and transforms its structure into a revolutionary statement. Sembène's *The Money Order* is a historical landmark because, for the first time in a film by an African director, the actors speak an African language. But it is in *Ceddo* that Sembène posits an archaeology of discourse in Africa. The richness of the language in proverbs and sayings, the power of the spoken word and of the speaker are all represented in *Ceddo*. In the king's court, the discursive space defines itself by including some as members of the discourse in a hierarchical order and by excluding others. The griot, to use the words of Camara Laye, is master of discourse. He controls its distribution and its impact. He is the one through whom the speaking members communicate.

Let's examine the manner in which the subject of orality determines the form of narration in the film. In order to represent the discursive space, the director creates a *mise en scène* in which the griot occupies the centre of the circle formed by the king's court, the imam, the missionary and the Ceddoes. The fast editing style of European films is replaced by long takes in deep-focus shots. It is as if the camera has taken the griot's position so as to reveal the directions of speech. There are very few camera movements and close-ups. Shot/reverse-shots are avoided so as not to give the impression that one is dealing with a dialogue scene similar to the ones in Western films.

However, Sembène, like the griot, also makes his presence felt at several points in the diegesis. He is physically present as a Ceddo, carrying firewood on his head, discussing the issue of exile with other Ceddoes, and during the imam's baptising of Ceddoes. The use of close-ups of human faces and of objects, in this film where long shots dominate the narration, reveals a didactic intervention on the part of the director. Thus Sembène, like the oral storyteller, determines the reading of the signs for the viewer.

The travel of initiation or the educational quest, which constitutes the structural cell of oral literature, is also an important motif in African cinema (see, among others, *Borom Sarret, La Noire de...* (Sembène, 1996), *L'Exile, Lettre paysanne* (Safi Faye, 1975), *Wend Kuuni, Njangaan* (Traoré, 1975), *Touki Bouki* (Djibril Diop Mambety, 1973). The quest defines itself as a movement from the village to the city and ends with the return to the village. One can also interpret it as an alienation and a return to authenticity, as is shown at the end of *Touki Bouki*, for example.

Ceddo also moves its characters so as to bring them to an awakening of consciousness. The princess, first kidnapped by the Ceddoes, realises the exploitation of her people by the imam and joins the Ceddoes in their resistance against the tyranny of the imam. What above all differentiates *Ceddo* from the oral narration is its closure. In the oral tradition, the physical return symbolises the return to the status quo. The griot is conservative and his story helps to reinforce traditional values. In oral traditions, the story is always closed so as not to leave any ambiguity about interpretations. In *Ceddo,* on the contrary, the

215

return denotes the union of the princess and the Ceddoes. Thus the end of the film, a freeze frame, announces the new day pregnant uith several possibilities.

Finally, I will end this study by showing the manner in which one of the best films of the Pan-African Film Festival (FESPACO 87), Cheick Oumar Sissoko's *Nyamanton*,[10] continues the African film language I have sought to define above. *Nyamanton* constitutes an educational quest, or an initiation trip for the two main characters, Kalifa and Fanta, who travel daily from their home to the neighbourhood where they work. The home symbolises the interior space where tradition is a refuge, safeguarding parental relations. The children play with their grandparents and the resulting laughs help the family go through their daily difficulties. The city represents the outside, the change of setting and imminent danger. The trips between home and the city enable the children to witness the injustice present in their society and to question its permanence.

Nyamanton, too, like *Ceddo*, goes beyond the mere imitation of orality to question the griot who is the master of discourse. In one scene Kalifa says to his friend, Aliou, that his father is the greatest liar after Jali Baba, Mali's famous griot. Aliou answers that griots do not lie, that what they say is the true story and that Kalifa ignores their value. Aliou then starts imitating Jali Baba and sings his friend's praises. One sees in this scene the definition of the griot as a historian on the one hand and, on the other hand, as an artist whose play with words ranks him with liars. But more important than this reference to the figure of the griot and his narrative is the fact that the director's world view takes the place of that of the griot as the most authoritative in the thematisation of the kids' relation to everyday life in Africa. In oral tradition, it is through the griot's point of view that one sees and realises the universe around one. In film, the camera replaces the griot as the director's eyes and constructs the new images of Africa for the spectator. It is in this sense that one says that the African film-maker has replaced the griot in the rewriting of history.

Nyamanton is constructed mostly with long shots. These shots show clearly the space occupied by the women at the house door and Kalifa's father under the tree. The father has to yell when he communicates with women because of the distance separating them. In order to remain within the limits of realism as regards the representation of such spaces, the camera occupies the centre between the women and the father, as was the case with the griot in *Ceddo*. Here, too, close-ups and shot/reverse-shots are avoided as much as possible.

At first sight, this narrative expedient may be dismissed as simply a primitive use of the camera in an attempt to economise on editing. Thus a hasty comparison with Western cinema might bring one to the conclusion that African films lack action. But an analysis based on the forms of oral tradition will highlight the originality of African film language in *Nyamanton*. First, one can see through an ethnographic insight that the long shots serve better to create the effect of verisimilitude in the narrative. The external space in Africa is less characterised by the display of emotion and closeness between man and woman, and more by a designation of man's space and woman's space in society. The narrator imitates this reality by using mostly long shots and by describing the emotion of the characters instead of showing it.

The griot's influence on the film-maker brings about the fact that subjective shots do not always have the same significance in African cinema as in Western cinema. Close-ups of a child's face or of a pack of cigarettes in *Nyamanton*, for example, are not objects seen by a character but their description by the director/narrator for the spectator. Even the flash-forward in the film is a description of the mother coming to an understanding of the situation in which she finds herself. Instead of effacing himself and realising the story through different characters' narrations, the director in *Nyamanton* always carries the camera on his shoulder and, like the griot, dominates the narrative with his presence. While Western directors often achieve recognition by letting the story tell itself, African directors, like the griots, master their craft by impressing the spectator with their narrative performance. This may be because, with the griots, one achieves fame not by being the author of new texts but by being able to reproduce the best versions of old texts. *Nyamanton* is a new version of such African films in which tradition clashes with modernity, and the popularity of its director lies in the manner in which he describes the most memorable episodes of the clash.

The choice of *Nyamanton* for the title of the film is also interesting in the context of oral tradition. Etymologically, *Nyamanton* comes from the prefix *Nyama,* which in Bambara and Mandinka may be translated as 'potentially dangerous forces released through the performance or violation of ritual'.[11] *Nyaman* with an 'n' at the end means trash. Thus a popular song in West Africa likens Sunjata, King of Mali in the 13th century, to a dump-site which hides everything underneath itself, but which cannot be covered by other things. Literally the song refers to Sunjata's vital force which protects his people and which harms his enemies like the plague released from a *Nyama* or from the violation of ritual.[12]

When the title of the film is interpreted in the context of *Nyama* as a West African trope, one sees how Sissoko positions the spectator to take a personal responsibility in reducing the children's future to trash collection, and to fear the retribution of *Nyama*. Sunjata, too, had a difficult childhood, and those who were responsible were punished. On the other hand, the likening of the children to Sunjata leads the spectator to identify them with the collective future of Africa. As in *Ceddo,* orality is here again made the subject of the film in order to arraign the repressive forces of tradition and modernism .

Finally, the oral tradition also influenced the French title of the film, *La Leçon des ordures* (The Lesson of Garbage). Sissoko wanted to oppose to 'The Lesson of Things' which students in francophone Africa learn every morning from French textbooks the lessons learnt about Malian society by Kalifa and Aliou through their work as garbage boys. As 'leçon des choses' becomes interchangeable with 'leçon des ordures', and both are little more than *Nyaman,* the film creates the necessity to question the lessons inherited from the former colonial powers. There is no doubt that the form of African cinema is influenced by its traditional content. Understanding the role played by the oral tradition in African film enables the critic to see how the film-maker has transformed this tradition into a new ideology. But it is also possible to study the way in which the African content has changed the cinematic language of the West. This is what transpires when one examines the strategies by which film has incorporated African traditions. The African director makes conscious and unconscious references to the griot's narrative techniques.

217

Notes

1. Robert Stam and Randal Johnson, *Brazilian Cinema* (East Brunswick, NJ: Associated University Press, 1982). Teshome Gabriel, *Third Cinema in the Third World: The Aesthetics of Liberation* (Ann Arbor, Mich.: UMI Research Press, 1982). Julianne Burton, *Cinema and Social Change in Latin America: Conversations with Film-makers* (Austin: University of Texas Press, 1986). for the recent debates on Third Cinema see Julianne Burton, 'Marginal Cinemas and Mainstream Critical Theory', *Screen*, vol. 26 nos 3/4, 1985. Teshome Gabriel, 'Colonialism and "Law and Order" Criticism', *Screen*, vol. 27 nos 3/4, 1986. For an overall review, see Roy Armes, *Third World Filmmaking and the West* (Berkeley: University of California Press, 1987).
2. Jean Rouch, 'Le Dit du cinéma africain', in *Films éthnographiques sur l'Afrique noire* (Paris: UNESCO, 1967), pp. 1–9.
3. In *Revue de Littérature Comparée*, vol. 3 no. 4, 1974, p. 536.
4. For recent discussion of codes that are specific to film language, see Jacques Aumont *et al.*, *Esthétique du Film* (Paris: Editions Fernand Nathan, 1983), pp. 138–43.
5. Jacques Binet, for example, argues that 'The African traditions were not prone to an art of images: no fresco, no painting and no drawing'. See 'Les Cultures africaines et les images', in *CinémAction*, no. 26, 1982, special issue, 'Cinémas noirs d'Afrique', p. 19.
6. *Revue de Littérature Comparée*, p. 549.
7. Mbye Cham, 'Ousmane Sembène and the Aesthetics of African Oral Tradition', in *African Journal*, 1982, p. 26.
8. In Jerome Rothenburg, (ed.), *Technicians of the Sacred* (New York: Anchor Books, 1969), pp. 184–191.
9. 'Oral Literature and African Film: Narratology in *Wend Kuuni*', in *Présence Africaine*, no. 142, 1987, pp. 36–49. Also in Jim Pines and Paul Willemen (eds), *Questions of Third Cinema*, (London: BFI, 1989).
10. See Manthia Diawara and Elizabeth Robinson, 'New Perspectives on African Cinema: An Interview with Cheick Oumar Cissoko', *Film Quarterly*, vol. 41 no. 1, Winter 1987–8).
11. Christopher L. Miller, 'Orality through Literacy: Mande Verbal Art after the Letter', *The Southern Review*, vol. 23 no. 1, Winter 1987, p. 84.
12. Massa Makan Diabate, *Le Lion à l'arc* (Paris: Hatier, 1986).

Further Readings

Gabriel, Teshome, *Third Cinema in the Third World* (Ann Arbor, Mich.: UMI Research Press, 1982).

Stam, Robert, and Shohat, Ella (eds), *Unthinking Euro-Centrism* (New York: Routledge, 1994).

Tajima, Renée (ed.), *Journey Across Three Continents* (New York: Third World Newsreel, 1985).

Willemen, Paul, and Pines, Jim (eds), *Questions of Third Cinema* (London: BFI, 1989).

Tradition orale et nouveaux médias (Bruxelles: OCIC, Collection CINEME-DIA/Cinémas d'Afrique Noire, No. 12, 1989). Published in collaboration with FESPACO.

Iris, no. 18, 1995. Issue on 'New Discourses of African Cinema'.

Research in African Literatures, vol. 26 no. 3, 1995. Issue on African Cinema.

PART V
Critical Perspectives

Africa from Within: The Films of Gaston Kaboré and Idrissa Ouédraogo as Anthropological Sources

FRANÇOISE PFAFF

Reprinted from *Society for Visual Anthropology*, vol. 6 no. 1, Spring 1990.

All films are cultural products, and thus vehicles of culture. Since 'Anthropology is the study of humankind in its various manifestations through time and across geographical space',[1] including arts and fiction (humankind's representation and expression), films can be the privileged object of anthropological attention. Based on this premise, all films, whether documentaries, feature films, raw visual footage or even home movies, can be examined from an anthropological perspective.[2]

Applying Lucien Goldman's theory of the novel to feature film, one can say that film is the product of individuals or groups influenced by the society in which they live.[3] Mainstream star-conscious American fiction cinema is often fast-moving, noisy, and technically intricate; and, usually, American films are less charged with emotion than European films. French motion pictures often stress the psychological facets of emotional problems, sociopolitically oriented films from the Soviet Union are frequently overtly propagandist, while progressive films from the Third World such as Latin America and Africa (South Africa excepted) aim at conveying a particular sociocultural and political message mirroring the aspirations and/or needs of their increasingly Westernised nations. If one applies Jung's theory, fiction film can be seen as the reflector of the collective unconscious, very much like former myths. The above and other theories would tend to substantiate the statement made by Hortense Powdermaker in her 1947 article entitled 'An Anthropologist Looks at the Movies':

> Through the study of American movies, we should likewise contribute to the understanding of the American society. We assume that movies will reflect values and goals of folklore; the theatre and literature have always reflected them.[4]

And, indeed, not only Northern American or French films, but also African films should contribute to the understanding of the societies which have generated them. The purpose of this paper is to demonstrate how one can make a legitimate and justifiable analytical and/or pedagogical use of African feature films within a visual anthropological framework, using fiction films made by Africans as documentation. It should be said here that this analytical strategy is far from being new, as evidenced by extensive studies of German and Japanese feature films in times of war, in an attempt to decipher the enemy's psyche[5] –

why not use the same methods to promote the understanding of foreign cultures in peacetime to avoid war on cultural, political and economic fronts? One should also note that prior reviews of African feature films (Ousmane Sembène's *Emitai,* 1971, and *Black Girl,* 1966) have appeared in such publications as *American Anthropologist.*[6]

The present investigation will focus primarily on the works of two African film-makers, Gaston Kaboré and Idrissa Ouédraogo, whose realistic motion pictures were produced in similar conditions and reverberate easily delineated geographic spaces and the cultural codes indigenous to social groups in Burkina Faso (formerly Upper Volta). Here, our examination will derive from the notion of anthropology as a tool and methodology entirely separated from the unscientific and harmfully condescending colonial context of Western cultural supremacy within which the discipline flourished in the 19th century.[7] And, in effect, a culture can be apprehended as objectively as possible, provided the observer does not apply a hierarchical value judgment (whether he or she wants it, he or she looks at the world through his or her own traditions) to the differences he or she may encounter and which may imply the superiority of Western culture over non-Western thoughts and behavioural patterns. Moreover, one has to be cognisant of the fact that the data presented in the film has been conceptualised, selected and contextualised by a film-maker who acts as a participant observer of sorts, a member of the ethnic group represented on the screen, which is in itself a significant departure from the culturally distant and culturally biased gaze of the alien Western observer. For, even if laudable efforts are made by anthropologists to integrate the culture they propose to study, they remain outsiders, which brings to mind the following declaration once made by the French ethnographer/film-maker Jean Rouch: 'We will never be African and our films will remain films made by foreigners.'[8] Yet intellectual honesty forces one to recognise that, if endogenous, an African film-maker's representation of his or her community is not necessarily completely objective and flawless because his or her thought patterns will also depend on such things as class, religion, gender, and so on.

Before dealing explicitly with the films of Gaston Kaboré and Idrissa Ouédraogo, it is important to place them within the larger context of African film-making, whose cultural nature and goals have been often reassessed in the course of its 35-year history. In fact, the advent of sub-Saharan African cinema coincided with the independence of many African countries after years of colonial subordination, and the African film practitioners were deeply concerned with the issue of culture and national identity. These directors often espoused the cultural doctrines expressed by such theorists as Frantz Fanon of Martinique and Amilcar Cabral of Guinea-Bissau. In 1973, Cabral stated that 'a people who free themselves from foreign domination will be free culturally only if... they return to the upward paths of their own culture'.[9] Similar concerns were included in *The Wretched of the Earth* by Frantz Fanon.[10] The cultural facets of African film-making were stressed at official gatherings of African film-makers and critics, and recorded in such documents as the 1975 Algiers Charter on African Cinema, which stipulated:

Contemporary African societies are still objectively undergoing an experience of domination exerted on a number of levels: political, economic and cultural. Cultural domination, which is all the more dangerous for being insidious, imposes on our peoples models of behaviour and systems of value whose essential function is to buttress the ideological and economic ascendancy of the imperialist powers. The main channels open to this form of control are supplied by the new technologies of communication: books, the audiovisual, and very specifically the cinema ... in the face of this condition of cultural domination and deracination, there is a pressing need to reformulate in liberating terms the internal problematic of development and of the part that must be played in this worldwide advance by culture and by the cinema.[11]

Significantly, the Algiers Charter was followed by the Niamey Manifesto of 1982, which stressed the need to express the cultural legacy of the African peoples through films as well as the need to use such a medium in the development process of African nations.[12]

The first film ever made by West Africans was *Afrique-sur-Seine* (1955), shot, edited and released in Paris. Yet, although the work depicts the aspirations and occupations of Paris's Black population, it was also the first time the French capital and its inhabitants were seen through non-Western eyes, by African students (Paulin Vieyra, Robert Carristan, Jacques Milo Kane and Mamadou Sarr) returning the anthropological gaze, first looking at their colonial metropolis and subsequently to their continent and the world. African cinema was to become a unique instrument of cultural self-examination and self-assertiveness (while rejecting the stereotypical images of Africa found in Western tarzanistic jungle melodramas) within a shifting context of modernisation and urbanisation. Férid Boughedir, of Tunisia, emphasises the cultural trend found within such African films as *Muna Moto* (1974) by Jean Pierre Dikongue-Pipa; *Saitane* (1963) and *L'Exile* (1980) by Oumarou Ganda of Niger; *Wend Kuuni* (1982) by Gaston Kaboré; *Yam Daabo* (1987) by Idrissa Ouédraogo; *Djeli* (1981) by Kramo Lancine Fadika of Côte d'Ivoire; and *Jom* (1981) by the Senegalese Ababacar Samb.[13] It is also an omnipresent theme in many works by Ousmane Sembène of Senegal and Souleymane Cissé of Mali. Moreover, as was the case for Oumarou Ganda, Mustapha Alassane (Niger) and Safi Faye (Senegal) were encouraged by Jean Rouch to develop their skills as film-makers. It thus comes as no surprise that their works are often ethnographic in content, style and format (16mm). Interestingly, this cultural/ethnographic trend in African film-making has recently been acknowledged and negatively criticised by younger film-makers such as Cheikh Ngaido Bah, of Senegal. Referring to the French funding of many West African motion pictures in the past, Bah stipulates:

What African film-makers do not talk about is the fact that they used to make films for Europe ... Europe dictated to them what African cinema should be. And Europe gave them a certain amount of money to finance some of their film projects based on scripts corresponding to European views of Africa. A lot of scripts were written or at least edited at the French Ministry of Co-operation. In the old days such motion pictures reflected village life, class conflicts or the clash between traditional mores and modern ways in Africa; now these films deal with African mystical beliefs, as happens in *Yeelen* by Souleymane Cissé.[14]

Here, even if one does not agree fully with Bah's views, one could very well not so much question the authenticity of the African film-makers' cultural representations but wonder if their selection of cultural icons was entirely theirs. One could also raise the issue of the convenience of emphasising cultural film components over political topics (such as the misdeeds of colonialism and neocolonialism), which may have adversely challenged the past and present policies of France towards its former colonies. However, expressing an entirely different viewpoint, which matches that of most African film-makers, the Ethiopian film critic Teshome Gabriel considers the cultural nature and role of film an essential part of African and Third World cinemas because 'the struggle to preserve the cultural make-up of a society constitutes a major concern for Third World film-makers'.[15]

In his article 'Feature Films as Cultural Documents', John H. Weakland stresses:

> There are several basic reasons why fictional films should be especially useful in the study of general patterns of culture. In the first place, they are useful precisely because they are not factual. Instead, they tell a story; that is, they present an interpretation of some segment of life by selection, structuring and ordering images of behaviour.[16]

Generally, this 'interpretation of some segment of life', this deconstruction/reconstruction of reality within the imaginative process of film-making is rather difficult to attribute to definite individuals in terms of Western commercial cinema because motion pictures are usually group products, the result of a collaborative effort between such people as a scriptwriter, a director and a producer. In the case of African cinema, films are often authors' works. The single most important creative force is the film-maker who, although he or she works with a technical crew and may have to abide by the wishes of financial sponsors (the French government, his or her own government or private funding sources), usually fulfils a multiple role: that of producer, scriptwriter, and director. It can thus be easily assumed that the personality and training of African film-makers, which this study considers as insider-informant, greatly influence the style and cultural content of their cinematic products. Before proceeding to the analysis of their works, it appears indispensable to see which elements in the lives and careers of Kaboré and Ouédraogo may have shaped their art.

An investigation into the background of the two Burkinabe film-makers reveals a number of striking similarities. Both were born in the early 1950s (does this fact explain their lack of thematic concern regarding Black/White Manicheanism or the issue of colonialism amply illustrated by older African directors?), and belong to the urban Westernised elite (their fathers are civil servants). Yet the two often stress their rural roots, which allow them to represent village lifestyles and beliefs with a great deal of accuracy. In addition, Gaston Kaboré and Idrissa Ouédraogo learned their skills at film schools. After his MA in history from the Sorbonne, Kaboré decided to acquire training in film-making with the primary intention of using film as a research instrument. In 1974, he registered at the Ecole Supérieure d'Etudes Cinématographiques, a French institution from which he graduated in 1977.

Idrissa Ouédraogo had also begun other studies (English) at the University of

Ouagadougou before engaging in a film-making career, which led him to study cinema at INAFEC, Burkina Faso's now defunct film institute. Then he went to film school in the Soviet Union, where he became acquainted with Soviet socialist realism, and finally he studied in France, at the Institut des Hautes Etudes Cinématographiques, from which he graduated in 1985. After working for his country's Film Production Services, Ouédraogo (unlike Kaboré, who lives in Burkina Faso) now resides in Paris, where he is working under Jean Rouch on a PhD dissertation on the theoretical problems of film-making. From the start, Ouédraogo, who in his student days had written 'plays about commitment', recognised film as a medium through which he could communicate his sociopolitical and culturally oriented views.[17] Such ideas remain unchanged, as he told an interviewer (alluding to the fact that his full-length film *Yam Daabo* had been featured at the Cannes Film Festival): 'I think that cinema is political, because when my film is presented at Cannes, it is Burkina Faso's culture which is represented there.'[18] The cultural nature and impact of African film is also recognised by Gaston Kaboré, who once said:

> My political choice forces me to take an active part in the struggle to restore the personality and dignity of African and Burkinabe people. In my opinion, cinema has a great role to play as a medium to promote our development policies and also as a means to rehabilitate our culture.[19]

Gaston Kaboré's directorial career began with the shooting of *Je viens de Bokin* (I Come from Bokin, 16mm, colour, 38 minutes, 1977), a film he made with a crew of INAFEC students, and which addresses the topic of migration from village to town. Next, Kaboré made a series of commissioned didactic documentaries: *Stocker et conserver les grains* (Stocking and Keeping Grain, 16mm, colour, 22 minutes, 1978), *Regard sur le VIème FESPACO* (A Look at the Sixth FESPACO, 16mm, colour, 40 minutes, 1979), and *Utilisation des énergies nouvelles en milieu rural* (The Use of New Energies in Rural Environments, 16mm, colour, 40 minutes, 1980). Most of these shorts promote the use of new agricultural techniques; one of them covers the various cultural events that occurred at the 1979 FESPACO (the biennial Pan-African Film Festival of Ouagadougou). Kaboré made his debut as feature director with *Wend Kuuni* (The Gift of God, 35mm, colour, 75 minutes), followed by *Zan Boko* (35mm, colour, 100 minutes, 1989).

As happened in the case of Kaboré, Idrissa Ouédraogo's first motion pictures were shorts: *Poko* (16mm, colour, 20 minutes, 1981), which denounces the poor medical infrastructure leading to the death of a pregnant village woman about to give birth; *Les Ecuelles* (The Wooden Bowls, 16mm, colour, 11 minutes, 1983), which shows the traditional craft of making wooden bowls; *Les Funérailles du Larle Naba* (16mm, colour, 30 minutes, 1983) on the ceremonial rites associated with the death of the king of the Mossi; *Ouagadougou, Ouaga deux roues* (16mm, colour, 16 minutes, 1984), a documentary on Burkina Faso's capital city, whose inhabitants favour the use of mopeds as a means of locomotion and transportation; and *Issa le tisserand* (Issa the Weaver, 16mm, colour, 20 minutes, 1985), a pessimistic statement about disappearing indigenous crafts. All these films have no dialogue or obstrusive authoritative/authorial voice-over commentary and rely solely, as communication medium, on the strength of their explicitly forceful images – a convenient and efficacious way to reach out to all segments of Burkina Faso where forty-two dialects and languages are spoken. *Yam Daabo* (The Choice, 16/35mm, colour, 100 minutes) and *Yaaba* (35mm, colour, 90 minutes, 1989) remain, to date (1990), Ouédraogo's sole feature-length motion pictures.

All of the works of Kaboré and Ouédraogo easily lend themselves to anthropological scrutiny. *Je viens de Bokin,* for instance, is a good study of culture contacts situations; *Stocker et conserver les grains* and *Utilisation des énergies nouvelles en milieu rural* both highlight traditional farming methods while advocating new techniques, thus depicting how the economic order, ideologies, as well as patterns of social relationships are changed within the broader context of modernisation. *Les Funérailles du Larle Naba* and *Les Ecuelles* illustrate George Marcus's theory of the 'redemptive mode', through which the ethnographer (in this case the film-maker) 'demonstrates the survival of distinctive and authentic cultural systems despite undeniable changes'; while *Issa le tisserand* could be conceived to be based on Marcus's 'salvage mode'. In this latter case, Ouédraogo, like the ethnographer, 'is able to salvage a cultural state on the verge of transformation'.[20] However, the present paper will focus primarily on the Burkinabe directors' feature films, which are more readily available in the West. Although film style is also related to culture, our approach will be primarily founded on thematic elements.

In content, *Wend Kuuni* is inherently different from most African motion pictures, whose plots are usually set in contemporary environments (this may reflect significant interest in present-day topics or may be attributed to the high cost of historical reconstruction). Kaboré, a former history student, points out:

> *Wend Kuuni* takes place in pre-colonial times [but] its exact time frame is not important. It could be 1420 or 1850 because the sociocultural reality which I depict remained unchanged for years ... [I chose] a past and autonomous society with its own oppressive forces and inner contradictions, a community which I did not regard as an ideal African society.[21]

Although based on Kaboré's original script, *Wend Kuuni* derives its general mood from African oral tradition, which the film-maker views as 'a cultural testimony of African history'.[22] The story of the film reflects an era of Mossi stability and wealth. One day a pedlar found a child lying, unconscious, at the foot of a tree. He then discovered that the young boy was mute and could not reveal his past. Soon thereafter, the child was adopted by a weaver and his family. They called him Wend Kuuni. Henceforth, the boy was lovingly raised by his foster parents. He developed a touching friendship with Pognere, his young adoptive sister, who was able to relate to him in spite of his impairment. Wend Kuuni shared village life and became a shepherd. Suddenly, the idyllic serenity of Wend Kuuni's new community was disrupted by a woman who accused her husband of impotence. Unable to bear this public shame, the husband put an end to his life by hanging himself. Upon the emotional shock of discovering the dead man's body, Wend Kuuni regained his power of speech. Finally able to tell his own story, he explained that he had become mute from the trauma of having seen his mother die in the bush after being expelled from her village as a witch because, hoping for the return of her husband who had disappeared

228

while hunting, she had refused to abide by tradition and remarry.

Wend Kuuni is told in a tale-like fashion. Here the film-maker, the narrator whose sporadic voice is heard, and Wend Kuuni are all storytellers reflecting West African orature.[23] Such a characteristic is amply recognised by both African and non-African critics, who see in Kaboré's work a fine example of fruitful symbiosis between film syntax (with its Western codes) and African oral narratology.

Zan Boko, Kaboré's second feature-length film, differs in content and form from *Wend Kuuni*. Like many African films, *Zan Boko* illustrates the contemporary social and psychological clashes that may occur between traditional lifestyles and Western-influenced modernity. The work's main themes include the adverse effects of urbanisation, nepotism and corruption, the issues of acculturation, social alienation and the freedom of the press. The plot focuses on the fate of Tinga, a peasant who is displaced from his ancestral land because of urban expansion, and the greed of his nouveau riche neighbour who covets his estate to build a swimming pool. In spite of a journalist friend's vain efforts to disclose the true circumstances of Tinga's eviction (his live television programme is suddenly ordered off the air by the Minister of Information), the former villager proves unable to resist the dubious transactions and pressures of the elite in power. *Zan Boko* is a sensitive, ironic and courageous film, whose images mirror the realities shown: long shots and slow pace match representations of the rural context while more frequent close-ups and medium shots, as well as a quicker cinematic rhythm, translate the urban world. Gaston Kaboré, in his production notes, stresses the sociocultural components of his work and its very title as follows:

> Amongst many black African cultures the birth of a child is accompanied by rituals that are designed to prepare the introduction and acceptance of a new member of the community. Among the rites practised by the Mossi in West Africa, is the burial of the mother's placenta. This act consecrates the first bond between the new-born child and the nourishing earth. It is also the home of the ancestors and of the spirits which protect the family and social group. The place where the placenta is buried is called 'Zan Boko'. These two words are used by the Mossi when speaking of their native land, with a meaning that is at once religious, cultural, historic and emotional but also signifies *a real* relation with place. 'Zan Boko' is an expression of the concepts of 'roots' and 'identity'. This film tells of the disappearance of a small African village which is engulfed by an ever-expanding urban sprawl. A rural community, which is characterised by its own rhythm of life and a specific vision of the world, is brutally disrupted and loses its identity.

To fully appreciate the content of Idrissa Ouédraogo's *Yam Daabo* (set in a present-day milieu), one has to take into account the fact that Burkina Faso, one of Africa's poorest states, is partly located in the Sahel. This region is sporadically affected by drought, and has areas of poor soil and scarce water which have made agriculture difficult and caused migratory movements from rural to urban areas and neighbouring countries such as Ghana and Côte d'Ivoire (this circumstance is illustrated in another Burkinabe motion picture, *Paweogo*, made in 1982 by Sanou Kollo). Thus, for a number of years, the nation has relied heavily on imported goods, raw material and foreign aid – a situation the government has sought to remedy in recent years. Significantly, Idrissa Ouédraogo's optimistic *Yam Daabo* conveys a message of self-sufficiency in tune with the revolutionary goals of Burkina Faso's leaders. *Yam Daabo* narrates the story of a peasant who decides he will no longer rely on international aid. With his family he decides to leave a dry area to find fertile land and a bright future. In his own words, the director wanted to rectify the one-dimensional image of Africa, often globally perceived by many as poverty-stricken and helpless.[24]

Ouédraogo's second feature film, *Yaaba,* espouses the tale-like aspect found in Kaboré's *Wend Kuuni.* Situated in a timeless framework, *Yaaba* is a humanistic story which encompasses dreamlike, mythic and legendary elements, as well as realistic illustrations of daily rural life in Burkina Faso. According to the film-maker's production-notes for *Yaaba:*

> 'Yaaba' in Moore means grandmother. 'Yaaba' is also the name that a twelve-year-old boy, Bila, gives Sana, an old woman abandoned and rejected by the whole village. *Yaaba* is above all a story about a friendship which is born and which grows between two people in a village society, where we see man as he really is: good, bad, generous, intolerant. *Yaaba* began with the memory of a tale of my own childhood and of a sort of nocturnal education. Where I come from, this nocturnal education is acquired between the age of seven and ten, just before falling asleep, if one is lucky enough to have a grandmother.

Both Kaboré and Ouédraogo, who belong to the Mossi ethnic group (which represents one-half of the country's total population), have placed their stories in Mossi surroundings, and their characters speak Moore, the Mossi vernacular and one of Burkina Faso's main languages. The careful portrayal of Mossi lifestyles on the screen undoubtedly facilitates character identification for Burkinabe viewers, but also communicates a wealth of ethnographic data to non-African observers. The film-makers' non-professional actors are Mossi, and convey with ease and a lot of naturalness the gestures and behavioural patterns of their ethnic group. Even though some of the actors may be Westernised (for instance the role of *Wend Kuuni*'s weaver is played by a high school teacher), their family roots lead to Mossi rural traditions in a not-so-distant past. Moreover, Kaboré and Ouédraogo's fiction works were filmed on location. *Wend Kuuni* and *Zan Boko* were shot in villages located in the vicinity of Ouagadougou as well as in the capital itself. *Yam Daabo* was made in a Mossi village on the edge of the Sahel as well as in Burkina Faso's more fertile southern area. *Yaaba* was shot a few miles from Ouahigouya, in the main town of the Yatenga province (north-western Burkina Faso), where Idrissa Ouédraogo was born. Ouédraogo says: 'There village life is exactly as we show it in the film, there is no reconstitution, everything was shot in natural settings.'[25] Here it may also be worth pointing out that the Ouagadougou region and the Yatenga province were two of the three precolonial Mossi states whose prestigious past was marked by political stability, economic wealth and a spirit of independence which opposed fierce resistance to Islamic as well as to Western penetration. One should bear in mind that French colonisation occurred in the region at the very end of the 19th century (in 1896), much later than in other parts of Africa. These characteristics of lasting prosperity, wealth and self-sufficiency are indeed reflected in *Wend Kuuni*.

Burkina Faso has two distinct seasons which regulate the life of its farmers – the dry season (from October to May) with its sun-scorched red soils, tall dry grass, dusty and barren fields, and the rainy season, during which all of nature becomes suddenly green. In order to take advantage of optimum weather conditions for their filming, most of the two directors' works take place during the dry season (as happens in *Wend Kuuni* or in the first part of *Yam Daabo),* or on rainless days, seemingly towards the end of the rainy season when the millet crops are ready to be harvested, increasing the villagers' field activities (in *Zan Boko* a woman stresses how difficult it is to pay social calls during the busy rainy season). In *Yaaba,* however, some lush vegetation indicates that the film's plot occurs during the rainy season. These surroundings are reflected in beautifully reflective visual compositions of solitary characters on semi-barren savannah landscapes, or in long shots depicting the villagers' communal labour activities (*Zan Boko*'s field clearing and harvesting, and the like).

The many geographic facets revealed through Kaboré and Ouédraogo's motion pictures correspond to the Mossi's attachment to their homeland, where their ancestors are buried and venerated. This factor renders even more significant the decisive migration undertaken by the ageing head of a family in *Yam Daabo*. In *Zan Boko*, the changes brought about by urban expansion deeply eaffect the people's relationship to their land. One of them deplores that the city has 'conquered' their homeland. The words of the griot, as he sings in a local outdoor bar, are: 'Ours is a sad story. What has become of us? Our land is dead, killed by the big city. Our ancestors are without a home. The monster has triumphed.' And Tinga tells his wife: 'What bothers me is being treated like outsiders on the land of our ancestors.' Finally, the issue of Tinga's relocation after having sold his land shows how Tinga's identity is affected. This offers a poignant illustration of the disruptions caused by modernisation, especially since in traditional Mossi culture land was collectively owned and assigned to individuals by heads of lineages. It is also noteworthy to point out that in such societies land could, traditionally, be borrowed or inherited but never sold.

Although the two Burkinabe film-makers describe urban environments whenever required by their plot (*Yam Daabo, Zan Boko*), they seem to have a predilection for the filming of rural lifestyles. And indeed the Mossi's residential units (with cylindrical mud brick huts covered with conical straw roofs, granaries, inner courtyards with sun shelters and grinding platforms), tools and cooking utensils (short-handled hoes, mattocks, knives, pestles and mortars, clay pots), clothing (often made with locally woven bands of cotton material), and lively markets (with their social role and economic function) are described with ethnographic care. Although village chiefs are mentioned in *Zan Boko* or briefly seen in *Wend Kuuni,* little is said concerning their actual authority. Instead, Kaboré and Ouédraogo focus their lenses on the day-to-day activities of their farming communities. They show us the structured workings of kinship within a patriclan system. Here, although women may take part in discussions with spouses, the major decisions concerning the welfare of families are eventually made by men, as in the case in *Yam Daabo*. This trait is also evident in *Zan Boko* when Tinga's wife seems unprepared to advise her husband. When Tinga asks, 'Nopoko, what do you think about the matter [the selling of the land] I discussed with you?', his wife quietly answers: 'You know very well the problem is beyond me.' In these villages, as seen on the screen, labour is divided along lines of sex and age. Men take care of the heavy tasks of clearing the land, planting, weeding and harvesting. During the dry season, men are more frequently present in their compounds, where they repair tools, huts and granaries, and engage in various crafts. Women generally participate in most of these activities, but in the four Burkinabe films (made by male directors) which are the object of our study women are mainly seen performing domestic tasks: grinding and pounding millet (even at advanced stages of pregnancy as depicted in *Zan Boko)*, the processing and preservation of food, cooking (a virtue for which women are complimented by their husbands and guests in *Yaaba* and *Zan Boko)*, caring for children, engaging in petty trade at the market place, braiding hair, sweeping courtyards, or fetching water from house wells, from public fountains or a distant river.

Breaking away from the commonly accepted notion of African women often perceived by the West as submissive, Kaboré and Ouédraogo have created several assertive female characters. In *Wend Kuuni*, Gaston Kaboré shows that precolonial Africa was not an idyllic era, but that it contained oppressive forces that were detrimental to women. Here the eponymous character's mother dies as a consequence of her determination not to remarry and as a result of the villagers' intolerance. Also in *Wend Kuuni*, another woman by the name of Timpoko boisterously challenges her impotent middle-aged husband.

In his motion pictures, Ouédraogo also includes forceful portrayals of Burkinabe women. In *Yam Daabo,* probably as a sign of changing times, the authority of the head of the family is challenged by his wife and his daughter Bintou. In *Yaaba,* Bila's mother is also shown as a woman of her own mind when she secretly sends her son to fetch Sana's medicine to cure Bila's dying young female friend, Nopoko, and when she quickly intervenes to put an end to her husband's punishment of Bila, who had been forbidden to visit the old and isolated woman. As in *Wend Kuuni*, a woman reacts against her husband's impotence, which she discloses publicly. Here, however, Koudi goes one step further and takes a lover. At first, she hides to meet him, without thinking of severing her marital ties as he suggests to her. She replies: 'I can't, it's a family matter.' Yet, after her conjugal unfaithfulness has been discovered, the woman leaves the village to escape people's scorn and disdain. Also in *Yaaba,* the repudiation of a woman by her husband (he accuses her of having poorly raised their sons who have wounded Nopoko in a fight) and the very ostracism suffered by Sana are more striking commentaries on the vulnerable position of some women in Mossi rural regions. Having lost her father and mother as a child, Sana has lived an unmarried and solitary existence and does not benefit from the protection of kinship. Thus, as happens in the case of Wend Kuuni's isolated mother, Sana is accused of witchcraft as well as of instigating sickness, and her hut is subsequently set on fire. For these Mossi women, a lack of kinship leads to ostracism. It deprives them of security and is even a denial of their very identity, which within their social groups seems to be defined primarily in terms of their function as wives, mothers and elders.

Gaston Kaboré and Idrissa Ouédraogo have given children meaningful parts in their productions. This is especially true in *Wend Kuuni* and *Yaaba,* where children are the protagonists and the symbols of new hope. In Ouédraogo's *Yam Daabo*, the family's young son, Ali (about ten), does not play such a prominent role as in the two other motion pictures. Yet, early in the film, the boy's death, as a result of being struck by a car in the city, is one of the first trials the family has to overcome to continue their journey towards greener pastures.

To meet the demands of communal village life, Mossi children are exposed to a sexually differentiated enculturation, and have been traditionally taught and encouraged to participate actively in a variety of tasks at a rather early age. Children may be punished by any member of the community on failing to comply with assigned activities. These have been noted by a number of observers. According to Peter B. Hammond:

> Boys begin early to run errands for their elder male kinsmen. They sit beside the old men as they repair tools, they are given greater responsibility than their sisters in the herding of animals, and well before adolescence they have begun to help in the millet fields ... By early adolescence a boy has learned all of the techniques of farm work and will shortly be assigned his own field. The small girls who remain to eat with their mothers and the other adult women of the patriclan soon begin to help with cooking as well as gathering firewood and wild foods. They are sent to the wells for water ... with their brothers they join their parents in farm work at the age of seven or eight. By the beginning of puberty, girls have acquired all the skills expected of a Mossi wife and mother, a role they usually assume at thirteen or fourteen, two or three years after the onset of puberty.[26]

Except for their work in the field, many of these children's occupations are depicted in the works of Kaboré and Ouédraogo. In *Wend Kuuni*, one notices the strictness of Pognere's mother, which might appear excessive to Western eyes. She has the chief responsibility for the daughter's discipline. She admonishes her when Pognere (who is about ten) does not get up as early as expected. The mother is also extremely upset when the daughter lingers on her way to delivering karité butter to her aunt, who lives in a nearby village. Usually, however, whether told to sweep the courtyard, clean the dishes or light the fire for cooking, Pognere efficiently complies with her mother's request. In *Yaaba*, Bila (seemingly twelve years of age) is disciplined by his father and does not rebel. Here, sex roles are defined at an early age, as exemplified by the joke of Nopoko (she appears to be about twelve). When Nopoko sees Bila carrying a water-filled calabash on his head, she tells him: 'With a nice pair of earrings you could pass for a woman.' Seeing that Bila gets truly upset at her remarks, she makes up by offering to carry the load on her head, which he readily accepts. In these timeless rural settings children do not attend school, but receive their informal and practical education from their parents and grandparents. The role of the elderly in the children's formative years is also described in *Zan Boko*, which takes place in present-day Burkina Faso. Here Tinga has to leave the compound to tend his fields, and he asks his father to watch over his son while checking the quality of the young boy's straw weaving. At times, Tinga and his elderly father converse or discuss family matters while under the traditional sun shelter. This proves that the old man's knowledge and advice are respected and sought after. In *Zan Boko*, this and other events corroborate Hammond's observations. According to him:

> Among the aged those too feeble to work in the fields remain in the patriclan residence. If they are able, the old men repair tools and weave mats. Old women tend the children and the kitchen fires. In the rainy months, when all able-bodied members of the patriclan are often away in the fields ... the old people guard the settlements from thieves and watch over any young children left behind. ...
>
> So long as they can function physically and socially, the old among the Mossi are valued for their accumulated wisdom and for the knowledge of traditional lore ... they retain formal authority as long as they remain mentally alert.[27]

It is in such a social framework that the isolation of *Yaaba*'s Sana takes all of its tragic significance. Without kinship or children, Sana is unable to perform the traditional role played by elders, and her wisdom is valued by no one except Bila. He relies on her initiatives to seek traditional medicine from a distant herbalist/healer in order to cure Nopoko. Sana also teaches Bila to be tolerant towards the village's adulterous woman because 'she may have her reasons'. Later in the film, Bila makes that same remark to Nopoko as she severely judges the unfaithful village woman. Indeed, Bila symbolically reinstates Sana's status and privileges by calling her 'Yaaba' ('grandmother' in Moore). The young boy's attention moves her, and she says to him: 'You know that's the first time someone has called me grandmother and this makes me very happy.' From then on, Bila becomes very caring and protective towards the old woman, to whom he occasionally brings food, and with whom he shares games and jokes as many children would do with their grandmother.

Since Gaston Kaboré and Idrissa Ouédraogo focus greatly on village life, viewers are made to witness other aspects of Mossi culture, including sundry social encounters, meals and conviviality, dance and craftsmanship. We are repeatedly made aware of the importance of lengthy and concerned greetings when people meet. This is effected by a handshake between men, while traditional women curtsy slightly, holding their right hand to their heart. On such occasions, news about the family or the village community is exchanged. Another factor the film-makers emphasise is the importance of gifts (often local products) and visits meant to strengthen village and kinship links. In *Yaaba*, Bila's gifts of food to Sana reflect the relationship he has established. In *Wend Kuuni*, the mute boy's adoptive mother gives karité butter to her sister, who promises to use it to make flat cakes which she will, in turn, send to the weaver's family. Also, in *Zan Boko,* a female visitor gives karité butter as a present to Tinga's wife, while another guest brings her salt. Tinga's wife brings 'soumbala' (a condiment which she customarily prepares and sells at the market-place) as a wedding gift to one of her friends' daughter. In the same film, millet beer (which is consumed in rural as well as urban areas) is prepared by women and appears instrumental in generating warmth and conviviality among men. As a rule, the films of Kaboré and Ouédraogo show that sexes separate at mealtimes in rural communities: women first serve food to the male members of the family, and then eat in a separate area of the courtyard with other women or female children. In contrast, *Zan Boko*'s Westernised bourgeois family eats at the same table, and men and women mingle at parties where food is served.

In the four films which constitute the core of our analysis, communal dancing is rarely shown. However, dancing does take place spontaneously in the evening after a day of work in the field (*Yaaba*), or on festive occasions such as a wedding (*Yaaba*). On the other hand, the crafts in which men engage are often presented. Several scenes of the weaver threading cotton and working at his small loom are included in *Wend Kuuni*. Here as well, a long sequence shows how the weaver's adopted son makes his flute out of a hollow bamboo stick. At the beginning of *Yam Daabo*, a blacksmith works on a red-hot iron blade over a charcoal fire built in front of a double bellows made of sheepskin. In *Zan Boko* Tinga weaves straw mats, a craft he teaches to his son. Later, Tinga's son ingeniously makes a toy car out of wood and straw, a skill the urban boy next door has lost. The latter plays with expensive imported toys and offers to buy the small car, an event which parallels his father's desire to own Tinga's land.

Mossi villagers, who abide by tradition, depend on the deceased members of their lineage, the ancestral spirits, for their welfare. If properly treated and venerated, through the sacrifice or chickens or goats, ancestral spirits are thought to secure the health and prosperity or their descendants. Likewise, rain and good harvests may be granted by deities, the Earth custodians, provided one honours them through well-defined ritual propitiations and adequate ceremonies.[28]

The omnipresent links between the Mossi's traditional secular and religious worlds – myths, supernatural beliefs and religious customs – are mentioned in Kaboré's and Ouédraogo's productions. As Wend Kuuni's mother flees from her community on being accused of practising adverse magic, she is haunted by the words of an eerie and ghostlike voice who tells her: 'You are cursed, you shall not find refuge.' Also in *Wend Kuuni*, Pognere, who wishes she were a boy, in order to spend more time with Wend Kuuni, tells him that she heard that spirits 'could make girls into boys'. Such a revelation does not surprise the boy, who tells her he also believes that 'spirits are powerful'. The only scene portraying the activitics of a diviner is included in *Yaaba* as the villagers feteh him to cure Nopoko. After receiving a rooster as payment for his services, and after performing rites, the diviner states: 'There is nothing wrong with your child, somebody has stolen her soul, I see an old woman. You must drive her out of the village, and sacrifice a bull.' The villagers soon come to believe that Sana is responsible for Nopoko's sickness, which increases their cruel attitude towards the old woman. Sana is not endowed with supernatural gifts, but she believes in a traditional polytheistic system as reflected in her well-wishing words to Bila: 'May the gods favour you.'

The role of men in the performance of animistic rites can be observed in *Zan Boko*. Here Tinga is worried by his wife's difficult delivery in spite of his male friends' reassuring words. One says to him: 'Don't worry, just trust the midwives and the ancestors,' while the other reiterates: 'Do not despair, the spirit of the ancestors will protect her.' Yet, as the condition of Tinga's wife worsens, the midwife tells Tinga's father: 'Your son must execute the water ritual,' which Tinga performs by drinking water from a calabash, and spitting three times on the ground. A few sequences later, Kaboré shows us Tinga's wife cradling her newborn baby girl. Does the film-maker himself imply the possible efficacy of the water ritual? An opposite view on the power of supernatural forces is evident in *Zan Boko* after the arrival of civil servants sent to make a topographical survey of the village to be incorporated within Ouagadougou's new city limits. At this point a conversation between Tinga's father and Tinga suggests that Tinga has resorted to occult forces for help. Yet, in this particular instance, nothing has the power to stop urbanisation.

This post-colonial modernisation and expansion of cities to incorporate rural sectors has inexorable and often damaging effects on the sociocultural facets of Mossi life. Idrissa Ouédraogo underscores the deadly impact of urban life (Ali's death) and its negative influence on customs (due to overcrowded housing, crime, and so on) in *Yam Daabo,* as the family merely crosses a town to reach its final destination. Likewise, Gaston Kaboré stresses the changes people's lifestyles have undergone in an urban milieu. In *Zan Boko,* the government officials belong to a bourgeois class imported from the West and unknown in a traditional milieu. They are literate, using French in professional situations and also frequently at home, while farmers are mostly illiterate and speak Moore, which creates an added language barrier between farmers and the urban elite (in Burkina Faso, 8 per cent of the people can read and write). This factor is superbly rendered at the end of *Zan Boko,* when Tinga is invited to participate in a TV round table on urbanisation organised by Tinga's journalist friend, who wishes to disclose government frauds in that area. Here, Tinga sits in a studio with city planners, a sociologist and government officials. Yet he is unable to understand what his compatriots say because they express themselves in French. In *Zan Boko,* Kaboré also contrasts meaningful differences in attire, lodgings and habits (for example, the bourgeois's male housekeeper sweeps his employer's house, while house cleaning is done by women in villages). He describes Ouagadougou as a place where corruption and nepotism victimise the newly urbanized villagers. In this context, some women are seen working as secretaries outside their homes, thus limiting their traditional role as homemakers and educators. Here, a benefit of urban life could be the availability of schools, but in this area, as in housing, slots are reserved for the children of the bureaucratic elite (one-fifth of all primary schoolchildren attend classes in Burkina Faso).

As they mirror various aspects of rural and urban life in past and present Burkina Faso, the works of Gaston Kaboré and Idrissa Ouédraogo are very informative ethnographic documents because, in Weakland's words:

> In projecting structured images of human behaviour, social interaction, and the nature of the world, fictional films in contemporary societies are analogous in nature and cultural significance to the stories, myths, rituals, and ceremonies in primitive societies that anthropologists have long studied.[29]

And, indeed, a close scrutiny of the recurrent images and themes in Kaboré and Ouédraogo's four fiction films provides viewers with some general traits and values found within Burkinabe society. The two film practitioners insist on their compatriots' solidarity, generosity, dignity and industriousness, but they also mention less positive characteristics such as intolerance, which can lead to cruelty whenever they think their securing and stabilising social or cosmological order is endangered. Subsequently, this attachment to tradition and the ancestors' homeland may create sociocultural alienation, particularly when people are

236

made to adopt technologies and views that do not always fit in with the patterns already existing in their culture (as emphasised in *Zan Boko*). Likewise, Kaboré and Ouédraogo's depiction of a very structured family and social life does parallel the strong adherence of the Mossi to lineage and kinship. The overwhelming belief in the power of ancestral spirits or occult forces is also culturally accurate, and may even have a symbolic meaning in terms of cultural identity and resistance to the penetration and domination of alien religious thoughts. One should consider that the Mossi have historically often been hostile to Islam, and minimally responsive to Christian teachings, which results today in limited minority groups of Muslims and Christians.[30] Interestingly, Kaboré (a Christian) and Ouédraogo (a Muslim) have both chosen to emphasise animistic religious authenticity in a country where two-thirds of the present population practises traditional African religions.

In creative works, what is unseen or masked is usually almost as important as what is seen. Thus films are the reflection of aesthetics, moral and ideological choices made by film-makers in terms of what they feel is important to show audiences. As such, Kaboré and Ouédraogo's egalitarian revolutionary ideas and male perspectives have totally filtered out issues related to polygamy, castes and ethnic rivalry, although these are still part of contemporary Burkinabe society. Also, their preference goes to the portrayal of nuclear family units over extended families, whose strength remains nonetheless the backbone of the Mossi community. Here one wonders whether this choice is due to their own Westernisation or to their wish to appeal to urbanised Burkinabe film-viewers, whose practice of polygamy and dealings with extended families are more limited than in rural areas. Moreover, in *Wend Kuuni*'s somewhat nostalgic rendition of a stable past, Kaboré does not even hint at the existence of slaves within precolonial Mossi societies.

Furthermore, perhaps to erase the often stereotypical folkloric/exotic facets linked to African agrarian ceremonies and rites of passage, Kaboré is not interested in presenting the funeral of Tinga's father in *Zan Boko*. Likewise, only very few dancing scenes from a marriage are shown by Ouédraogo in *Yaaba*. And neither alludes to the Mossi festivals which mark their seasonal cycles (for example, the rain-making ritual and ceremonial).[31]

These observations about *Wend Kuuni*, *Yam Daabo*, *Zan Boko* and *Yaaba* confirm that motion pictures are selected reflections or constructed slices of reality rather than reality itself. Thus, in using Kaboré and Ouédraogo's fiction films, or any films (since all films are mediated art forms), as cultural communication and anthropological data, one should definitely assess not only the works but their indigenous authors, as well as their authors' purpose in making their films (for no camera is objective). Furthermore, one should be aware that the film critic's personality, perception and vision will impact upon all the elements he or she notices in the directors' works. The Burkinabe films that have been studied here were not made with specific ethnographic intentions, yet their authors' concern to present accurate facets of their society make these works valuable tools for exploring components of Burkinabe culture, especially rural lifestyles. It is as such, and within a critical anthropological perspective, that *Wend Kuuni*, *Yam Daabo*, *Zan Boko* and *Yaaba* should be considered. Indeed, these fiction films highly facilitate the humanistic encounter with and the knowledge of the long ignored, neglected or disdained culture of the Other.

Notes

1. Judith Lynne Hanna, 'The Anthropology of Dance', in James H. Humphrey and Lynette Y. Overbury (eds), *Dance, Current Selected Research* (New York: AMS Press, 1989), Vol. 1, p. 219.
2. Mostly Kaboré and Ouédraogo's feature-length fiction films are be considered in this study.
3. Lucien Goldman, *Pour une sociologie du roman* (Paris: Gallimard, 1964).
4. Quoted in Françoise Pfaff, 'Film and the Teaching of Foreign Languages', *College Language Association Journal*, vol. 22 no. 1, September 1978, p. 26.
5. John H. Weakland, 'Feature Films as Cultural Documents', in Paul Hockings (ed.), *Principles of Visual Anthropology* (The Hague and Paris: Mouton, 1975), pp. 231–51.
6. David Sapir, 'Emitay' (*sic*), *American Anthropologist*, vol. 76 no. 3, September 1974, pp. 693–7. Also Risa Ellovich, 'Black Girl (La Noire de)', *American Anthropologist*, vol. 79 no. 1, March 1975, pp. 198–9.
7. Anthropology as justification of White supremacist policies of Western nations in their domination of Third World peoples is amply illustrated in such nineteenth-century essays as that of James Hunt, 'On the Negro's Place in Nature', in Ashley Montagu (ed.), *Frontiers of Anthropology* (New York: Putnam's Sons, 1974), pp. 203–53.
8. Jean Rouch, 'L'Afrique entre en scène', *Le Courrier de l'Unesco*, no. 3, 1962, p. 15.
9. Amilcar Cabral, *Return to the Source* (New York: Monthly Review Press/Africa Information Service, 1973), cited in Roy Armes, *Third World Filmmaking and the West* (Berkeley: University of California Press, 1987), p. 25.
10. Frantz Fanon, *The Wretched of the Earth* (Harmondsworth: Penguin, 1967), pp. 178–9.
11. See pp. 25–6, above.
12. Jacques Binet *et al.* 'Cinémas noirs d'Afrique' *CinémAction*, no. 26, 1983, pp. 168–9. See also pp. 27–30, above.
13. Férid Boughedir, *Le Cinema africain de A à Z* (Belgium: OCIC, 1987), pp. 42–3.
14. From an interview with Cheikh Ngaido Bah conducted by the author in Dakar, Senegal, 1 July 1988.
15. Teshome H. Gabriel, *Third Cinema in the Third World – The Aesthetics of Liberation* (Ann Arbor, Mich., UMI Research Press, 1982), p. 16.
16. Weakland, 'Feature Films', p. 246.
17. Françoise Pfaff, 'Africa Through African Eyes – An Interview with Idrissa Ouédraogo', *Black Film Review*, vol. 4 no. 1, Winter, 1987–8, p. 11.
18. Laurence Gavron, 'Ouédraogo et sa grand-mère d'Afrique', *Libération*, 10 May 1989.
19. Cherifa Benabdessadok, 'Wend Kuuni, le don de Dieu', *Afrique-Asie*, no. 319, 9 April 1984, p. 57.
20. George E. Marcus, 'Contemporary Problems of Ethnography in the Modern World System', in James Clifford and George E. Marcus (eds), *Writing Culture* (Berkeley: University of California Press, 1986), p. 165.
21. From an interview with Gaston Kaboré conducted by the author in Washington, D.C., 3 May 1985.
22. Ibid.
23. For a further examination of the correlation between African cinema and African oral traditions see Manthia Diawara, 'Oral Literature and African Film: Narratology in *Wend Kuuni*', *Présence Africaine*, no. 142, 2nd Quarter 1987, pp. 36–49, and in Jim Pines and Paul Willemen (eds.), *Questions of Third Cinema* (London: British Film Institute, 1989), also see another article by the same author, 'Popular Culture and Oral Traditions in African Film', pp. 209–18, above.
24. Pfaff, 'Africa Through African Eyes' pp. 1–12.
25. Gavron, 'Ouédraogo et sa grand-mère d'Afrique'.
26. Peter B. Hammond, *Yatenga* (New York: The Free Press, 1966), p. 86.
27. Ibid.
28. Ibid., pp. 163–79.
29. Weakland, 'Feature Films', p. 240.
30. Elliot P. Skinner, 'Christianity and Islam among the Mossi', *American Anthropologist*, vol. 60 no. 6, December 1958, pp. 1102–19. According to Skinner, Muslims and Christians represented above 10 per cent of the Mossi. This number is probably higher now.
31. Hammond, *Yatenga*, pp. 185–203.

History and Actuality in Ousmane Sembène's *Ceddo* and Djibril Diop Mambety's *Hyenas*

MAMADOU DIOUF

Translated by Robert Julian. This paper was presented at the University of Victoria, Canada, in October 1994 and has not previously been published.

The moment of independence is a time to rebuild, a time of material and symbolic restoration in order to overcome colonialism and abolish the logic of assimilation, subordination and alienation which comes with the imposition of the metropolitan culture and its stand-in, colonial culture.[1] The arts and letters must contribute to this work of renovation and reinvention.[2] And, following the example of the novel in particular, cinema has taken on a specific role: on the one hand to contribute to the nationalist ambition of building African states – independent, national and sovereign – and, on the other, to participate in the reconstruction of African societies lastingly traumatised by the 'long nightmare', as this historical period has been called, of the process of colonial subjugation and its modes of governance based on brutality and dispossession.[3]

Passions were unleashed upon independence, and the recovery of international sovereignty was accompanied by a cultural effervescence, a restoration of traditional and/or specifically African values and symbolic architectural and aesthetic procedures contributing to the reinvention of the social imaginary and traditions. These procedures found expression in plastic creativity (painting, sculpture, dance), in sound and rhythm, as well as in the means of staging and image making. In short, the post-colonial moment opens out onto the reorganisation and the reordering of the collective memory in order to imagine another history, to write history differently – a history against the colonial and/or assimilated imaginary of the technicians of empire and the carriers of a certain kind of modernity (bureaucrats, politicians, policemen) the portrait of which has been cruelly drawn and exposed in Ousmane Sembène's *Borom Sarret* (1963), and held up to ridicule in the cruel chase games of *Badou Boy* (1970) designed to escape from the panting gendarme while trying to make his lungs burst.

This paper aims to follow closely and to trace the vicissitudes of the imagination and the production of a historical memory, or, more adequately, of a historical consciousness, and to identify its features in post-colonial times. The reference points for this quest are provided by the films of Ousmane Sembène and Djibril Diop Mambety, and, in particular, the former's *Ceddo* (1976) and the latter's *Hyenas* (1992).

Although voices, words and writings[4] have reverberated widely throughout the world, conveying a multiplicity of African identities and grievances, the images, the landscapes and faces of Africa try to re-establish the truth of a continent, of its women and men, in order to contest the images of an Africa invented by occidental knowledge.[5] Consequently, this paper does not aim to offer an aesthetic or a cinematographic reading of the two films in question. Besides, I am not competent to do so. Starting instead from my own discipline, I propose a reading of *Ceddo* and *Hyenas* which tries to detect and reveal the way these two films approach and treat history, understood both as a restored and restorable past and a memory (deeds, gestures, sayings and customs), but also actuality – that is to say, the way these films narrate their content and meanings in order to account for identity and evolution in Senegalese societies. Therefore, neither the *mise en scène* nor the image-making process are at the heart of this commentary, even though both underpin the discourse which sustains the cinematic writing of Ousmane Sembène and Djibril Diop Mambety. Besides, the existence of a plurality of discourses expressing the plurality of the groups and their ideological, sociological, religious and political moorings justifies the use of the plural when we speak of histories and actualities. Indeed, cinema, more than the other arts and letters, has been more effective in the way it has ordered the competing modernities, be they religious, ethnic, political or economic, wherever they find their platform, whether in the city, the urban peripheries or the countryside. My questions are concerned more particularly with the knowledges, the representations and the modes of expression which are essential to the process of the constitution/restitution of one's self-image and its trajectory through time. These are the sites where a memory specific to a group manifests itself. To read such an intellectual history in filmed material does, of course, have consequences. However, what matters is that images which speak of the past summon us to read the present. It is this very Augustinian dialogue between past and present in *Ceddo* and *Hyenas* that I would like to uncover here.

Connecting the two film-makers and these two films is rather daring, since they are opposites in every way, stylistically as well as thematically. Sembène inscribes his work into the geography of the Sahel,[6] opening out onto the Arab world and the Atlantic. It is a zone of contacts and cultural transactions between ways of living, of producing and of praying, a zone of confrontations, of racial intermingling, of co-operation and alliance as well as of competition for the control of long-distance trade as much as for the local, steadily degrading, environmental resources. In short, a zone in which conflict is endemic, tracing the Saharo-Sahelian dividing line as a border drawn in fire and blood from the Atlantic to the Horn of Africa. Djibril Diop Mambety's films, on the other hand, are woven into an urban framework:[7] the roofs and streets, with all their architectural diversity, sheltering various kinds of misery. His first film, *Contrast City* (1969), all irony and breaks, clearly parks the film-maker in the city. The breathless chases of *Badou Boy* (1970) through the streets and the errancy on wheels of Mory and Anta in the city (*Touki Bouki*, 1972) confirm the film-maker's address of urban spaces. In his latest production, the author continues on that path, confining the action of *Hyenas* almost entirely to the closed space of Draman Drameh's grocery-bar.

The two Senegalese film-makers, each with his own style, positions, prejudices and personal history, confront the same official history: that of the dominant sectors of Senegalese society. To that history they oppose, first of all, regimes of truth and representations the veracity of which resides in the authority of the images and in the *mise en scène* of their plurality. They then go on to propose alternative images of a social order by replacing the nationalist narrative with other founding events, constructing another kind of historicity in opposition to the post-colonial imaginary.[8] Diop Mambety and Sembène also share a way of accounting for the present, the former starting from the past, the latter from a mythification of the present, both creating a temporal rhythm for actuality which consists of the imbrication of different temporalities. That approach allows for clashes between costumes from different eras and musical idioms with different tonalities and rhythms, stemming from different epochs. In this way, both demonstrate that one cannot dissociate the history of actuality from the actuality of myth in their cinematic idioms.

This paper addresses the way these two film-makers deal with these contradictory ways of appropriating history and constructing, on a daily basis, the singularity of social groups and national formations, tracing it back from the present to the past.[9] The point is to show that the parallelism between Sembène and Diop Mambety is not all that incongruous in spite of their positions at opposite extremes of Senegalese cinematography. However turbulent he may be, Diop Mambety is undeniably the eldest son in Sembène's lineage. Indeed, there is an obvious kinship between Sembène's non-Sahelian films, such as *Borom Sarret* (1962), *Taaw* (1970), *Mandabi* (1968) and *Xala* (1974), and Diop Mambety's work, all the more when their themes draw on Senegalese society's social and ideological margins in order to produce discourses of rupture and/or imbalances, the one relying on women, the other on marginal and/or asocial figures.

Ceddo or the Inversion of Memory

Sembène's aesthetic, intellectual, ideological and political enterprise is deployed in that space where the human individual struggles against the ruling powers and which is, according to Milan Kundera, a struggle of memory against forgetting.[10] It adopts as its vocation the construction of a discursive terrain which opposes and/or disrupts/reorganises the nationalist discourse, demanding to be read and to be understood in the context of the present. This no doubt explains why Ousmane Sembène has to suffer the hostility of politicians and professional historians which caused the film to be banned in Senegal for a number of years due to a question of the doubling of consonants.[11] What is at issue in Sembène's film?

To present the film, extracts from two books on African cinema will suffice. In *Le FESPACO 1969–1989: Les Cinéastes africains et leurs oeuvres* we read:[12]

Two years after *Xala*, Ousmane Sembène presented *Ceddo*, a Fulani word signifying 'the outsiders'. The 'ceddo' is a man who says No. In *eighteenth-century* Senegal, Dior Yacin, the daughter of king *Thioub*, is kidnapped by a ceddo. This event serves as a catalyst exposing the power relations between people and social groups. *The ceddos [sic] are those who refuse to be Islamised... Their power steadily decreases. The kings and chiefs convert. And the marabouts want to go farther, extending the Islam of the chiefs to the whole population*, even if that means resorting to assassination.

Various rivals for the princess, and to the title of chief, confront one another. *Customs die... Islam kills them. The matrilineal inheritance of power is said to be contrary to the teachings of the Prophet.* Men kill other men, men betray their brothers. In the village, the world of the whites consists of only two people: *the merchant and the priest.* The merchant trades slaves and commodities for his imported goods. The priest tries to save souls. Islam achieves power by assassinating the chief. It will have the ceddo murdered in order to free Dior Yacin, the schemers having decided that she will be the Imam's bride. The ceddos [*sic*] are killed, sent into slavery or converted... *But where men were defeated, a woman will succeed.*[13]

In the *Dictionnaire du cinéma africain*,[14] *Ceddo* is summarised as follows:

The film is set in the 17th century, when Islam and Christianity penetrated West Africa. To both religions, all means fair or foul are acceptable to fill the mosques or the churches: *firearms, alcohol and trinkets of all kinds. Having converted the royal family and the leading dignitaries, Islam comes up against the refusal of the 'ceddo'. To them, adherence to a foreign religion means renouncing African spirituality.* In order to achieve his aims, the Imam usurps the throne and reduces the recalcitrants to *slavery. The princess, incarnating her people's resistance throughout the film, kills the marabout-king.* A thought-provoking film deploying *actual events* spread over *several centuries.*

One may begin by remarking an indeterminacy in the time frame of the narrative. There is a choice between the 17th century, the 18th century and 'when Islam and Christianity penetrated West Africa', which are not identical. Perhaps the action takes place over several centuries. This temporal indeterminacy has a precise function. It permits the film-maker to inscribe his reflections into a general framework, enabling a reading addressing the present and allowing for other ways of imagining the past. Nevertheless, it is impossible to detach oneself from a genuinely historical, at times even anthropological reading of Sembène's film, although he cares little for meticulous reconstructions of costumes, dwellings or physical attitudes. By stressing temporal indeterminacy, he thus introduces a geographical indeterminacy. The indices of a genuinely historical 'reality effect',[15] those actual events mentioned in the dictionary, are the designations of 'marabout', merchant, priest, slavery, African spirituality against Islam/Christianity, and, yet more directly, names such as Ceddo, Dior Yacin and Thiub, which refer to a specific ethnic identity, that of the Wolof. The mention of firearms, alcohol, trinkets of all kinds and commodities for trade exchanged for slaves evokes three centuries of the Atlantic trade (the 16th, 17th and 18th centuries), while the Arab appearance of the marabout refers to the Saharan or Arab trade and to domestic slavery. If Dior and Yacin are very common names of lingeer in Kajoor and Bawol,[16] the latter echoes Yacin Buubu, who allied herself with the Muslim party in the Kajoorian epoch of the war of the marabouts (1673–4). Thiub,[17] on the other hand, recalls very specifically the patronym of the mother of a Kajoorian damel (1809) and a Bawol teen (1817),[18] Birima Fatma Cubb, who died in 1832.

The relevance of such a reference allows us to grasp the thrust of Sembène's project, which is to produce a historical 'reality effect' as the basis for his analysis. The film-maker gives a historical colouring to his narrative in order to break with the post-colonial order, that of the Empire.[19] By opting for such a way of writing history, which D. W. Cohen[20] calls 'history production', the author of *Ceddo* verifies in an anticipatory manner one of the great advances of modern historiography:[21] the affirmation that the mapping of history not only restores intelligibility, but can also obscure, hide, confuse and especially question what happened in order to open up the coherence and the meaning of narrated events to dialogue, to argument and contestation.[22] The temporal indeterminacy allows for the selection of pertinent sequences of events within a fictional duration. It is indeed a story spread across several centuries, taking in the marabouts, the opposition between Islam and African spirituality, the components of the lingeers' name, Yacin, the trade goods and the trinkets, all referring to different episodes of Senegambia's history.[23]

The film refers to the war of the marabouts which started in 1645 in the Senegal river valley and extended to Kajoor in 1673–4. That year, a marabout occupied the throne of Kajoor until he was defeated thanks to the intervention of the king of the neighbouring Saalum. A coalition of slave traders and traditional aristocrats failed to put a stop to the war of the marabouts and the latter managed to triumph at Fuuta Tooro in 1776, creating the first theocracy in western Senegambia. The second marabout revolt in Kajoor happened in 1795 and the last one in 1827, in the reign of Birima Fatma Cubb.

The conversion to the Muslim religion by aristocrats and dignitaries is also alluded to, together with the decline of religious spirituality and African values, a state of affairs which does not do justice to the ability of Senegambia's Wolof societies to achieve compromises. In fact, the political and social logic of the ceddo is concerned more with a way of life of pillage, war and power struggles than with religious practice. In theory, conversion marked the end of the secular and emblematic tradition of pillage as a way of affirming aristocratic and warrior status. In this respect, Sembène clearly stages – assuming that his narrative occurs during the reign of Birima Fatma Cubb – the tension between a reputedly Muslim sovereign allied with Sheikh Bunama Kunta[24] and the increasing recourse to pillage as a way of exercising power as well as of acquiring new resources after the abolition of the Atlantic trade in 1815. As for the other two questions related to the issue of conversion, Sembène takes a position opposed to that of the historians. Regarding the decline of African spirituality, I have already indicated that this is more a matter of negotiated and selective compromises than of impositions; the issue is one of religious precepts rather than simply the ajurs' religious affiliation, which was undoubtedly Muslim. Similarly, historians interpret the revolts against the religious leaders as popular revolts. Obviously, in the way he renders popular resistance and revolt in the film, Sembène clearly calls the professional historians' account into question. In this respect, and in the matter of the defeat of the traditional chiefs, Sembène turns historiography upside down. Institutional historiography teaches, on the contrary, that Kajoor successfully resisted the jihads from the 18th century up to the colonial conquest.[25] Regarding the systems of filiation, succession and genealogy, the same point applies: this was a matter of negotiated transactions and compromises between the patrilineal and matrilineal orientations rather than the one simply replacing the other.

Any number of passages in the narrative of *Ceddo* could be reread in this way. For instance, the priest symbolises the presence of Catholic missionaries in

Kajoor although their last efforts to settle in Kajoor/Bawol failed in 1850, when the damel-teen destroyed the chapel at Mbour.[26] These corrections of 'historical truth' in no way alter the force and truth of the film, which is built on the ruins of nationalist history and political itineraries based on patronage in the service of a group of authoritarian leaders, their imperialist bosses and their allies, the marabout brotherhood involved in peanut production and other claimants to historico-ethnic legitimacy. Inverting all of this, Sembène challenges the historians, upon whom he bestows the dishonourable title of 'chrono-phages', thus relegating them to the role of undertakers, associating their activity with death and the refusal to take a stand in the struggles of the present, in the passions and conflicts of life – in short, in the human enterprise in which history is at stake.

Ceddo purports to tell the story of the wars between the aristocracies and Muslim communities in the 17th and 18th centuries, but it in fact relates to the involvement of religion, marabouts and bishops in the political conflicts of Senegal today. The film-maker employs a variety of techniques, including an inversion of the standard readings of certain historical facts, a radical critique of the post-colonial compromise, such as Senghor's advocacy of both striking root and opening out, and a variety of gauges for social groups and power relations. These telescoping procedures give rise to an abstract discourse on class struggle, social relations and exploitation, and ideological, cultural, religious and economic dependency. The film denounces the persistence of an imperialist logic and the rejection of the notion of passive resistance, embodied by the religious dignitaries, which has slowly gained force in ideological debate in Senegal. This resistance aims to restore an identity which the Muslim communities first defended with weapons against the aristocracy and the French conquest, and then preserved during the long night of colonial rule. Especially at the time of its release in 1981, *Ceddo* was a majestic uprising and provocation against the arrogant versions of memory propagated by the brotherhoods, claiming to replace the memory of the agents of empire and post-colonial modernisation, while at the same time redefining and appropriating the oral traditions.[27]

Ceddo's message is an intentional staging of history, a wilful formulation of contemporary identities in Senegal which displays their small acts of cowardice and compromise, but it also obliquely affirms values which are ancestral only on the surface. Sembène neither recites nor depicts history; he invents new historical traditions against the oral traditions and imperial culture, both of which produce social and political situations he cannot accept. In this way, the film-maker performs the work of a historian, because history and memory are the product not only of control and repression – what the Wolof consider worthy of memory – but of creation and re-creation as well. With *Ceddo*, Sembène restores the pluralism of African societies and of nationalist discourse by bringing to light the unspoken and concealed elements even as he insists on the importance of nationalist discourse and the logic of competition which arises from it. The plurality of historical interpretation lies at the heart of Sembène's message, which calls on spectators to break with the images sanctioned or organised by an authority. Even if this message remains somewhat dogmatically stated, its sonorous polyphony is instilled in the images. Indeterminacies delimit the possible fields of interpretation and lay the ground for breaks which can lead to new balances, in order to contest and/or propose other productions of history.

Along with the elements serving as catalysts (Islam, the priest, the slave trader, aristocrats), a sense of subversion comes with the choice of actors and with displacement from the very masculine and brutal orientation of the ceddo's world to that of the lingeer, who solves and resolves the story. Here too Sembène decides to invert the ceddo and Islamic ethical orders, as well as the relation between gor (dignity, rectitude) and goor (man/masculinity/violence). This is certainly familiar ground for Sembène, both in his novels (*Les Bouts de bois de dieu/God's Bits of Wood*, 1960) and his films (*Emitai*, 1971). The inversion is double-barrelled, operating via the radical formality of reading for 'breaks' and as a technique for subverting the established order. Manu Dibango's music contributes to this general provocation, which is like sand flung into the eyes of the well-informed spectator who expected lyrical, masculine transport from the Wolof bards. By way of this displacement, which is very close to Foucault in its way of unveiling the truth of a society, Sembène works in a direction akin to that of another analyst of the history of nationalisms, Jacques Berque. In a rather surprising way, and long before the current fashion (which is no doubt legitimate and indispensable) for gender and women's problems, Berque wrote about the Maghrebine women at the time of independence:

> Now that she leaves her cave shouting and gesticulating, after having fought, she poses for the historian the problem of how to deal with the participation of the mute, the separate and the preserved. She is supposedly bound by taboos. 'Taboo' is the meaning of the word 'harem', cherished by Crébillon the younger. This wall, which is meant to protect her, has never been as strongly defended as now that it is crumbling. Polygamy and isolation are hardly more than propaganda themes. But on the 13th of May, when the Psychology Section displayed Muslim women with their faces bared, the shock was great. It was decried as a rape. But let us be clear. It was not the women who were raped; long ago they won the right to be seen. What was raped was the idea of the veil, of preservation, of meaning. In fact, everyone understands this, while the polemic storms on the surface of white sheets.[28]

Sembène thus raises a twofold question about the perception of women in Senegalese society, regardless of whether it was founded on religious, social, traditional, economic or other considerations. The question is put brutally, by introducing women where normally they are present only as objects of pleasure (Xawaré and/or of sin), circulating like political resources within the network of alliances. Dior Yacin chooses the ceddo. She literally allows herself to perceive and to approach him as an object of her pleasure. His body is for consumption. And so an inversion holds to the very end of the film. The inversion in sexuality and war – she kills the marabout – overthrows the system of values derived from masculinity and leading to femininity, even as the physical and aesthetic attributes of both sexes are overstated. Like the Penda in *Les Bouts de bois de Dieu*, she is a text from that borderline culture which, once displayed, reveals the ambiguities and paradoxes of the cultural bricolage which nationalism legitimised in its hour of triumph. The construction of *Ceddo* leaks noise into the midst of the totalitarianism of post-colonial historical interpretation. It reproves the ambitions of the state and the dominant groups in the writing of history.

245

Seen in this way, Sembène's film provides an echo of *Hyenas* by Djibril Diop Mambety, on the path opened by Jacques Berque's analysis of incipient nationalisms and the role of social actors. Where Sembène claims to account for 'the participation of the mute, the separate and preserved... she [the woman] accompanied history. She gave it a pledge which exceeded the political sphere, by far'.[29]

Diop Mambety leads us into borderline worlds, sticking our faces into the mud and the theatre of the everyday, where nature and human misery take the stage to play out a single plot, survival.

Hyenas or the Detours and Drifts of the Present

Djibril Diop Mambety's film will provide more of a counterpoint than a comparison to this analysis of the treatment of history in *Ceddo*. The theme of *Hyenas* has been described in this way:

> Colobane is a little town in the Sahel, lost amid the hot sands, clouds of dust and dazzling light of the desert. In Colobane, misery is the daily lot, and poverty is shared by the leading citizens and the rest of the population. At the time of day when boredom is general, the inhabitants meet at the grocery of Draman Drameh. Hope appears on the horizon in the form of Linguère Ramatou, who previously lived in Colobane, but left after being rejected by Draman, who had made her pregnant. Inexplicably transformed from whore to multimillionaire, Ramatou offers the inhabitants of Colobane a colossal sum if they will do away with Draman.
>
> Accompanied by a lovely score of African music which makes no concession to exoticism, *Hyenas* is the re-reading of a play by the Swiss writer Durrenmatt which keeps to the essence of the text while incorporating local particularities.[30]

We could pursue the parallel between the two films by Ousmane Sembène and Djibril Diop Mambety. Both have the same dramaturgical basis or nub. *Ceddo* presents a woman who is 'the guardian of emotions where the primordial is always stronger than what is acquired, the cradler of children, the symbol of refuge, the keeper of the immemorial [who] had remained affirmative... She had stayed virginal and fecund, like nature.'[31]

Dior Yacin executes the marabout and compensates for the shortcomings and cowardice of man, 'harried, broken, destroyed, remade'.[32] In *Hyenas*, another woman holds the population hostage and requires a man's death before she will save them from misery. The two dramas unfold in two different scenes of memory: on the one hand, the vast spaces of the Sahel and their economies based on the Sudano-Saharan and Atlantic slave trade and, on the other, a small town in the Sahel, Colobane, in the days of structural adjustments and conditions laid down by the World Bank and the International Monetary Fund. The two narratives relate the destinies of two lingeer: Dior Yacin, the symbol of an ethics which claims descent from a long aristocratic line, and Lingeer Ramatou, a majestic whore who returns from her odyssey confirmed by endless wealth. She is richer than the World Bank. Where Dior Yacin picks up a lost historical thread, Lingeer Ramatou does not purchase a new virtue. She catches up with a story to wring its neck through the sacrifice of Draman, the flesh-and-blood incarnation of the story of her life. She calls for a new order in the stories and histories of Colobane, the invention of an unstained present. Seen in this way, the two films appear to echo and enter into dialogue with each other.

However, they represent two opposite poles of cinematographical writing in Senegal. Whereas Sembène remains an 'African' film-maker, Diop Mambety is 'Senegalese' or, to be still more precise, from Dakar. The inherent didacticism of Sembène's films is answered by Diop Mambety's painful, disaffected poetry. A cosmic laugh in the form of a barren, ochre cityscape which resembles a garbage dump, a bar which seems to have gathered up life's cripples – no, the poets of the present. This cinema exhibits modernity without its make-up, the very one which tourists are not supposed to see, though it is the stuff of urban anthropology. Diop Mambety's cinema is deliberately urban, full of an urbanity without the conventions of civility, made up of borderlines, sex and drugs,[33] with its detours and drifts. This situation is conveyed too by the costumes by Oumou Sy and the overexposed shots of exteriors. Here creativity arises from within the social and economic logic of recovery in impoverished suburbs, of daily making-do (*bricolage*) on the verge of collapse, according to a rhythm of social life based on alcohol, in a grocery-bar where urban civility is reinvented in the absence both of the 'traditional' signposts Sembène talks about and of homogeneous communities. Diop Mambety presents figures from communities made up by ephemeral encounters, the uprooted whose identities are gaudy and fractured, whose only bonds are money and debts. Always ready to spin a fable, this version of humankind can construe life only in the present.[34]

It is likewise in the form of a fable that Diop Mambety casts his narrative, as if to ask us, spectators and onlookers, if the World Bank, the International Monetary Fund, structural adjustments, debt, aid and prostitution are not ingredients of a mythology which is hard to swallow for people who are used to tales which always lead to the sea and the promise of eternity. *Hyenas* cannibalises reality and offers a physical restitution of Colobane in which forms of misery are combined while the ambitions and life stories of individuals, with all their base acts and signs of passing solidarity, are cut off from each other. In small brush strokes, Diop Mambety launches the fiercest of critiques against the theatre of power, the inanity of political and economic discourses for reform and good government. One must finally ask if the World Bank is not a high-class prostitute, with identical conditions to those of Lingeer Ramatou, calling for blood, sweat – as the mayor and deputy-mayor abundantly prove under the hot, dusty sky of Colobane – tears and death. What value can be ascribed, in this tale, to the prostitution of famished peoples, us, totally imprisoned by our errancy since, as soon as the grocery-bar becomes the place where discourse is produced, the sense of honour turns into a derisive, pretentious sentiment before gut-wrenching hunger? Diop Mambety hurls in our faces our total submission to money, in a society (he adds fiercely) where ostentation is a rule of life or death.

The role of the woman in Sembène's narrative has a precise cathartic and didactic aim. Her body, 'a challenge to man' like her revealed nudity, is, in Jacques Berques's words, successively 'a curse, a benediction, [an] overflowing, that surplus which woman offers to the point of surprising and frightening the happy beneficiary, swelling today's public exhilaration. On these summits, or at these depths, of collective gesture, women triumph by means of the sacred.'[35]

247

And she attests to the absolute necessity of exhuming the actress as the carrier of disruption in dependent societies. A 'break', a disruption, is the key word in the message of *Ceddo*. In contrast, the urban setting of *Hyenas* permits Diop Mambety to play on the ambiguities of the city, the place where the primordial and the immemorial vanish, the place of passage, death and resurrection. The nowhere country where individual destinies cross paths and lives destroy each other or rebuild themselves. The naked landscape where every architecture is possible, where people build on wind and humiliation, where different kinds of modernity mingle and collide with extreme brutality: the brutality which justifies Lingeer Ramatou in putting a price on Draman Drameh's life. A rainbow-coloured city where stray destinies overlap and blind despair is buried in the dirt. Stylised, aristocratic despair, theatricality as a stand-in for history and myth, indissolubly part of the cinematographical writing of Diop Mambety which constitutes an archaeology of the present.

In Conclusion

If contemporary aesthetics conceives of history as a play of mirrors, a power struggle and a site of contestation and competition within the political sphere, both *Ceddo* and *Hyenas* provide catalysts for a society in distress which has become disoriented and gone adrift on a rough sea, a Senegal in which history and fable call out and insult each other as in the sabbar[36] or, more prosaically, in the historico-political elucidations and the mimickry of El Hadji Mansour M'Baye, bard, traditionalist, journalist and unavoidably the historian of Abdou Diouf, the 'guardian of the constitution'.[37] Ousmane Sembène reports on an itinerary. He has an acute sense of history and an extraordinary aptitude for translating class struggle into cinema. In contrast, Diop Mambety makes great efforts to track the excited surge and definitive collapse of Senegalese society, reduced to the recuperation and prostitution of souls. To Sembène's possibility of a break, Diop Mambety opposes an aesthetics of despair and absent purpose, a horizonless geography where the destinies of those who wash up on the edges of the city mingle. He speaks of an everyday life of inclemency and intemperance; he treats of 'indocility', in the sense given that term by Achille M'Bembe.[38]

Sembène's message is fashioned at the heart of ideology even if he subverts it. For the author of *Borom Sarret*, the desire to build and transform subsists, in spite of political disillusion and the ravages of economic adjustment. As for Diop Mambety, he is satisfied

> to take an interest in the world of the unexpected and the surprising, in those productive moments during which pleasure is associated with terror, whereas individuals and societies now experience the unexpected, disgust, indigence, the absence of shame, the abyss, even horror, all at once; in short, they are speechless and disfigured . . . through a twofold process whereby the individual becomes a subject in post-colonial Africa, undergoes subjection and affirms his or her impotence, all at the same time.[39]

From this dialogue of two film-makers situated at the antipodes and yet in some ways so very close, we have derived a sketch of the contemporary production of the history of Senegal, a restructuring/regeneration of identities which have been undone. This history is more plausible than the better constructed, and therefore more truthful, history of the historians. This history is fashioned from images and metaphors which displace the interpretation from the centre towards the margins where all societies may be read, a fable in the service of subversion. There is no risk of a mistake in concluding that where Sembène seeks, as always, to direct his reflections and his action towards the necessity of freeing Senegalese societies from all oppression, Diop Mambety continues to entangle figures of pain and moments of jubilation. Far more than Sembène, his post-nationalist writing sets off an allegorical explosion of cunningly poetic animism.

Notes

1. In this respect, very useful sources are Edward Said's *Culture and Imperialism* (New York: Vintage Books, 1993) and the special issue of *American Ethnologist*, 'Imagining the Past: Nation, Culture and the Past', Vol. 19 no. 4, November 1992.
2. In his book *An African Voice: The Role of Humanities in African Independence* (Durham, NC: Duke University Press, 1987), Robert July provides a comprehensive survey of the way the arts and literature have participated in the nationalist enterprise. It is relevant to know that this book is the sequel of *The Origin of Modern African Thought* (New York: Praeger, 1967).
3. See Jacques Berque, *La Dépossession du monde* (Paris: Seuil, 1964).
4. See Mamadou Diouf, 'Les Paroles politiques africaines: Des luttes anticolonialistes aux conférences nationales', in GEMDEV, *L'Intégration régionale dans le monde: Innovations et ruptures* (Paris: Karthala, 1994).
5. See V. Y. Mudimbe, *The Invention of Africa: Gnosis, Philosophy and the Order of Knowledge* (Bloomington: Indiana University Press, 1988); and Kwame Anthony Appiah, *In My Father's House: Africa in the Philosophy of Culture* (Oxford: Oxford University Press, 1992).
6. This generalisation is somewhat abusive. Sembène's work is not devoted to Sahelian themes as exclusively as I suggest. The most significant exceptions are *Borom Sarret* (1963), *La Noire de...* (1966), *Mandabi* (1968) and *Xala* (1974). I have included *Emitai* (1971) and *Camp de Thiaroye* (1988, co-directed with Thierno Faty Sow) in the Sahara-Sahelian vein; the former being a story about the clash between ways of living and colonial encounters, the latter concerning itself with a pan-Africanism inscribed in the colonial designs of war. The Sahelian characterisation of Sembène's work is strongly confirmed in the major work still to come, *Samory*.
7. This radically urban inscription of the director of *Touki Bouki* emerges in the pervasive irony of *Parlons, grand-mère*, the film made about the shooting of Idrissa Ouédraogo's *Yaaba*, another cineaste of the Sahelian spaces.
8. Regarding the question of the relations between the past and the present and the issue of the construction of a historical consciousness, the following essays are of great interest: Veit Erlmann, 'The Past is Far and the Future is Far: Power and Performance among Zulu Migrant Workers', *American Ethnologist*, vol. 9 no. 4, November 1992, pp. 688–709; J. L. Comaroff and Jean Comaroff, 'The Madman and the Migrant: Work and Labor in Historical Consciousness of a South African People', *American Ethologist*, vol. 14, 1987, pp. 191–209; Mamadou Diouf, 'Représentations historiques et légitimités politiques au Sénégal', *Revue de la Bibliothèque Nationale*, no. 34, Winter 1989, pp. 14–24.
9. E. Balibar and I. Wallerstein, *Race, Nation, Classe: Les Identités ambigües* (Paris: La Découverte, 1990).
10. Milan Kundera, *Laughter and Forgetting*, quoted in David William Cohen, *The Combing of History* (Chicago: University of Chicago Press, 1994), p. 13.
11. *Ceddo* was not publicly shown in Senegal until 1981, after the resignation of president Léopold Sedar Senghor, who had decided to ban the film on the grounds of an orthographical device: Cedo instead of Ceddo. Sembène's refusal to correct this 'spelling mistake' was the apparent reason for the ban. The real reason is more likely to reside in the film's message.
12. Patrick G. Ilboudo, *Le FESPACO 1969–1989: Les Cinéastes africains et leurs oeuvres* (Ouagadougou: La Mante, 1988).

13. Ibid., p. 380. The emphases on the phrases, expressions, names and dates in this passage and the following one are mine. The aim is to show clearly the inflections of Sembène's cinematographic discourse and to compare it to the perspective of professional historians. This extract allows for such a reflection because, although no typographic sign indicates it, it appears to have been taken from a publicity statement and/or from a declaration by the director/producer, on the evidence of the text's form and the suspension points.

14. 'L'Association des trois mondes', *Dictionnaire du cinéma africain* (Paris: Karthala, Ministère de la Cooperation et du Developpement, 1991), Vol. 1, pp. 303–4.

15. Roland Barthes, 'L'Effet du réel', *Communications*, no. 11, 1968, pp. 40–51.

16. Kajoor was one of the most powerful Wolof kingdoms of the slave-trading era, for a long time resisting the colonial conquest in the 19th century; Bawol was the other Wolof kingdom, Kajoor's neighbour.

17. Thiub is the transcription of the Wolof patronym rendered in that language as Cubb.

18. In between the first name and the patronym of Wolof princes and dignitaries, the first name of their mother was inserted to facilitate identification. This form of the name is therefore a sign of protocol and status. The kings of Kajoor and Bawol had the title, respectively, of damel and teen. It was the ambition of every damel to unite the two Wolof crowns of Kajoor and Bawol and to bear the prestigious title of damel-teen. This was achieved by Birima Fatma Cubb from 1817 onwards. For further information, see Mamadou Diouf, *Le Kajoor au XIXième siecle: Pouvoir Ceddo et conquête coloniale* (Paris: Karthala, 1990).

19. The French title of Ousmane Sembène's last novel is *Le Dernier de l'Empire* (Paris: L'Harmattan, 1981).

20. Cohen, *The Combing of History*, pp. 1–23.

21. See, for instance, E. Hobsbawm and T. Ranger (eds), *The Invention of Tradition* (London: Cambridge University Press, 1983). This book opened up a whole new area for research to African and Africanist historians and anthropologists, such as Shula Marks, Stanley Trapido, Bogumil Jewsiewicki, Atieno Odhiambo, Frederick Cooper, Achille Mbembe, Mamadou Diouf and others. This work, and especially that of D. W. Cooper, has been the subject of acerbic criticism by Jan Vansina, who calls all this work 'postmodern history'. According to Vansina, this approach maintains 'that both culture and historical evidence are the creations of the present moment and only have meaning in this moment. Hence culture and history are perpetually 'invented', now steadily disseminated as a position by the journal he edits' ('Some Perceptions on the Writing of History, 1948–', *Itinerario,* vol. 16 no. 1, 1992, p. 89, quoted in Cohen, *The Combing of History*, p. 16, note 8.

22. See R. H. Canary and H. Kozicki (eds), *The Writing of History* (Madison, Wis.: Wisconsin University Press, 1978), especially the contribution by L. Mink, 'Narrative Form as Cognitive Instrument', pp. 129–49.

23. For this history, a useful source is Boubacar Barry's *Le Royaume du Waalo: Le Senegal avant la conquête* (2nd edn; Paris: Karthala, 1985); Abdoulaye Bathily, 'Islam and 19th Century Resistance Movements', in *Senegambia: Proceedings of a Colloquium at the University of Aberdeen* (Aberdeen University, African Studies Group, 1974), pp. 67–81; C. Becker and V. Martin, 'Royaumes sénégalais et traite des esclaves au 18ième siecle', in *Revue Française d'Histoire d'Outremer*, vol. 62, 1975, pp. 266–99; Lucie A. G. Colvin, 'Kajoor and its Diplomatic Relations with Saint-Louis du Senegal, 1763–1861', PhD, Columbia University, 1972; and Diouf, *Le Kajoor.*

24. On the Kunta family and the role it played in the Islamicisation of West Africa, see Diouf, *Le Kajoor,* pp. 136–9, and Philip Curtin, 'Jihad in West Africa: Early Phases and Interrelations in Mauritania and Senegal', in *Journal of African History*, vol. 12 no. 1, 1971, pp. 11–24.

25. Lucie A. G. Colvin, 'Islam and the State of Kajoor: A Case of Successful Resistance to Jihad', *Journal of African History*, no. 4, 1974, pp. 587–607.

26. The future of Christianity in Wolof countries was definitively sealed between 1843, the year in which missionaries penetrated into Kajoor and (on grounds of Islamisation) requested authorisation to set up missions, and the time when the Sereer agreed to receive these priests without the authorisation of the damel-teen. Cf. Diouf, *Le Kajoor*, pp. 150–3.

27. The best illustrations of the Muslim/brotherhood's recovery of the oral traditions are the narratives dealing with the death of Lat Joor NGone Latyr Joop, damel of Kajoor (wearing the robes given him by Amadou Bamba, the founder of the Mourides Brotherhood,

and with the latter's blessing, the damel announced on the way to his last battle that he would pray with his marabout before sunset); Maba Jaxu Ba (jihadist marabout of the early 19th century); and the traditions relating to Albury Njaay, the last Wolof buurba, who died at Kuduru (Niger) of a wound from a poisonous arrow after refusing to break his fast to take an antidote. The two most prestigious Wolof sovereigns died Muslim deaths.

28. The title of the chapter in which Berque addresses this question has a new resonance in the light of today's fundamentalist violence: 'L'Histoire et la danse' (History and dance) (*La Dépossession*, pp. 9–20). The author admits that his description is partly imaginary. Here, too, his, project intersects with Sembène, who ascribes to the nudity of the lingeer a roles analogous to dance. Nudity also is imaginary. In fact, according to the travel narrative of G. T. Mollien, Ajoor women covered themselves from breasts to legs. Cf. *L'Afrique occidentale en 1818 vue par un explorateur français*, presented by H. Deschamps (Paris: Calmann-Levy, 1967), pp. 39–40.

29. Ibid., p. 15.

30. This description is taken from a brochure entitled 'Echange culturel Suisse-Sénégal: Pro Helvetia et Xenix présentent: Cinéma itinérant au Sénégal', Dakar, 4 May–2 July 1974.

31. J. Berque, *La Dépossession*, pp. 14–15.

32. Harried by the empire, as Berque says. I add this to be consistent with the message of Sembène and of Islam. *La Dépossession*, p. 14.

33. In Marges, *Sexes et drogues à Dakar: Enquète ethnographique* (Paris: Karthala, ORSTOM, 1994), Jean-François Werner relates a prostitute's slow descent into hell in the suburbs of Dakar, with a wound in the buttock replacing the golden cast on Lingeer Ramatou's foot.

34. The same approach may be found in the novels of Ben Okri, especially *Stars of the New Curfew*, 1988.

35. Berque, *La Dépossession*, p. 15.

36. The sabbar is both a Wolof dance and a percussion instrument. The dancer matches his or her steps to the percussion rhythms which dictate movements on the ground or in the air as the feet, legs and arms wheel about in short arabesques.

37. El Hadji Mansour MBaye rose to prominence in the media just as Abdou Diouf took power in 1981. As with the profession of faith 'peace be upon him', which accompanies the name of the prophet of Islam every time it is pronounced, the grand bard of Senegal has tacked on the phrase 'guardian of the constitution' to the name of the president of Senegal in his religious, sports, political, musical and high-society chronicles on radio and television.

38. Achille M'Bembe, *Afriques indociles: Christianisme, pouvoir et état en société postcoloniale* (Paris: Karthala, 1988).

39. Achille M'Bembe and Janet Roitman, 'Des figures du sujet en postcolonie', unpublished manuscript.

Eroticism and Sub-Saharan African Films

Françoise Pfaff

Reprinted from *ZAST*, nos 9/10, 1991.

Since the beginning of time, and on a universal scale, eroticism has been a sig-nificant and integral part of art. In most societies, the use of sexually suggestive symbolism was initially linked to fecundation. In such cases, graphics of sculp-tured representations of a couple engaged in the sexual act may not primarily have had sexually arousing characteristics or intentions, but rather magic and/or religious attributes – to conjure or channel fertility onto an individual or a group. These representations were commonly used in ceremonies, or were kept in households to invoke gods or the forces of nature to ensure the fertility of a woman or the yielding of heavy crops.[1]

Likewise, the representation of a sexual organ may have had religious implications rather than libidinous connotations. The many phallic objects engendered by the worship of Dionysus and other Greek divinities in antiquity testify to the development of erotic cults devoted to fertility. One can thus say that the very concept of eroticism is socially and historically defined and that it varies. What is erotic to a twentieth-century man in North America may have appeared pornographic to a Victorian man of that same geographic area. What is now erotic to a Western urban dweller is not necessarily so to an African villager. Therefore, eroticism has to be related to the values and aesthetics of the society which generated it. In some countries, eroticism is linked to nudity; in other regions clothes or partial clothing may be sexually arousing. Contemporary Western societies generally perceive the exposed female breast as being erotic while other cultures may not:

> In Africa, the erotic function of the breast is much less important than in Europe or America.... In all African societies, breasts are the symbol of female fecundity... One must note that in most rural African societies the breast is regarded as a strictly utilitarian appendage for feeding the young.[2]

Deriving from historical and cultural circumstances, eroticism also differs according to class, race, gender and age, even within the same society. In the USA, for instance, sexual symbolism and physical attractiveness are often con-nected to race, class and age (the media primarily glorify the standards of beauty and eroticism linked to the young White middle or upper-middle class). And obviously what is sexually enticing to a man may not be so to a woman. These considerations are essential to an unbiased study in sub-Saharan African

252

cinema, whose societal and aesthetic canons are often different from those of the Western world. It should be stated here that the films of South Africa will not be incorporated in this analysis because of their unavailability in the West (with the exception of the *The Gods Must Be Crazy*, Jamie Uys, 1980), and the fact that Black South African film-makers have been gagged or altogether kept away from movie-thinking and/or movie-making in their country (a number of them, like Nana Mahomo and Lionel Ngakane, are in exile and may or may not practise their trade).[3]

Since the advent of film, eroticism (which appeals to the viewer's voyeurism and provides vicarious sensuous gratification) has been an essential and often very profitable component of numerous Western motion pictures. Interestingly, most of these movies have been made in societies of a sexually repressive Judaeo-Christian tradition where, at one time, the ultimate justification for sexual intercourse was procreation and not erotic pleasure *per se*. In such circumstances is eroticism the necessary, even indispensable, illustration of love within the story that unfolds on the screen? Does it match a new social permissiveness? Is eroticism in film a way to confront visual taboos and fulfil, without punishment, sexual fantasies or drives? Does eroticism lend itself to cinema because of its aesthetic qualities? Should eroticism be analaysed in a realistic context or in a metaphoric, even subversive, perspective? These questions and others should be considered when attempting to delineate the nature and function of eroticism in sub-Saharan African films. And, indeed, the purpose of this paper is not merely to tally and describe the most significant erotic senses found in that cinema, using solely universal symbolism and imagery, but rather to link its visual representation to the socio-religious and cultural fabric within which they were conceived.

The most common examples of controlled sexually suggestive postures in sub-Saharan African cinema are shots of heterosexual couples walking hand in hand (homosexuality is very rarely depicted by African directors), as seen in Kramo Lancine's *Djeli* (Côte d'Ivoire, 1981) or Ababacar Samb's *Et la neige n'était plus* (Senegal, 1965); and/or couples kissing while standing and embracing as filmed in Timité Bassori's *Sur la dune de la solitude* (Côte d'Ivoire, 1964), Jean-Pierre Dihongue-Pipa's *Le Prix de la liberté* (Cameroon, 1978), Ola Balogun's *Black Goddess* (Nigeria, 1978) and Kwaw Ansah's *Love Brewed ... in the African Pot* (Ghana, 1980). Bed scenes, though prudish, are much less frequent. They are to be observed in such films as Bassori's *La Femme au couteau* (Côte d'Ivoire, 1968), where actress Danielle Alloh is merely sitting on a bed (fully dressed) and leaning towards actor/director Timité Bassori, who is lying under a sheet covering his pyjama-clad body; or Souleymane Cissé's *Baara* (Mali, 1978), in which a woman and her lover are seen lying naked under sheets in the bed of a comfortably furnished room after their adulterous sexual encounter.

In this latter film, very few signs of passion or even affection are noticeable between the two: the woman is smoking while her companion holds her briefly before pouring himself a glass of whisky, a scene which duly accentuates their status as Westernised middle-class urban dwellers as well as the sexual independence of a married woman who manages a shop and is a member of the nouveau riche class. In *L'Herbe sauvage* (Côte d'Ivoire, 1977), Henri Duparc's triangular love story which also portrays a man and his mistress, the man shows more sustained and affectionate interest in his partner. Although naked in bed, the couple are covered by a sheet to the waist and bosom. The film-maker, however, stages this scene so as to emphasise a sensuous contrast between actress Vivien Touré's full and erect dark-skinned breast and the light-coloured sheet. Her physical attributes are stressed at another point in the film as she is taking a shower. Here the tactile beauty of her glistening bronze body is increased by her slow movements, and by a continuous flow of translucent running water. Somewhat shyly, nevertheless, Duparc's frame only shows Touré's nakedness from head to waist. In a rural context, such love scenes take place outdoors, conferring on couples a primeval harmony with nature, thus reducing the cultural taboos linked to sex between unmarried partners. In Oumarou Ganda's *Saitane* (Niger, 1973), a woman meets her lover in the savannah, far from her urban neighbours' attention. But, here again, the film-maker merely depicts the lovers' initial caresses (both are lying down fully clothed), after which the camera swiftly pans away towards grass and river waters.

In their large majority, the sexually intimate scenes in sub-Saharan African films are rather static and emotionless. Exceptions are nonetheless observed in such films as *Sur la dune de la solitude* and Dikongue Pipa's *Muna Moto* (Cameroon, 1974). *Sur la dune de la solitude* is a modernised version of the legend of Mamy Watta, the seductive mermaid-like temptress who lures men into her deep-water realm. In this early work, Timité Bassori offers several lyrical and even poetic shots of an urban and Westernised couple's amorous games. Walking at night on one of Abidjan's beaches, Elia attempts to embrace Enje, the beautiful woman he has just met, but she playfully escapes. After he catches up with her, the two finally disrobe (both wear bathing-suits but the camera lingers lasciviously on their slender and well-shaped statuesque bodies) and enter the sea, where they kiss. Then, Elia slowly lifts Enje, carries her out of the water before laying her down on the moonlit white sand. After such intertwining moments of seduction and conquest, Enje reveals to her would-be lover that she is a reincarnation of the legendary West African mermaid. The dialogue ends with Elia and Enje embracing one another, half-naked. Here the director cuts the shot.

In *Muna Moto*, Dikongue Pipa gives similar attention to flirtation. He does so in a flashback where Ngando, a villager, is arrested for having tried to reclaim his own child. As he is handcuffed and taken away to prison in a police van, Ngando's thoughts go back to the time of freedom, love and hope before an arranged marriage separated him from Ndomé, the mother of his child. In this love scene, Ngando and Ndomé, partially dressed in local wraparounds, embrace and roll down dunes to the inviting foamy waters of the nearby sea. As well as reflecting Ngando's indomitable love for Ndomé, the couple's pristine and natural laughter, happiness and togetherness in a wide and natural open space accentuates Ngando's despair and present isolation within the confines of a police wagon.

Another technique used by sub-Saharan African film-makers is the exchange of languorous love-filled gazes as a part of the characters' seductive process. Fitting particular plots, these looks may convey a subdued erotic content to viewers as occurs in Ousmane Sembène's *Black Girl* (Senegal, 1966) between Diouana and her boyfriend, and in his film *Ceddo* (1976) between the ceddo and the princess during the dream sequence in which she offers him water to drink; in Med Hondo's *Soleil-O* (Mauritania, 1969) and Cissé's *Finyé* (Mali,

1982), a film in which the director illustrates the story of a forbidden love between two adolescents. Since interracial relationships are a very rare occurrence in African cinema, of particular interest is a scene in *Soleil-O* which describes the casual affair between an African accountant and a Parisian woman. Seduction is initiated by the woman as the two wait for a bus. She slowly walks around him and looks at him with insistence. He notices her and smiles before following her as she departs. At one point, a close-up shows the woman with a slightly open mouth and twitching lips, an image which reflects sexual desire in many Western films. Also, this representation of sexually inviting attitudes on the part of a woman is indeed more frequent in Western than in sub-Saharan African film-making. One has to remember, however, that *Soleil-O* was shot entirely in France by an expatriate film-maker whose aim was probably to reach non-African as well as African audiences.

Since most sub-Saharan African directors are men, frequently the naked female body is the primary object of desire offered to viewers. This can be achieved in an incidental, even utilitarian fashion which culturally blends into the narrative, as occurs in the opening shot of *Ceddo*, where a bare-breasted woman goes to fetch water, or in Henri Duparc's *Bal poussière* (Côte d'Ivoire, 1988), when topless female characters are bathing in the sea. In *Yeelen* (Mali, 1987), once more during a bathing scene, Cissé shows the male protagonist's naked body in its entirety as well as his mate's naked breasts; yet in both instances their gestures are brisk and practical and are not erotic. Naked female bodies have also been used by these film-makers in a static fashion, thus heightening their symbolic presence rather than their sexually arousing characteristics. In *Xala* (Senegal, 1974), a film which describes the sexual and economic impotence of a middle-aged polygamous Dakar businessman, Sembène offers a back shot of the businessman's third wife, lying motionless and indifferent on the nuptial bed. Likewise, the middle third of the wife's naked back appears in the foreground of *Xala's* poster. In both instances the erotic content linked to the female body is kept to its minimum, while its symbolic meaning is increased.

A different approach to the filming of a woman's body is used by Désiré Ecaré in his 1970 *A nous deux, France* (Côte d'Ivoire), which satirically portrays the life of Ivorians in Paris. The acculturated African protagonist is married to France, a Frenchwoman by whom he has a child. A scene of the film shows France's husband, Tarzan, strumming her undressed body. Here, in spite of France's quasi-immobility, Tarzan's rhythmic hand movements and the colour contrast of the couple's skins should be perceived as erotic by both African and non-African audiences, especially since Ecaré visually transgresses the taboos usually connected with interracial love. This perception was probably shared by the director, who used a still from the sexually titillating scene on his promotional poster.

Since most West African film-makers have lived and/or studied in Europe like their Western counterparts, and in spite of cultural differences, African cineastes are very aware of the fact that a prolonged shot of a naked body in motion has highly erotic connotations. Sembène timidly illustrates this in *Black Girl* when he shows, from the back, Diouana in the process of undressing slowly. Later, in *Ceddo*, a stylised and otherwise stern epic, the Senegalese film-maker stages a scene which celebrates the harmonious and sensuous figure of the princess kidnapped by an insubordinate villager (ceddo), who thereby protests against the king's political weakness and the increasing penetration of Islam. Here Ousmane Sembène lingers, with his camera, on the majesty of the princess's quasi-naked body as she goes towards the sea near her place of seclusion. As she is about to bathe, she removes the short piece of cloth wrapped around her waist. At this very moment, the director opts for suggestive and indirect eroticism (a shot of the piece of material falling at the princess's feet) rather than its actual visualisation. Then the viewer is offered anew a full shot of the princess's partially covered body as she unhurriedly and lasciviously goes back to her hammock under the ceddo's watchful eyes (her actions are also witnessed by Tara, the male griot). Shortly thereafter, the princess goes to get a gourd (incidentally phallus-shaped) of fresh water, which she offers to her captor. The ceddo, still under the charm of her former gesture, and sensitive to this unexpected attention, approaches her until he realises that her apparent concern is but a play to get close to him and pull an arrow from his quiver. As the princess's design is thwarted, she returns to the hammock, sizing up her guard with her usual inscrutable look.

Similarly, Cissé's handling of nudity in *Finyé* is far from being offensive. The film's bathing scene, in which Batrou (a Westernised high-school student) invites her boyfriend to join her, is staged with restraint to emphasise the purity and beauty of the young couple's amorous adventures. Yet Cissé's extreme close-up of Batrou's breast dripping with water (thus isolating and stressing it) appears more as an erotic celebration of her beauty than a mere description of her bathing or a reference to her future fecundity (as seen before, full and pointed breasts symbolise fecundity in traditional African statuaries).

In sub-Saharan African films, sexual desire can be expressed verbally. In *Ajani Ogun* (1975), *Muzik Man* (1976) and *Black Goddess* (1978), the Nigerian film-maker Ola Balogun makes ample use of songs and serenades (sometimes in the manner found in Indian melodramas, which are highly popular in Africa) to express the love of his male characters for the woman of their dreams. Sexually explicit and humorous references are contained in *Xala*, where older men discuss jokingly the deflowering of a virgin; in Hondo's *Sarraounia* (Mauritiana/Burkina Faso, 1986), as African women exchange views about the intimate attributes and preferences of the 19th-century French soldiers; and in *Yeelen*, when the young protagonist declines responsibility for the seduction of the wife of the village chief by emphasising the autonomy of his penis (a statement which triggers roars of laughter among African and non-African audiences). Likewise, Duparc's *Bal poussière* contains an unusual number of off-colour jokes. Humour (and its distancing qualities) is also used by sub-Saharan African film practitioners in some of their bed scenes, which might otherwise have been erotic. One remembers how the middle-aged male protagonist of *Xala* becomes comical, to the point of being pitiful, in his vain attempts to deflower his new bride. In *Bal poussière*, the erotic content of one of the intimate scenes is considerably reduced as the two partners refer to a French card-playing expression (belote, rebelote) before engaging in the sexual act (unseen on the screen).

Although sex-related images are contained in a number of sub-Saharan African films, *Touki Bouki* (Senegal, 1973) by Djibril Diop Mambety and *Visages de femmes* (Côte d'Ivoire, 1985) by Ecaré are the motion pictures most often pointed out by critics for their erotic components. Mambety presents an intellectualised, ritualistic and metaphoric portrayal of intercourse, while Ecaré offers a naturalistic rendition of it.

Touki Bouki opposes the rules of conventional narrative African cinema and denounces the sociocultural alienation suffered by young Africans. The film portrays the wanderings of Mory, a former shepherd who now lives in Dakar, where he meets Anta, a young university student. *Touki Bouki*'s love scene between Mory and Anta is thematically and stylistically erotic because it discontinues and defers (through cuts and repeated action) the viewer's vicarious sexual and voyeuristic desire: Anta undresses on the beach, revealing only the upper part of her body, but the scene is unexpectedly interrupted as she prepares to lie down (Mory's body is never shown in the entire sequence). This scene is followed by images of a sheep being slaughtered, perhaps metaphorically sacrificial (sexual violence, rupture of the hymen?), and a full shot of foaming waves hitting black and shiny rocks – here the surge indicates the couple's youthful and passionate rapport. A subsequent close-up of Anta's fingers clenching a Dogon cross (a Malian symbol of fertility) on the rear of Mory's motorbike, accompanied by off-screen orgasmic sounds, finally confirms that Anta has actually lain with Mory and that the viewer has indeed witnessed a love scene where Eros meets Thanatos. This is undoubtedly the most innovative and puritanical love encounter of African cinema.

Visages de femmes depicts, in an often humorous mode, the changing conditions of women in the Côte d'Ivoire. It also includes the most explicit scene of intercourse in the whole history of African cinema – views of a sin-spared Eden in which bronze bodies dive and emerge lustfully and acrobatically in the luscious bed of a nearby river surrounded by dense, erect trees. These actions are initiated by a young African village woman (a rare occurrence in African films), who seduces her Westernised lover. Furthermore, *Visages de femmes* offers the only instance in which one sees both partners' genitals, and diversified sexual postures. Although some critics considered the scene a pantheistic representation of love in its primeval beauty, *Visages de femmes* was banned in the Côte d'Ivoire for eight months, probably because of its sexual audacity. Also, the film triggered a significant controversy between the film-maker and festival participants at the 1987 Pan-African Film Festival of Ouagadougou (FESPACO). One suspects that primarily because of its prolonged love scene, which lasts about eight minutes, *Visages de femmes* has met significant commercial success in Paris, where it was simultaneously seen in eight film theatres. Ecaré's film drew large audiences, whose essential concern might have been to verify the widespread stereotypical myth of uninhibited and insatiable African lust. It is probably based on such a marketable premise that Alphonse Beni had directed *Saint Vouyou* (Cameroon, 1982), an erotic detective movie with interracial sex.

Even when expressed, eroticism still appears to be incidental and scarce in sub-Saharan African films. Can this fact be related to their sociopolitical nature or the puritanical aspects of the cultures from which they emanate? Is it a conscious or subconscious effort on the part of film-makers to 'rehabilitate' the image of their compatriots, and thus overcome the stereotype of the sexually potent African intensely propagated during the colonial era? Or could it be that these motion pictures have an inherent eroticism which would not necessarily be obvious to a non-African observer?

According to a Senegambian interviewed for this article, African films are interspersed with objects and icons which bear erotic connotations within their cultural spheres and may not elsewhere. He cites the wooden and ceramic beads which Senegalese women wear round their waist; when women are naked these beads click and emit a distinct perfume said to be sexually arousing to men. Thus, when such beads are noticeable on the third wife in *Xala* (a dramatic and painful irony in view of her husband's impotence), they have an unmistakable reference for local audiences, which they do not for others. Likewise, *Baara*'s scene in which the woman is preparing to meet her lover by standing over an incense burner is sexually suggestive to Malians or Gambians because in their country incense *(tchulai)* is widely used as a perfume by women to attract and/or seduce men.

Few would deny, however, that sub-Saharan African films (and written literatures) are generally characterised by a rather pious chastity, which is especially surprising given the fact that many initiatory erotic tales are contained in African oral literatures.[4] Could one therefore relate such austere traits to the influence in Africa of Islam and Christianity, two religions which have linked sex to procreation rather than erotic pleasures? For Abiyi Ford, a film theorist and practitioner who teaches at Howard University, eroticism is not often found in these films because they derive from an environment in which 'sex is not the mysterious taboo it is in the West, where showing publicly something that should be hidden and done in the dark is a prime force and device to sell anything from cars to movies. In other cultures sex is a natural thing, nothing to be frowned upon, and it does not have the same voyeuristic impact it has on Judaeo-Christian Westerners.'

A number of critics have linked the relative absence of eroticism in African films to their political nature, implying that their authors would be more interested in analysing the forces at work in a given society than the amorous frolicking of romantic heroes. The Senegambian observer insists that 'sexualness is often associated with decadence, therefore some political film-makers do not want to introduce it in their work. It is a reaction against the kind of gratuitous sex of Hollywood films.' For Abiyi Ford, 'African film-makers illustrate subject areas that cannot be best dealt with in an erotic framework, so erotica is not a priority in their agenda so far as the message is concerned.' They would be hard pressed to include eroticism in motion pictures on colonialism and neo-colonialism. Yet there have been occasions when eroticism has been used to serve a larger context, as happens in Sembène's *Xala*.

Yet, increased film eroticism is to be expected in the forthcoming years in Africa because its societies are changing, and so are people's attitudes towards sex. Tourists bring in their own views of it. Africans travel abroad, and they are also greatly influenced by foreign and X-rated films. Based on his screening of *Visages de femmes*, Ford senses that:

African directors are going to give a more important part to eroticism in their films because the West sells everything with that. In order for their works to be commercially viable you may find African film-makers beginning to throw some sex here and there to satisfy the Westernised appetites of audiences... up to this point African cinema has been mostly a subsidised cinema (financially sponsored by local governments, the French Ministry of Co-operation

258

and the like). Its driving force has not been a need to make money, and it is a cinema that has a sense of purity to it. However, when African cinema reaches a point where it has to respond to the tastes of its audiences, it will maybe become more erotic in order to sell.

Asked why one does not find more sexually suggestive images in African cinema, the Ethiopian director Haile Gerima responded:

In our societies, sex is not the point of departure for everything. There is more to life than sex. In the West it is the point of reference for everything. People can't sell a sweater, bread or a bathtub without advertising it with a woman's leg ... even religion is studied from the angle of sex. In Africa people don't wake up for sex, they wake up to find out where they are going to get their next meal. I think it has to do with the nature of society – its intentions and orientations, what is expected and what one wants in life. Sex is only one of the things that you go through in the initiation of life. In the West, sex is a decisive factor. So every movie has to abide by that... I think this has a lot to do with the fact that sex is viewed as a commodity... In southern Ethiopia, there is a region that has a very interesting erotic expression. This art may include a phallic symbol pointing towards the Sun God, but it has a religious meaning. Eroticism is strongly linked to societal circumstances.[5]

Gerima (who made such films as *Harvest: 3000 Years*, 1976) has never included any sexually enticing representation in his motion pictures because he is first interested in the 'psychological, physical and social liberation of people'. Nonetheless, he does not dismiss using eroticism in his future works, provided that it closely fits their dramatic context.

To conclude, one should postulate that eroticism (defined according to both African and Western standards) is indeed scarce or at best generally quite benign in most sub-Saharan African films because of their sociopolitical nature, as opposed to the psychological intricacies of Western love triangles, which tend to generate erotic scenes in Western films. One should also consider that screen eroticism would drive away potential non-professional actors and actresses in areas where acting is still frowned upon and not considered a serious or dignified professional activity. Furthermore, this lack of eroticism in African films may also be related to the fact that eroticism does not seem to be a dominant or publicly displayed trait in the collective agrarian societies from which they have emerged. And, since sexually oriented gestures (kissing, embracing, and the like) would tend to isolate a couple from other members of the community, these are not as customarily observed as in Western countries, where relationships are more individualistic, thus more expressive. In most African societies, sex is usually practised within marriage (even though it may be a polygamous one), it is closely regulated through initiation rites and social rules imposing abstinence (during menstruation, pregnancies and so on), and its aim is primarily procreation rather than erotic pleasure alone (irremediably reduced in the case of excised women). And, according to Thérèse Kuoh Moukoury of Cameroon,[6] lovemaking, as performed in many regions of Africa where collective life is the rule, has no long foreplay. It is a brief intimate moment which takes place in the dark and in silence, a moment during which a respectable woman is not expected to exhibit signs of pleasure. One understands how this may subdue amorous behaviour, especially in the case of a polygamous marriage where visible indications of love could arouse jealousy and anger among co-wives. Moreover, arranged marriages, which are still practised (especially in villages), are not as conducive to flirtation as other matrimonial customs in different parts of the world, where future mates engage in a variety of seductive processes which may then be represented in literature or on screens as reflections of these lifestyles.

According to a number of Africans interviewed on the subject of eroticism in African literature,[7] this same scarcity of sexually explicit scenes is to be observed in contemporary African writings. Should one believe that these writers and film-makers are still strongly marked by the puritanical teachings they may have received in koranic or missionary schools? And, although there may be a certain degree of eroticism in initiatory tales told during circumcision or stories told or sung by women among themselves at the wells, while fetching wood or going to the marketplace, a close scrutiny reveals that such eroticism has its strict codes and limitations. These stories may be spicy and suggestive but a lot remains untold, and the graphic details of intercourse are unspoken or the narrative ends when intercourse occurs. It also happens that the storyteller skilfully uses euphemism and metaphors to mention the sexual act. In all cases, the narrator is more at ease naming sexual parts of the body than depicting intercourse.[8] Much of the same is to be noticed in sub-Saharan African film-making. One remembers how, in *Xala*, the second wife confronts her husband and jealously refers to the third wife's vagina, while Sembène shies away from presenting any sexually explicit scenes in that same film, thus reinforcing the symbolic meaning of what is unseen. Likewise, there are many instances when African film-makers suggest or briefly show erotic scenes whereas their European or American counterparts may choose to dwell on them for the sake of realism, artistry or commercialism.

Inasmuch as sub-Saharan film-makers are to a large extent still influenced by traditional values and a sense of sociopolitical commitment, eroticism appears as rather limited in their works. Nevertheless, as these film practitioners and their audiences become increasingly Westernised and urbanised, it is to be expected that their motion pictures will give a larger place to the kinds of commercially beneficial sexually suggestive scenes which are rather frequently found in present-day Western cinema. Let us hope that in so doing such works will not achieve a cultural bastardisation which may prove highly detrimental to sub-Saharan African societies and to their budding cinematic identities.

Notes

1. Phyllis and Eberhard Kronhausen, *Erotic Art* (New York: Bell, 1968), p. 204.
2. G. Balandier and J. Maquet, *Dictionary of Black African Civilisation* (New York: Leon Amiel, 1974), pp. 69–70.
3. This paper was written before the end of apartheid in South Africa as symbolised by the release from prison of Nelson Mandela on 11 February 1990.
4. S. Lallemand, *L'Apprentissage de la sexualité dans les contes d'Afrique de l'Ouest* (Paris: Edns de l'Harmattan, 1987).
5. The interviews upon which the latter part of this paper is based were conducted by the author at Howard University, Washington, DC, April 1989.

6. G. Clavreuil, *Erotisme et littératures* (Paris: Acropole 1987).
7. Ibid.
8. Lallemand, *L'Apprentissage*, pp. 19–21.

Further Readings

Armes, Roy, and Malkmus, Lizbeth, *Arab and African Filmmaking* (London and New Jersey: Zed Books, 1991).

Gadjigo, Samba, *et al.* (eds), *Ousmane Sembène: Dialogues with Critics and Writers* (Amherst, Mass: University of Massachusetts Press, 1993).

Naficy, Hamid, and Gabriel, Teshome H. (eds), *Otherness and the Media – The Ethnography of the Imagined and the Imaged* (Chur, Switzerland: Harwood Academic Publishers, 1993).

Ukadike, Nwachukwu Frank, *Black African Cinema* (Berkeley: University of California Press, 1994).

Notes on Contributors

Farida Ayari is a journalist who writes regularly on women and cinema.

Claire Andrade-Watkins is a film-maker and teaches at Emerson College in Boston, Massachusetts, USA. She is co-editor of *Blackframes: Critical Perspectives on Black Independent Cinema* and author of many articles on African cinema.

Imruh Bakari is a film-maker and writer. He teaches at King Alfred's College, Winchester, England.

Sambolgo Bangré is a journalist and a regular contributor to *Ecrans d'Afrique*.

Nouri Bouzid is from Tunisia and is the director of many films, including *The Man of Ashes*, *The Golden Horse Shoes* and *Bezness*.

Mbye Cham teaches at Howard University in Washington, DC, and writes on African and Caribbean literature and cinema.

Tahar Chériaa is a pioneer and champion of African cinema. He is the founder of the Journées Cinématographiques de Carthage (The Carthage Film Festival in Tunisia) and the author of *Ecrans d'abondance ou Cinéma de libération en Afrique*, as well as numerous essays on African cinema.

Manthia Diawara teaches at New York University, where he also directs the Africana Studies Programme. He is the author of *African Cinema: Politics and Culture* and editor of *Black American Cinema*.

Mamadou Diouf teaches at Cheick Anta Diop University of Dakar, Senegal, and is also an officer at CODESRIA (Council for the Development of Social and Economic Research in Africa) in Dakar. He writes on history, politics and culture, and is the author of *Le Kajoor au XIXième siècle: Pouvoir ceddo et conquête coloniale*.

Med Hondo is a film-maker from Mauritania, and is the director of *Soleil-O*, *West Indies, Sarraounia* and *Lumière noire*.

Joseph Ki-Zerbo is an eminent historian and cultural scholar from Burkina Faso. He is the editor of the University of California's *General History of Africa, Vol. 1, Methodology and African Prehistory*.

Sarah Maldoror is a pioneer of African cinema and an activist in liberation struggles. She is the director of many documentaries and features, including *Monangambee, Sambizanga, Un Dessert pour Constance, L'Hôpital de Leningrad, Léon G. Damas* and *Aimé Césaire, la masque des mots*.

Anne Mungai is from Kenya and is the director of *Saikati* and many documentaries.

Mweze Ngangura is from Zaire and is the director of *Kin-Kiesse, La Vie est belle* (with Bernard Lamy), *Changa Changa* and *Le Roi, La Vache et Le Bananier*.

Sheila Petty teaches at the University of Regina in Canada where she chairs the

Department of Film and Television. She has written extensively on various aspects of African cinema and television.

Françoise Pfaff teaches at Howard University in Washington, DC. She has written numerous essays on African and Caribbean literature and cinema, and is the author of *Ousmane Sembène, A Pioneer of African Film, Twenty-Five Black African Filmmakers* and *Entretiens avec Maryse Condé*.

Emmanuel Sama is a journalist and a regular contributor to *Ecrans d'Afrique*.

Ndugu Mike Ssali is a historian from Uganda.

Camillo de Souza is a Mozambican film-maker. He was a Manager-Producer at the Instituto Nacional de Cinema in Maputo (1987–8).

Rod Stoneman is a former Deputy Commissioning Editor of independent film and video at Channel Four Television. He is now Chief Executive at the Irish Film Board.

Jean-Marie Téno is from Cameroon and is the director of both fiction and documentary films, including *Bikutsi Water Blues, Afrique, je te plumerai, Le Dernier voyage, Mister Foot* and *La Tête dans les nuages*.

Keyan Tomaselli teaches at the University of Natal in South Africa, where he also directs the Centre for Media and Cultural Studies. He is founder and editor of the journal *Critical Arts*, and is the author of numerous articles and books, including *The South African Film Industry, Myth, Race and Power* (co-author) and *The Cinema of Apartheid*.

Mahama Johnson Traoré is from Senegal. He is former Secretary General of FEPACI (1978–82) and the director of *Diankha-Bi, L'Enfer des innocents, Diegue-Bi, Lambaaye, Reou-Takh, Garga M'Bosse* and *Njangaan* (also spelt *N'Diangane*).

Nwachukwu Frank Ukadike teaches at the University of Michigan in Ann Arbor. He has written extensively on African cinema and television, and is the author of *Black African Cinema*.

Index

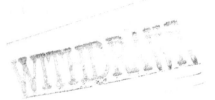